Lynchings in Missouri,
1803–1981

Lynchings in Missouri, 1803–1981

Harriet C. Frazier

McFarland & Company, Inc., Publishers
Jefferson, North Carolina, and London

LIBRARY OF CONGRESS CATALOGUING-IN-PUBLICATION DATA

Frazier, Harriet C.
Lynchings in Missouri, 1803–1981 / Harriet C. Frazier.
p.   cm.
Includes bibliographical references and index.

ISBN 978-0-7864-3668-2
softcover : 50# alkaline paper ∞

1. Lynching — Missouri — History.   I. Title.

HV6465.M5F73 2009   364.1'34 — dc22   2009023177

British Library cataloguing data are available

On the cover: Frank Embree and his lynchers, July 22, 1899, Burton, Howard County
(State Historical Society of Missouri); *inset* mob mills about
at Frank Embree's murder (State Historical Society of Missouri);
background Missouri counties (courtesy Missouri State Archives)

Manufactured in the United States of America

McFarland & Company, Inc., Publishers
Box 611, Jefferson, North Carolina 28640
www.mcfarlandpub.com

For Hattie and Robin

Acknowledgments

My thanks begin with continuing praise for the decision which the University of Central Missouri's library made to purchase the Kansas and Missouri execution files of Watt Espy. Working with his material on Missouri's death penalty got me started on what has been nearly 20 years of research on this state's dark side. Although I have a great deal of formal education, Watt showed me the way to document Missouri's legal executions and, by extension, its lynchings. I salute him for his pioneering work.

His friend and collaborator, Daniel Hearn, aided my research for this book. He sent me a list that he compiled of Missouri lynchings reported in the *Savannah* (GA) *Daily Herald*, 1866–1895; the *New Orleans Times-Picayune*, 1900–1911; two items from the *San Francisco Examiner*, both from 1892, and three from the *Arkansas Gazette*, 1903–1914. Characteristic of Danny's work, he listed all entries by name if known, town if known, month, day, year, page, and column. His information was especially helpful in bringing specificity to the vagueness of many Missouri county histories regarding when an event, such as a lynching, took place. Had the writers of these histories had microfilm of old newspapers, their dating of incidents would be more far more precise. Since microfilm was basically invented as a spy technique of World War II, it was not available when the many Missouri county histories I checked were written.

From Michael J. Pfeifer's website, "Partial List of Lynchings in Missouri, 1836–1981," I added five names, all between 1869 and 1874: (1) Harry Howard, Clay County, (2) James Cline, (3) Jehiel Stevenson, (4) Thomas Detroe, Cass County, and (5) Dr. Rush, Lafayette County. Each entry on Pfeifer's website contains the date, name of the lynched, town and county where the mob murder took place, and the alleged crime of the lynched person. No item gives any sources; the user of this website must locate, if it can be found, any and all documentation.

Linda Reckart is thanked for telling me that Mid-Continent Library, Independence, Missouri, has a magnificent website for locating, among much else, stories in old newspapers about my subject matter. Because this library services my zip code, all I had to do was apply for a card. Once I obtained it, from my home, I could and did locate numerous otherwise inaccessible news stories about Missouri lynchings from a large number of newspapers.

At the Missouri State Historical Society, its director, Gary Kremer, steered me to useful material on several occasions. In its photographic department, Christine Montgomery, as in the past, was immensely helpful with many of my illustrations for this book. The staff member who repeatedly did the heavy lifting for me was Kimberly Harper, reference librarian. In addition to locating, photocopying, and mailing me numerous newspaper stories concerning my subject, she answered my many e-mail questions with speed, efficiency, wit, and consideration. Without Kimberly's help, this book would be far less well documented. She is a jewel. Her predecessor, Laurel Boeckman, retired senior reference specialist, is thanked for the invaluable assistance she gave me in the early stages of my research.

Among the many helpful librarians at the Johnson County (KS) Public Library, its interlibrary loan librarian Linda Riehle, a warm and witty person, hunted down for me multiple obscure and out-of-date books. Without her persistence, much of my documentation for this book would never have been located. Other Johnson County librarians who aided me include Scott Vieria and many other helpful persons in reference and at the front desk.

At the University of Central Missouri's library, as with earlier books, I received assistance from its dean, Molly Dinwiddie, its special collections director, Naomi Williamson, and its interlibrary loan librarian, Patty Morrison.

At Mid-Continent Public Library, Janice Schultz, manager of the Genealogy and Local History Branch, is thanked for her astonishing knowledge of the material and for her part in making certain that an astounding variety of books and other material is available for this library's patrons. Glen McAnavery, reference assistant in genealogy, and Jan Cosner, reference librarian in the general part of Mid-Continent Public Library, are thanked for their assistance.

At the Kansas City (MO) Public Library, Mary Beveridge, head of Special Collections, Missouri Valley Room, and her staff are thanked. At the reference desk, Dennis Halbin, Judy Klamm, and Bill Osment are thanked for their repeated assistance in answering my questions.

At the Missouri State Archives, Robyn Bumett is thanked for locating and sending me the prison record and parole papers of Lonnie Taylor and Missouri State Senator Kenny's Senate Bill 259 (1931), one of this state's attempts to pass anti-lynching legislation.

At the University of Missouri–Kansas City Law School, of which I am a graduate, Kathleen Hall, Lawrence MacLachlan and Nancy Morgan are thanked. All have been huge helps on this and earlier books about Missouri.

Jeff Blackman has been, as with earlier books, my computer-fixer. He has made it possible for me to write a book on what is for me a new-fangled piece of equipment. Kate Martin, a graphics expert, made possible the sectional names and lines in my map of Missouri and all my charts. Her work is excellent.

Judy Gerber, at Memorial Park Cemetery, St. Joseph, helped me locate the grave of Kenneth McElroy, and Frances Chelline accompanied me on this photographic mission.

Andy Hannas recalled and told me about all the horse metaphors used in railroad and automobile transportation. Finally, the late Tom Fairclough helped with this book's title and many other aspects of it, and as in the past, I thank him for his assistance.

Table of Contents

List of Illustrations

Preface

My research for my fourth book on the dark side of Missouri's history began nearly 20 years ago. I was then a law professor in the Criminal Justice Department, University of Central Missouri, Warrensburg. Watt Espy personally placed his Missouri and Kansas legal execution files in the university library when he visited the campus in October 1989. I immediately began verifying and adding to his Missouri research; among other additions I made to Espy's work, I collected accounts of the lynchings that took place here. I did so largely by reading seemingly endless reels of microfilmed Missouri newspapers. I took or had taken, depending on the type of microfilm reader on the premises, readable copies about a wide variety of mob murders featured in these newspapers. I also checked numerous Missouri county histories, and some yielded amazing, detailed descriptions of the extralegal deaths of undesirables.

In the early 1990s, I spent sufficient time in the Chicago Public Library to locate the *Chicago Tribune*'s placement of its annual lists of the executed and lynched nationwide. Amidst compilations of bankruptcies, heavy losses by fires, shipwrecks, suicides, and other disasters, either early the next year or late in the ending year, this newspaper compiled and published annually, from the early 1880s through 1918, the number of people executed and lynched nationwide. (It ceased publishing such lists after 1918. Presumably the millions of World War I dead rendered insignificant the double, or at best triple, digits of the annually executed and lynched in the United States.) Throughout its collection of these domestic catastrophes, and under the headline, "Lynchings," the paper listed the total number of known "strung up victims" for the year; the number in each state and territory; and the date, name (if known), race, alleged offense, city, and state of those who died at the hands of "Judge Lynch," the category under which the newspaper often placed the particulars of fatal mob violence. Not surprisingly, most of these awful events took place in the South, and they overwhelmingly involved males, both as mob members and victims. I collected every available particular of the *Chicago Tribune*'s annual lists. At my request, my library (University of Central Missouri) obtained on interlibrary loan the Chicago Public Library microfilm of each relevant *Chicago Tribune*. I made a copy of each and marked it as to page(s) and column(s), and I retain these valuable lists to date. I checked every name in every year which contained a Missouri locale in one or more Missouri newspapers. As should be expected with such a giant undertaking by any newspaper with a deadline for publishing its findings, there are a number of errors in the

Chicago paper's compilations. Not invariably, but often, the NAACP publication *Thirty Years of Lynchings in the United States, 1889–1918* (1919) took over many mistakes initially made by the *Chicago Tribune.* Subsequent researchers often adopted the errors of the newspaper and the NAACP.

I have used both the Chicago paper's compilations and the NAACP's as starters. I have at least one in-state source that a lynching took place here, or I have not included it in the 229 confirmed events that make up my Appendix 1, "Lynchings in Missouri, 1803–1981." That source may be a letter; a journal entry; a federal or a state court record, either printed or handwritten; a county history; an in-state newspaper; or a combination of two or more of these items. Most often, my sources have been newspapers, and the total numbers of different newspapers I have used to write this book is at least 150.

I have also included on a chapter by chapter basis a discussion of alleged mob murders that did not take place here. They are listed in Appendix 2: "Falsely Reported, Doubtful, and Foiled Lynchings in Missouri, 1857–1930." I located 50 between 1857 and 1930 that do not qualify as Missouri lynchings, and they fail to do so for a number of reasons. Among many others, the victim was lynched, but not in Missouri. (I was born and raised in the tri-state area of Wheeling, West Virginia; the state of Ohio was immediately west across the Ohio River, and the state of Pennsylvania was 15 miles to the east. The *Wheeling News Register* and the *Wheeling Intelligencer* reported numerous out-of-state happenings by town or village, without mention of Ohio and Pennsylvania; the newspapers' readers were presumed to know their location, be it in West Virginia, Ohio, or Pennsylvania. My West Virginia residence of nearly 20 years put me on the alert for misclassification of mob murders by state). When the lynching took place in a jurisdiction that bordered Missouri, usually, an in-state newspaper reported an out-of-state event, one that occurred in Arkansas, Kentucky, or Tennessee. The in-state paper never explained to its local readers that this event did not occur in Missouri; obviously they knew the area and what was and what was not in-state. The compilers of the *Chicago Tribune's* annual list of the lynched did not know the area, and they placed these events in the wrong state. Other researchers copied incorrect information from the Chicago newspaper's lists.

Other deaths listed as Missouri lynchings may lack the minimum number of three in the mob to qualify. Crimes committed by individuals or a pair of perpetrators, who killed without back-up support, do not qualify as lynchings. More events go into my Appendix 2 from the 1880s forward because the *Chicago Tribune's* collection of them began in this decade.

However, lynchings did not begin in the 1880s; only the collection of data about them nationwide did. My first four chapters concern earlier deaths at the hands of Missouri mobs. Despite my best efforts, my work is incomplete. Many Missouri newspapers that once existed are no longer extant, and local and contemporary newspapers are the primary means by which any investigator documents most of these wretched events. An accurate number of the lynched from the first through the last for any state is impossible. I regard all offered *totals* of lynchings, in any state or territory or the nation as a whole, from whatever source derived, with a great deal of skepticism. We simply do not have the complete picture of all those who were mob-dispatched, nor shall we ever.

My research is the first investigation of Missouri's full history of lynchings. It is better to document these knowable atrocities than to neglect the task, because the available sources yield incomplete results. It is to be expected that someone else will locate additional deaths at the hands of Missouri mobs, horrors which I never managed to stumble across.

The definition of a lynching is not as elusive as is the accurate number of lynching victims in any state, territory, or the entire United States. Two capable historians, James R. McGovern in *Anatomy of a Lynching* and Richard Maxwell Brown in *Strain of Violence,* have defined parts or aspects of exactly what is and what is not a bona fide lynching. As a starter, the victim must die; otherwise, the incident should be classified as an attempted lynching. Always the event is the work of a mob that, without any legal authority, fatally harms another human. No court authorizes the action against the victim, and no sheriff or other law enforcement officer carries out the destroyed person's punishment pursuant to a warrant, which specifies the method, date, time limitations, and place of death. The mob never acts in self defense, and it never kills in order to prevent the imminent death of others. The general public perception is that a lynch mob always hanged its victims by the neck until dead. Often enough this occurred. However, the nature of the torment is not its essence; hanging, burning, shooting, dragging, drowning, a combination of these methods, or any other manner of causing intentional death that is utilized by the mob, qualify. The event is characterized by community approval of the result(s) and/or fear that the lynchers would also finish off disapproving talkers who named names. The wealthiest and most prominent citizens of the community may not have been involved in any aspect of this extralegal killing, but their disapproval of it was likely mild. After all, the extralegal dispatching of the unwanted always kept low the taxes to combat lawlessness. Mob members either remained unknown to coroners' juries; or if they were arrested, grand juries did not indict them; or if tried, trial juries did not convict them. Two exceptions to this rule exist; both are products of the U.S. District Court for the Western District of Missouri, one in 1874 and the other in 1985.

War, especially a civil war, does not provide the proper venue for what we term a lynching. By its nature, a civil war fractures the community; things fall apart. The multiple deaths which result from this splintering are usually described as the product of sectarian violence and secessionist activity. The perpetrators of such lawlessness are termed criminal gangs, bushwhackers, death squads, and militia. Their members come from disaffected groups who oppose the central government. Their hostile actions are often random attacks against another community, whom the attackers consider enemies. In turn, these enemies retaliate. The results on all sides are often deadly, characteristic of civil strife, and the despicable actions of enemy combatants fall outside the definition of a lynching as used in this book.

Prior to the commencement of sectarian strife which eventually becomes a civil war and after the warring parties have signed a ceasefire, it is proper to use the term *lynching* for punishing misdeeds or perceived misdeeds of those whose lives were considered of little value. However, the community must regard the punished person(s) as criminal or highly disreputable. For example, if a gang of desperadoes murders a physician, sheriff, cabinet minister, or any other respected citizen who has not misbehaved or is not perceived as misbehaving, his death at the hands of the gang is not a lynching. The community never approves this form of lawlessness.

I relate the history of lynching in Missouri in 12 chapters, and discuss the final — or last—Missouri lynching in the Conclusion. Chapter 1, "One Native American and 17 White Victims, 1803–1861," begins shortly after the Louisiana Purchase with the lynching of an Indian, and it stops early in the Civil War. During the antebellum period, mobs are known to have dispatched 17 white persons. Offenses such as horse stealing led to the lynching of white males, and only rarely of black persons. Vigilantes also punished murderers by lynching them. Any falsely reported, doubtful, or foiled lynchings included in a chapter are discussed.

Chapter 2, "Slaves and Free Blacks, 1818–1862," concerns a sizeable number of bondpersons (including the only females ever known to have been lynched in Missouri) whom mobs put to death, principally in the 1850s. In two counties, the story of a slave's mob murder may be fused with an earlier killing of that same slave. As a result, there are 20, 21, or 22 known lynchings of African Americans covered in this chapter. Though my Appendix 1 lists 229 names, there may be an actual total of 227 or 228. Missouri mobs definitely lynched more blacks than whites during Missouri's antebellum and early Civil War period. In the slave jurisdictions which formed the Union, the colonial and later the state legislatures passed statutes which compensated the slave owner when the colony or the state put his property to death. Once American rule of what is now Missouri began, there was never government-ordered compensation when slaves were capitally punished. Generalizations about how slavery protected blacks from mob violence are not applicable here, or in other states, whose laws never provided that owners be paid when the state hanged their human property. Lynching by burning began in this time period, and mobs only burned blacks, never white persons.

Chapter 3, "Civil War Aftermath, 1866–1869," describes what was often score-settling from the conflict that had recently ravaged the rural areas of Missouri. Five that we know about took place in eastern Missouri and 28 in the western section of the state. Most likely, the courts and law enforcement officers in these western rural counties were functioning, if at all, just barely. Thirty-three whites and two blacks died at the hands of mobs. This chapter and all those subsequent through Chapter 12 discuss mob murders by the section of the state in which they took place, clockwise: southwest, northwest, northeast, and southeast.

Chapter 4, "More White Victims Than Black, 1870–1879," suggests, sketchy as the evidence may be, that blacks in rural areas fled the state in droves. By 1860, Missouri had the second smallest percentage (10 percent) of its population in bondage of any of the 16 slave jurisdictions, 15 states and the District of Columbia. This trailed only Delaware, which had just under 2 percent of its population in slavery. Furthermore, between 1870 and 1910, the African-American population of Missouri declined; our knowledge of this decline is based on census information collected by the federal government every ten years since 1790. Altogether 16 blacks and 36 whites were murdered by mobs between 1870 and 1879. This decade is the high water mark for known mob murders, with 52 in all.

Chapter 5, "Law vs. Mob: Strenuous Efforts to Punish Lynchers, 1872–1879," examines three cases wherein the documentation is especially good. Federal handwritten court records, a Missouri governor's determination to establish law and order, and the Missouri legislature's new law to aid the prosecution of lynchers (ruled unconstitutional by the Missouri Supreme Court) make clear that high officials and many other Missourians did their best to curtail lynchings. This chapter describes the only known mob murder of a Missouri sheriff. At the time of his fatal shooting, this law enforcement officer was escorting and protecting a prisoner who had pleaded guilty to stealing two mules and was en route to the penitentiary.

Chapter 6, "'The brute seized her': Black Victims, 1880–1889," details the lynching of black persons for sex crimes, murders, and frightening a white lady. For the first time, black lynch mobs killed other blacks. Charges of rape, whether founded or not, account for most black victims of mob violence.

Chapter 7, "Railroads End Lynching of Horse Thieves: White Victims Decrease, 1880–1889" discusses the discontinuation of horse stealing as an offense for which mobs put men to death. By the 1880s, both freight and passengers frequently traveled by railroad throughout rural Missouri; as a result, horses were no longer the primary means of transportation. Hog stealing, bank robbery, mistreatment of family, murder, and rape were offenses for which whites were lynched in the last decade of the nineteenth century. In all there are 21 known white victims and 12 black for a total of 33 known mob murders in Missouri in the 1880s. Because the *Chicago Tribune* began its annual lists of the lynched in the early 1880s, 11 events that belong in Appendix 2 took place in the 1880s. Alleged lynchings of blacks are discussed in Chapter 6 and whites in Chapter 7.

Chapter 8, "Arranged Media Coverage and Other Obscenities: Black Victims, 1890–1899," discusses the 17 black victims of lynch mobs here, three more than the number of white victims in the same decade. One black man died two years after he allegedly raped a white woman. She only remembered that a black man attacked her after her husband decided that their child was not entirely white. In the 1890s, the state of Missouri executed more persons than in any other time period; this probably reduced the number of mob murders. In all there were 31.

Chapter 9, "White Victims, 1891–1900," discusses the 14 known white victims of lynchings here during the 1890s. Most white persons whom mobs put to death were, rightly or wrongly, thought to be murderers, but suspected hog thieves and a man known to have mistreated his family were also victims of mobs. In all, 15 falsely reported, doubtful, or foiled Missouri lynchings occurred in the 1890s, more than during any other decade. The names, dates, and places of the 1890s non–Missouri lynchings involving blacks are discussed in Chapter 8 and those involving whites in Chapter 9.

Chapter 10, "Racism as Scholarship to Justify Violence: 1900–1909," discusses the three white and 16 black victims of lynchings in Missouri during this decade. As the total numbers declined from the high water mark of the 1870s, the percentage of blacks increased dramatically. This chapter describes the poisonous writings of supposed white experts on the criminality of blacks, especially those that committed sex crimes against whites. It also discusses the seven events of this decade that are listed in Appendix 2.

Chapter 11, "Black and White Victims, 1910–1919," begins with accounts of the only known lynchings of white men, both in western Missouri, during this decade, one in 1915 and the other in 1919. Both had killed law enforcement officers. Otherwise, all eight known victims of lynchings here during this time period were black, and their alleged offenses were assault, burglary, robbery and murder, and stealing. Significantly, the Missouri General Assembly abolished capital punishment in 1917, and it reinstated it in 1919. Violence waned considerably here during this decade.

Chapter 12, "Declining Numbers, and Black Victims Only: 1920–1942," does not yield a single white victim of fatal mob violence in the state. All whites put to death in Missouri died pursuant to a court order. All lynched persons over a 22-year period were black, and their alleged victims were white females whom they were accused of raping, attempting to rape, and/or murdering. This chapter discusses both federal and state legislation to punish lynchers; all bills introduced at both the state and federal level failed to become law. In 2005, 80 members of the United States Senate apologized for that body's failure to enact any anti-lynching laws of the many introduced over a 105 year period.

A conclusion includes the most recent lynching in Missouri, the mob murder of a white man, arrested by his own count on 53 felonies, all without a conviction. When he was finally convicted of assault, he quickly posted bail during his appeal, and he was once more free to torment his townspeople in Skidmore, Missouri. They believed that he needed to be killed, and while his homicide was investigated by every law enforcement agency — city, county, state, and federal — with even remote jurisdiction to look into the matter, the perpetrators remain unknown.

With the exception of two western counties that ceased to be sites of mob murders in the 1870s, the conclusion links the top nine counties, those with the greatest number of mob murders from start to finish, with pre–Civil War events in them: either the execution, the lynching, or both the execution and the lynching of slaves. These nine areas account for slightly more than one-third of the total known mob murders in Missouri. All nine of these counties were scenes of lynchings before the Civil War and at least as late as the 1890s, and most were places of mob violence in the twentieth century.

Finally, I am certain that another researcher will be able to document from an in-state source or sources other mob murders that took place in Missouri. I am confident that I never found all of them.

CHAPTER 1

One Native American and
17 White Victims, 1803–1862

One might as well begin with a letter, one that Amos Stoddard (1762–1813) wrote to his superior. The writer was a Massachusetts attorney, Revolutionary War veteran, and the first American governor of territorial Missouri. He had represented the French in their transfer of Upper Louisiana on March 9, 1804, at the remote St. Louis Post, and the next day, March 10, as the American representative at these same transfer events, he received the northern portion of the Louisiana Purchase in the name of the United States. President Jefferson had earlier appointed W.C.C. Clairborne (1775–1817), another attorney and governor of Mississippi Territory, as one of two commissioners to receive the southern portion of the Louisiana Purchase from the French in New Orleans on December 20, 1803. Clairborne, in turn, appointed Stoddard to his position as captain, first civil commandant, and governor of the area, which eventually became Missouri.

The new governor's responsibilities included communicating to Clairborne "incidents worthy of notice." In a letter dated May 19, 1804, he wrote to him in New Orleans that in November 1803, some Creek chiefs met with the commandant of New Madrid District about "15 or 20 vagabond Creek or Muskoe Indians," whose crimes had troubled both white and Native American residents. As the chiefs were meeting with the commandant, one of the Indian vagabonds "stole a Rifle from a white man in the neighborhood." The Creek chiefs pursued, captured, and returned him to New Madrid. Stoddard described what happened next: "They [the Creek chiefs] requested leave of the commandant to punish him — which they did by beating him to death with clubs." Stoddard's letter to Clairborne continued, "I mention these circumstances to show in what light these stragglers are viewed by their own nation.... They have lately killed no less than 8 persons, and they have hitherto eluded their pursuers." We have no way of ascertaining the clubbed man's connection, if any, to these unnamed eight recently killed persons.

I believe this incident involving the rifle thief can properly be described as a lynching. It was the activity of Creek chiefs against another Creek or a Muskoe Indian. Further, the mob first secured permission of the commandant. Its motive in acting as it did appears to have been to curry favor with white authorities. Surely there has never been any Native American law that mandated capital punishment by chiefs beating the condemned to death for stealing a rifle from a white man. Should it be insisted that the clubbed-to-death Indian was guilty of a more serious crime or crimes, no proof of his involvement in any other criminal activity is included in Stoddard's letter. All we know is that the unnamed Indian was a thief, and he died at the hands of other Indians.

Just how many other native people might have died similar deaths, we have no way of knowing. Nor do we have any tally on similar incidents involving white men as killers of Indians. There are no Missouri newspapers until 1808. However, from Stoddard's same letter to Clairborne, we know about several incidents in which white men killed Native Americans in Missouri. In one, in the town of St. Louis, a drunken white man shot to death an Indian, "and no punishment [was] inflicted on the criminal." In another, in January 1804, white men killed five Indians in the belief they had killed relatives of one of their attackers. Stoddard knew that there was little reason to bother with any legal proceedings against these white men because the grand jury "cannot be prevailed on to find a bill of Indictment against [them]."[1] From his mention of two unrelated events by May 1804, it seems obvious that there must have been a sizeable number who met unwarranted deaths at the hands of white men. Otherwise, President Jefferson's secretary of war, Henry Dearborn, would never have authorized a payment to the tribe ranging from $100 to $200 for the wrongful death of each Indian at the hands of white men.[2] Such payments were necessary if any semblance of justice was to be achieved here. White men, as Amos Stoddard noted, sat as grand and petit jurors in the courts of the territory and later the state of Missouri, and they would neither indict nor convict other white men who killed Indians. However, the men who governed Missouri and the United States understood the necessity of maintaining excellent relations with Native Americans. To insure this, among other benefits, Indians received scrupulously fair treatment when they were tried in American and Spanish courts. My research for *Death Sentences in Missouri, 1803–2005* unearthed only three natives who were executed for killing white men, one executed by Spain and two by the United States. The Spanish sentenced to death at least three others in what is now Missouri prior to the Louisiana Purchase, and after it, in St. Louis, the Americans condemned three additional Indians to death. However, all six were either pardoned or escaped from jail, and efforts to recapture them were abandoned. The reason Indians received lenient treatment at the hands of both Spanish and American rulers is not complicated. Alliances could be formed with their tribes against various belligerent European nations.[3] Perhaps the chiefs who beat to death the rifle-thief Indian had already formed one, or soon would, with the white commandant's government. Otherwise why bother to punish, especially fatally, someone whose only proven crime consisted of taking personal property from a white settler.

There may have been other lynchings of Indians in Missouri, but I could discover no documentation for any such event. William Foley, an expert on early Missouri history, attributes the decline after 1815 of any Indian threat to the steady increase in white settlers.[4] Native Americans appear to have moved out of the territory and later the state of Missouri. As will be shown in subsequent chapters, large numbers of African Americans also left the state of Missouri in later time periods.

When we turn to the lynching of whites, there are no extant accounts of successful mob action until the 1840s, and during this decade there are two. The first came very close to making it into the record books as a legal execution, but not quite. On June 17,

1843, a crowd of 3,000 persons assembled in Farmington, St. Francois County, to watch the hanging of James Layton, convicted on a change of venue from Perry County for the January 1841 murder of his wife. The mob did not understand that the governor's reprieve of the condemned until the first of September would not cheat justice. It burst open the county jail, secured Layton, built its own gallows, and its members hanged him and went their separate ways.[5]

The second lynching of the 1840s was of Abraham Smith, in Fredericktown, seat of Madison County. Smith had killed another white man, Thomas Vinson, in late 1843, and he confessed his crime. An early twentieth century newspaper from Fredericktown dates the death of Smith as having occurred a few years after the legal execution of John Duncan. Since Duncan's hanging was the first use of capital punishment in the state of Missouri, it received sufficient publicity to fix its occurrence on April 5, 1821. The county history comes closer to the mark when it states that the lynching of Smith took place in February 1844, or more than 20 years after the execution of Duncan. Another date is given in a contemporary St. Louis newspaper as August 6, 1844, and this news story seems to be the most reliable dating.

A collateral descendant of Smith's victim's daughter gave me some early twentieth century Fredericktown news stories about this case. One published on January 15, 1900, is signed by Vinson's daughter, from Brunot (Wayne County), Missouri.[6] In it the daughter dates the murder of her father as December 28, 1844; she was mistaken by approximately one year. It must have been late in 1843 that Abraham Smith shot her father. Although the daughter assigns no motive for this homicide, we know from her account that the perpetrator and his victim were neighbors. Often enough the disagreements of men in such proximity proved deadly. By all accounts, Smith was tried during the winter of 1844 in Fredericktown, and the jury found him guilty of the first degree murder of Thomas Vinson; the county history misnames the murdered neighbor John Vincent. Smith appealed his conviction to the state's only appellate court, the Supreme Court of Missouri. Before it issued any decision, law enforcement officers in Madison County, fearing mob action, removed their prisoner for safe keeping to the nearby Cape Girardeau County jail in Jackson. However, Smith was returned to Fredericktown for a court hearing in the summer of 1844.

Here the story becomes sadly familiar. The crowd, composed mainly of the victim's friends, fearing that somehow Smith would escape the sheriff's noose, marched to the jail and demanded that the sheriff give up his prisoner. He refused and was overpowered, and after several hours of intensive labor, the mob forced the jail's door open and dragged Smith out of his cell. Its leader asked the assembled crowd to vote on whether or not to hang him, and either unanimously or by a large majority, it decided in favor of hanging him. Forthwith, Abraham Smith was lynched by being strung up to a nearby walnut tree between 3 and 4 p.m. Not surprisingly, neither the county history nor the daughter of the victim names any member of the mob. A St. Louis newspaper does. It describes the arrest in the city of St. Louis of a John Sinclair on September 30, 1844, as a principal in the lynching of Smith; Sinclair's arrest and confinement on a judge's order in the St. Louis City jail; and his planned removal to Madison County. The story concludes: "Eight or ten of the mob are now in jail, and if justice is done them, they will share the fate of the criminal whom they executed."[7] At this early date, the city of St. Louis had already ended its enthusiasm for mob punishment of wrongdoers. As will be shown through this book, lynchings were mostly carried out and approved in rural areas and small towns in this state. As is entirely expected from the brief extant accounts of this early event, there is no known legal penalty which John Sinclair or any other member of the mob who strung up Abraham Smith suffered at the hands of the law.

From these two known lynchings of white men in Missouri in the 1840s, several features of the circumstances of the extralegal killing of whites emerge. Both men had been found guilty of first degree murder by a court of law. There was no question of their guilt. Equally important, the method the mob used to end its victims' lives was the same as the legal method of executing criminals. In 1790, the First Congress passed and President Washington signed into law a major crimes bill. One section of it specified: "The manner of inflicting the punishment of death shall be by hanging the person convicted by the neck until dead."[8] In 1808, the Missouri territorial legislature adopted this statute verbatim when providing for the capital punishment of all offenders, both slave and free.[9] Both the federal and the territorial legislature did so because, during the late eighteenth and throughout most of the nineteenth century, death by hanging was considered the most humane method of executing the condemned. It remained Missouri law until the gas

Missouri counties divided into Northwest, Northeast, Southwest and Southeast, with names of adjacent states indicated (courtesy Missouri State Archives)

chamber replaced the county gallows in 1938. Overwhelmingly, and throughout most of Missouri's history, mobs here chose to kill white men by hanging them to death. Occasionally they shot or drowned them. They did not burn these victims; this hugely cruel punishment was not the proper way for white men to die. Death by burning was used for some African Americans.

During the 1850s, another aspect of the lynching of white men emerges here. Mobs put them to death for horse stealing. This crime looms large in the mythology of the untamed West. In that glorified version of events, no real man would actually deliberately ride off on another man's horse. To do so, as the myth went, was to leave that unhorsed individual to almost certain death. Without his trusty mount, alone in the wilderness, surrounded by wolves, bears, cougars, and other dangerous animals, the man on foot was thought to be a certain goner. Given the peril that the theft of a man's horse exposed him to, horse stealers richly deserved death. That was the campfire version of events.

That it was largely a white, not a black man's crime, is less well known and probably not a part of any mythology. The disassociation between horse stealing and slavery in Missouri can be found as early as in 1808 legislation. In that year lawmakers continued from the previous 1804 law the crime of larceny (stealing), but they added the separate offenses of horse stealing and hog stealing. Hog theft was a criminal act expected of both slave and free defendants. Though its $100 fine was unsuitable for those in bondage, its designated whipping of no less than 25 and no more than 39 lashes was tailored for slave offenders. In addition it carried no enhanced punishment for a second conviction. Horse stealing, on the other hand, was wrongdoing expected of free persons, all but a few of whom were white. From its initial appearance in 1808, it was a more serious crime than hog stealing. First, offenders were required to pay the owner double the value and receive no less than 50 and no more than 100 stripes. For a second conviction, the offender could be imprisoned for up to seven years and fined $1,000.[10] The primary use of stolen swine was food, but equines were means of swift, and always for slave runaways, forbidden transportation.

The next year, 1809, the town of St. Louis passed "An ordinance Concerning Slaves." One of its sections contained the following prohibition, "No slave shall take nor ride the horse, mare or gelding of his master or mistress, or that of any other person without permission first had and obtained from the owner thereof." The law further required every person to be watchful and report infractions to owners, and if these owners refused or neglected to punish "by whipping on the naked back of such slave twenty stripes," then the owner was required "to forfeit and pay the sum of ten dollars."[11] The intent of this prohibition against bondpersons riding horses as a pastime was to stop would-be fugitives from the service of their masters before they started.

The disconnect worked; few runaway ads that appeared in Missouri newspapers over a 50 year or greater period mention any animals. Usually they described the clothing, physical features, sex, and approximate age, and from these descriptions it is clear that most runaways were on foot. Every slave-rich county had patrollers on the alert for, among other bondpersons' misbehaviors, runaways. Black persons on horseback were eye-catching. White men traveled the roads, and their mission was to apprehend blacks without passes who appeared to be in the wrong places. As best they could, runaways avoided

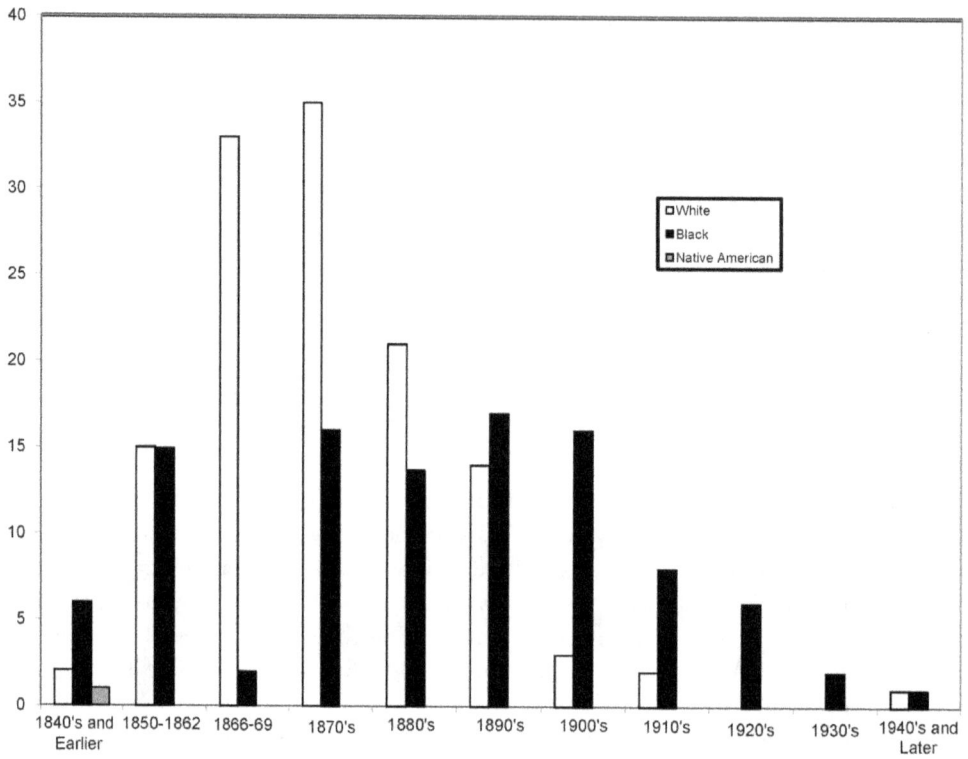

Decade-by-decade chart of lynchings in Missouri by race, 1803–1981

the highways. The smaller the fleeing slaves could make themselves as they silently blended in with foliage, the more likely they were to remain free. Hiding and eluding captors would be far more difficult for escaping bondpersons if they were encumbered with a mount. Equally important, if any unfamiliar black was in possession of a horse, he was likely to be charged with a crime. One notice which a sheriff placed in a newspaper advised that a black man who claimed he was free had been jailed in the town of St. Charles. Because, as the piece continued, "He has an old bay horse, saddle, and saddle bags, he is now charged with larceny."[12] The law enforcement officer assumed that black men did not own horses. They were the property of white men.

   That the horse played almost no role in the slaves' running away from this state can also be shown with reference to the two best known Missouri runaways, William Wells Brown and John Anderson. Narratives of their lives exist; Brown wrote his own, and an English abolitionist, Harper Twelvetrees, wrote Anderson's. Brown's master, a steamboat owner and St. Louis resident, allowed him to work as a steward on a steamboat. In 1834 Brown escaped across the Ohio River from Covington, Kentucky, to Cincinnati, and he appears to have walked northeast in Ohio until he eventually reached Cleveland. There he found employment on a Great Lakes steamboat. There is no mention of a horse or mule in Brown's account of his escape from bondage. John Anderson began his journey from Saline County in 1853; he took, among other property of his owner, a mule and a bridle. He rode the animal only a short distance. Once he reached the Missouri River,

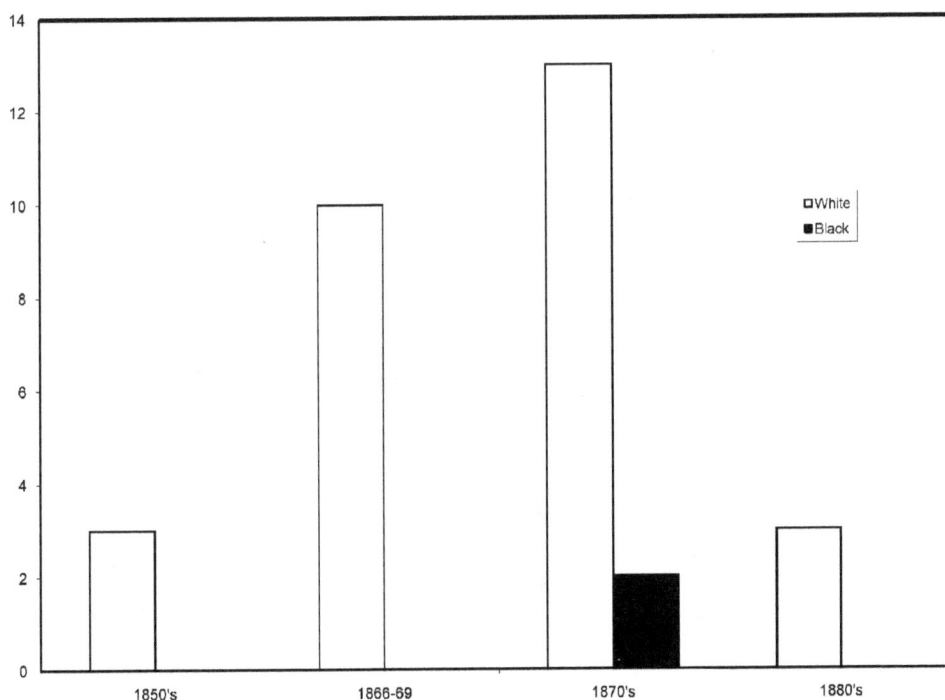

Chart showing four decades of lynchings for horse and mule stealing, 1850–1881

he crossed from Saline to Howard County in a small boat, using a piece of bark as an oar. He left the mule behind rather than either swim it across the river or tether it to his boat for the journey. Once Anderson arrived in Howard County he was on foot, and he remained a pedestrian until he reached the middle of the state of Illinois. From this location, he rode a team of horses to Rock Island. Within a few days of his arrival, abolitionists paid his train fare to Chicago. Eventually he reached Detroit, presumably by railroad, and we know he crossed from Detroit to Windsor, Ontario, Canada.[13]

Clearly, there was no need to write laws against fugitives taking horses with them when they fled the service of their masters. When the Missouri General Assembly passed major legislation in 1835, including the punishment of horse thieves, it did not write the law to punish slaves. Blacks were rare among prison inmates throughout the antebellum period. Because slaves had no liberty to lose, they could not be punished with imprisonment. The new law was mainly intended for white offenders. The statute provided that "Every person who shall be convicted of feloniously ... stealing ... any money, goods ... of the value of ten dollars or more..., any slave..., any horse, mare, mule ... cattle, sheep ... [and] hogs belonging to another shall be deemed guilty of grand larceny." It set the punishment for stealing any livestock at not more than seven years.[14]

The 1835 criminal statutes of Missouri were written for a state that finally had a penitentiary in which to confine wrongdoers. The year after the 1835 legislation was passed, Missouri's newly completed prison began receiving inmates. As early as 1830, the Ways and Means Committee of the Missouri General Assembly was issuing reports on a penitentiary; by 1833, an act for establishing the prison in Jefferson City had become law.[15]

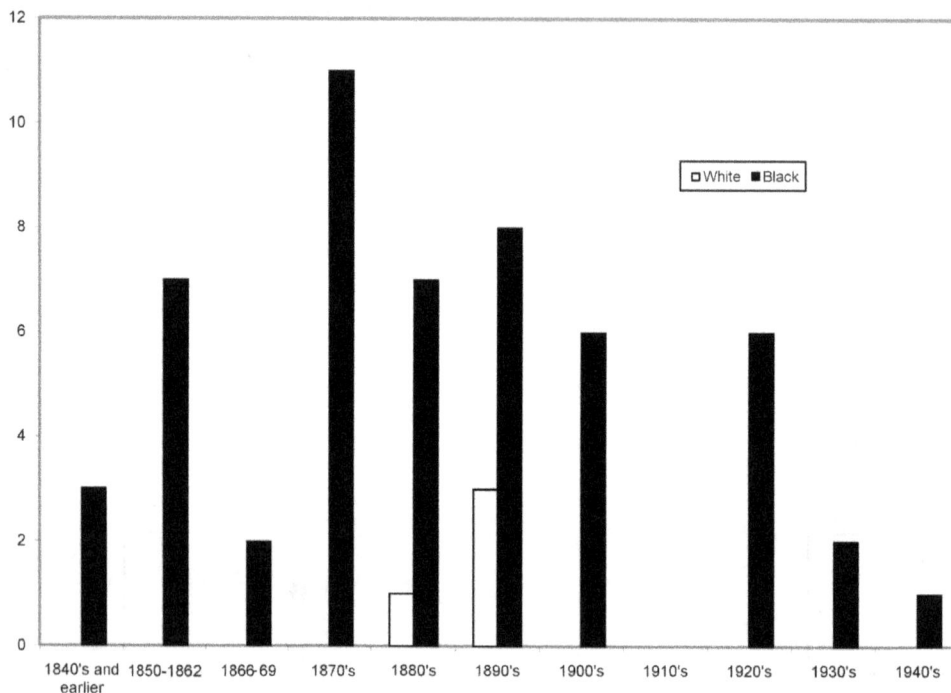

Decade-by-decade chart showing lynchings for sex crimes in Missouri, 1818–1942

The prison door was open wide for horse thieves, among many other wrongdoers. Because the Register of Inmates, Missouri State Penitentiary, almost invariably listed as "grand larceny" the offense of persons convicted of stealing an extremely wide range of personal property, there is no way of ascertaining from prison records what the now incarcerated inmate had carried off. He might have stolen money, a slave, a horse, a mule, some sheep, or choice hogs. The legislature defined the crime of grand larceny so broadly that it covered the felonious taking and carrying away of almost any imaginable personal property of another, so long as there was the intent to deprive the victim permanently of his possession(s). It seems a reasonable assumption that a fair number of convicts at the Missouri State Penitentiary did time for stealing horses. Throughout the antebellum period, these thieves were white, as were almost all other prison inmates in Missouri.

Horse or mule stealing appears to have been an easy and profitable crime to commit. By modern standards, the nineteenth century fencing for livestock here must have been totally inadequate; poor or non-existent security for barns and stables was apparently commonplace. Missouri newspapers contain numerous ads for strayed animals, principally horses, and the ad often features a crude cartoon of a horse. From the territorial period on, the law provided that the "householder" (one with a residence, not a vagabond) finding the stray shall, within ten days, give notice to a justice of the peace, and he in turn was required to locate three disinterested householders to describe and appraise the found property. The clerk of the court had to record the information. The law further required that should the owner not claim his property within 40 days then the finder must advertise the strayed animal in a newspaper. If no owner appeared within two years, the finder became the rightful owner of the property, but he was required to pay the court costs. In 1817, if the owner claimed his missing animal, he owed the finder of any horse a reward of $2.[16] The 1835 law gave "any person" who found livestock certain benefits and burdens concerning them; it contains no mention of race. By 1845 there were requirements that the finder post a bond if "not a free white person and householder." This "free white person and householder" language continued in all revisions of Missouri stray law throughout the antebellum period.[17] These laws were yet another way that blacks were denied possession of equines.

The newspaper advertisements contained the age of the horse, usually between five and eight years, the height, ranging from 14½ to 16 hands high, and the appraised value, $25 to $80.[18] The men who placed them were honest, were following the law, and wished to unite the out-of-place horse with his rightful owner. Horse owners purchased other ads. After a headline outlining the reward (ranging from $5 to $20), they began, "Strayed or stolen." One continued, "A Black Horse five years old, fifteen hands high ... an additional reward of twenty dollars for the thief."[19] Another, "A large sorrel HORSE.... I will give twenty dollars to any person who will return said horse and give me information of the villain that carried him off, as will enable me to convict him."[20] Though some of the newspaper notices mention a brand on the equine, typical now of cattle, not all did, and if there were a brand, it could be altered. Equally important, farm animals, including horses, were personal property, and their sale was not registered, as real estate was, with the county office of Recorder of Deeds. It seems a safe assumption that the men arrested for this crime in the antebellum period, and especially those who were lynched, were not novice horse stealers. No youthful ages are mentioned in any pre–Civil War accounts. They had probably succeeded with this particular thievery a number of times before they were finally apprehended.

The lynching of horse thieves prior to the post–Civil War era is not a detailed record. What we know derives from contemporary newspapers and later from county histories. The earliest mention is a news story from September 20, 1850. It refers to "several individuals [who] have recently been taken out and lynched in St. Joseph, Missouri, for horse stealing."[21]

The second mob death involving this crime is the first known triple lynching in Missouri's history. It took place in Smithville, Clay County, on August 7, 1854. Three men, William Shackelford, his brother, Samuel Shackelford, and John Callaway, had been accused of horse stealing. The residents of Smithville ordered them to leave the county. They refused, and in the process the accused men shot and killed two Smithville men, John W. Douglass and S. J. Ross. According to county history, William Shackelford was hanged first and Callaway next, and he stated before his death "that Samuel Shackelford was to blame for all the trouble; that Sam ... had induced him into stealing horses, that Sam stole the mule he was arrested for, and he took it and sold it in St. Joseph."[22] The last to die was Samuel Shackelford. Although these men probably would have remained alive had they not shot to death two Smithville citizens, their horse thievery set in motion the train of events which led to their deaths. The men were lynched on a Monday, and their bodies were still hanging on Tuesday morning on the limb of a tree in Smithville.[23]

In Palmyra, Marion County, in October 1859, an unnamed man was caught with a stolen horse in his possession. The mob who found him soon hanged him.[24] This was

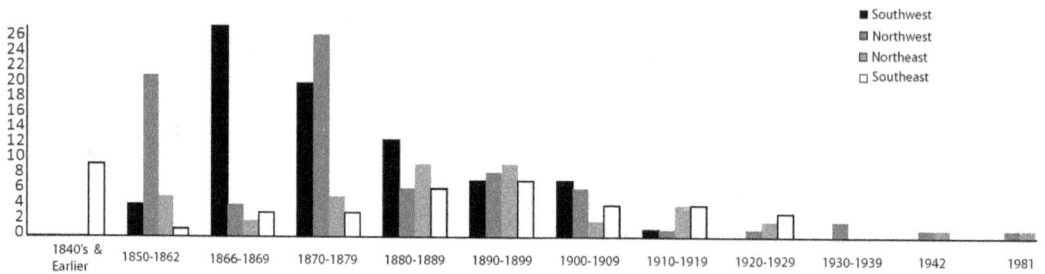

Decade-by-decade chart showing lynchings in Missouri by section of the state, 1803–1981

the only lynching in Marion, the county of Mark Twain's childhood, I located. On October 22, 1859, another horse thief and escaped prison inmate, Sim Sexton, earlier accused of robbery and assault, was seized by between 300 and 400 men near Renick, Randolph County. The men voted, and the motion in favor of hanging him carried. He was soon strung up. His history, according to a newspaper account, included "horse-thieving operations from Boone County to the Iowa line for a number of years past."[25]

In the early 1880s, the *Chicago Tribune* began its annual lists of the executed and lynched nationwide. Once this newspaper's detailed compilations were underway, a Howard County incident would likely have been carried in it as a completed lynching. As a result, subsequent compilers would add another name to its list of Missouri's victims of Judge Lynch. However, in 1857, there were no annual lists. In June of that year, a George Matheny, alias Tucker, was arrested for horse stealing in Howard County and confined in the jail in Fayette. He had earlier lived in Johnson County, was suspected of the same crime there, and had killed a member of a mob trying to drag him out of his residence in order to lynch him there. His Howard County neighbors believed that he was a member of a band of horse thieves. On September 5, a Saturday, 300 to 400 persons gathered in Fayette, of which 50 or 60 were active participants and the remainder silent sympathizers. The mob marched to the jail and began the work of breaching it. The prisoner heard the sounds of angry men and jail door demolition, knew his fate if the mob secured him, and according to the newspaper, "took a strong linen towel, tore it in two, and succeeded in hanging himself before an entrance was effected.... Upon hearing that the prisoner had taken his own life, and being convinced of the fact, the mob quietly dispersed."[26] This incident was not a lynching, but because it has many of the elements of one it is carried in Appendix 2, "Falsely Reported, Doubtful, and/or Foiled Lynchings in Missouri, 1857–1930."

One white man was strung up here on May 9, 1850, for criminal behavior rooted in abolitionism. Because his case is thoroughly entwined with that of his slave companion, it is discussed in the next chapter.

Mobs put to death four additional white men and planned to kill two others between 1853 and 1859. Three of the four were believed guilty of the murder of a worthy person. Both a newspaper and a county history relate the crime and lynching of Obediah W. Wingo in Richmond, seat of Ray County, on October 10, 1853. Wingo, according to the newspaper, had been drunk for approximately a week prior to his shooting and killing Benjamin R. Allen. When Allen and Wingo happened to meet on a Richmond street, they exchanged a few words about a blacksmith causing a young horse to be thrown and bound in order to shoe him. Allen, a passerby on horseback, thought it a cruel method for shoeing. After Wingo remarked that he saw no alternative, he left the vicinity of the blacksmith's shop. Moments later, he returned with a double-barreled gun and asked Allen to retract his remarks. Allen refused; thereupon Wingo shot him in the head, immediately causing his death. The murdered man was married, the father of four young children, and the community thought him a fine gentleman. Wingo had a very different reputation. In addition to several run-ins with the law, as the newspaper notes, Wingo's "general habits and associations were of the worst and most vicious sort; being seen, even on the Sabbath, playing cards with negroes and disturbing the quiet and peace of families by seeking intercourse with their slaves, for the most disgusting and vicious purposes."[27]

Immediately following Wingo's shooting and killing Allen, he was arrested and placed in the Ray County jail. Four days later, while he was being returned to his cell after a court appearance, a mob of 250 snatched him from the sheriff and several guards, placed a rope around his neck, and dragged him on his face and hands to a tree. There, on October 14, 1853, it hanged him by the neck from a limb, and his lifeless body dangled from it until the corpse was removed and buried the next morning. The newspaper describes the men who lynched Wingo as including "recognized members of the various Christian Churches, and many of the most respectable, intelligent, order-loving, and law abiding citizens of the county."[28] The county history, published 28 years later, says of Wingo, "He was a very quarrelsome, desperate, and dangerous man, and the community was well rid of him."[29] Obviously, the community approved of this lynching long after the fact.

The next known lynching of a white man, James Ray, took place eight miles from Florence in Morgan County, on July 8, 1856. Ray had a bad reputation and had filed a civil suit. Witnesses in it gave testimony that they would not believe him under oath. He vowed revenge. Perhaps coincidentally, perhaps not, children and their teacher who drank from a spring near their school house became dangerously ill. The community believed that Ray had poisoned the water. After all, he was, as the newspaper reported, "the greatest rascal in the neighborhood," and parents of some of the "suffering children" had sworn in court that they would not believe him under oath. Finally, Ray had removed his own children from the school shortly before "the spring was poisoned, pretending he wished them to thin corn."[30] Ray's neighbors arrested him, but he managed to escape to adjacent Hickory County. From it, a mob returned him to the school with the poisoned spring in Morgan County. Approximately 100 men participated in Ray's lynching. Among the leaders were several Baptist ministers, one of whom the newspaper names, Rev. Thomas Greer. The assembled allowed Ray one hour to prepare for his death. When his time expired and he insisted for the last time that he was innocent, he was hanged, probably from a tree limb, near the schoolhouse, where the mob believed Ray had poisoned the spring water.[31]

The last known white men accused of murder who died at the hands of a mob during the 1850s were Jeff Kessler, on June 25, 1858, and James Milligan, about two weeks later, on July 5. Both men were put to death in Albany, seat of Gentry County, near the Iowa border. Kessler allegedly shot and killed Samuel Timmons, a constable of Bogle

Township, who happened to have committed a minor offense. A justice of the township issued the warrant for Timmons, and it was handed to his old enemy, Kessler, who enlisted Milligan to help him. While Milligan stood guard, as the story goes, Kessler shot and killed Timmons in mid–June 1858. Both were arrested and indicted, and their trial was set for June 24 in Albany. Kessler had engaged two capable attorneys from St. Joseph, one of whom, 39-year-old Silas Woodson, was later governor of Missouri (1873–1875). Kessler's lawyers obtained a continuance for him, and the state's attorney agreed to one for Milligan. The citizens were displeased that their trial was delayed. A "great crowd," as the newspaper phrases it, had assembled, and once court was adjourned, "Kessler was immediately seized by the crowd, and taken a short distance from the courthouse, and hung by the neck until he was dead."[32]

On July 5, the mob removed Milligan from jail. Features of his lynching are remarkably similar to a legal execution of the time. He asked to be baptized, and his wish was granted. He was taken to a stream nearby, and a minister submerged him. He was then given a new and dry suit, and the crowd hanged him from the same tree from which, several weeks earlier, it had strung up Kessler. Approximately 300 persons watched the extralegal hanging of Milligan.[33]

One account of the lynching of white men in Missouri during the 1850s is fictional. The editor/publisher of a Platte City, Platte County, newspaper, no longer extant, learned of a plan to murder two men from one or more of the mob's leaders. Its intended victims, then inmates in the Platte County jail in Platte City on charges of enticing slaves to leave their masters, were a former physician from Rochester, New York, Dr. John Doy, an abolitionist resident of Kansas, and his 25-year-old son Charles. A young circuit court judge, Elijah Norton, stopped the mob in its tracks, but the already published newspaper reported in great detail the lynching as if it had occurred. The *St. Louis Republican* published the matter as accomplished fact, and the *New York Times*, relying on the St. Louis newspaper headlined its account, "Lynch Law in Kansas — Execution of the Doys." The *Times* story includes, "The crowd, more than three hundred strong, ... attacked the jail, taking the prisoner, and then forced the son to drive the cart ... about two miles from the city, where they were hung to a tree. The old man begged very hard for his life, but they would not hear him. The son was hung first."[34] A recent book of death records from Missouri newspapers contains this entry: "Doy,___ and son lynched in Platte Co. for 'running off Negroes,' *California Weekly News* [Moniteau County], March 5, 1859."[35] A full account of the anti-slavery adventures of Dr. Doy, before, during, and after his and his son's imaginary lynching, can be found in my *Runaway and Freed Missouri Slaves and Those Who Helped Them*, Chapter 9.

Three other known lynchings of white men occurred here in the early 1860s. A fourth from 1861 has too brief a record to determine whether or not it should be classified as a mob murder; it is listed in Appendix 2. Marcellus Harris was tried in St. Clair County Circuit Court for the murder of Dr. James Smith in Osceola, and he was acquitted. Approximately a year later, in 1861, according to the county history, Harris was "waylaid and assassinated ... not over one-fourth of a mile from the Court House."[36] The silence of this account regarding the identity of the assassin(s) and the proximity of Harris to the place where he was found not guilty of murder suggest that his death was planned and carried out with community approval. However, a single gunman may have killed

Harris, and nothing in this book is classified as a lynching unless it seems likely that at least three persons participated in the death of the victim.

A similar incident took place in either February or March of that same year in Johnson County. Dr. Judson G. Stewart was tried in Warrensburg for the murder of Miles Cary, and he was also acquitted. A few days after Stewart was released from the Johnson County jail, his body was seen hanging from a tree near Rose Hill, Johnson County. The newspaper account adds that Stewart was "the notorious Dr. Jameson, the Kansas Outlaw."[37] Once more the community approved, and the method of death, hanging, suggests that at least three determined men ended Stewart's life shortly after he was found not guilty of murder in a court of law.

In Livingston County, Samuel Husher murdered his neighbor, William Avery, near Spring Hill, on August 31, 1861, by lying in wait for him and killing him with a shotgun. He then dragged his victim's body into the brush to conceal his crime. When Avery's body was discovered, Husher was immediately suspected. He had earlier threatened Avery. The county history relates of the matter, "Husher was tried by a sort of lynch court, partly legal and largely illegal." The defendant chose his own jury, but he was not tried at the courthouse in Chillicothe; rather the proceedings against him took place near the crime scene. The evidence against Husher included his threats to Avery, his discharged shotgun, and his 12- to 14-year-old daughter's testimony that he came home on the night of the murder with his weapon and blood-splattered clothing, removed and burned his clothes, and warned her never to speak of what she had seen. She spoke, and the jury found him guilty, and it fixed the sentence at death by hanging within the next 24 hours. Though the Union Army occasionally dispatched men with amazing speed, no court under civilian control in the history of Missouri ever carried out a death sentence with such speed.

Husher gave directions regarding his property and hired a coffin-maker. On September 4, 1861, he was hanged on a gallows near Spring Hill in the presence of hundreds of spectators. Until 1938, all legal executions carried out under state authority took place at the county seat. This man's did not. The county history contains a high level of approval of Husher's lynching: "There were no continuances, changes of venue, dilly-dallying, or subterfuges, tolerated in that court.... The verdict and the sentence were applauded by nearly every man in the county. The verdict was universally approved."[38]

The final case covered in this chapter began in 1858, when William Legrand Hall stabbed Andrew Bullock to death in Franklin County. After one trial in Union, he received a second on a change of venue to Washington County. At his trial in Potosi, he was sentenced to 15 years in the Missouri State Penitentiary. At both evidentiary hearings, his defense was insanity. After several years in prison, he was transferred to the lunatic asylum in Fulton. After 10 months at the state's mental institution, its officials, presumably one or more of whom were medical doctors, pronounced him sane and released him.

In due course, Hall killed his sister; she was then caring for their terminally ill father. His daughter's murder so shocked the father that he died within six hours of her death. Next, Hall attempted to kill his brother; his motive for these crimes against his family was his wish to become his father's sole heir. He was arrested, brought to Union, the county seat, placed in jail, and, in the middle of his preliminary examination, on July 18, 1862, in the Franklin County courthouse, the lynching party began its work. As the county history phrases it, Hall "was seized by about fifty quiet, determined, silent, unmasked men, taken to a wagon ... [and in it] to the southeast part of town, where a rope was fastened about his neck, the other end thrown over the limb of a large elm tree and fastened and the wagon driven out from under him, and he [was] left to choke to death."[39] The mob of silent men returned to the courthouse grounds and went their separate ways. The county history concludes of Hall's case, "There is no doubt in the minds of many of the best citizens that the victim of this lynching was insane."[40] Contemporary newspaper coverage was less sympathetic. One wrote of Hall, "He had no friends and met with very little compassion."[41] Another stated the truth of many lynchings, "None of the authorities interfered."[42] There are no other known fatal mob actions against white persons in the early 1860s.

The records of an Indian and various white men dying at the hands of a mob here before the war years do not total 20. There are probably other instances in this state of white men dying at the hands of a large number of others during the antebellum period, but I have no documents to substantiate that such violence ended the lives of any other whites during the pre–Civil War years. The likelihood is great that other Indians were lynched during the territorial period and even more white men during the four decades before the war began. Most of rural Missouri was Southern in its sympathies. Many of its citizens were born in the Carolinas, Kentucky, Tennessee, and Virginia, and they retained their Confederate loyalties. Newspaper editors and publishers reflected the views of their readers. When the Civil War began, the Union Army marched into these little towns, and to quash anti–Northern sentiments, its members destroyed many rural newspapers and their presses and jailed the papers' editors. Otherwise, we would know a great deal more about vigilante justice here before sectarian strife engulfed Missouri during the Civil War years.

The next chapter discusses African Americans, mostly slaves, whom mobs put to death in the pre–Civil War years.

CHAPTER 2

Slaves and Free Blacks, 1818–1862

The record of African Americans being lynched in Missouri during the antebellum period is considerable — 20, 21, or 22, depending on whether an early event is fused with a later one in both Franklin and Jefferson counties. Mobs put more blacks than whites to death here before the Civil War. After the war and until the 1890s, rabble violence ended more white than black life in this state. Historians and other experts on this subject usually explain that slavery protected blacks from mob violence because bondpersons were valuable properties. An early twentieth century authority on lynching, James Cutler, states, "The summary execution of Negroes did not ... become a serious evil previous to the Civil War."[1] Lawrence Friedman notes that "Lynching was hardly necessary as an instrument of terror and domination during slavery."[2] Michael Fellman writes, "Lynching of blacks commenced in Missouri at the end of the War."[3] Edward Ayers views it in this light: "The crime that haunted so many ... white Southerners in the late 1880's and 1890's [was] the rape of white women by black men."[4] White Missourians worried about black fiends ravishing their girls and women far earlier than the end of the nineteenth century. The fact is that none of these scholars have done all of their homework on the pre–Civil War lynching of blacks, most of whom were slaves. They, as many others, have far more extensively studied the slavery of the eastern seaboard states than newer places of bondage, such as Missouri. Slaves were lynched here, and these horrid events took place with some frequency.

A distinction not made by any of these authors is useful. In the states which formed the Union and retained slavery as late as the 1860s — Delaware, Georgia, Maryland, North Carolina, South Carolina, and Virginia — the colonial and later the state legislatures passed statutes that compensated the owners of bondpersons when the colony and later the state took their human property for the purpose of execution. In what later became the Louisiana Purchase, the French also compensated masters and mistresses when they put their slaves to death. Records exist of these payments in what is now the state of Louisiana. No records are extant for the areas that later became the states of Arkansas and Missouri. English and French colonial laws had nothing to do with the U.S. Constitution's Fifth Amendment requirement that just compensation be made when private property is taken for public use. The first 10 amendments to the U.S. Constitution became law in 1791. By this time the compensation statutes of the Southern colonies had been in effect almost a century. They remained on the books throughout the antebellum period and helped to protect bondpersons from being lynched.

In jurisdictions where the law authorized the compensation of the slaveholder when a court condemned his human property to death and a sheriff carried out the sentence, the murder of slaves at the hands of a mob was probably uncommon. After all, the *lawful* execution of bondpersons was fortuitous for the owner. Any rabble that ended a slave's life wrongfully interfered with the master's right to the state's (or the District of Columbia's) compensation to the slaveholder for his property loss. Arkansas, Missouri, and Tennessee never paid owners when slaves were legally put to death. Mississippi restricted the amount to one-half of the slave's value; Texas hemmed it in with other restrictions. For the most part, the antebellum lynching of slaves occurred in states that paid the owner little or nothing when a county sheriff executed his human property. This was so because in slave states that joined the Union, the franchise was never as restrictive as in the original Southern colonies. For example, in South Carolina as a prerequisite for running for the legislature, the candidate had to own at least ten slaves. In Missouri neither slave nor real estate ownership was required for voting or serving in the General Assembly. To be sure, in the newer places of slavery, lawmakers continued to serve slave owner interests. However, they never made laws with the same total devotion to these interests as did legislators in the states that formed the Union.

Another distinction between Missouri and the older slave states concerns the legal method of executing bondpersons. Because this state was a territory from 1803 until 1821, federal law applied here, and as mentioned in Chapter 1, the only approved method of legally executing was by hanging the condemned by the neck until dead. Once Missouri became a state, the noose remained the state's only means of executing any death-sentenced person, slave and free, black and white, male and female. On the other hand, states which formed the Union retained their older and far crueler methods of carrying out slave death warrants. In 1709 a woman was burned alive on charges that she set fire to her master's house in the colony of South Carolina.[5] In 1745 in Orange County, Virginia, Slave Eve was convicted of petit treason in the poisoning murder of her owner, and her death sentence required that she be carried "upon a hurdle to the place of execution and there to be burnt."[6]

Much nearer to Missouri, according to one nineteenth-century Illinois county history, the sheriff of the District of Kaskaskia, Illinois (then a town across the river from Ste. Genevieve), was instructed to burn Slave Manuel to death for witchcraft on June 29, 1781.[7] At this time, Illinois was a county in Virginia. Just two months before Missouri's 41 delegates met in St. Louis to write Missouri's first constitution in 1820, at least two Missouri newspapers, one in St. Louis County and the other in Cape Girardeau County, carried front-page reprints of an out-of-state news item about the execution of Slave Ephraim and Slave Sam for the murder of their master in Edgefield District, South Carolina. As the account makes clear, these slaves' separate death warrants required Sam's death by fire and Ephraim's hanging and decapitation so that his head could be publicly displayed. The news story says, "It must be a horrid ... sight to see a human being in the flames.... From some of the spectators we learned that it was a scene which transfixed in breathless horror almost everyone who witnessed it."[8] In 1830, under state law in Abbeville, South Carolina, a young male slave was burned to death for the attempted murder of his mistress.[9] By state statute in South Carolina as late as 1840, judges retained the discretion to decide "the kind of death to be inflicted" when capitally sentencing bondpersons.[10]

Judges in Missouri could only order death by hanging, and they did so until the last decade of the nineteenth century, as punishment for one crime, murder.

In contrast to Missouri, the state of Virginia in 1856 listed no fewer than 73 capital offenses for slaves, and only one of them, first-degree murder, was also a capital offense for a convicted free white.[11] The model for the older slave states' proliferation of death penalty crimes and punishments was English. Though England never experienced slavery, Blackstone wrote of English law in the 1760s: "It is a melancholy truth, that among the variety of actions which men are daily liable to commit, no less than a hundred and sixty have been declared by act of Parliament to be felonies ... worthy of instant death."[12] By the end of the eighteenth century the number of capital offenses under English law had climbed to more than 200.[13] When the early settlers came from England to America, they brought a great deal of English law with them, including many of the mother country's capital offense statutes and methods of carrying out various capital punishments.

That female slaves in America convicted of petit treason suffered death by burning is directly traceable to English law. Blackstone clarified the law on the subject of treason, both high, as in the murder of a king, and petit or small. The latter was the crime an inferior committed when he or she murdered a superior. He wrote, "For a wife to kill her lord or husband [and] a servant his lord or master ... is denominated petit treason.... The punishment for this offense, in a man is to be drawn and hanged and in a woman to be drawn and burned."[14] As the law developed in colonial America, the punishment reserved in England for servants who killed their mistresses or masters was easily and logically transferred to African slaves who killed their white owners. We shall also see that in the antebellum cases in Missouri when mobs burned their victims to death they did so in the belief that an inferior black had killed a white who was, if not his owner, certainly his superior.

Behind the English law were various Biblical injunctions pertaining mainly to sexual offenses, which required burning the offender to death. To cite but a few, prostitution: "Bring her forth and let her be burnt"; "if she profane herself by playing the whore ... she shall be burnt with fire"[15]; and adultery with one's mother-in-law, "If a man takes a wife and her mother, it is wickedness; they shall be burnt with fire, both he and they."[16] The Middle Ages built on later Biblical interpretations, and heresy, homosexuality, witchcraft, and sorcery were fire-punished offenses. Such a punishment was intended to extirpate the root and branch of heterodoxy. Perhaps the most famous of many who perished in the flames was 19- or 20-year-old Joan of Arc, found guilty of heresy and witchcraft, and burned at the stake in 1431.

Four hundred years later, it was unthinkable that either an American government or an American mob should end the life of any white person by burning him or her to death. Blacks, mainly slaves, were a different matter. The barbarity of fire remained a viable option for ridding the earth of them. In *Uncle Tom's Cabin* (1852), the cruel master, Simon Legree, taunts his slave, Tom, by asking him, "How would ye like to be tied to a tree, and have a slow fire lit up around ye — wouldn't that be pleasant — eh Tom."[17] Fiction yes, but Harriet Beecher Stowe reported what was actually going on in real time in her famous novel. For example, a news story out of Arkansas from December 1849 relates that the master was murdered by "two of his negroes. The body was found the next day, and the guilt of the negroes being satisfactorily established, they were taken out, tied to a tree, and burned to death."[18]

When Francis L. McIntosh was lynched in the town of St. Louis, on April 28, 1836, he too was tied to a tree and burned to death. He was a free mulatto from Pittsburgh, Pennsylvania, and he happened to be in St. Louis because he was employed as a riverboat man on the steamer *Flora*. On the last day of his life, he had earlier intruded when St. Louis law enforcement officers arrested a couple of sailors for disturbing the peace. Thanks to him, they escaped. Very likely, he was drunk, or at the least, had far too much to drink. When Deputy Sheriff George Hammond and Deputy Constable William Mull took him into custody for interfering with the arrest of the sailors, en route to jail and on the courthouse square, he broke loose from these officers and drew a knife with which he wounded Mull and cut the large arteries in Hammond's neck, causing his immediate death. Shortly, he was captured and placed in jail, but his stay was brief. A mob took him from jail and carried him to the edge of town. A contemporary physician's eyewitness account of this burning mentions that McIntosh sang and prayed while chained to a tree, where the crowd "built a slow fire around him. The lower part of his legs were burnt partly off and when the flames had burnt him so as to let out his bowels, some asked him if he felt any pain, he said yes, great pain. It was 18 minutes after the fire was kindled before he died."[19]

The sheer horror of this lynching gave St. Louis one black eye. The Honorable Luke E. Lawless, the circuit court judge who presided at the May 1836 grand jury investigation of McIntosh's death, blackened the town's other eye. Lawless's charge to the grand jury required it to decide whether the killing of the free mulatto was "the act of the few" or "the act of many." If the latter, then "it is beyond the reach of human law. The attempt to punish ... would ... be fruitless.... How are we to indict ... two or three thousand offenders? ... If the thousands congregated round the fire were the actors, ... it would be impossible to punish and absurd to attempt it." Lawless laid the blame for McIntosh's crime of wounding one law enforcement officer and killing another on the attempts of outsiders to end slavery. He discovered "the abolitionist influence [in] the peculiar character of [McIntosh's] language and demeanor" and "his rabid denunciation of the white man ... his hymns and prayers" as he slowly roasted to death. The judge also discussed the dangers of Indians and Negroes uniting against whites. As one would expect, when a grand jury composed entirely of white men was so charged, its foreman's report of May 24, 1836, concluded of McIntosh's murder, "It was the act of the populace, an assemblage of several thousand persons, for which five or ten individuals could not be made responsible."

The burning of McIntosh was denounced near and far. It is one of the best documented and widely known lynchings in the history of the United States. The abolitionist Elijah Lovejoy, then a resident of St. Louis, wrote of it that "the spirit of mobism ... forces a man ... from beneath the aegis of our constitution and laws, hurries him to the stake and burns him alive."[20] His condemnation of McIntosh's death cost Lovejoy his press; a mob threw it in the Mississippi River on July 21, 1836, and he was forced to move to Alton, Illinois. There another mob eventually murdered him on November 7, 1837.

Word was out that McIntosh had died an agonizing death. William Lloyd Garrison wrote several articles about it; a lengthy one concluded, "What was his offence! What in a white man under the same circumstances would have been called only manslaughter."[21] Theodore Weld, a famous and effective abolitionist, included condemnatory excerpts about McIntosh's demise from both an Illinois and a New York City newspaper in his *American Slavery As It Is* (1839), a book that sold 100,000 copies its first year in print.[22] When Abraham Lincoln deplored mob rule in a Springfield, Illinois, speech in 1838, he mentioned that "a mulatto man by the name of McIntosh was seized in the street, dragged to the suburbs of the city, chained to a tree, and actually burned to death."[23] The English novelist and economist, Harriet Martineau (1803–1876), journeying in Missouri and Illinois at the time of this lynching, wrote of McIntosh in her book about her American travel, published in 1838 in England: "No one would have dreamed of treating any white man as this mulatto was treated." She also observed that "the charge of Judge Lawless (his real name) to the Grand Jury is a sufficient commentary upon the state of St. Louis society."[24] In April 1842, the English novelist Charles Dickens, who had earlier read Martineau's book about her western American travel, visited St. Louis, and on a steamboat from there to Cincinnati wrote a friend about "the mob ... among whom were men of mark, wealth and influence [who] *burned* [McIntosh] *alive*. This I say, was done within six years in broad day; in a city with its courts, lawyers, tipstaffs [court criers], judges, jails, and hangman; and not a hair on the head of one of those men has been hurt to this day."[25] In early newspaper accounts of the wounding of Mull, the death of Hammond, and the incineration of McIntosh, the St. Louis *Missouri Republican* ended its coverage, "Let the veil of oblivion be drawn over the fatal affair."[26] It was not. For many years following, St. Louis's white population remembered 1836 as the "year the nigger was burned."[27] In his 1906 book on American lynchings, James Cutler devotes five pages to this St. Louis incident.[28] Truly, the slow burning to death of McIntosh lives in infamy. In all fairness to the city of St. Louis, it never had another lynching in its entire history, and its population at the time of McIntosh's murder was approximately 16,000.[29]

Stories of other early mob action against African Americans in Missouri are problematic. According to a retrospective in an 1897 newspaper, Slave Leonard, a 6' 4", powerfully built man owned by Miss Sarah McDonald, raped a Mrs. Tiematin and murdered a Mrs. Buse near Campbellton, Franklin County, in 1818. He was captured and jailed in Union, and outraged citizens broken open the jail and seized and hanged him from a black walnut tree in the northeast part of town, in what remained a vacant lot when the news story about this early event was published.[30] The history of Franklin County narrates the April 1847 lynching of Slave Eli in Union: "He attempted to rape a Mrs. Teaman, afterwards murdered her, and attempted to kill her young son, Henry. He was indicted for murder in March 1847, but prior to his trial, angry citizens took him from the jail and hanged him a little to the northeast of the present post-office building."[31] The absence of an antebellum Franklin County newspaper makes resolution of the discrepancies and similarities between these accounts impossible. A county history could easily misdate an event by 19 years; likewise a news account written nearly 80 years later could also be in error. The alleged crimes of the slave, the name of the victim Tiematin or Teaman, and the location of the stringing up, "the northeast part of town" and "a little to the northeast of the present post-office building" suggest that Slave Leonard and Slave Eli were the same person. However, they may be different bondsmen, one lynched in 1818, and the other in 1847, both in Union, Franklin County.

Other accounts of the lynching of black men here in the 1840s are also problematic. According to a brief statement in a county history, "About the year 1842 a Mr. Jeude, living near the present village of Pevely, was murdered by a negro, who killed him for the purpose of getting his money. The negro was not annoyed with a trial as the citizens caught him and hung him until he was dead."[32] Presumably this lynching took place in or near Hillsboro, seat of Jefferson County. In this same county, two years later, another African American identified as an asset of the estate of Phillip Coontz was arrested for the murder of a Dutch shoemaker and his wife, Mr. and Mrs. Yeider, and taken to the jail in Hillsboro. On March 5, 1844, a mob of 300 persons broke open the jail, seized the black man, placed him in a cart, drove him in it to the place of his alleged murders, tied a pole to two trees, fastened a rope around his neck and to the pole, and drove the cart off, thereby hanging him to death. One newspaper reports this event without editorial comment.[33] Another, a St. Louis newspaper, ran two stories on it. The first concludes, "It is much feared he will be taken out of jail and hung, but I hope the law may take its course."[34] The second ends, "We cannot approve of this violation of the law, but the murder appears to have been so deliberate and cold blooded, that the only wonder is that the community did not proceed more rashly."[35] The rasher mob behavior was almost certainly burning him to death.

By the time the county history was initially published in 1888, its authors may have misdated the 1842 lynching of an unnamed slave and confused the name Jeude with Yeider. Time and again, it is apparent that the compilers of county histories relied on the memory of old-timers when describing early events in their counties. Microfilm of newspapers which narrated these then contemporary happenings was not available to these nineteenth century writers of county histories. Just as Slave Leonard and Eli may be the same or different men, likewise, the unnamed Negro lynched about 1842 in or near Hillsboro may be the unnamed asset of an estate lynched in or near Hillsboro on March 5, 1844. However, there is always the possibility that these may be separate mob actions, one in 1842 and the other in 1844, in or near Hillsboro, Jefferson County.

During the 1840s, one additional mob death of an African American in Missouri can be documented. It took place in Caledonia, Washington County, in 1840. The newspaper names neither the slave nor his owner. Instead we read that a slave, belonging to a Mrs._____ of Belleview, raped her in late March, and on April 12 either raped or attempted to rape another woman, unnamed in the news account. The slave was captured on April 13 and taken to his mistress, and she in turn gave the rabble permission to do with him as it wished. In imitation of the law of a state such as Virginia, five persons appraised his value at $300; the mob collected this sum among its members and paid her, and on April 15, 1840, approximately 60 persons voted unanimously to hang him. At high noon in the village of Caledonia and in the presence of 300 to 400 persons, he was, as the newspaper reports, "swung off."[36]

The record of African Americans being lynched in Missouri is at its most uncertain during the 1840s. There may be documents for as few as two or as many as four, depending on whether the lynchings in Franklin and Jefferson counties are counted as one or two events. The 1850s and early 1860s are a different story. The possible confusion of one event with another does not occur, and the many incidents taken as a whole tell a horrifying story in a way that no individual case can. As a starter, this time period is the only one in Missouri's history in which not one, but two, slave women were lynched in separate and unrelated cases.

The first took place in Clay County. The most intriguing aspect of the case is the victim's possible relationship to a slave woman named Annice. Sheriff Shubael Allen hanged her in Clay County in 1828, following her conviction for the drowning murder of five slave children belonging to her owner, Jeremiah Pryor's. Two of them, Bill, aged five years, and Nelly, aged two years, were the culprit's own children. Did Annice have a daughter, also named Annice, aged about 16 years when her mother was put to death? Did Jeremiah Pryor sell the daughter to Shubael Allen, her mother's hangman?

The year after his hanging execution of Annice, Sheriff Allen placed a runaway ad offering a $60 reward in several Missouri and Illinois newspapers for the return of two Negro men (Ben and Rafe) and one girl (Annice), "about 17 years old, common size, of a yellow complexion, down look, well grown, and likely, her clothing is not recollected."[37] Sheriff Allen's runaway ad achieved its purpose, at least in the case of the "likely girl" who ran away; the daughter Annice was returned to him. When her owner, a prominent early citizen of Clay County, died in 1842, aged 48 years, his widow, Dinah Allen, became the administrator of his estate. In April of that year, she petitioned the probate court that she be permitted to retain his goods and chattels and to pay all debts of the estate from the sale of land her late husband had owned. In the court order granting her petition, the document specifically mentioned "Annice" as one of four slaves who were not to be sold.[38]

Eight years later in 1850, Annice the daughter remained a bondwoman of Dinah Allen. In the first newspaper article about Mrs. Allen, headlined "Daring Attempt to Murder," she is described as "universally esteemed and beloved, ... a favorite among all who know her." The story explained that on April 1 about 3 A.M., she was awakened by "what she supposed [was] the bite of a rat." The victim went into the bedroom where her sons were sleeping and exclaimed that she was bleeding to death. Someone had struck her in the face with an ax or a large knife. Two physicians were summoned, and she survived the wounds inflicted by a person or persons then unknown.[39] Four weeks later, the newspaper states of the attack on Mrs. Allen: "The general impression [is] that the author of this brutal and unheard of outrage is a negro woman and servant to the unfortunate sufferer." The story continues, "If the law which takes cognizance of such offences is not sufficiently rigid to prevent their commission, then it is time that some signal measures should be taken.... This thing should be looked into."[40]

The Allen sons suspected that the younger Annice was involved in the attempted murder of their mother, and on the basis of their suspicion, she became an inmate in the Clay County jail in Liberty. Once she was incarcerated, an unnamed minister visited her "at different times" and gradually obtained her confession, as the newspaper phrases it, "voluntarily and without any description of compulsion" that she axed her mistress, Dinah Allen. She told the minister that "a white man by the name of McClintock" suggested to her that they kill Mrs. Allen so they could get all the money she had, and afterward "he would take her to California and make her his wife and she would be "free." Annice agreed to McClintock's plan. According to her statement, he brought the murder weapon, an ax, with him when he came into the Allen kitchen, where she was sleeping; together they left the cook room, a separate building. Next, McClintock opened Mrs. Allen's bedroom window, and both assailants entered the house through it and saw her sleeping form. According to Annice, McClintock described to her Dinah Allen's position in bed and directed her to strike her owner in the face. When the victim struggled rather than died, the pair fled the crime scene. The white man made his getaway over the yard fence, and Annice returned to her pallet in the kitchen.

The presentation of this story and evidence corroborative of it to a jury in a court of law had an immense difficulty; Missouri law from 1804 until the end of slavery barred a black or mulatto from testifying against a white person. Further, because their intended victim survived their attack on her, neither Annice nor McClintock was death-eligible. The sheriff could only legally hang persons convicted of murder. Had they been tried and found guilty of attempted murder in Clay County Circuit Court, the most severe punishment possible for Annice was a whipping, sale, and transportation out of state. For McClintock it would be 10 years in the penitentiary.

As the newspaper saw it, "The statute laws of the state afford no adequate remedy ... to protect [the people] against the villainous machinations of negroes and their white abettors." As a result, the county's white male citizenry, comprising "farmers, mechanics, merchants, lawyers, physicians, and others" (surely including the Allen sons, unmentioned in all coverage) met at the Clay County courthouse to decide on an appropriate extralegal remedy. In the presence of the assembled, Annice appeared, as did McClintock, and she accused him of being a willing partner in the plot to murder Dinah Allen. After those present made "a full and deliberate investigation of all the facts and circumstances," by acclamation the "ablest and most respectable citizens" decided that both Annice and McClintock "should be publicly executed, and there was not a voice against it." Some present opposed the lynching, "but they remained silent when the vote was taken." Accordingly, on Thursday, May 9, 1850, and "in broad open daylight, by men of as much respectability as can be found in the United States, Annice and afterward McClintock were taken half a mile from town and hung." The paper says of the men who lynched the black woman and soon afterwards, her white male accomplice: "The term 'mob' cannot with any degree of justice be applied in this case. No people on the face of the earth are more law-abiding and more respectable than the people of Clay County, but they will no longer witness the butchery ... of their best citizens, by their own households, instigated ... by those devils in human shape, called abolitionists."[41]

Though a Clay County history published in 1885 and an out-of-county newspaper of the time[42] terms the hanging of Annice and McClintock a *lynching*, in all local and contemporary newspaper coverage their deaths at the hands of the county's most respectable citizens are termed *executions*. According to the county history, "McClintock denied to the last that he was guilty, but the negro asserted that her confession was true."[43] Neither newspapers nor the county history gave a first name for McClintock. He seemed to have been a pariah in his own county. As for Annice, any person about 17 years old in 1829 was about 38 years old in 1850. She was unsuccessful in her one known runaway attempt as a teenager, but her desire to be free was never extinguished. Her love of liberty left her open to the blandishments of the mysterious McClintock, whom the best, but unnamed, citizens who put him to death termed an *abolitionist*. This was a standard term of contempt for any white person or free Negro in a slave state known to be unenthusiastic about slavery. However, he was lynched because the white citizenry believed a bondwoman when she accused him of assisting her in the attempted murder of her mistress. McClintock did not meet a violent death because, standing alone, he attempted to entice Annice to leave Missouri, journey to California with him, and become his wife. Whether Annice lynched in Clay County in 1850 was an older daughter of Annice executed in this same county 22 years earlier remains speculation.

Less is known about the other slave woman, Teney, whom a mob hanged ten years later in Callaway County. In its county seat, Fulton, at least six slaves, two of them women, had earlier been sentenced to death; we are certain that three were legally executed, including one woman. The county's failure to bring Slave Teney to trial may have resulted from its citizens' increasing fear that the good old days of slavery were slipping away.

Her crime took place on Saturday, October 27, 1860, and her lynching appears to have occurred the next evening, October 28, a Sunday. On a day when all the white members of the household except one had gone to church, someone bludgeoned Miss Susan Jemima Barnes to death. She was first attacked in the east room as she sat knitting, and she fled to the kitchen and from there to the west room, where, as the *Boonville Weekly Observer* says, "She was completely overpowered, her head beaten into atoms, not a bone remaining whole save the right cheek bone. Her brains lay scattered over the floor.... Marks of bloody hands were on the wall, blood was on everything about the house." The coroner's jury surmised that the murder weapons included a shovel and fire tongs. The handle of the shovel was straight in the morning and later "very much bent." Gashes on Miss Barnes's hands and elsewhere on her body suggested that her attacker also used a knife, but it was not located.

Suspicion fell on Teney, a leased bondwoman, who in the absence of the man of the house, Miss Barnes's brother, as the newspaper continues, "was very impudent.... She had had several difficulties with her young mistress." On the morning of the crime, Teney was sent to a field to shuck corn, and she resumed her work that same afternoon. She initially wore a copper-colored garment, the tuck, or pleat, of which was ripped some five or six inches. When she returned to the cornfield, a neighbor, Mrs. Miller, observed that Teney had on a different dress. On Sunday, the coroner resumed his investigation of Miss Barnes's murder. Meanwhile, two men, William Booth and Solomon Thomas, searched for Teney's copper-colored dress; they found it splattered with what appeared to be blood, concealed in a corn sheaf near her place of work the previous day. Mrs. Miller identified the recovered dress as one Teney had first worn the day of the murder. When confronted with all the available evidence against her, she admitted that she killed her young mistress. She was immediately arrested, and a deputy constable, Henry Willing, obtained a horse for her journey to the Callaway County jail in Fulton, some eight miles distant. However, he never brought in his prisoner.

Despite Willing's "entreaties, threats, and persistent efforts," a "large and excited crowd" took Teney from him to a lonely stretch of remoteness and hanged her from a tree. The Boonville paper ends its story, headlined "Horrible Murder. A Negro Girl Hung by a Mob ... Under the excitement of the occasion, some of our best, and most responsible citizens engaged in the mob. It seems to have met the approbation of the owners of the negro."[44] A Callaway County history quotes from a local newspaper, which estimates the strength of the mob at "some forty or fifty exasperated men." This history reports that "Teney's body was taken down and buried the same evening."[45] Just as no African-American women were legally executed in Missouri after slavery perished, likewise, no mob, acting with community approval, is known to have lynched any white female.

In addition to the two slave women murdered by mobs, one in 1850 and the other in 1860, mobs in Missouri put to death at least 13 male slaves after 1852. With the exception of one in 1862, the other 12 took place between 1853 and 1859. In November 1862, near Hackberry Ridge in Andrew County, in the northwestern section of the state, an unnamed slave belonging to Edmund Gee allegedly raped and murdered an 11-year-old girl and almost murdered her brother as the children were returning from school. After the slave confessed his crime, as a news story describes it, he "was hung by the citizens at the place where he committed his crime."[46]

When the crime was a less serious offense than murder, namely attempted rape, rape, and first-degree assault, the vote to burn the offender never carried; he was always hanged. Missouri was the only slave jurisdiction as the Civil War neared in which a bondman's or bondboy's rape of a white female was not legally punished with death. This state's official punishment required the slave's castration under the direction of the sheriff by some skillful person.[47] Despite a diligent search, I never located a single incident of this dire punishment being carried out in this state. Usually the court, if a court was even involved, reduced the charge of rape to a lesser offense, such as assault, and sentenced the slave to a whipping and transportation. The owner would have used a middleman or trader to sell his slave down the river, and sold intact, not mutilated, he fetched a far higher price than he would have if a buyer knew that his new property had raped or attempted to rape a white girl or woman in Missouri.

The first known of these sexual offense cases not involving murder took place in Boone County. On August 12, 1853, Hiram, owned by Edward Young, allegedly attempted to rape 15-year-old Nancy Hubbard as she, her married sister, and her sister's small daughter were returning from a funeral. This is the first case I discovered in which contemporary newspapers mention that the accused was young, although how young was unstated. The assailant appeared out of the bushes completely naked and assaulted his victim, but she fought him off. Initially, the suspected slave was brought before several justices of the peace and discharged. However, he was reexamined and held in the Boone County jail in Columbia for trial. After what a newspaper describes as Hiram's "full confession," debate ensued among the leading citizens as to whether he should be burned or hanged. Mr. Hubbard, the father of the victim, was opposed to burning; he favored hanging. The vote to burn Hiram was only six, and the hanging motion carried. A committee was appointed to force the jail doors, take Hiram prisoner, and obtain a rope, a cart on which to convey him to the place of his death, and a coffin in which to bury him. Accordingly, on the western edge of Columbia and in the presence of a crowd estimated as high as 1,000 persons, on Monday, August 22, 1853, Hiram was, as one newspaper describes it, "deliberately hanged with nearly as much order as usually attends legalized executions of criminals. He was buried and thus ended the summary punishment."[48] Not only did a contemporary newspaper list Christian and surnames of the lynching committee, the chairman merited a middle initial, George *N.* King.[49] Nearly 30 years later, *The History of Boone County, Missouri* was published in 1882, and its four pages devoted to Hiram's lynching includes all names of the committee in charge of his death. Lynching is murder, and it has no statute of limitations. It can be prosecuted many years later. By the time the Boone County history was published, enthusiasm for lynching in the former slave states and the West was in full swing. Obviously neither the lynchers, members and chair of the committee, nor the compilers of the county's history ever imagined any legal action would result from the publication of these many names. As far as we know, no Boone County prosecutor ever brought any criminal charges.

On August 13, 1859, Slave Martin or Mart, an asset of the estate of Finley Danforth, allegedly raped Mrs. John Morrow in Greene County, in southwest Missouri. She threw scalding water on her assailant, and a wound on his chest matched the area of his body where she dashed the hot water. In addition, he confessed, despite the fact, notes a newspaper, that "no force or threat was used to induce him to tell."[50] After he was indicted, but before his trial began on August 17, a crowd of 300 to 400 men surrounded the place of Mart's lockup, Temperance Hall in Springfield, the county seat, took him from this place to the edge of town, and as the county history phrases it, "strung him up. Shortly, he was dead. The body was cut down and given hasty burial. Afterwards, it was 'resurrected' and dissected by a Springfield physician."[51] It could be argued in these cases that the mobs knew that the law would never put these rapists to death. This is a feeble explanation; mobs lynched a number of persons who were legally death-eligible.

In three separate incidents in different counties, the mob hanged a slave whom it believed was guilty of murder. In Clay County on February 12, 1855, Peter gained entrance to William O. Russell's home and slashed him with a corn knife. Russell had severely beaten a slave woman he owned, Peter's wife. Approximately two weeks later, Russell died from his injuries. Peter was arrested, indicted, and committed to the jail on first-degree murder charges. His trial was scheduled to begin at the April term of the Clay County Circuit Court. When a mob first assembled to lynch Peter, his owner, Major Lightburne, persuaded its members to abandon their plan, but on March 5, 1855, they reassembled, dragged Peter from his jail cell, and hanged him from a tree in the courthouse yard.[52]

When the clerk of the Clay County Circuit Court submitted bills for costs in two slave capital cases, Peter's and one other in which a slave indicted for murder escaped, the state auditor refused to pay them on the grounds that the state was not liable for them. Both the Clay County circuit clerk and Missouri's attorney general agreed that fees in both cases accrued under laws passed in 1845. One relevant statute read, "If a slave be convicted of any capital offence and executed, costs shall be paid by the state."[53] The Missouri Supreme Court upheld the state auditor's refusal to reimburse the county. It wrote of Peter's lynching: "The lawless violence of a mob, in its impatience to inflict punishment, taking the life of slave, is not the execution contemplated by this [1845] statute, even if the slave had been convicted before he was hung by the mob."[54] The court construed legislation already in existence when Peter was hanged. Nonetheless, and in obvious reaction to the Clay County claim and the potential for the claims by clerks of other Missouri circuit courts, the General Assembly amended the law to accommodate any county's collection of fees in slave cases, including those that were capital, whether or not the sheriff officially hanged the bondperson. Under legislation approved December 5, 1855, among other changes, the state would pay court costs "for a conviction of a slave in capital cases."[55] The lawmakers silently omitted the earlier requirement that the sheriff officially execute the condemned bondperson(s). As a result, the law required that either the state or the county pay court costs in some cases in which mobs lynched slaves. The amount depended on what services, if any, each county official actually performed. This legislation proved immensely beneficial for Saline County a few years later.

In some lynchings no court costs accrued. On October 10, 1855, George murdered his master, Judge Thomas Plenmons, in Carroll County, in the northwest section of the state. Plenmons had acquired George several years earlier by marriage, and the union of master and slave was a disaster. As one newspaper explains, the day before the murder, the judge had "corrected [whipped] this Negro for some dereliction of duty." When George was ordered to dig potatoes 200 yards from the house, he lured his owner to the patch on the pretext that he needed to be shown where to begin his potato digging. Once the judge was in the field, George struck him in the back of the head with his hoe. Afterward, the slave repeatedly struck his speechless but still living owner with his gardening tool until the judge finally died. That night he put his owner's body on a horse and conveyed it one and one-half miles from the house, dragging the corpse several hundred yards to create the illusion that Plenmons had been thrown from his horse and dragged to death. When his family missed him the morning of October 11, George was the prime suspect in his master's disappearance. After the slave was "severely thrashed," he led his interrogators to his owner's body. Once George made a "full confession," many of the neighbors took him out and hanged him from a tree. As for the cause of the judge's murder, one newspaper decided that Plenmons "was very indulgent to his negroes and allowed them to have their own way, till they were ruined.... If you wish your slaves to respect and honor you, they must be kept in their place. They cannot stand indulgence."[56] Garrison's *Liberator* ran a short article about the killing of Judge Thomas *Clingman* and the slave being "instantly hung by Lynch Law." Instead of the surname *Plenmons*, the garbled name remained *Clingman* in Cutler's early twentieth- century study of American lynchings.[57]

The remainder of the cases involves five bondmen being burned to death. The first took place in Pettis County, in northwest Missouri. It occurred after Slave Sam, aged 19 or 20 years, allegedly murdered a woman who was in late stages of pregnancy, Mrs. John Rains, of Heaths Creek Township, on July 3, 1853, when he was unable to rape her. In order to eliminate witnesses against him, he also attempted to kill, and believed that he had, her children. However, one child lived and was able to identify the perpetrator as the property of a neighbor. The slave was arrested and lodged in the jail in Sedalia, and a young attorney, George G. Vest (1830–1904), later U.S. Senator Vest (1879–1903), was appointed to represent him. In the middle of Sam's trial a mob removed him from jail, and General Smith, the founder of Sedalia, persuaded it to cease and desist. It dispersed, only to come together a second time about 100 men strong. On July 6, 1853, they took their prisoner from the jail approximately one-half mile from town. They invited all the slaves in the vicinity to witness their actions, tied Sam to a walnut sapling, built a circle of wood shavings and other combustible material around him, lit the pyre, and burned him to death.[58]

In Carthage, Jasper County, in extreme southwestern Missouri, two slaves purchased from Cherokee Indians — Colley, owned by John B. Dale, and Bart, owned by John J. Scott — on July 16, 1853, allegedly robbed and murdered a physician, Dr. John Fisk, raped and murdered his wife, choked their infant to death, and set fire to the physician's home.

Dr. Fisk had scolded Colley on several occasions for the slowness with which this former Native American slave performed various tasks. Colley persuaded Bart, then a runaway, to help him eliminate the John Fisk family in return for Colley's assistance in helping Bart commit another murder. When these miscreant slaves were arrested, the citizens of the surrounding country took them from law enforcement officers and burned them to death on July 30, 1853. In Sam's burning in Pettis County, slaves were invited to witness. In the Jasper County burning, they were rounded up as unwilling spectators, given the closest proximity to the scene, and required to light the blaze. Crowds from Arkansas, Kansas, and Indian Territory, now Oklahoma, assembled to watch Colley and Bart die chained to the stake in the bonfire.[59]

In Lincoln County in eastern Missouri, on December 24, 1858, Slave Giles stabbed his owner, Simeon B. Thornhill in retaliation for being "reprimanded" (i.e. whipped). The white man survived two days, named his killer, and the slave was arrested and placed in jail at Troy. On January 1, 1859, a mob forced its way into this facility, removed Giles, conducted him to a convenient locale, and there burned him to death. The county history contains this relevant detail: "When the funeral pile was completed, it was set on fire.... But death did not satisfy the wreakers of vengeance. They added fuel to the flame and ... persevered in the fiendish work until the body was all reduced to ashes. It is said that the scene was horrible to behold." Unlike the vast majority of these slave cases, court proceedings resulted from this Missouri burning. According to the county history, in March 1859, three men, presumably mob leaders, James Callaway, James Segrass, and Samuel Carter, were indicted for the murder of Slave Giles. In fall 1859, they were arraigned; jurors were empanelled, and an attorney was appointed to prosecute them. Not surprisingly, he dismissed the case, and that ended the prosecution of these men.[60]

The final known incineration of a slave here occurred on July 19, 1859, in Marshall, the county seat of Saline County. His name was John; he had been convicted at a special term of the Saline County Circuit Court of the first-degree murder, on May 13, 1859, of Benjamin Hinton. He was in jail awaiting sentencing when a mob removed him and burned him to death. John was one of four slaves lynched in this county within 24 hours.

On the previous day, July 18, 1859, a 14-year-old white girl, daughter of a Mr. Lamb, whom one newspaper terms "one of the most worthy citizens of Arrow Rock," was raped by an unnamed slave as she and other children returned from picking blackberries. The alleged assailant was cutting grass near the patch, and the children asked him questions regarding its locale. He came naked out of the bushes, grabbed the child and after "the villainy had been perpetrated," returned to cutting grass. The other children ran and spread the alarm; soon a number of black men were placed in a lineup. A minister and other respectable citizens investigated the crime, and they concluded that Dr. William Price's Negro man was the culprit. After a committee decided his guilt, his owner locked him in a stable, posted a guard over him, and planned to have him taken to the county jail in Marshall the next day. However, while the prisoner was under lock and key, he confessed, "corroborating the statements of the children in all particulars." That same evening, four or five men, dressed in women's clothing, came for the accused rapist, forced the key to the stable from the guard, entered, took out their prisoner, and in the presence of a large concourse of citizens, hung him from the limb of a tree, where they left him hanging, near the town of Arrow Rock.[61]

No court records exist in the Arrow Rock hanging on July 18, but they are extant for the three slaves lynched in Marshall the next day, only one of whom, John, convicted of murder, was burned to death. Each slave had a different owner. Dr. William Price owned the one hanged in Arrow Rock, and Giles Keister owned John, valued at $1,500; Mrs. Virginia Howard owned Holman, valued at $1,000; and James White owned James, valued at $1,000. All these bondmen committed their crimes on different dates and in different locales within the county. John murdered Benjamin Hinton of Waverly, Lafayette County, on May 13, near Miami in Saline County. Holman was being detained in the jail in Marshall prior to his trial for the attempted murder of William S. Durrett on June 21. In Holman's assault of Durrett, he cut his arm so deeply that he crippled him for life. James was on trial at the courthouse for an attempted rape of Mrs. Mary Habecot on July 12.

On July 19 a mob broke into the jail in Marshall and gained possession of John and Holman, and it also seized James at the courthouse. It hanged Holman and James and burned John approximately 200 yards north of the public square in broad daylight. Judge Russell Hicks, later a law partner of George G. Vest, was holding a special term of court in this county for these three bondmen, and he resigned his judgeship to protest the mob's lawlessness in burning one and hanging the other two.[62]

Thanks to the General Assembly changing the law following the lynching of Peter in Clay County in 1855, circuit court records exist of the three lynchings that took place in Marshall. Each contains a detailed listing of fees for personnel such as the clerk of the circuit court, the sheriff, the jailer, and justices of the peace. In John's case the record specified that the sheriff "placed him within the walls of said jail & locked the door of said jail from which place said Negro man John was by force and violence taken from said jail & publicly executed."[63] In Holman's, a grand jury had indicted him, but "before he was brought into the courthouse and placed upon his trial, [he] was forcibly taken from the jail and by the people publicly executed."[64] In James's, "said Negro man was placed upon his trial ... and whereas after the adjournment of said Court for dinner [the noon meal], the ... defendant was forcibly by the people seized [and] taken from the custody of the sheriff and his deputies and publicly executed."[65] At the November 1859 term of the Saline County Circuit Court, bills of costs were itemized in the cases of the three slaves lynched in Marshall on July 19, 1859. In Holman's and James's noncapital cases, court costs were certified to be paid by the county. Because John's was capital, fees in it were certified to be paid by the state.

The Saline County lynching of four slaves is the largest known number put to death in Missouri's history within 24 hours, and it probably is the largest because the sheer numbers generated a great deal of publicity. Equally important, the handwritten court records survive. These cases are also the subject of a lengthy article. The author mentions that in the 12 years between 1847 and 1859, "at least eleven slaves were lynched in various parts of the state."[66] There were more, several more. Likewise, his blaming the mob violence of 1859 in Saline County primarily on events which took place on the Missouri-Kansas border following the U.S. Congress passing the Kansas-Nebraska Act in May 1854 seems a stretch.[67]

The mini–Civil War which ensued following this federal legislation is the subject of two chapters in my *Runaway and Freed Missouri Slaves and Those Who Helped Them*

(2004). These events were no doubt a factor in the sheer number of slaves lynched in Missouri, but they are only one. The extralegal death of slaves began in Missouri some years before the Kansas-Nebraska Act became law. Other causes are equally important. The pro-slavery power, once so firmly in control of all three branches of the federal government, was losing its tenacious grip. Texas and Florida were the last places of slavery admitted to the Union, and they became states in 1845. Thereafter, new states were free. The list is impressive: Iowa (1846), Wisconsin (1848), California (1850), Nebraska Territory in 1854 (admitted as a state in 1867), Minnesota (1858), Oregon (1859), and Kansas (1861). Even earlier and on Missouri's eastern border the free state of Illinois joined the Union in 1818. This state's proximity to these many places of freedom gave slave-owning Missourians the fantods.

In 1852, Judge Scott wrote for the Missouri Supreme Court that Dred Scott was not free. In so doing he swept away nearly three decades of Missouri Supreme Court decisions favorable to the slave's suit for freedom. Judge Scott reasoned, "Times now are not as they were when the former decisions on the subject were made. Since then not only individuals but States have been possessed with a dark and fell spirit in relation to slavery, whose gratification is sought in the pursuit of measures, whose inevitable consequence must be the overthrow and destruction of our government."[68] His concepts are somewhat murky, but he was obviously concerned about the increase in the number of free states and, with their greater numbers, their greater power in the halls of government. Perhaps he even imagined that eventually the federal government might abolish slavery.

If a border state, such as Missouri, with three of its sides flanked by free states, did not have sufficient problems to increase the anxiety of its slave-owners, a publishing event occurred in New York City that made all their earlier worries seem insignificant. In March 1852, *Uncle Tom's Cabin* went on sale. It was an almost overnight success. Edmund Wilson wrote of it that it was one of the most influential books "that have ever appeared in the United States. A year after its publication ... it had sold 305,000 copies in America and ... two million and a half copies in English and in translation all over the world." Wilson added to these remarks that when President Lincoln greeted its author at the White House, he is supposed to have remarked, "So this is the little lady who made this big war."[69] In her famous book, Harriet Beecher Stowe spoke truth to slave power about human bondage. There is not a single scene depicting the mistreatment of bondpersons that cannot be replicated several times over with reference to events that took place in Missouri, a state that plays no part in her novel. Apologists for the peculiar institution had busied themselves propagating the myth of the contented slave; they were especially diligent after 1850. Their shrill voices explained, as one Missouri newspaper phrased it, "Slavery is the highest state of Civilization the negro has ever enjoyed in the history of the world. In Africa he is a brute.... In the slave states he has a home; ... has the protection of the laws; has friends and associations among the most refined of the land; has religious instruction."[70] At the same time these bald-faced lies were being believed, spoken, written, and almost considered holy writ, a fictional account of the truth of slavery became reading material and the talk of the nation and Europe.

In January 1853, the *Southern Quarterly Review* in New Orleans published Louisa S. McCord's 40-page review of the book. Among a staggering number of other silly comments, she pronounced *Uncle Tom's Cabin* "loathsome rakings of a foul fancy."[71] It is impossible to know how many Missourians actually read this novel. Wilson mentioned as late as the early twentieth century that a South Carolina teacher made "his pupils hold up their right hands and swear that they would never read *Uncle Tom's Cabin*."[72] Of equal interest, the silent movie, *The Birth of a Nation* (1915) was intended as Southern rebuttal to this novel 63 years later. Whatever actual knowledge of her book slave-owning Missourians may have had, its author, Harriet Beecher Stowe was known and detested here.

Three slaves were lynched by being burned alive and a fourth was lynched by hanging in this state during the summer of 1859. Six years earlier, at least two newspapers in Missouri published defamatory articles about Mrs. Stowe. She was then having an immensely successful tour of Europe. One claims that "in France she is totally unknown," and no respectable French person would receive her.[73] Another says that "there are hardly a dozen people in the United States that cannot see through Mrs. Stowe and her barefaced fiction.... She occupies as insignificant and disgraceful a position as her bitterest enemy would desire."[74] Among the multitude of others Mrs. Stowe met in Paris, as her biographer notes, were "such luminaries as a granddaughter and great granddaughter of Lafayette,"[75] the French hero of the American Revolution, for whom a Missouri county seat, Fayette, and a county, Lafayette, are named. The energy these Missouri newspapers — and likely a number of others subsequently destroyed by the Union Army — expended in their attempted destruction of Mrs. Stowe goes far to demonstrate the unreality and unfitness of things in this border state. The winds of change were blowing the privileged way of Missouri slave owners, and the Kansas-Nebraska Act had not yet become law.

What of the Fugitive Slave Law? Its passage in 1850 did little or nothing to stem the flow of runaway slaves from this state. They left in droves. As the 1850s became the early 1860s, encounters between slave runaways and their catchers here became increasing violent: One newspaper reported that a "Negro ... who recently ran away ... was shot and killed ... in Naples, Illinois."[76] Another about runaways to Iowa read, "Capture of Eleven Runaway Negroes — Thirty Revolvers Recovered from them."[77] No fewer than 30 inmates, imprisoned because they were convicted of abolitionist activity in Missouri circuit courts, were received at the Missouri State Penitentiary between 1850 and 1862.

Likewise, in the 1850s, the Missouri General Assembly passed laws that reflected the anxious state of its slave-owning citizens. Always, the belief existed that if slavery was not winning friends and influencing enemies, then it must be someone else's fault, never the institution of slavery itself. One law of 1855 dealt especially harshly with persons charged with raising an insurrection of slaves, free Negroes, or mulattoes. Conviction of any aspect of this crime carried a death sentence. Likewise, any person who published, circulated, spoke, or displayed any picture or device which, among other matters, had "the tendency [t]o excite any slave, or other colored person in this State to insolence or insubordination toward his master ... or to escape from his master" was, upon conviction, sent to prison.[78] Though some unlucky inmate may have served time for *exciting* a slave to escape from his owner, there were no death sentences carried out under these statutes. When the legislature got worried enough in 1860 to required that every free black person and his descendants who arrived in Missouri after 1847 be sold into slavery, the governor vetoed the law.[79] For many years free Negroes in Missouri and other slave states had been considered public pests; they set unacceptable examples for enslaved persons. The pro-slavery Missouri Supreme Court judge, William Napton, wrote that the presence of free blacks tended "only to dissatisfy and corrupt those of their own race and color remaining in a state of servitude."[80]

In the 1850s and early 1860s, no pro-slavery Missourians seemed to notice that at least 11 legally executed and lynched slaves killed their owners, lessors, or a wife's owner. The county sheriff hanged six of them. Among lynched slaves, one slave woman, Annice, attempted to murder an owner, and the other, Teney, a lessor. Among male slaves whom mobs put to death, Peter in Clay County, George in Carroll County, and Giles in Lincoln County, each killed a person with power over him, or, in Peter's case, power over his wife. These men's victims were whip-wielders and tongue-lashers, and their punishments of their bondpersons cost them their lives. After slavery ended, there were neither owners nor lessors of human beings. One form of violence was no more.

No one really saw it coming, but one day, all the lynchings of slaves, the legal hangings, the newspaper articles praising slavery and condemning writers such as Harriet Beecher Stowe, the Missouri Supreme Court's Dred Scott decision, the abolitionists serving time in the Missouri State Penitentiary, and the laws concerning human servitude really ceased to matter. All the king's horses and all the king's men could not put slavery back together again. It took a bloody war, and because Missouri never left the Union, the Emancipation Proclamation never applied in this state. Finally, the Missouri State Constitutional Convention met early in 1865. It elected Arnold Krekel its president, and on January 11, it signed an ordinance abolishing slavery in Missouri.

Slightly more than two and a half months later, on March 31, President Lincoln appointed Krekel, a German, a naturalized citizen who played such an active role ending human bondage here, judge for the Western District of Missouri federal court. As will be shown in subsequent chapters, Judge Krekel presided over two criminal trials relevant to this study. One involved lynchers who took their victims from a train and the other some members of a very large vigilante organization, whose activities included mob murders.

CHAPTER 3

Civil War Aftermath, 1866–1869

The lynching deaths of three males discussed in my first two chapters took place after the April 12, 1861, firing on Fort Sumter, the event which officially began the Civil War. Two white men, Samuel Husher in Livingston County, on September 4, 1861, and William Hall in Franklin County, on July 18, 1862, and an unknown slave in Andrew County, in November 1862, comprise the total of known mob murders here during the war years that are unrelated to the presence of the federal army in this state. Moreover, these three isolated events took place relatively early in the conflict.

In Missouri the Civil War began in earnest in 1862, and it continued for several months after Lee surrendered to Grant on April 9, 1865. The Union Army's first known execution here of a civilian, John Owens, took place in Monroe County on June 8, 1862. He was convicted of bushwhacking, or secessionist activity. The Union Army's last execution was of G. P. Wright, convicted of guerrilla activity, in Warrensburg, Johnson County, on June 2, 1865. The 89 known executions of the Union Army here seem a paltry percentage of the nearly 13,000 Missouri men and boys who perished in the war, mainly as a result of battlefield deaths, wounds, and the ravages of disease.[1] To browse death records in Missouri newspapers during the Civil War years[2] is to be struck by the inordinate numbers who died here in Union Army prisons and hospitals of diarrhea, typhoid, measles, pneumonia, consumption, and the like. These deaths were not lynchings.

When soldiers and civilians together hanged a man or a boy during the war years, his offense was almost invariably related to the conflict. Such persons were put to death for actual or perceived guerrilla activity. Often their executioners were members of county militias, groups allowed to kill only because of the war. For every active guerrilla or bushwhacker, there was a community of background supporters. When the population split into various groups, as it will in any civil war, otherwise united Missourians fought and killed each other. The term *lynching* is not applicable to the resulting carnage. It can only be used to describe deaths before the hostilities began, unrelated to them, and after their cessation.

Before discussing any of the 1866–1869 mob murders here, it is useful to explain why hundreds of blacks were lynched during this time in one former slave state, Mississippi, and only a few in another, Missouri. It is generally assumed that mobs putting African Americans, mainly ex-slaves, to death, achieved their first significant head of steam after the Civil War. This was probably true in states where blacks vastly outnumbered whites. However, excluding Delaware, with only 1.9 percent of its population slave,

Missouri had the smallest percentage of bondpersons of all 16 slaveholding jurisdictions in 1860, 10 percent.[3] In fact, in all federal antebellum censuses starting in 1820, the percentage of Missouri's population that was Negro declined: from 18.3 percent (1820), to 15.9 percent (1830), to 15.6 percent (1840), to 13.2 percent (1850). On the other hand, in Mississippi the percentage of the population that was Negro increased, with the exception of one dip in 1850: from 44.1 percent (1820), to 48.4 percent (1830), to 52.3 percent (1840), to 51.2 percent (1850), and to 55.3 percent (1860).

The free black population of both states was small, but Missouri had a significantly larger percentage than did Mississippi. In 1860 in Missouri, out of a total of 114,931 Negroes, 3,572 were free. In 1860 in Mississippi, out of a total of 436,631 Negroes, 773 were free. These figures mean that 3 percent of Missouri's blacks were free in 1860, and in Mississippi that same year, slightly more than one-hundredth of one percent. In Jackson County, the 1850 federal census reveals that there were 41 free persons of color, and by the 1860 census, 69.[4] However, most free blacks in Missouri lived in the city of St. Louis. By 1860, this metropolis, with a population of 162,000, was the seventh largest city in the United States. According to the State Census Returns, by 1864, St. Louis County had 7,628 free persons of color and only 1,785 slaves.[5] We can be certain that the number of free blacks in this area increased after the war. Though African Americans suffered other indignities in the city of St. Louis, after 1836, lynchings were not among them. By the 1850s, so many successful blacks and mulattoes lived there that one, Cyprian Clamorgan (1830–1906?), wrote and published *The Colored Aristocracy of St. Louis* (1858). No such book was imaginable in any Mississippi city, town, or village in the pre–Civil War years.

It is well known that Dred Scott lost his suit for freedom before the Missouri Supreme Court and the U.S. Supreme Court. Less publicized is his win before the original St. Louis jurors who heard his case. Their jury instructions were based on case law favorable to the slave's quest for freedom. Judge Mathias McGirk, a man who served on the Supreme Court of Missouri longer than any other antebellum member, 1820–1841, wrote most of this excellent law. His decisions, among other factors, helped to increase the free black population of Missouri, especially in St. Louis. It was in this city that Taylor Blow, Dred Scott's longtime benefactor, freed Dred Scott and his family in May 1857. Of equal interest, with the help of a $175,000 federal grant, the Missouri State Archives has located and preserved 283 handwritten freedom suits filed in St. Louis County courts between 1806 and 1865.[6]

In Mississippi, no one wrote appellate law to help slaves achieve freedom, such as Judge McGirk had done. There the policy was to prevent the increase of free Negroes in the state. Moreover, in reaction to an 1840 decision of the Mississippi Supreme Court holding that it was not the policy of Mississippi to prevent emancipation, in 1842, the legislature decided that taking any slave out of the state with the intent to emancipate him or her was unlawful. In 1859, the appellate judges ruled by a divided vote that a slave woman who was taken to Ohio and resided there for 18 months was not free. The hysterical rhetoric of the majority decision makes Justice Taney's language in *Dred Scott* seem almost elevated discourse. The Mississippi Supreme Court wrote: "Suppose that Ohio ... should ... claim to confer citizenship on the chimpanzee or the ourang-outang (the most respectable of the monkey tribe), are we ... to ... lower [our] citizens and institutions in the scale of being to meet the necessities of the mongrel race? ... Ohio [cannot] confer freedom on a Mississippi slave."[7] With law of this demeaning quality, it is not surprising that on the eve of the Civil War, Mississippi had 99.93 percent of its black, mulatto, quadroon, and octoroon population in bondage.

Mississippi had no adjacent free borders, surrounded as it was by Louisiana, Arkansas, Tennessee, and Alabama, all slave jurisdictions. To be sure, a portion of it faced the Gulf of Mexico, but all slave runaways from Mississippi had either to make their way to the North through other slave states or somehow acquire navigational skills for escaping by open sea through the Gulf of Mexico. The federal census figures loudly proclaim that few bondpersons ever managed to run from this place of slavery; successful flight was not doable. Far too many obstacles obstructed the Mississippi slave's path to freedom, no matter which way he, she, or they turned. In contrast, Missouri was the runaway capital of American slavery. To the west, northwest, north, and east it was bordered by places of freedom, and in them were many abolitionists eager to lend helping hands to slaves escaping their bondage here. Though the Missouri River separated at least the first 75 miles of Missouri from Nebraska in the north and a sizeable stretch of Kansas, when this river flowed to the southern boundary of Platte County, it turned east, traversed the state, and became a tributary of the Mississippi River in St. Louis. Once the Missouri River no longer separated Missouri from Kansas, the border became a straight line separating western Missouri and Arkansas from eastern Kansas and Oklahoma. Anyone could walk or be carried across this border, and many slaves made their way west from Missouri by putting one foot in front of the other. For those required to cross a body of water, either the Missouri River or the Mississippi, the canoe, mackinaw, bullboat, keelboat, and especially the steamboat were all in use on these rivers prior to the Civil War. Some slaves paddled or rowed their way to freedom by going west to Kansas; others headed their watercraft east to Illinois. Likewise, a number of them reached free soil as passengers or as crew on the many steamboats that then navigated these waters. Finally, in February 1863, a time well before global warning, the Missouri River became such a solid mass of ice that a number of Platte County's slaves walked across this frozen river in order to become members of the Union Army in Kansas.[8] No one has ever suggested that slaves in a state such as Mississippi secured their freedom by walking on or across the Gulf of Mexico.

The number of slaves still remaining in Missouri were counted by the state auditor at 73,811 in 1863.[9] Most who remained enslaved here by this year could only have been women, children, and the elderly. In addition to those who gained their freedom legally and remained at home and the even greater numbers who ran from Missouri to a northern state or still farther north to Canada, President Lincoln, the 38th Congress, and the Union Army offered other outlets. He issued the Emancipation Proclamation on January 1, 1863, and it freed all slaves held in most of the Confederacy, a would-be nation which Missouri never joined. On February 24, 1864, the 38th Congress passed and Lincoln signed a law which mandated drafting into the Union Army and simultaneous freeing of all able-bodied male persons of color between the ages of 20 and 45. Loyal masters were to be compensated for their former slaves at rates not exceeding $300 per man.[10] On June 28, 1864, this same congress repealed the 1850 Fugitive Slave Law.[11] No longer was there any federal authority in place to facilitate the return of runaway slaves to their owners.

No completely accurate figures exist for the number of black boys and men who served in the Union Army. Ron Chernow sets the number who served in the American Revolution on the side of the patriots at "about five thousand."[12] What were the figures four score and seven years later? As one might expect, not one Negro man or boy from Mississippi joined; the state was too far south for any black person in it to become a member of the army of Abraham Lincoln. All African Americans from slave jurisdictions who served in his army came from either the District of Columbia (3,269) or a border state that never left the Union: Delaware (954), Kentucky (23,703), Maryland (8,718), and Missouri. We can infer that many Missouri slaves flocked to Kansas and there joined the army of their choice. No fewer than 2,060 colored troops served on the side of the North from Kansas; most could only have been Missouri bondpersons. The 1860 federal census of Kansas shows a total of 627 Negroes in Kansas Territory, two slaves and 625 free persons. This figure would have included women, children, and the elderly as well as those of draft age. The total of colored troops who joined the Union Army in Missouri was 8,344.[13] Add to this number at least 1,700 Missouri slaves who joined in Kansas, and we have a figure that exceeds 10,000. This means that at least twice as many African-American men and boys from Missouri fought for the Union as the total number who fought in the American Revolution on the side of the patriots. Nothing in my research suggests that colored troops who enlisted in this state—all of whom were initially sent to St. Louis[14]—were stationed in Missouri in any appreciable numbers. Of the 268 known U.S. soldiers whom the Union Army executed during the Civil War, an especially high number were black. All Union Army executions of Union Army soldiers that took place in this state were of white boys and men, not of black.

When we look at all the evidence, we find that only 10 percent of Missouri's population was Negro in 1860. From an early date, most free blacks who remained in the state lived in the city of St. Louis, a town with a lynch-proof jail, at least after 1836. In addition, runaway slaves left Missouri in large numbers throughout the antebellum period. Adding to this exodus were more than 10,000 Missouri slaves who won their freedom by joining the Union Army. Once blacks left Missouri, the available evidence suggests that they mostly stayed gone. The 1870 census lists 6.9 percent of Missouri's population as Negro, and subsequent censuses continue to show declines in the percentage of Missouri's population that was black. On the other hand, 53.7 percent of the population of Mississippi remained Negro in the 1870 federal census. Under these circumstances one would expect the lynching of sizeable numbers of blacks in Mississippi and few, very few, in this state. The reason is simple. In areas of Missouri wherein the riffraff strung up lawbreakers and other undesirables, namely small towns and rural areas, large numbers of African Americans had already left before the Civil War came to its dribbling end here.

Exact figures for mob murders in Mississippi in the late 1860s are not available, but scholarly estimates are high, perhaps too high. Quoting scholars who quote other scholars, Julius E. Thompson states that "perhaps hundreds of blacks were lynched." He places the number at two to three per week,[15] and over a four year period these weekly figures add up to somewhere between 400 and 600 lynched blacks in one state in approximately 208 weeks. In Missouri, there must have been a few more than I located, but my research uncovered only two in this same four-year period.[16] Moreover, the documentation for one case is slight, if not suspect. The same newspaper that may have fused an 1818 with an 1847 lynching in Franklin County is my only source to substantiate that a post–Civil War lynching of a black took place there. The 1897 retrospective news account states, "Just at the close of the war, a negro man was hanged by a mob, near Boles, for we believe, assaulting a white woman. They finished their job so well that we believe it has never been known publicly what disposition was made of the remains."[17] It should be noted that Franklin was adjacent to St. Louis County, and in the immediate aftermath of the war most African Americans who remained in Missouri lived in or near the city of St. Louis.

The second and only other lynching I discovered of a black in Missouri between 1866 and 1869 took place in St. Louis County. On Saturday, September 11, 1869, a Mrs. Dwyer decided to visit her parents in Kirkwood, while her husband was absent from home on business. She hitched the horse to a spring wagon, and on the highway, she met a Negro on horseback. He followed her into an area where trees obscured the scene, dismounted, got in the road in front of her, and as the *St. Louis Times* reports it, made "an indecent proposition to her." She managed to get away from him. Its coverage continues that when word of "the attempted outrage" spread, "the neighbors became highly enraged and at once determined that the perpetrator should answer before a legal tribunal."[18] The next day, a Sunday, September 12, Mr. Dwyer and one or more of his neighbors visited a home where the Negro, Anthony Colman, was employed. The visiting white men closely questioned him, and he admitted that he had attempted the outrage, but he vehemently denied that he had used any force.

At this point, Mr. Dwyer and his companions placed Colman in a wagon in order to take him to the authorities in the city. They refused to allow his 60-year-old father, who asked to ride with them, to join them. About six miles from the city of St. Louis, a party of 10 to 15 men rode up on horseback and demanded Colman. The *St. Louis Times* notes that "from the darkness," Mr. Dwyer and his party "were unable to distinguish whether the mob was composed of white or black men." A gun battle erupted between the men in the wagon and those on horseback, and in the confusion the Negro disappeared. The wagon party continued to the city and reported the matter to the police. Two officers went to the scene; there, they found Colman dead with bullets in his head, face, and spine. The police took his body to a police station, and the next day the coroner conducted an inquest. At this relatively early date, news coverage makes no mention of the coroner's jury. It will later.

The *St. Louis Times* gives the age of the deceased as 16 years. The *Missouri Republican*, relating essentially the same facts, lists him as 18 years of age, and its story concludes, "Probably some persons will be arrested."[19] This killing was subdued. The husband of the indecently propositioned woman was not a mob member. His intent was to surrender his prisoner to the police, not to lynchers. From the newspapers' accounts it seems more likely that the young black man did not proceed far enough with his plans to term his actions an attempted rape. What he did was more on the order of preparing to attempt a crime, and such is not a crime. A judge would probably have released him with a stern lecture. However, this legal nicety was lost on the men that attempted to take him from the wagon, and in the confusion shot and killed him. As for the inability of Dwyer and his neighbors to discern their race, we will never know if they were protecting the identity of other white men whom they knew, or if the group was composed of black men.

This is the earliest mention of a possible black lynch mob in Missouri; it will not be the last.

St. Louis County remains important when we turn to legal executions here after the war. Between 1866 and 1869, I discovered only six: three were of black men, one in Clinton County, another in Monroe, and the third in St. Louis, and three of white, one each in Morgan, Buchanan, and St. Louis counties. These latter two locales were Union Army strongholds. Legal trials and executions *under state authority* were carried out in both St. Joseph and St. Louis City during the war years. Their civilian courts never ceased to function. It is not accidental that one-half of the legal executions after the war (1866–1869) took place in Buchanan and St. Louis counties. Their seats of governments never lost the necessary facilities and personnel to dispatch some form of justice.

Most of the remaining communities of this state had few or no civilian courts in the conflict's immediate aftermath. Once the Union Army departed and with it, its rule of martial law, there were precious few means of maintaining law and order other than by vigilantism. Excluding the lynching of two black men, both in eastern Missouri, in the immediate aftermath of the Civil war, all the lynchings I discovered were of white men. With three exceptions, one near the Callaway/Montgomery county line and two in Jefferson County, all known mob murders between 1866 and 1869 took place in western Missouri counties. To be sure, support for the Union existed here, there, and elsewhere, but there was also considerable Confederate sympathy, and among much else that was greatly diminished in the course of the war were effective civilian law enforcement officers and functioning circuit courts. All known lynchings from this period and those of most subsequent chapters are discussed by the section of the state in which they occurred: southwest, northwest, northeast, and southeast.[20]

In southwestern Missouri, mob murders occurred in seven counties: Greene, Morgan, Camden, Vernon, Jasper, Bates, and Barry. The earliest took place in Greene. A group of men who called themselves "Regulators" or the "Honest Men's League" organized there, and the group's avowed purpose was to rid its area of criminals. The Regulators' first victim was Green B. Phillips, a former Union Army officer suspected of being an accomplice of wrongdoers. Either the night of May 20 or 21, vigilantes met in secret session, passed a death sentence against Phillips, and assigned three gun-wielding men to carry it out. They did so on the morning of May 23, 1866, by shooting him to death on his property as he attended to chores. A few days later, on May 26, the same group targeted two additional men, both former members of Union militias, John Rush and his son-in-law, Charlie Gorsuch, persons whom the Regulators believed to be thieves and robbers. At an executive session, the mob's top men passed death sentences against Rush and Gorsuch, and the designated assassins carried out their killing mission on May 26, 1866. They entered the village of Walnut Grove, took these men prisoner, and hanged them from a redbud tree approximately a mile south of the town. In early June of this same year, 280 Regulators met in Springfield in front of the courthouse on the public square to display their power and defend their actions. Some condemned them, but among their public defenders, who made speeches justifying their actions, were a Presbyterian minister, Reverend Brown and J.W.D.L.E. Mack, a former state senator who represented the district which included Greene County in 1862 and 1864 in the Missouri General Assembly. Needless to say, with these bigwigs speaking on behalf of this group, no member of the

Regulators was tried for any one of the three murders this group committed in late May 1866.[21]

One mob murder is known from Morgan County. During the war years, Ewing Tucker served on the Confederate side, and as the years passed with no word of or from him, he was presumed dead. His wife married Elijah Slocum, and after the arrival of their baby, Tucker returned. Mrs. Tucker/Slocum briefly lived with her first husband, but she soon returned to her second. Slocum treated her more kindly than Tucker. This former Confederate soldier sought revenge, and early on a Wednesday morning, August 29, he went to the Slocum residence, and there he shot and killed his rival and threatened to kill their wife. She summoned neighbors, among them Constable Shockley. They tracked Tucker to his residence by a peculiar mark on his shoe. Shockley arrested Tucker, but the hour being late, he kept him at the Shockley residence that evening. The constable intended to bring him to the sheriff in Versailles, the county seat, the next day. That same evening about midnight, 15 to 20 face-blackened and disguised men showed up at the constable's home and demanded that he give them his prisoner. He attempted to reason with the mob, but no avail. He was told to shut up, or as the newspaper phrases it, "his brains would be ventilated with a bullet." The mob forced Shockley's front door and seized Ewing Tucker. It took him a short distance from the house and shot and killed him. The constable found Ewing Tucker's body the next morning, August 30, 1866. According to the news story, it was located "in almost the identical spot where his victim was shot the day before."[22]

One dual lynching can be documented from Camden County. It took place on June 23, 1867, when a group of 30 to 36 men on horseback and the owner of some stolen horses, Frank Hickox, in a buggy, all from Moniteau County, took custody of Allen Conner and Daniel I. Jones, alleged horse thieves. The Moniteau County men had promised Camden County officials that they would take these culprits to Jefferson City for safekeeping before their trial. Word had been received on June 17 that men with stolen horses were traveling through Camden County. Several Camden deputy sheriffs tracked these alleged horse thieves to Dallas County, captured them, and on June 19, confined them in the Camden County jail in Camdenton. There they remained until they were turned over to Frank Hickox and his friends. On June 23, the hanging bodies of Conner and Jones were found a few miles from Linn Creek, Camden County.

Information about this event is found in a letter written by the circuit attorney of Camden County to the editor of a Jefferson City newspaper. The editor omitted the verdict of the coroner's jury concerning the deaths of Conner and Jones, so he stated, for lack of space.[23] Presumably, he feared retaliation from Frank Hickox and his many friends if he printed the findings of the Camden County coroner's jury, namely that Hickox and friends caused the death of Conner and Jones.

The coroner's office has very old English roots, and from earliest times, in both England and the United States, the coroner's duties have been to inquire into the cause of death of any body found within his jurisdiction when there is reason to believe the deceased died a violent or unnatural death. The earliest Missouri laws regarding the coroner were passed by the territorial legislature on July 3, 1807. Among other provisions, they established the office, set the number of jurors at 23, and required the coroner to put them under oath. Additionally, "The jurors being sworn, the coroner shall give them a charge ... to declare of the death of the person, whether he or she died of felony.... And if felony who were principals and who were accessories, with what instrument he or she was struck or wounded, ... and of all other circumstances relating to said death."[24] The law, though modified as to the number of jurors, six in all revisions after the Civil War, and changed now so as to allow women to serve, has basically remained unchanged in rural counties. These statutes concerning coroners and their jurors are Missouri law in 2008. What we shall see as this narrative proceeds is the essentially lawless and cynical use made of this ancient feature of English and American law, the findings of coroners' juries, when the cause of death was a lynching.

Four mob murders from Vernon County can be confirmed as taking place immediately after the war. The earliest occurred in the spring of 1867. The galvanizing event for it was the March 26, 1867, murder of Joseph Bailey, the county's 41-year-old sheriff, a distinguished Union Army brigadier general during the Civil War. He was born in Wisconsin and raised in Ohio, and his military service was mainly outside Missouri. However, he came to this southwestern Missouri county, and the people elected him sheriff. The news account of his death describes him as "our much esteemed citizen ... kind, affable." The paper gives this detail. On March 24, a citizen complained before a justice of the peace that the Pixley brothers, Perry and Lewis, had stolen a hog from him and despite his request, they refused to return it. The JP issued a warrant for them, and the recently elected sheriff went to their home to arrest them. In a most gentlemanly but unwise fashion, he allowed them to retain their weapons as he, on horseback, began to bring them, on their horses, to Nevada, the county seat. Shortly, his bullet-riddled body, missing $250, was found in a creek bed, and almost immediately, a reward of $3,000 was offered for Lewis and Perry Pixley, dead or alive. Apparently they were never captured, but it was assumed that their friends and associates knew details of their escape. Several were questioned, and some were arrested as accessories after the fact, including Tom Ingram, the current husband of a woman who had earlier been married to a notorious bushwhacker, killed in Arkansas after the war. The night of March 29, 1867, a posse brought Ingram to Nevada, but members of a vigilante committee took him from the men armed with legal authority. The next morning his body was found hanging from a tree at the edge of town.[25]

The other Vernon County lynchings of the late 1860s concern a familiar offense. In the spring of 1867, shortly after the hanging of Ingram, mobs put to death three people: an unidentified man accused of horse stealing; John Chrisman for mule stealing; and John Wilson, who was hung on Clear Creek on unstated "general principles," according to the county history. Perhaps his lynchers believed Wilson was a thief. The county history clarifies contemporary attitudes: "The unwritten law, generally recognized in the West, that a horse thief is worse than a murderer, has found recognition in Vernon County; it is almost certain death to steal a horse."[26] From the account of mob murders in the county history, stealing a mule in this county and elsewhere in Missouri merited the same punishment.

Turning to another southwestern county, Jasper, in the spring of 1868, George Hutton left the area with Margaret H. Fullerton, his mother-in-law, a widow possessed of some valuable property; she lived in nearby Lawrence County. He was supposed to leave her in Sedalia, a town to the northeast, on his trip to Ohio. Nothing more was heard of or from Mrs. Fullerton, and once Hutton returned to Jasper County after his 17-day trip to the Buckeye State, he was arrested. A contemporary news account states that he was being held in a house; such a facility implies the absence of a jail. On the night of April 28, 1868, a group of armed and disguised men took him from the house and shot and severely wounded him as he attempted to escape from them. Next, they took him three miles east of Sarcoxie and hanged him on a blackjack tree, still within Jasper County but very near the Lawrence County line. The reporting newspaper writes what most others of the period did; it deplores the rash act, but added that at times extralegal remedies were necessary "for cut-throats, horse-thieves, and men of that class."[27]

Two deaths from Bates County can be documented in the 1866–69 time period; the alleged offense was the usual. According to the county history, on February 27, 1869, a citizen complained that William H. Simmons had stolen two horses. The sheriff and a posse arrested him, brought him to Butler, the county seat, and confined him in the jail. The next morning, for $500, his father bailed him out; this sum guaranteed the young man's court appearance for trial. On March 2, 20 to 25 disguised men demanded the persons of William and his brother, David J. Simmons. As the boys came out of the house, the mob seized them, and their bodies were found hanged on a couple of trees, approximately 100 feet apart. On the ground near one of their corpses was a piece of paper; someone had written on it, "We hung them for horse thieves." At the inquest which followed these events, as the county history notes, "The jury returned a verdict that the two men came to their death by violence at the hands of men unknown to the jury."[28] This history was published in 1883; by this date, the verdicts of coroners' juries were a routine feature of the local newspaper's coverage of these events.

The last known lynching from southwestern Missouri in the late 1860s took place in Barry County. George Moore killed Jack Carney and his wife, 18 miles southeast of Cassville, in December 1869. Presumably, within a short time, a mob hanged him in Cassville, the county seat, according to the county history, "from the old bell-post, which at that time stood at the southeast corner of the courthouse."[29]

In the northwest section, post–Civil War mob deaths took place in Atchison, Johnson, Pettis, Clay, Lafayette, Saline, and Ray counties. The first precisely dated one occurred in Atchison. The incident began on March 22, 1866, when two men argued over the sale of cord wood. S.A. Hunter had purchased some from William R. Robertson in an area near the Missouri River, and Robertson resold it to a passing steamboat. The original buyer and seller had words, and Robertson, a man who did not, according to the county history, "enjoy a very good reputation in the neighborhood in which he lived," shot and killed Hunter, a man "well and favorably known in Northwest Missouri." By early April, Robertson was arrested in Linn County and taken to Iowa, and from there to the Holt County jail in Oregon, Missouri, to be confined until his trial. On April 4, 1866, he was returned to Atchison County, a locale that appears to have lacked both a jail and a usable courthouse. The sheriff and his posse had stopped with their prisoner at a dwelling a distance from Rock Port, the county seat, when, as the county history describes the scene, "directly after dark the house was suddenly surrounded and entered by a band of armed men who took Robertson away and doubtless hung him, as he was found hanging from a tree in the neighborhood." Bill Lewis was charged with murdering Robertson, but as the county history notes of Lewis, "He managed as did others concerned in the outrage, to have his trial moved from place to place ... until finally the matter was worn out, and he escaped justice."[30]

By far the county with the largest number of mob murders immediately after the war was Johnson. Between March 1 and August 1, 1867, a total of nine boys and men were lynched within its borders. Six of these killings took place in March. The event which set off this wholesale Gestapo action was the February 25, 1867, murder and robbery of David Sweitzer, a farmer who lived six miles north of Warrensburg. Besides shooting and killing him, the bandits took $130 from him; most of it they managed to lose while making their getaway. No less than $120 of it was found in the road the next morning near Hazel Hill. After leaving Sweitzer's house, the thugs also shot at Jack Radford; their bullets missed him but killed his horse. Presumably they tried to kill Radford to avoid detection and apprehension. The first local newspaper coverage of Sweitzer's murder concludes: "We dislike lynch law ... but we should feel like letting the halter draw on these fellows without either judge or jury. We are confident it would have a salutary effect and let murderers and robbers know that if the law cannot deal out justice the people will."[31] By the newspaper's next issue on March 8, it lists the "execution" of three men: Dick Sanders, identified in the paper as one of the murderers of Sweitzer; Bill Stevens, "father of the desperate character, Tom Stevens, whose house is a harbor for a number of desperadoes"; and Jeff Collins. The story concludes with the hope that additional horse thieves and murderers within the county would also be hanged.[32]

Prior to the spree that led to the separate hanging of three men, 400 Johnson County citizens met early on March 1, 1867. The county history named their leaders: Colonel Isaminger, N.B. Klaine, and Professor Biggar. According to the history, Biggar told the assembled, "We have not the same advantages that larger cities enjoy, and whatever action is taken now, is for our safety."[33] The county history states that at least 100 of the 400 were involved in the hanging death of Dick Sanders, believed to be one of David Sweitzer's killers. His lynching occurred on March 1, some time after the early morning meeting. Presumably with his hands tied, Sanders was placed on a horse, a rope around his neck was attached to a tree limb, and the horse was driven out from under him. Three days later, 20 men gunned down Bill Stevens, "a desperate character," as the county history notes, who, with others, 10 months earlier, had attempted to kill Francis Preston Blair, Jr. Blair was a former Union Army general, and the attempt on his life was made to prevent him from speaking to an assembled audience in Warrensburg, on June 1, 1866. Bill Stevens was also believed to be second in command of a band of horse thieves, of which Dick Sanders was the chief.

The third victim, Jeff Collins, whom the county history describes as a "notorious character," had threatened the lives of several Warrensburg merchants and was also believed to be a horse thief and a murderer. On March 4, 1867, 20 citizens captured Collins, and after a pseudo-trial, they hanged him from a blackjack tree in or near Warrensburg and left his body dangling that night and the next day. It disappeared the next night, and the county history reports that Warrensburg physicians dissected it.

Shortly, a party of 400 men also put to death two additional males, Tom Stevens, son of Bill Stevens, and Morg Andrews, persons believed to be accomplices in the murder of David Sweitzer. Both were young, aged 18 or 19 years, and at the time their fate was sealed, they were inmates in the Douglas County, Kansas, jail in Lawrence. As James

J. Fisher describes the matter, the vigilante committee applied to Jefferson City and obtained the necessary extradition papers. The boys were taken from the jail in Lawrence, brought by train to Warrensburg, and hanged outside town. Their bodies were left dangling, with their feet a few inches above the ground. The driver of two couples in a closed carriage passing on the road believed that he saw two men standing on the highway. When the women in the carriage saw the faces of the swinging remains, both fainted.[34]

According to the county history, as the killing spree continued, the original 400 who decided the fate of the first five boys and men neither approved nor participated in the remaining four lynchings that shortly followed in their county. A man named Hall was next. Detail in the county history is sparse: he was "arrested, confessed killing several men, and was accordingly hanged in late March 1867." Hall was followed by a man unmentioned in the county history. However, a Kansas City newspaper contains this story, "Bill Scott, a desperado, was found hanging dead at Rose Hill, Johnson County, last Sunday morning [May 12, 1867]. A few nights before some horse thieves attempted to break into the stable of a Mr. Barnes at Greenton Valley, this same county. Mr. Barnes fired a double-barreled shotgun at them, killing Henry Clemmings in his tracks."[35] There the news story ends; the implication was that his partner in crime, Bill Scott, escaped, and shortly an unknown mob captured and hanged Scott. It did so in the belief it had rid the county of one more horse thief.

Several months later, in August 1867, Thomas A. Little was arrested by the Committee of 400, brought to Warrensburg, and charged with knocking a man down and robbing him of a few dollars. Surprisingly, the big committee acquitted him by a vote of 233 to 28, and it sent him off to the jail. Shortly a splinter group of 15 to 20 men battered down the jail door, removed Little, carried him down Main Street and hanged him from an elm tree. In September 1867, the ninth victim of lynching died in Johnson County. He was James M. Sims, a person whom the county history describes as a "half crazy fellow charged with stealing a horse." He rode off on it after the owner declined to sell it. Law enforcement officers captured him southeast of Clinton in Henry County, but they never managed to confine him in the Johnson County jail in Warrensburg, Fifty armed men demanded Sims outside town, and the officers gave him up. Shortly, these 50 placed him in a wagon with his hands tied, a rope around his neck, and the other end tied to a tree, and they drove the wagon out from under him. There, at least for a while, the lynchings finally ended; nine boys and men in mostly separate mob murders in one rural county in a period of seven months, March to September 1867. The results established a record in the history of lynchings in Missouri. Neither before nor after were so many put to death in one area in such a short time span. However, vigilante justice or injustice ceased in this county with two additional mob murders, one in 1872 and the other in 1874.

At approximately the same time, Pettis, Clay, and Lafayette counties were the scene of one lynching each, and Ray accounts for a dual mob murder. The first lynching of the late 1860s took place in Pettis County, on March 23, 1867, in Sedalia, the county seat. Joe Wood, whom a newspaper describes as a "desperate character," assaulted a fellow customer in the saloon of Joseph Geimer. When the proprietor complained, Wood shot and killed him. Shortly, as the paper reports, "A number of citizens collected, ... put a rope around Wood's neck, took him to the woods and hung him—as he richly deserved."[36]

Another newspaper contains considerable gory detail. It relates that enraged citizens nearly beat Wood to death before they dragged him through Sedalia to the place of his death, and after they hanged him, to make certain he was dead, someone shot him in the head. The coroner's jury held an inquest, and it determined that Joe Wood had died at the hands of unknown men. Wood was suspected of other crimes, including bank robbery, and the man he killed, Joseph Geimer, as the paper notes, "was respected by all who knew him."[37]

In Clay County, on June 15, 1869, a vigilante committee chased a confidence man named Harry Howard from the small town of Harlem to the *Lizzie Campbell,* a ferry boat on the Missouri River. It tied a rope with a heavy stone around his neck and threw him overboard. He managed to free himself and caught hold of the boat's rudder. Mob members fired at him six times, and his body disappeared in the water. The precise form of the confidence game Howard played on the residents of Harlem is not explained. Instead, the news story says, "When a town becomes infested with thieves and law breakers and no officers within six miles of the scene of their operations, it is natural for honest quiet people to protect themselves."[38]

In Waverly, Lafayette County, Bill Budd was shot and killed the evening of July 24, 1868, by a party of armed men as he stood on a street. They snatched his dead body, and it was found the next day, hanging from a tree outside town. The inquest produced no evidence as to the identity of his killers. According to the newspaper, "Budd had been a Confederate soldier throughout the war years. His friends said bushwhackers were his enemies, and they had killed him; his enemies that he was a robber and a habitual disturber of the peace." Another explanation was his stated willingness to appear as "a witness against every rebel who attempted to register as a legal voter."[39] At this time in Missouri, those who voted and/or sought public office, lawyers, teachers, and preachers were required to take a loyalty oath to the Union.

On January 6, 1869, in Saline County, a friendly encounter between a man identified only as Carlisle, termed a "habitual drunk" and a German cobbler, Charles Crytill, proved deadly. Carlisle shot and killed Crytill in a saloon in the town of Cambridge because he refused to continue drinking with him. Carlisle was immediately arrested, but the constable who attempted to bring him to Marshall, the county seat, never arrived with his prisoner. Angry citizens took him, as the newspaper notes, from "the clutches of the law and disposed of him by either drowning or hanging."[40] His body could not be located. The proximity of Cambridge to the Missouri River makes wholly plausible that if the mob did not end his life by drowning him, it disposed of a stiff by tossing his remains in the river, a body of water that flowed east to join the Mississippi River near the city of St. Louis.

The final incident that can be positively identified as a lynching in northwest Missouri in the late 1860s took place in Richmond, seat of Ray County, on March 18, 1868. Two men, James M. Devers and Andrew McGuire, were jailed on a charge of aiding in a Richmond bank robbery. A party of unidentified men met little resistance at the jail, locked up the sheriff's deputies, and, as the newspaper reports, "walked off with the prisoners, who were found hanging, next morning, dead, in a hollow east of the negro school house." At the subsequent inquest, the jurors determined "that the parties implicated were from abroad and unknown to the sheriff, jailer, and guards in charger of the prisoners."

The newspaper does more than the usual deploring; it contains no winks and nods about the necessity of mob murder. Rather, it denounces "this whole affair as dastardly ... injurious to our community, which has hitherto had the reputation of a quiet law-abiding place."[41]

From the northeast section of Missouri there is only one known lynching from these years. Its precise location cannot be ascertained; either Callaway or the county to its immediately east, Montgomery, was the place of the death of Lewis Myers in mid–April 1868. He was in possession of a horse stolen in Callaway County, but he was arrested in Montgomery and committed to its jail, then in Danville. As the newspaper reports, "while on his way to Fulton in the custody of a constable, Myers was taken out of the hands of that officer and hung by a mob."[42]

From the southeast section of the state, in addition to the two already discussed blacks, there are two other lynchings in Jefferson County. Both men were accused of murder and lynched in 1868. The first involved James Quick. He was charged with the murder of George W. Higginbotham in Washington County, arraigned for trial in Potosi, and granted a change of venue to Jefferson County. While he was awaiting his trial, he was held in the jail in Hillsboro. As the county history describes it, "Judge Lynch and his disciples took Quick from the Jefferson County jail and hung him without the sanction of law."[43] On November 3, 1868, Charles H. Bickford allegedly shot and killed Alexander Walker, a cabin-dweller, near Vineland, in Jefferson County. The two had been involved in a lawsuit, which the victim won. Shortly, Bickford was arrested and placed in the jail in Hillsboro, to await his trial. According to the county history, "Bickford was taken out of the jail and hanged at the same time and by the same parties that took Quick from the Hillsboro jail and hung him."[44] There may be a dating problem with these mob murders. Quick was indicted in April 1868, and Bickford did not commit his alleged crime until November 1868. Ordinarily, a session of the circuit court of any county in the nineteenth century would take place sooner than seven months after an indictment for murder. Even allowing for the disruption of the Civil War, the time lapse between Quick's indictment in Washington County and his lynching in Jefferson has problems. The county history clarifies only that a mob took two men, both arrested for murder and awaiting trial, from the jail in Hillsboro and hanged them in 1868. Very likely the members of the mob were the same men, but they may have done their dirty work in the spring of 1868 in Quick's case and the late fall of that same year in Bickford's.

One additional known violent death of this time period took place in Clay County, but its brief coverage in the local newspaper makes its classification as a lynching doubtful. All we know is contained in a single sentence. Perhaps from a confidential source, the paper reports, "We learned that Redmund B. Munkirs was killed at his residence in this county on Saturday last [May 18, 1867], by a band of unknown men."[45] Any contemporary Clay County reader of this single sentence would have understood exactly why Munkirs was killed and would have had a good, if not excellent, idea of who did it. On the surface, and this is all we know, it would appear to be a score-settling murder from one or more untoward acts during the Civil War, but this guess is an insufficient basis to include it in the tabular summary of Appendix 1. It is placed in Appendix 2.

The lynching of two black males between 1866 and 1869 for the rape and/or attempted rape of a Caucasian girl or woman seems an almost timeless event. Their mob murders might have taken place here any time after the French first brought bondpersons to southeastern Missouri to work in the lead mines in 1720. Or, it could have happened as late as World War II. These mob murders of African Americans for real or imagined sexual offenses against white females here were likely most any time over a period of at least 220 years. They are not easily tied to any particular event, such as the Civil War.

This is not the case with the 33 white men and boys lynched in Missouri between 1866 and 1869. The suspicion lingers that a contributing factor, if not *the cause*, in many of these extralegal deaths was the recently concluded war. To be sure, mobs hanged horse thieves and murderers well before the war began, and they continued to do so with renewed energy after it concluded. It is a fact that war unleashes criminal elements that might lack the courage to plunder and kill if constituted authorities remained in charge. After the conflict ended, there were neither functioning courts nor effective law enforcement officers in most of western Missouri to curtail the nefarious activities of the evil ones. Vigilantes punished genuine wrongdoers, if there was any punishment. Nonetheless, one wonders if many of the lynched victims, whatever the offense(s) they allegedly may have committed, were of the other sides during the war. Both the county histories and contemporary news coverage mention with some frequency that someone was a Union Army officer (up to and including several generals), or a member of a Union militia, or on the Confederate side, or a bushwhacker. Alexander Hamilton expressed it well in Federalist No. 34, written January 3, 1788, "The fiery and destructive passions of war reign in the human breast with much more powerful sway than the mild and beneficent sentiments of peace."[46] The residual rage from the recently concluded conflict cannot be discounted as a factor in many of these 1866–1869 mob events.

This anger did not exhaust itself in the late 1860s. Multiple killings continued here into the 1870s. In fact the first five years of the 1870s saw more lynchings than at any other time in the history of Missouri.

CHAPTER 4

More White Victims Than Black, 1870–1879

Contrary to expectations, the 1880s and 1890s were not the times of the greatest number of lynchings in Missouri. Rather, this distinction belongs to the first five years of the 1870s. Between the start of the decade and December 1874, at least 45 victims of lynchings here can be documented, and there are almost certainly others. I attribute the continuing violence to the aftermath of the Civil War, a conflict that, apart from the cities of St. Louis and St. Joseph, devastated all areas of the state.

A St. Joseph newspaper documents the first lynching discussed in this chapter, one that cannot be precisely dated. That Civil War battles were vividly remembered, if not still being fought in this locale, is made clear by the headline, "A Notorious Bushwhacker Hung." Bushwhackers were mortal enemies of Union Army troops, and during their occupation of this state, these guerrilla fighters probably committed crimes against both members of the military and the civilian population. Once the war ended, the insurgents sometimes continued their predatory lifestyle. The news story attributes no specific offense to the deceased, Bill Childs. We know only that in Buchanan and adjoining counties, he was known, as the newspaper phrases it, as a "desperate outlaw [who will be] remembered by the militia of this county, some of whom had frequent chases after him." The paper names no members of the mob; rather we read that a "party of civilians who knew their man and appreciated his fame" hanged Childs in a barn on a farm his mother owned in Lafayette County. His death took place either in late December 1869 or in early January 1870.[1]

The number of lynched blacks whose deaths can be documented dramatically increased from those of the late 1860s, to 16, but the overwhelming majority of mob victims between 1870 and 1879 continued to be white males. According to the 1880 federal census, Missouri contained .2 of a percentage point *fewer* Negroes than in the 1870 census. The black population dropped from 6.9 percent (1870) to 6.7 percent (1880). On the other hand, Mississippi saw the percentage of its Negro population increase from 53.7 percent in 1870 to 57.5 percent in 1880. Translated into actual numbers, Missouri's total population in 1880 was 2,168,176, and of this number 145,350 were African Americans. Most Missouri blacks continued to live in or near the city of St. Louis. In contrast, Mississippi's total population in 1880 was 1,129,689, and of this number 650,291 were African Americans. Further there was no municipality in Mississippi that remotely resembled St.

Louis, a metropolis that acted as a magnet for African Americans, among other minorities. In Mississippi, black folks basically remained in rural areas. Julius E. Thompson states, regrettably without any documentation, that at least 769 persons were lynched in Mississippi during the 1870s. His chart which details these numbers of the lynched, 1870–1879, includes only three whites.[2] Though 769 seems extraordinarily high, given the black to white ratio in the 1880 federal census of Mississippi (57.5 percent to 42.5 percent), one would expect far larger numbers of lynched blacks there in the 1870s than in Missouri. Here, 93.3 percent of the population was white and only 6.7 percent African American in the 1880 census. For the most part, blacks continued to stay gone from areas of the state they left before, during, and after the Civil War.

We know that civilian courts and effective law enforcement officers were far more numerous in Missouri than in the late 1860s. Nonetheless there continued to be more lynchings here during the 1870s than legal executions. During this decade, county sheriffs hanged, pursuant to court order, 31 known persons, including one white man for the first-degree murder of a black man. These legal gallows deaths took place throughout the state, but 15 were in its southeastern section. This left the remaining 16 in three other sections: southwest, three; northwest, nine, and northeast, four. Most legal executions were of white men who killed other white persons; most of their victims were male. Sheriffs hanged only five known black men here during the 1870s. Two were convicted of the murder of their wives, two of killing a white man, and one of killing another black man. These legal executions of blacks for wife-murder took place in Howard (1873) and Clay counties (1874); in neither was there an appeal. The other three death sentences of black men were affirmed on appeal: a black male perpetrator and a white male victim in St. Louis County (1875) and in Warren County (1877), and a black perpetrator and a black male victim in Jefferson County (1879). Though the black wife murders took place many miles west of Missouri's major city, the other three capital cases involving black perpetrators took place in or near St. Louis.

When we turn to lynched blacks of this decade, we are struck by the locales of these incidents. Unlike the legal executions, three out of five of which were in the state's eastern section, with five exceptions, most lynchings of persons of color took place in western areas of the state. Two occurred in the southwest section of Missouri and nine in the northwest. The two southwestern mob murders took place in Henry and Greene counties.

In Henry County, on July 5, 1870, John Sears, alias John Coleman, allegedly raped an 18-year-old white girl named Miss George in broad daylight, as she returned from picking blackberries. The Henry County history describes Sears as having "some Mexican blood in his veins"; the Warrensburg newspaper terms him a "half-breed Mexican," but his primary race was Negro. Sears threatened and controlled his victim with a knife. When the young lady reached her home, she told her married sister what had happened, and her sister told her husband. As the Sedalia newspaper describes it, "The news spread with lightening velocity.... Negroes about Clinton, to their praise, turned out to hunt down one of their own color ... and very soon he was captured by a negro and was brought to Clinton." According to the Warrensburg newspaper, Sears was placed in a lineup outside the jail with five other black men, and Miss George identified him as her assailant. The mob was ready then and there to hang him, but the authorities managed to keep him safe by confining him in the jail. By the next day, according to the Sedalia paper,

"The people flocked in from the country by the hundreds, armed with pistols, guns, and filled the courtroom and yard." When the victim identified a particular knife as the weapon her assailant had wielded during his crime against her, the enormous crowd had heard enough. It snatched Sears from the courtroom in the midst of his preliminary hearing and hanged him in the middle of the day from a tree on the courthouse yard. The Warrensburg paper describes the excitement in these terms: Sears "was seized and dragged to a locust tree at the southeast corner of the courthouse square, ... strangled [by the crowd] and afterward suspended in the air until he was dead — dead."[3]

In Greene County, on June 19, 1871, Bud Isbell, a 21-year-old black male, allegedly raped a white woman, Mrs. Peter Christian, at her home in Springfield, while her husband was gone. The perpetrator asked his victim for a drink of water. She handed him a cup and pointed out the well; he returned from it, and as the county history describes it, "made to her an outrageous proposal." She refused, but since she was small and frail, he worked his will upon her. She immediately let be known what had occurred, but he was gone. A reward was offered for him, and five days later, Saturday, June 24, two men from Newton County who had captured Isbell in Newtonia returned him to Springfield. He was taken to Mrs. Christian, and after she positively identified him as her attacker, he was brought to the public square. In remembrance of things past, as the county history relates, "The crowd decided to hang the black-skinned and black-hearted ravisher ... near the spot where twelve years before, [Slave] Mart Danforth was hung for a similar offense." Forthwith, the mob placed Isbell on a horse, fastened one end of a rope around his neck and tied the other to a tree limb, and led the horse away. The rope was too long; Isbell's feet touched the ground. He was lifted up while the rope was shortened, and the mob strung him up a second time. To insure that the hanging man was dead, someone in the crowd shot him. The newspaper's retrospective describes what came of the coroner's inquest: "No attempt was made to arrest the men who did the hanging."[4] Both the county history and a newspaper relate that Isbell was believed to have perpetrated the same crime on a young colored girl a short time earlier. Standing alone, the rape of a Negro female, child or adult, either a prostitute or the county's most respectable and beloved black woman, was almost never sufficient to trigger either a completed lynching or a legal execution. The extreme punishment was 99.9 percent reserved for alleged rapists of white females.

The northwest section of Missouri accounts for nine known lynchings of blacks in the 1870s, and seven of them were believed to be sexual attackers of white women. Three lynchings took place in Saline, two in Lafayette, and one each in Livingston, Carroll, Johnson, and Platte counties. The incident which triggered the first of the 1870s lynchings of black men in Saline County occurred on September 21, 1870, when West Hawkins attempted to rape an unidentified white woman in the middle of the afternoon. At that time, her husband and other family members, excepting a two-year-old, were away from the home. Carrying a double-barreled shot gun and a squirrel, Hawkins approached her residence and lingered about the premises. A 15-year-old boy, named in the story, happened to come by in search of some horses. When the boy left the vicinity, the black man rushed his victim, but as the newspaper explains, "She resisted him with all her might and prevented him from accomplishing his hellish designs." Meanwhile the young horse-searcher, upon hearing the woman's screams, reappeared, and her assailant ran off.[5] The headline of another news account states: "Mob Law in Marshall — Attempted Rape the Perpetrator Hung by an Infuriated Mob." Perhaps the new mob included members from the county's lynching of four black men within 24 hours in 1859. We will never know, but we do know that a very angry bunch removed West Hawkins from the easily breached jail and hanged him from a tree just north of town.[6] In the 1870 action, the men did not proceed as they had in 1859 by doing their dirty work in broad daylight. West Hawkins was strung up under cover of darkness. The county history dates his lynching as September 20, but the contemporary news account places it on October 20, 1870. The latter date is more likely to be accurate.

Less than a month later in this same county, according to a news story and the county history, an unnamed Negro waylaid a 16-year-old white girl and, as the paper phrases it, "attempted to outrage her person. The young lady was considerably bruised from the violent grasp of the fiend to prevent her getting away [and] has since been seriously ill." The story concludes, "The enraged populace took the brute at night and hanged him from a tree ... about five miles below Miami."[7] The newspaper and county history agree that this lynching took place on November 18, 1870.

The third mob death of a black male in Saline County in the 1870s was that of John Sweney, also spelled Swinney elsewhere in the only newspaper story I located about the incident. As the paper relates the matter, three black men, Clark Coiner, owner of an Arrow Rock saloon, Sweney and Reuben Elder hatched a harebrained scheme to eliminate competition in the bar business by setting other drinking establishments in town on fire. Not only does fire burn, it also spreads, and the conflagration in Arrow Rock's downtown business section was considerable. The enraged people got their hands on Sweney, and they hanged him on January 22, 1873, in or near Arrow Rock. Law enforcement officers managed to pass through Marshall, the seat of Saline County, at night, and they got their other prisoners, Clark Coiner and Reuben Elder, confined for safekeeping in the Lafayette County jail in Lexington.[8]

In Lafayette County, on June 6, 1870, the first of this county's two lynched males in the decade, John Tolliver, allegedly raped a seven-year-old Irish girl and threatened to kill her if she told anyone. The news account mentions that the child's mother finally discovered what had happened to her daughter five days later, on Saturday, June 11, and her discovery included noticing not only, as the paper phrases it, "the wounds inflicted by the brutal wretch, but also ... a loathsome disease, which had been contracted from [her assailant]." The mother relayed the facts of this assault to her husband, the child's father, and he located the Negro and took him before a justice of the peace. Before the JP, according to the news story, the black man confessed his guilt and was placed in the county jail in Lexington. The newspaper describes what happened next: on Monday evening, June 13, 1870, "the indignation of the citizens at the terrible outrage knew no bounds.... They gathered in large numbers, went to the jail, took the wretch out and hung him to a locust tree.... [The next morning] the carcass of the inhuman monster was still swinging on the tree."[9] The other Lafayette County mob murder of a black in the 1870s was the lynching of Joe Hardice/Hardin for horse stealing near Higginsville on August 17, 1874. One news account is short on details. It states that citizens in the vicinity "have long been troubled with horse thieves," and it concludes, "No particulars were learned except the lynching took place."[10] Another, aptly named *The Weekly Caucasian*, supplies more detail:

"A nigger named Joe Hardin has for a long time borne a bad character in the Higginsville neighborhood. Last Monday night, he was seized by a party of unknown men, upon the charge of horse-stealing, and hung near the railroad.... As the train came up Tuesday morning, his body could be seen still dangling from the limb of a tree."[11]

Another documented hanging of a black male for the rape of a white female took place in Johnson County. Newspaper coverage could be located because a Warrensburg resident, Henry C. Fike, kept a diary. For August 8, 1874, his entry reads as follows: "Last night some parties (unknown) hung a colored lad by name of Divers till he was dead, dead, dead. He had ravished E.A. Blodgett's little girl six years old." Two news stories supply Divers's Christian name, Monroe, and they also state that an integrated mob of unknown men hanged him. One newspaper describes him as the "rascally negro," and after assuring the reader that the culprit confessed, it concludes with the usual *general* condemnation of lynching, "but in this instance the act is justified, and there is no excitement over the matter whatever."[12] The other newspaper relates essentially the same facts, but its headline, "SHOULD HAVE BEEN BURNED,"[13] is a far more startling editorial than one typically finds in 1870s news coverage of these events. With the murder of Divers in 1874, Johnson County ended its lynching spree. In all, 12 can be documented within its borders. However with the exception of Johnson and Vernon — a county that also saw the last of its lynchings with its seventh in 1875 — all other Missouri counties with six or more mob murders continued to see extralegal killings at least as late as 1895.

Two other mob deaths of blacks in northwestern Missouri in the 1870s took place for the usual reason: the victims allegedly committed a sexual offense against a white female. One brief news story reads as follows, "George Brezan, a negro was hung by a mob at Chillicothe, Mo. [Livingston County] on Wednesday night [March 26, 1873] for committing a rape upon Miss Fisk, a highly respectable young white lady, living about 20 miles from that place."[14] Likewise, at Dewitt, Carroll County, another newspaper reports, "A large body of masked horsemen hanged a black male, Jim Callaway, and riddled his body with bullets on April 4, 1875, for the [April 3] alleged attempted rape of a 16-year-old white female, Miss Ruckel."[15]

The final known lynching of a black male for a sexual offense in 1870s northwest Missouri took place in Platte County. On July 27, 1876, Raphael or Ralph Williams allegedly raped a Mrs. Davis at her home in Camden Point. According to the county history, on July 31, 1876, the accused was "taken by a mob from the Platte City jail at night, and hung on an elm tree, on the road to Weston, near Tracy. It was afterwards charged that the negro was innocent." The newspaper account is more detailed. It specifies the number of armed men, 120, who posted pickets around the jail to avoid any interference, while five roused the sheriff and forced him to deliver the keys to the cells. A deputy sheriff unlocked Williams's cell, and the prisoner was hanged from a tree near the depot in Platte City. When the coroner cut the body down the next morning, a card was found pinned to it. It complained that "owing to the inefficiency of the laws of Missouri ... the Avengers who numbered among them some of the oldest and most respectable citizens of Platte County had deemed it advisable to take into their own hands and administer the justice the case so richly deserved."[16]

Perhaps in reaction to the lynchings for sexual offenses of the 1870s, either perpetrated or alleged to be perpetrated by black males against white females in Missouri, the legislature changed the law. In 1879 it added death as a punishment option in rape convictions. Excluding the years 1917 to 1919, when Missouri had no death penalty, this law remained in effect in this state for almost a century. In 1977 the U.S. Supreme Court ruled that a death sentence for the rape of an adult woman is unconstitutional. The High Court held that executing for this offense violates the Eighth Amendment prohibition against cruel and unusual punishments. In 2008, it held that capital punishment for the rape of a child also is unconstitutional; it too violates the Eighth Amendment.[17] The capital punishment option in Missouri's rape law of 1879 did not prevent additional lynchings of black males for real or imagined sex crimes against white females. Mob actions continued for this offense here as late as 1942. It was another 12 years after the statute was passed before the state of Missouri legally executed anyone for rape. With the exception of four white rapists of white women, one who attacked a biracial five- or six-year-old child, and one who attacked both a white and a black woman, when mob action punished this crime, the accused was black and his victim white.

In northeastern Missouri, there are three known lynchings of black men in the 1870s. The first was a sexual assault, an offense as often attributed to black men as horse stealing to white. It took place on June 21, 1873, outside Augusta in St. Charles County. George Fields allegedly raped, as the newspaper's brief coverage phrases it, "a young German girl, named Lizzie Kock." He was arrested near Labadle, Franklin County, and returned to Augusta where, as the news story concludes, he was "hung by a mob. Everything is quiet now. The negro is still hanging."[18] The second took place in Chariton County. On September 23, 1876, Edmond Moore allegedly raped Mrs. Samuel Virgin, while her husband was away from home on a Saturday evening. The newspaper notes that the victim "is a delicate lady, the daughter of Judge John W. Price, and a near relative of the late General Sterling Price," a former governor of Missouri and a former major general in the Confederate Army. Mr. Virgin and his neighbors brought Moore before her, and she positively identified him as her assailant. He had lived on a farm adjacent to the Virgins that summer. Moore managed to escape from the mob, of which Mr. Virgin was a member, and he surrendered to some black men. They in turn delivered him to the sheriff. On September 28, 1876, a newly formed mob removed the black man from the jail in Keytesville and hanged him, as the news account states, "with as little compunction as they would a sheep-killing dog and with vastly more satisfaction."[19]

The third northeastern case occurred in Howard County's Franklin Township. According to the newspaper, in the latter part of August 1879, Port Cason, a 30-year-old black male, went to the home of a white couple, Mr. and Mrs. Lon Capito, on whose farm he was living, presumably as a tenant worker. In the absence of her husband, "who had ordered him off the place," Cason "cursed and abused Mrs. Capito, who was in a delicate condition, so frightening the lady that she was taken suddenly ill and came near dying." Assuming the truth of the news story, Cason's behavior was not criminal. Since he initially resided on the Capito farm with the owner's permission, he could not be charged with trespassing, nor could he legally be ordered off the place without proper notice. As for frightening Mrs. Capito, the Negro's behavior might have rendered him civilly liable; perhaps he committed the tort of intentional infliction of mental distress, but doing so was not a crime. In virtually all other lynchings in Missouri of both white and black, the behavior complained of, if true, was criminal. This was not the case in

Port Cason's lynching. On Friday evening, August 29, 1879, "the citizens of the neighborhood" went to his residence and seized him for the purpose of whipping him, but when he resisted, they shot and killed him. His bullet-riddled body was subsequently found in the woods, and the shooters remained unknown. The news story concludes, "There are not a more law-abiding people in the state than the citizens of Franklin Township." The paper pronounced Cason, "worthless";[20] it clearly considered his death good riddance to bad rubbish. Needless to say both of the Howard County histories published in 1883 omit a number of disquieting events dealing with African Americans, including the lynching of Port Cason.

The first southeastern case of the 1870s involving an African American took place in Washington County. It concerned the February 1868 disappearance of a 40-year-old white woodchopper, Robert Cole. The newspaper's first headline states: "Partial Development of a Horrid Mystery of Nearly Two Years." A black child revealed a conversation he had overheard in the past two months between two black adults, Ben Walton and his son-in-law, Francis Hines. According to the boy, as the men passed a large and decayed log near the road, one remarked to the other, "That's the log and his things are behind it yet." Following this overheard and repeated remark, citizens of the neighborhood began investigating. They found property subsequently identified as that of the missing man: clothing, a pistol, and a watch. Shortly, both Walton and Hines were arrested, but citizens, not law enforcement officers, appear to have taken them into custody. The son-in-law stated that his father-in-law had murdered the missing man; afterwards Walton asked him for assistance in removing and secreting Cole's body. According to Hines, they dropped it in a mineral hole. Meanwhile, the first news story ends, "The two [Walton and Hines] were under arrest, and the citizens still actively at work in the effort to find the remains of the missing man." Then came a second headline: "Later — The Body of the Missing Man Found, Identified, the Father-in-Law Convicted upon Evidence of the Son-in-Law, and Hanged to a Tree." The story relates that on Tuesday, November 1, 1870, "a party of citizens took Ben Walton out, and required him to exhume the remains of the murdered man." That same evening, an indefinite number of unnamed men "took Walton near the road from Blackwell's Station to Bellefontaine, and left [him] hanging to the bough of a large hickory tree."[21] The coroner supplied the paper with details of the lynching. He held an inquest the next afternoon, Wednesday, November 2. Though the account does not so state, presumably the coroner's jury concluded that Ben Walton came to his death at the hands of unknown men.

I located only two accounts of blacks lynched for horse-stealing in Missouri. This crime was infrequently committed or suspected of being committed by African Americans. In the earlier case, vigilantes found Joe Cox, a black resident of Osceola, St. Clair County, in possession of a stolen horse near Wheatland, Hickory County, in either late December 1873 or early January 1874. The newspaper comments that Cox's "minor thieving propensities longed for more remunerations than mere trifles." The mob hanged him from the limb of a tree. The news story concludes, "Horse thieves should learn a lesson from black Joe's sure and swift punishment."[22] The second took place on August 17, 1874, in Lafayette County, near Higginsville, when a mob hanged Joe Hardice/Hardin from a tree near the Sedalia and Lexington Railroad.[23]

All other known lynching victims during the 1870s were white; mobs murdered more white males, 36, than the state legally executed in these years, 26. The greatest number of legal hangings of white men took place in the southeastern section of the state, 12 in all. Next in order for legal hangings of whites was the northwest section with eight; the southeast had three and the northeast two. Several reasons explain the comparatively large number of legal executions in the southeastern section of the state. More people lived there; it was home to the city of St. Louis. Equally important was the inability of *any* lynch mob to breach the jail in St. Louis. Not only were the county's capital prisoners held there during court proceedings, including appeals, they were hanged in this facility after all judicial matters and a request of the governor for a pardon had not succeeded. This jail was also used to confine prisoners from other Missouri counties, whenever there was a serious threat of a mob murder. For example, on November 19, 1870, two cousins, among other crimes, killed five members of a family in Washington County. The jury deliberated only three minutes before returning with first-degree murder convictions against them. Immediately after their trial, to avoid their being lynched, the condemned men were taken to the jail in St. Louis and held there until shortly before the sheriff of Washington County hanged them in Potosi, on January 27, 1871. Eventually, Kansas City's jail would serve as a secure holding place for capital prisoners from the southwestern section of the state, but no such facility existed in Kansas City, population approximately 30,000, in 1870 and 1871. Similarly, the Buchanan County jail in St. Joseph also housed potential lynching victims, and though this county had an execution in the 1870s, there were no known successful rabble actions during the 1870s in Buchanan County.

Between 1870 and 1879, mobs murdered the largest number of white men in the southwest section of the state, 16 in all. It would be 17 if it were not necessary to eliminate a Vernon County murder. Out-of-town news coverage is its only source. There is no extant newspaper from Vernon County during this time, and though its history, published in 1887, lists three unrelated lynchings within the county from the 1870s, it does not mention a January 30, 1877, murder of a man named Markham, near Donnegan's Grove, Vernon County. The news story relates that the victim was from Texas and had recently arrived for a visit with his brother, Buck Markham, and family. About 8 P.M. on a cold winter night, two strange men knocked at the Buck Markham residence and asked permission to warm themselves, and their request was granted. Immediately before the unknown men arose as if to leave, they asked the Texas man if his name was Markham. He replied in the affirmative; they immediately drew revolvers, removed him to the yard, shot him four times, and hanged him from an oak tree. Four other men were in the yard and prevented any assistance. As the newspaper phrases it, "no reason has been assigned for this terrible transaction. It is believed by some to be parties from Texas. Others say it was the work of a desperado lot of vigilantes from a neighborhood to the north of here."

The time period from the late 1860s through the early 1880s was the heyday of Midwestern outlaws. The most famous in American history were Jesse and Frank James, sons of a preacher, begot, born, and raised in Clay County, Missouri. There were a number of other lesser known gangs. The murder of a Texan named Markham was likely the work of one of them. We have no idea why he was killed, but a news story labeling the murder "a terrible lynching affair"[24] does not make it one.

Local newspaper coverage of most of these southwestern Missouri lynchings is not available from the 1870s. One must primarily rely on out-of-town newspapers and county histories. We know about a number of mob murders from this area from single sources, and they are likely to contain precious little. One history, which combines happenings in five counties, contains the following entries: "In June 1870 Dr. Taylor was hanged by Judge Lynch and company at Medoc, Jasper County, the charge being ill treatment of his family."[25] Without any explanation, this same history records that in Barry County, "in October 1871 a vigilance committee ... was said to have tried and hanged Aleck King."[26] It also mentions that in Newton County, "vigilantes hanged Lewis Swany and Buckskin in December 1871." Its only additional detail is meager: "During that year Buckskin killed eleven men"[27] A Kansas City newspaper supplies more information about this dual lynching. It relates that on December 30, 1871, two men, Morris Martin, better known as Buckskin, and Louis Swinn, beat and robbed a hard working German, Henry Solbyman, in Newton County. They were capture and jailed in Neosho. On January 2, 1872, a mob removed them from the jail and lynched them.[28]

In October 1874, according to the Vernon County history, a constable, James Quick, arrested James Harris. While the law enforcement officer was guarding his prisoner at Quick's home, about midnight, as the history relates, "a band of men came and took him out and riddled him with bullets."[29] No explanation is offered for either the arrest or the death of the deceased. Likewise unsatisfactorily short on facts is this same history's mention that in July 1875, "a young man named Dudley, only 20 years of age, was killed at Balltown by a party of men from Bates [County]who accused him of theft in that county."[30] The county history does not state what Dudley was suspected of stealing.

Three other southwestern lynchings of the 1870s involve either murder or robbery. In order of their occurrence, the first was set in motion on June 17, 1871, a Saturday. On this date, Jacob Fleming allegedly shot and killed James Hughes at a saloon in Osceola, seat of St. Clair County. Shortly he was jailed and indicted for first-degree murder, and on June 21, he was granted a change of venue to Benton County. This legal maneuver enraged the locals. On June 30, 75 to 100 men demanded the keys to the jail, and when they did not acquire them, they beat down the jail door, seized Jacob Fleming, put a rope around his neck, led him from the jail, and hanged him. No witnesses at the coroner's inquest recognized even one member of the mob.[31] The second took place on November 13, 1873, in Minersville, Jasper County, when a "disguised band of fifteen men," as the county history phrases it, "hung [Alfred T. Onan] for boldly attempting to rob the house of a man named Hunter, and [Onan] is said to have been a member of Quantrill's band."[32] Once more a grace note sounds from the Civil War. William Quantrill is best remembered as a guerrilla fighter who, with his gang in 1863, conducted the infamous raid against Lawrence, Kansas, in which large numbers of men, women, and children were murdered. He and his cohorts were also involved in a number of skirmishes with Union Army troops on the western Missouri and eastern Kansas border that same year. Ten years later, any white male from western Missouri might easily have been a member of Quantrill's band.

The third was set in motion near Rich Hill in Bates County, when 200 men joined to avenge the murder of Constable C.A. Wilson on the previous day, June 27, 1874. He had attempted to arrest David Hardy for stealing boots and jewelry from Addy Robinson, a resident of Osage Township. Wilson and one of his hired men went first to the residence of Hardy's father, but not finding their man there, they continued to search for him and found him in a field near his father's house. Hardy fired at Wilson with a double-barreled shotgun, killing him instantly. On June 28, 1874, the mob captured Hardy; 70 men took him to Rich Hill, and they hanged him from an elm tree approximately a mile from town.[33]

The other southwestern Missouri lynchings in the 1870s involve the most common reason for mob murders of white men, the theft of livestock. In one, the alleged crime was sheep stealing, and it was coupled with selling the animals' meat to butchers in Greene and Polk counties. The alleged sheep thief, Greenberry Buis, was arrested in Barry County. He was being taken to Polk County in July 1873, when, according to the Greene County history, "A body of about twenty-five armed men [in Greene County] rode up, took the prisoner out, and hung him to a tree." News coverage also places the lynching near the residence of Buis's mother in Greene County's northwest corner. Buis had earlier been arrested in Cass County for horse stealing, convicted therein, and served time in the Missouri State Penitentiary for this offense. The Greene County history dates his mob murder as July 7, a Monday, and an out-of-county newspaper of July 17 places his death on a Sunday, either July 6 or 13, and the paper numbers the mob at 50 to 60, a figure likely to be accurate. However, both sources agree that he died in early July 1873 because he was believed to be a sheep thief and had a prior felony conviction for horse stealing.[34]

Four southwestern counties were scenes of the lynchings of alleged horse thieves. In Pulaski County in July 1870, a party of men captured Henry Shadle, alias Henry Wright. He was suspected of having stolen a horse from a Mr. Hollis in Webster County. While returning Shadle to Webster County, the party with its prisoner stopped for the night near Lebanon, Laclede County. A mob took Shadle and hanged him from a tree on July 6, 1870. The newspaper reporting the incident did its customary condemnation of lynchings in general, but it added that "mob violence ... is about the only protection farmers have against horse thieves."[35] On August 30, 1873, in Benton County, near Cole Camp, a mob hanged two unnamed men accused of stealing horses. In this case, no law enforcement officers had arrested them and placed them in the jail in Warsaw. One news story relating this matter describes the theft of a dozen horses in late August near Appleton City, Bates County. Another concerns the escape of a man committed to the Saline County jail in Marshall for horse stealing. The prisoner managed to remove a sizeable rock from the outer wall of his cell, and by fashioning a rope from blankets, he slid down it to his freedom.[36] Given the rickety condition of most county jails, there was no guarantee that their inmates, once deposited in them, would remain confined. On October 27, 1873, Thomas Box did not escape summary punishment. Ten years earlier, he had been sent to prison from Cedar County on charges of passing counterfeit money. When he returned, he was believed to have taken up a new line of dishonest work. On October 20, a Mr. Vincent of Cedar County discovered that two of his valuable farm horses were missing. He and his friends investigated, and they found them in Box's possession. The news coverage is careful to disassociate Vincent and his friends from the death of Box. It states of them, "They, at least, it is said, did not lay hands upon Box in violence." However, on the morning of October 28, 1873, as a man was riding in to Virgil City, Cedar County, he saw, as the paper phrases it, "a man's body swinging in the wind." On closer inspection, it was Tom Box's corpse. The news story concludes, "The people have suffered ... much of late from horse stealing.... Box should have been hung long ago. His brother-in-law, as guilty as he was, has fled the country and others are preparing to leave. It is believed that Box made a confession before he died."[37] Repeatedly, newspapers covering these violent events add that the man about to be murdered confessed; always, there was the expressed hope that the right man had been put to death.

Less than two weeks later, there was a follow-up to Box's mob murder. On either November 8, a Saturday, or November 9, a Sunday, according to the Sedalia newspaper, vigilantes in Cedar County went to the home of Steigall, Box's brother-in-law, and they removed him and two other men, unknown to the local citizens. On Sunday morning, the body of one was found hanging from a tree near the road. The deceased may have been Box's brother-in-law or one of the unknown men. The newspaper removes any doubt regarding the reason for this second Cedar County lynching: "It is the universal belief that a thorough[ly] organized band of horse thieves infest that portion of the country, and the citizens are determined to clean them out, in self-protection."[38]

On July 19, 1874, in Vernon County, approximately one-half mile from Nevada, the county seat, eight men took Oliver Frakes from the arms of his mistress, strung him up, and shot their guns into his hanging corpse. Frakes was believed to have taken part in the robbery of an old man somewhat earlier, but more important, as the county history notes, Frakes was believed to be "a horse thief.... He wore good clothes, seemed always to have money, but was without visible means of support, and associated with improper characters. It is asserted now, however, that he was not a horse thief or a robber, but was only a gambler and a loafer."[39] Thus ends this recounting of the lynchings of the 1870s from the southwest section of the state, at least 16, and almost certainly there were others I did not discover.

I began this chapter with details of Bill Childs's imprecisely dated death for an unstated offense in either 1869 or 1870 in Lafayette County. It is one of 22 lynchings in northwest Missouri during the 1870s. Others include those of nine already discussed African Americans and three white bond swindlers, discussed in the next chapter. The remaining 10 include five for the crime a la mode of the period, horse stealing. The earlier of these lynchings for alleged equine theft was Martin W. Black's on April 14, 1870, near Kansas City, Jackson County. He was seized by a party of approximately six men, including one from Cooper County from whom Black was believed to have stolen several horses. The men hanged Black from a tree by the side of the road until he was dead. The newspaper account of this event has a typical conclusion, "It is said this man Black was a daring thief, and perhaps has met the right fate, though the mode may be questioned."[40]

In the summer of 1874, mobs put four horse thieves to death in separate incidents. The first and the most detailed news coverage concerned James Ross in Holt County, on July 17, for the theft of a valuable grey mare. Ten days earlier the animal had been returned to her owner. Contrary to the usual newspaper reporting of such matters at the time, the local papers are censorious regarding the lynching of Ross. He was 17, the son of respectable parents who lived in Iowa, had already pleaded guilty to his crime at his preliminary hearing, and had asked to be turned over to the circuit court judge for punishment. Earlier he had met a man whom one newspaper termed a "judge" on the road near Mound City, and the paper quotes this official as describing Ross as "not very bright,"[41] a suggestion that the "red-headed boy" or the "red-headed prisoner," as the press referred to him, may have been retarded. The lynchers took Ross from Constable Rice as he was attempting to bring him and another man in a hack to Oregon, the county seat. About six miles north of Forest City, five or six men stopped the constable and his prisoners, demanded Ross, took him 50 yards, and hanged him from the limb of a walnut tree.

One newspaper writes, "Taking the life of a defenseless prisoner is an outrage.... The opinion is universal among all classes of our people that the hanging of this boy was unwarranted, disgraceful in the extreme and the guilty parties must be held responsible for their bloody deed."[42] Another, "There is no excuse for the act.... The idea that it is right to take life for life is beginning to become too abhorrent to the people of this age, and how much more should it be where life is taken for property."[43] Despite the disapproval of this lynching, when a coroner's jury was impaneled to ascertain the circumstances of Ross's death, no one recognized any of the lynchers, rumored to be "some of the best men of the central part of the county."[44] In this case, community approval does not explain the failure to bring the bullies who hanged a young, perhaps retarded, white, and admitted horse thief to justice. Community fear probably accounts for the impunity of the mob.

The other lynchings of horse thieves in northwest Missouri the summer of 1874 took place in Lafayette County. The first left a slender record. One newspaper reports that on August 16, 1874, near Mayview, a mob repeatedly hanged a 25-year-old, identified only by the surname Hall, in order to extract information about his horse stealing activities. He died from fright and strangulation.[45] The second has already been discussed, that of the African-American Joe Hardice/Hardin on August 17, 1874. The third took place 10 days later. On August 26, 1874, 30 armed men took Harvey Osborne from his bed, and they hanged him from a tree limb in the vicinity of Higginsville Road, near Aullville. A note was found pinned to the corpse; it read, "Here is a thief. He came from Benton County." The news story explains the motivation of the mob: "The farmers throughout this section have long suffered the depredations of horse thieves." The paper is careful to add of the evildoers, "None were known or recognized, and they were supposed to be from some other county."[46] This careful non-reporting reflected community support for the death of yet another man believed to be a horse thief.

One additional lynching in the 1870s also took place in Lafayette County. On December 3, 1874, a mob in Concordia ended the life of a man named Dr. Rush, no Christian name given in the newspaper accounts of his death by hanging. He was alleged to have been detected trying to set the town on fire and to have attempted to poison a rival physician, Dr. West, who, upon his recovery, left town.[47]

In Nodaway County, on August 18, 1872, Alexander Worth Tansey allegedly murdered two men, one woman, and two small children. Their bodies were discovered in a decaying state in a broken down freight wagon south of Quitman. Tansey's motive for this massacre was robbery; he said he needed money, and he believed that he could obtain it by taking his victims' property. A mob, 300 to 400 members strong, slowly extracted details of his crimes from him. He gave one fanciful version after another, as the mob repeatedly yanked him up in order to get the truth from him. Finally, the mob had heard enough, and as law enforcement officers were taking him toward Maryville, the county seat, it seized Tansey and hanged him from a tree near the village of Clearmont. The county history's account of this lynching is lengthy. It includes this startling piece of information: "After Tansey was dead, his head was severed from his body and conveyed to Maryville, where it was for some time preserved in alcohol. It is related that a negative was taken of his head, from which many photographs were taken."[48] None are known to now exist. His death cannot be dated more precisely than the later part of August 1872.

The hanging of James Sharp for the murder of John Erskine in late July 1872, near Warrensburg, is Johnson County's only known lynching of a white man during the 1870s. The news account of it says that "several of the most respected citizens were among the mob."[49] One incident from the northwest section, on December 17, 1873, accounts for the lynching of three men, only one of whom newspapers name, Tom Stanton. It is the final known mob murder of white men in northwest Missouri in the 1870s. It took place near Cambridge, Saline County. Five men robbed a farmer of $1,000, which he received for the sale of hogs. A neighbor of the victim passing by found the murdered man and overheard the robbers quarrelling about the division of the proceeds. He quietly left the crime scene, raised a party of neighbors, and they captured and hanged three of the five men involved in the murder and robbery. Two of the culprits escaped.[50]

Two mob deaths of white men took place in the northeastern section in the 1870s. In Jefferson City, James M. Teague was arrested for the theft of a horse from Isaac Ellis, a resident of Lincoln County. Teague had a criminal history; he had served two terms at the Missouri State Penitentiary for theft. As Constable Robert F. Waters escorted him to Auburn from Jefferson City for examination, in or near Auburn, on November 13, 1874, a 50-member mob with blackened faces attempted to seize Teague, but the lawman protected him. At Teague's examination the next morning, the horse thief admitted his crime. When the constable and a posse of four later started with him toward Troy, the seat of Lincoln County, four men appeared out of the bushes. One knocked the constable off his horse, and another shot Teague. He fell to the ground, but his feet, tied to the saddle, kept him tethered to his frightened horse as the animal ran down the road, dragging him over rocky terrain. He was taken to a nearby cabin, patched up, and then brought to the jail in Troy on November 14. He died there from his injuries on November 19, 1874. The county history ends its account of this incident in typical fashion: "An effort was made to capture members of the mob, but they could not be found."[51]

On a Saturday, July 6, 1877, two miles northeast of Roanoke, in Randolph County, John W. Green shot and killed his wife, mother of their seven children, allegedly because of his sexual liaison with another woman. He claimed the shooting was accidental, that he was trying to kill a dog, but his bad aim caused the bullet(s) to hit his wife. She lived long enough to state that he intentionally shot her. The constable of Silver Creek Township brought Green to the home of the constable's father, G.W. Dameron. Green remained there until Monday, but fearing mob action, the constable moved him to another house. That same evening a party of men estimated at between 40 and 75 scoured the neighborhood until it located its victim. The mob easily overpowered the constable and one guard, and it issued a written order to the constable not to follow his prisoner. The mob said that Green's hanged body would be found the next morning near Silver Creek Church, and it was. The county history speculates that the mob probably came from Howard County because Mrs. Green's relations lived in that locale. It ends its coverage: "The people of Randolph are peaceful and law-abiding, and while it is the general belief that this mob was from Howard ... we doubt not that every man who engaged in hanging this man felt that he was discharging a sacred duty conscientiously and for the good of the community and his fellow man."[52] This lynching has a minor dating problem. An out-of-state newspaper gives a St. Louis dateline of July 11, states Green's shooting of his wife took place "on Friday last," or July 6, and his lynching happened on Monday, July 9.[53] The county history, published in 1884, places the death of Green's wife on Saturday, July 12, and his death on July 14, 1877. I adopt the newspaper date because it is contemporaneous with the events, and as such, more likely to be accurate.

A third incident from this section lacks sufficient documentation to confirm that it was an actual lynching. On December 31, 1870, Governor McClurg offered a $300 reward for the capture of each of the persons who took William White "from the custody of the officers of the law and brutally murdered [him] in Macon County on the 10th day of November last [1870]." There is no mention of this matter in either the 1884 or 1910 history of Macon County, and no extant contemporary newspaper coverage of the event.[54]

Counting the Washington County death of the black man, Ben Walton, discussed earlier in this chapter, there are three known lynchings from this time period in southeastern Missouri. There would be a fourth, but it is too short on detail to classify it as much of anything. There is no extant newspaper from the county, Dunklin, at the time of the event, February 1878. An out-of-state newspaper relates that the case arose out of an old family feud in Malden, Missouri, in which a Robinson, surname only, shot a man who shot two on the other side. Score-evening for feuding and fussing may be just that, and not a lynching. We have no knowledge of the community's opinion about any of these killings. The news story, headlined "Supposed Lynching in Missouri" concludes, "A posse pursued and caught Robinson, who was held under arrest until the affray was investigated and then disappeared. It is known that he did not escape."[55]

Only two white men were known to have been lynched in southeastern Missouri in the 1870s. The first was Dayho, surname only, a German resident of Ripley County, who so abused his two- or three-year-old ward that the child died after terrible punishments that may have extended over days, weeks, or even months. After his arrest and owing to the poor quality of the jail in Doniphan, seat of Ripley County, he was initially held in the jail in Potosi. He secured a change of venue to Butler County, and at his trial in Poplar Bluff, he was acquitted. Within a few days of his return to Ripley County in July 1870, as the newspaper phrases it, "a band of disguised men" came to Dayho's house, and when he refused to come out, the mob set it on fire. When he was forced to leave the burning structure, he was shot dead. The news story ends on an approving note: "We do not learn of any suspicion as to who were the murderers."[56]

The other known lynching from this section is for the most common crime of this decade, livestock theft, specifically horse stealing. A Union newspaper retrospective of 1897 that misdates events and garbles the names in almost every lynching it described from earlier times in Franklin County places the mob murder of *Hopkins* in Pacific in 1874 and describes him as "a leader of a gang of horse thieves."[57] A newspaper contemporary with the event dates the lynching of the horse thief Joseph C. *Howard* as occurring in Pacific City, Franklin County, on June 17, 1873. It notes, "An inquest was held this morning ... and a verdict was agreed upon that Howard came to his death by strangulation at the hands of parties unknown to the jury." It estimates the mob at 200 to 300 armed men.[58]

Newspaper coverage of some lynchings that took place in the late 1860s and most that occurred from the 1870s on mentions that the coroner's jury found that the deceased came to his death at the hands of persons unknown to the jury. Despite the legal requirements regarding inquests, including the oaths of jurors that they will inquire "by whom" the deceased came to his death, nothing in the law prevented members of the lynch mob from also serving as coroner's jurors on the very homicide they had recently helped commit. Surely, with some frequency, good and lawful men served in this dual capacity, and under these circumstances, lynchings thrived.

When we add the 35 mob murders of the late 1860s to the 45 that took place in the 1870s by December 1874, no fewer than 80 occurred in this state in less than 10 years after the Civil War ended. This is somewhat more than one-third of the known lynchings in this state between 1803 and 1981. No other time period remotely approaches these numbers for mob murders here. Missouri was fractured by the Civil War in a way that most jurisdictions were not. Without the internecine strife that took the lives of nearly 13,000 of Missouri's boys and men during the war years, it is not imaginable that these figures would be this high. Moreover, at least 83 percent of those murdered by mobs were white. The decade, 1870–1879, remains the high water mark for known mob murders, 52. This figure exceeds any earlier or later ten-year period by at least 17 lynchings that can be documented as taking place in this state.

The next chapter discusses three extensively covered mob murders from the 1870s. They differ from those in this chapter because strenuous efforts were made to punish the lynchers in courts of law, both state and federal.

CHAPTER 5

Law vs. Mob: Strenuous Efforts to Punish Lynchers, 1872–1879

Three incidents from the 1870s have sufficiently detailed records to warrant a separate chapter. Always the community approved, or was afraid to disapprove of, the extralegal deaths of those suspected of wrongdoing, but in each of these cases, either elected or appointed officials made extraordinary efforts to bring the lynchers to some kind of justice. That the victims in the three cases were white was probably a factor, but not determinative; as the last chapter demonstrates, nearly 70 percent of those whom a mob put to death in the 1870s were white. Each of these three lynchings has special circumstances that distinguished it from other Missouri necktie parties during this decade.

The first took place on April 24, 1872, in Cass County. Estimates of the mob's size vary. According to one Cass County history, published 45 years later, 50 armed men were involved. Contemporary newspaper coverage places the participants at 70 to 80, and it also states that 200 unmasked persons viewed this frightening spectacle. It began with a locomotive on the Missouri, Kansas, and Texas Railroad, which originated in Paola, Kansas, eastbound for Holden, Missouri. When it reached Harrisonville, seat of Cass County, several gentlemen connected with the Memphis and Kansas City Railroad boarded. The train consisted of four cars: two for passengers (containing approximately 30 persons), one for baggage, and the engine. About 12 miles east of Harrisonville, it reached a locale called Guntown or Gunn City; shortly, the engineer saw an immense obstruction on the tracks: rails, logs, and rocks. While he gave his full attention to stopping his vehicle, masked men began pumping bullets into it. When the engineer managed to halt the train before it crashed into the barricade, other disguised men boarded it. At gunpoint they required the engineer and fireman to hold up their hands, and while these railroad employees were carefully guarded in one car, others of this daring mob sought out the objects of their wrath. According to the newspaper, as they made their way through the cars, they broke doors, smashed windows, and threatened to burn the train. They screamed, "Where's the bond robbers? Turn out the bond thieves." Their first victim was James R. Cline, an attorney for the Memphis and Kansas City Railroad. According to the newspaper, he stepped off the train "into the midst of the yelling, shrieking mass," and told the assembled, 'Here I surrender myself to you. Take me. I am unarmed and am willing to be tried before any tribunal if I have done any man wrong.'

He threw up his arms while he spoke to show he was defenseless ... he fell, riddled by 40 bullets." The next victim was Judge Jehiel C. Stephenson/Stevenson, presiding justice of the county court; he was shot dead in a passenger car. Last, the lynchers found Thomas E. Dutroe, a bondsman for Cline, in the baggage car; they shot and severely wounded him, threw his body to the ground, and allowed him to bleed to death over the next four hours. The killers then threatened to eliminate anyone who either sympathized with their victims or revealed the name of any man they might have recognized. One newspaper clarifies, without naming him, that "the leader of the gang was recognized as a citizen of Harrisonville. About 20 others were recognized and will doubtless be brought to justice and punished for this, the blackest and foulest massacre of the age." This paper's extensive coverage concludes, "The strong arm of the state authorities will no doubt be invoked, and the terrible disgrace wiped from the fair fame of western Missouri."[1] Shortly, a lengthy article about this brazen crime appeared in *The New York Times*. According to it, "A trembling coroner's jury brought in a verdict of death at the hands of persons unknown.... The mob emboldened by these successes threatened ... to hang the Governor himself should he attempt to interfere.... Governor [Brown's] sole action [was] to dispatch one small company of militia to contend with a mob of over a thousand desperate men." This newspaper's article ends, "It is time that disorders of this sort should cease, and that the amateur executioners of the border should be taught that there is one law for rogues and honest men alike."[2]

The matter did not end with the verdict of the coroner's jury. Because both Cass County Circuit Court records concerning this case and local newspaper coverage of Cass County Circuit Court proceedings are no longer extant, county histories are the most readily available source for the background and subsequent proceedings in state court. According to a history published in 1917, the Missouri legislature authorized the county courts in 1868 to issue bonds favorable to the development of the railroad. Out of this, the Land Grant Railway Construction Company contracted to build, and completed, the railroad from Holden, Missouri, to Paola, Kansas, the very route upon which the three train passengers were murdered. The mob's anger over the indebtedness of its county was not complicated; Cass County's citizens were given no opportunity to vote on the issuance of the bonds. They regarded the chicanery of these bonds as robbery with fancy pens. Hence the enraged mob took bold action in stopping the train.

County Court Judge Stevenson had received $12,000 in ill-gotten gains and Cline, $55,000. A Mr. Ladue, not a train passenger and apparently unharmed, received for himself and R.S. Stevens, another unharmed non-passenger, $127,000. The county recovered Cline's $55,000 and Ladue's $127,000. At the time they were murdered, Cline and Stevenson had already been indicted, made bail, and were due in Cass County Circuit Court to face charges, presumably of bond fraud. The 1917 history of Cass County devotes an entire chapter, "County Bond Trouble," to the intricacies of the matter; it details the sums by which the murdered men enriched themselves and recounts their subsequent indictments. According to an 1883 county history, the Cass County Court legally obtained the bonds, cancelled them, and ordered their destruction by burning on May 6, 1878. The judges consented to spare several as souvenirs. One went to a drugstore in Gunn City, and its proprietor framed and displayed it. He did so, states this history, so "that the public servants of old Cass may remember, when they trample upon the rights of the people and refuse to hear their prayers, that they will appeal to a higher power and serve an injunction that will stick — which means death to tyrants."[3] This awkward prose clarifies that for the most part, the citizens of Cass County approved the dire events of April 24, 1872. Forty-one men were eventually arrested in connection with the Gunn City Massacre, as it came to be known. At trial, if legal matters even advanced to that stage, there were neither convictions nor guilty pleas obtained in any state court proceedings. According to the 1917 history, when "persons supposed to be in the mob were tried, they were acquitted."[4] Thus far, this case resembles the majority of other lynchings.

One man watched this blatant and unpunished display of lawlessness with special interest. His name was James S. Botsford (1844–1915). When he was 16 years old, he joined the Union Army as a private in the Fifth Wisconsin Volunteers. Soon after Private Botsford arrived in Washington, D.C., in July 1861, he and several other young recruits paid a visit to the White House and there met President Lincoln. Following this visit, Botsford's unit saw considerable action during the war. It fought at Antietam, Fredericksburg, Chancellorsville, and Gettysburg. By the spring of 1864, he was fighting and badly wounded in the Battle of the Wilderness under the ultimately victorious general, Ulysses S. Grant. When Botsford's war wounds healed, he settled in Illinois and began the study of law; in 1867, at the age of 23, he was admitted to the state bar of Illinois. The next year he moved to Sedalia, Missouri, and there he practiced law as a junior partner of Johnson & Botsford. After several years as a Sedalia attorney, his former commander offered him a new job. In January 1871, President Grant appointed 27-year-old James Botsford as the U.S. Attorney for the Western District of Missouri Federal Court.[5] This court was first established in 1857, and its jurisdiction included the 66 western counties of Missouri. Its counterpart was the U.S. District Court for the Eastern District of Missouri, initially established as the District of Missouri in 1822, divided in 1857, comprising the 68 counties of eastern Missouri.[6]

At the time of the Gunn City Massacre, Arnold Krekel (1815–1888) was the federal judge for the Western District of Missouri. With his family, he was a German immigrant to St. Charles, Missouri, in the 1830s. He was admitted to the Missouri Bar in 1845, remained a staunch Union man, and became president of the Missouri State Constitutional Convention that abolished slavery in this state on January 11, 1865. Three months later, President Lincoln appointed him the federal judge for the Western District of Missouri, a position he occupied until poor health forced his resignation in 1888.[7] Judge Krekel presided over two criminal cases involving lynchers. One was the Gunn City matter, and the other is discussed in the next chapter.

I first became aware that the prosecution of the Gunn City lynchers continued after their acquittals in Cass County Circuit Court by reading the *Sedalia Daily Democrat.* This newspaper was eager to cover any matter involving two prominent attorneys with a Sedalia connection. Botsford had practiced law in this town for approximately three years before President Grant appointed him a U.S. Attorney. Equally important, George G. Vest (1830–1904), later U.S. Senator Vest (1879–1903), had, as a young Sedalia attorney, been appointed to represent Slave Sam, accused of murder and lynched by burning in Pettis County in 1853, a case discussed in Chapter 2. When the Civil War began, Vest served as a judge advocate with the Confederate forces in Missouri. After the war, he moved back to Sedalia.[8] He was a practicing attorney there when he represented one or more of the defendants in *U.S.* v. *Robert Brown, Jr. et al.*, the federal criminal case involving the Gunn City lynchers.

How did a federal court, years before any member of congress considered anti-lynching legislation, get subject matter jurisdiction over a case in which an enormous mob of white men killed three members of their own race, none of whom were federal employees, in the state of Missouri? Even though at the time it would not have made any difference, no one crossed state lines in order to lynch these men. Federal kidnapping legislation which required crossing a state line with the victim(s) came much later. Botsford found a basis for indicting a large number of defendants in the U.S. Constitution. Among the enumerated powers of the U.S. Congress is the authority to "establish Post Offices and Post Roads."[9] Out of this power evolved the exclusive federal authority to transmit the mails and to conduct other postal matters of the United States. In 1825, the 18th Congress made it a federal crime to "knowingly and willfully obstruct or retard the passage of the mail."[10] When the train that departed Paola, Kansas, on April 24, 1872, bound for Holden, Missouri, was stopped by a lynch mob in Gunn City, Cass County, it had in addition to two passenger cars, one for baggage. Among other items of cargo were the U.S. mails: letters, packages, and the like. The federal court had geographical jurisdiction because Cass is one of the 66 counties that comprise the Western District of Missouri Federal Court, and it had subject matter jurisdiction because there was mail in the baggage car and it was retarded long enough for the mob to stop the train; lynch three men by shooting them to death, including one victim that bled to death over a period of four hours; and swear the many witnesses to these murders to secrecy.

By good luck, although the federal court records in this case appear to be incomplete, they are extant. There are neither a series of questions and answers for each witness nor a summary of his testimony. The file lacks both opening and closing arguments; the only motion it contains is one in which the government moved the court to try a portion of the defendants. Botsford advanced a number of reasons for the severance: (1) he was prepared with evidence and witnesses to try a portion of the defendants, (2) these government witnesses would not be needed in any future trial, (3) if all defendants were given continuances, this would greatly increase the expense to the United States, and (4) not all indicted persons were currently in custody. However, even if this motion were not extant, what survives of this case makes clear the immense difficulty the prosecutor had in herding a bunch of alleged lynchers, both respected and/or feared in their community, through the federal criminal justice system. The minor nature of the charges against these men in no way prevented them from mounting a vigorous defense against the federal charges that arose in connection with their murderous activities on April 24, 1872. The flavor of their defense can be shown in the Sedalia newspaper: "The defendants claim that they have not had a fair trial ... that Judge Krekel has treated them as a vindictive man would treat a personal enemy."[11] Despite their whining, these lynchers were lucky; the handwritten federal court records contain absolutely no mention or even the hint that three men were murdered at the same time these accused defendants allegedly retarded the mail.

What survives in *U.S.* v. *Robert Brown, Jr. et al.* (Case No. 857) is the grand jury's indictment of 13 men. It charges that on April 24, 1872, in Cass County, Missouri, they "knowingly and willfully did obstruct and retard the passage of a carriage carrying the mail of the United States, to wit a mail car passing through said county as [a] mail route from Paola, Kansas, to the town of Holden in said Western District of Missouri, contrary to the ... statute ... and against the peace and dignity of the said United States."[12] This indictment was handed up during the March 1873 term of the Court when it met in Jefferson City on March 21, 1873. The 13 men named in this indictment and in this order were Robert Brown, Jr., Giles J. Cockrall, John C. Smith, William P. Barnes, Jr., Giles Beck, John W. Shuey, William A. Smith, Thomas Clifford, Timothy Clifford, Douglas McCall, William P. Barnes, Sr., Samuel Brown, and John Pierson. Presumably, U.S. Attorney Botsford chose these 13 because they were among the 41 men arrested on state charges of murder in Cass County. Most likely the federal case was strongest against these 13.

The bulk of extant documents in Case No. 857 consists of arrest warrants for these many defendants and details of the U.S. marshals' successes and failures to take these men into custody. They were not all found in Cass County. Several had moved. One was living in Stockton, Rooks County, Kansas, and later arrested in Jackson County, Missouri. Another had moved to Clarksville, Red River County, Texas, but he was eventually arrested in Cass County, where most of these indicted men were located. As the file attests, all those arrested made bail effortlessly. To have either denied it or required a large amount on the minor charge of retarding the passage of the mail would have been a violation of the Eighth Amendment to the U.S. Constitution. The defendants' recognizance bonds were each set at $1,000. All of the arrested men pledged themselves, as the file indicates, "as sureties jointly and severally in the sum of one thousand dollars to be levied of their respective goods and chattels, lands and tenements, and to the use of the United States" (208). All pledged "to appear personally at the September 1873 term of the Court and/or during the pendency of said indictment" (208). No money changed hands because each of the indicted men owned sufficient real and personal property from which the government could take the $ 1,000 should any one of them not appear for trial. At approximately the same time these multiple recognizance bonds were being posted, these many defendants, all represented by counsel, were arraigned, and each pleaded not guilty (207).

In addition to the $1,000 recognizance bonds for each of the defendants, the file contains a number of recognizance bonds of $500 for each the many government witnesses Botsford needed to present his case. The U.S. marshals' subpoenas for these men are also a part of the file. The marshals and their deputies principally located the witnesses in Cass County, but not all. One was found in Johnson County, Missouri. The U.S. marshals for the District of Indiana and the District of Michigan were asked for assistance in rounding up the 40 persons the United States eventually assembled in this case, at a cost of $1,720.20. Although the trial was initially scheduled for September 1873, it was continued, and in the interim, Botsford dropped charges against several of the defendants.

In March 1874 in Jefferson City, the trial against nine of them finally began. The file contains the names of all the jurors (216), but because we have no information about them other than their names, and not all of them could be located in the federal censuses, it is not possible to trace them through these documents. As a result we do not know in which of the 66 counties of the Western District of Missouri these jurors resided. We do know that the nine defendants who were finally brought to trial in March 1874 were represented by four attorneys; the most famous of them was George G. Vest. Presumably because of the skill of their lawyers, Judge Arnold Krekel directed verdicts of not guilty in favor of four of the defendants: John E. Smith, Douglas McCall, Samuel Brown, and John S. Pierson. As a result the jury never deliberated the case against these four.

The trial appears to have lasted at least three days. In mid–March, the *Sedalia Daily Democrat* ran brief articles about the proceedings. One includes this mention: "The United States Court is in session this week and engaged in trying the parties indicted for stopping the mail at Gunn City, in Cass County, at the time when the bond swindlers were killed."[13] We know from the newspaper that only defendants Robert Brown, Jr., and Giles Beck were convicted. As for the other defendants, either the judge directed a verdict in their favor or the jury found them not guilty. The jury's verdict survives on a single, otherwise unmarked piece of paper: "We the jury find the defendants Robert Brown, Jr. and Giles Beck Guilty as charged in the Indictment and the Jury further finds the defendants W.P. Barnes, Sr., William A. Smith, John W. Shuey, Timothy Clifford & Giles J. Cockrall not Guilty as charged in the Indictment." It is signed L.G. Shellidy, Foreman. The sentencing phase of the case appears to have begun shortly after the jury returned its verdict. Brown and Beck were each fined $100 plus costs, unspecified in the record as to any dollar amount, and the defendants' recognizance bonds were discharged (218).

The 1917 Cass County history states of the matter, "At Gunn City a mob stopped the train, and Stevenson and Cline received the just punishment for their conduct." It continues, "Indictments of persons supposed to be in the mob followed, their trials were had, and they were cleared. Perhaps two parties received small fines, which were readily paid."[14] More than 40 years after the lynching of three men and the state and federal proceedings against these murderers, the county history names no names of any mob members. Clearly the majority of Cass County residents continued to approve of the Gunn City lynchings. Despite the denouement of two $100 fines, the federal case should not be dismissed as much ado about nothing. Because of Botsford's determination to see some kind of justice done, we at least know the names of the guilty. Given the lack of Cass County circuit records and multiple missing newspapers, without the handwritten records in *U.S. v Robert Brown Jr. et al.*, no names of mob members would survive. We owe a debt of thanks to the prosecutor, the judge, the U.S. marshals and their deputies, and the witnesses who, no matter how badly intimidated, appeared and testified for the government.

A second extraordinary lynching of the 1870s, one that generated enormous newspaper coverage, began on June 21, 1873. As handwritten Callaway County Circuit Court records indicate, on that date, a farmer, James Brown, filed a complaint charging Peter Kessler and his son, Augustus, better known as Gus Kessler, with "willfully stealing and taking from James Brown on June 19, 1873, two large mules of the value of four hundred dollars."[15] On that same day, a warrant was issued for their arrest. *The New York Times* quotes a lengthy story from the *St. Louis Times* regarding the St. Louis police force's role in this case. In late June, the owner of the mules, James Brown, notified the St. Louis police of the theft of his livestock and his suspicions that the Kesslers were the thieves. At this time the father, Peter Kessler, and two of his sons, George and Gus, were living 12 miles from the city of St. Louis. On July 25, an alert St. Louis police officer recovered the stolen mules; they had been traded for another team plus $30. Initially, three Kesslers were arrested, but George was released. He convinced the police that he had been living in Indiana and was not complicit in the mule theft by his father and brother. Peter and Gus Kessler were confined in the St. Louis jail, and Callaway County Circuit Court records regarding them include fees for their capture and incarceration.

Once these men were in custody, the St. Louis police notified James Brown of their arrest; shortly he arrived in St. Louis. According to the *St. Louis Times*, "The chief of police [St. Louis City] told [Mr. Brown] very plainly that the police force could not be used to catch thieves who would be lynched as soon as they were out of the city. He [related] the recent hanging of Howard at Franklin, [discussed in the last chapter] as an instance in which his department had been compromised." The news story continues that "Mr. Brown gave the most solemn assurances that the Kesslers should have a fair trial, and was even willing to give bond if required." On July 28, Brown started back to Callaway County with the Kesslers, and a St. Louis police officer as an extra guard, On July 20, they arrived in Jefferson City; a telegram warned them to delay the trip to Fulton. When they arrived in Fulton the next day, they were met at the depot by 100 armed men who escorted them to the courthouse. Brown told the assembled that he was under a $2,000 bond for the safe delivery of the Kesslers to the sheriff of Callaway County. This information temporarily restrained the mob. Once the sheriff received his prisoners, he took them to the woods for safekeeping and returned them to Jefferson City.[16] Peter and Gus Kessler were confined in the Cole County jail. On the evening of August 14, the mule thieves were returned from Jefferson City to Fulton by train. En route, father and son were handcuffed together. The son, Gus, asked permission to use the "water closet," i.e. the restroom, and his father, from whom he was separated, remained outside. Once inside the small bathroom, Gus managed to slip off his handcuffs and escape through the window of the train.[17] In due course, the governor of Missouri would be blamed for the escape of Gus and other problems. Ostensibly his failure to provide sufficient guards for the journey of the mule thieves from the Cole County jail to Fulton was the reason Gus escaped. Meanwhile, the father, Peter, remained a prisoner on the train, and he was escorted from the railroad depot to the courthouse under heavy guard. As the county history clarifies, on the advice of his appointed attorney and to spare his client the lethal wrath of the mob, on August 15, 1873, Peter Kessler pled guilty to the charge of stealing two mules, and the judge sentenced him to six years in the Missouri State Penitentiary.

The judge appealed to the large crowd in the courtroom to maintain law and order. The sheriff, Colonel George Law, was determined to convey Kessler safely to the prison in Jefferson City by train. Once outside the courthouse, Kessler was placed in a carriage that was to carry him and his guards to the train station. The mob demanded that the sheriff relinquish his prisoner. He refused, and one or more members of the lynching party fired a number of shots into the carriage. The wounded occupants of the hack included Sheriff Law; John G. Provines, prosecuting attorney and editor of the *Fulton Press*; John Watson, a young merchant; and a young man named W.W. Dundon. In the midst of this hullabaloo, the mob seized Kessler from his wounded guards, dragged him from his seat in the carriage, and hanged the confessed mule thief on the outskirts of Fulton on August 15, 1873. One newspaper reports of this calamity, "A gang of armed men, without disguise of any kind whatever, shot the sheriff as he was conveying a prisoner, and after wounding that official and two or three others, forcibly took the prisoner.... What is very singular is that none of the perpetrators ... were recognized, although it occurred in broad daylight."[18]

At this time, the governor of Missouri was Silas Woodson. It will be remembered that, as discussed in Chapter 1, a man named Jeff Kessler, charged with murder in Gentry County, hired a 39-year-old attorney then practicing law in St. Joseph. His attorney secured a continuance for his client, and the delay so displeased the mob that it seized Jeff Kessler and hanged him from a tree near the courthouse in Albany on June 25, 1858. Now, 15 years later, Jeff Kessler's then-helpless attorney, Silas Woodson, was governor of Missouri, and he did all within his power to bring the lynchers of Peter Kessler to justice. Though there may have been some relationship between the Kessler lynched in 1858 and the Kessler lynched in 1873, as far as I know, the identity in the surnames is coincidental.

On August 16, Governor Woodson issued a proclamation to the people of Callaway County. In it he requested that anyone with knowledge regarding the lynching of Peter Kessler render all aid possible to the officials he was appointing to investigate the matter, Judge Burkhardt, whose circuit included Callaway County, and Attorney General of Missouri Ewing. The governor stated in his proclamation "that anyone who can and declines to give information respecting the matter shall be treated as having participated in the crime."[19] On August 17, Woodson wrote strong and angry letters to Burkhardt and Ewing. To the judge he wrote, "It will not do to leave this matter exclusively to the local authorities in Callaway," and the governor ordered the judge to "issue writs for the arrest of every man engaged in the affair, hear the cases, and all who are found guilty should be committed for trial by you." On this same date, Woodson wrote the attorney general, "The perpetrators of this great crime have not been arrested, nor are the local officers of the county of Callaway, so far as we are advised, making any effort to have them arrested, tried, and punished." The governor continued his letter to Ewing, "The strong arm of the state government must be interposed, and offenders against the law punished. I desire you to proceed to the county of Callaway and investigate the facts ... [and] bring the guilty violators of the law to trial and punishment."[20]

By August 20, the condition of the sheriff was critical. He had been shot in both the left hip and his spine. Paralyzed, he lay dying at his home. On August 23, death came to George W. Law, sheriff of Callaway County and a Civil War veteran who served on the Confederate side. The young man, W.W. Dundon, also a member of the party guarding Kessler, died from his wounds sometime after the sheriff expired. In a news story relating the grave condition of the two men, the paper writes of the mob that it "was led evidently, by a party of irresponsible young men who ... will be far beyond the possibility of immediate arrest."[21] On the same day the sheriff died, 400 citizens of Callaway County met at the courthouse to express their great regret regarding the death of their esteemed sheriff, their abhorrence of mob law, and their determination, as the local paper phrased it, "to see that the honor of the county is vindicated and the disgrace of the mob wiped out."[22]

On September 9, the new sheriff of Callaway County arrested E.C. Wood. The other members of the mob, the Fulton newspaper reports, left town by August 20, and "therefore neither the citizens nor officials of the county are responsible for their non-arrest."[23] A few days later the Sedalia paper writes that "several persons say that [Wood] was in the crowd who followed the mob on foot, and that his assertions that he was one of the lynchers were prompted by the amount of whiskey he had imbibed. Some even say that he is not altogether in his right mind.... He is now in jail to await his trial."[24] The *Fulton Telegraph* details the brief October 1873 trial of E.C. Wood. The lead prosecutor was Mr. Ewing, the attorney general of Missouri; he was assisted by two other attorneys. The defendant was represented by three lawyers. One witness after another testified to Wood's drunken condition the day Kessler was lynched, and each placed Wood at least one-fourth of a mile from the scene of Peter Kessler's murder at the time the mule thief was strung up. Following this testimony, Attorney General Ewing made a few remarks on the insufficiency of the evidence and dismissed the case, and the judge discharged the jury.[25] As for the actual perpetrators, the citizens of Fulton believed, as the newspaper indicates, that "those who were engaged in the lynching have taken warning and have all left the county.... It would be more than useless to send troops here, where there remains no one to arrest, amendable to the law."[26] The local paper printed a letter from a Callaway County citizen who believed, or at least professed to believe, that Kessler's lynchers were, by mid–September, "now in Nova Scotia, or some other foreign land."[27] By late September, Governor Woodson offered a reward of $1,000 each for the arrest of three young men, Porter Gregory, Mote Moore, and Robert Kemp. They had been indicted for the murder of Peter Kessler, George W. Law, and W.W. Dundon. The reward of $1,000 per culprit, if ever paid, could not have come from state funds. By statute, the amount the governor was able to pay from state funds was limited to $300 per fugitive.[28] Most likely friends or business associates of the governor helped finance the incentive for the lynchers' arrest. The governor also offered a reward of $300 for the arrest of anyone who could be identified as having participated in the mob that claimed three lives. Needless to say, a fat lot of good it did. The Sedalia news story concludes that the three indicted men "have long since fled the state."[29] The criticism of the governor continued. The *Fulton Telegraph* reprints unfavorable remarks about him from several other newspapers. The *Palmyra Spectator* said, "Our governor is entirely too ready with his militia doings. We see no necessity for any such proceedings." The *Mexico Leader* thought it evident that "Callawegians despise [Governor Woodson's] long winded efforts at threatening them into submission." The *Montgomery City Standard* suggested the governor forget about bringing the lynchers to justice; rather he should "put on petticoats and take charge of some orphan asylum or go forth as a lecturer on women's rights."[30]

Not surprisingly, this mob murder attracted the attention of out-of-state press. *The New York Times* reprints an opinion editorial piece originally run in the *St. Louis Democrat*. The article laments the inability of local law enforcement "to prevent the terrible crimes committed in our vast agricultural districts.... They [vigilantes] hang horse thieves sentenced to the penitentiary and kill officers of the law taking these thieves to the penitentiary, and at the same time they permit murderers to strut about in public places unmolested." The article goes on to suggest that the state of Missouri "organize a public State Police in every township and county. Such a police would make a mob organization, now so shamelessly usurping the functions of justice, useless and impossible."[31] Nearly 58 years later, on April 24, 1931, the bill creating the Missouri State Highway Patrol was signed into law. The relationship between Governor Caulfield's veto of an anti-lynching bill that year and his signing the statutes which created this new statewide policing agency is discussed in Chapter 12. The hope was that the new law enforcement agency would curtail, if not entirely eliminate, lynchings.

Meanwhile, in 1873, Governor Woodson continued his concern that the law punish the guilty parties in Callaway County. An out-of-state newspaper reports he had issued an order to convene a special term of the Circuit Court of Callaway County to investigate the lynching of Peter Kessler.[32] A number of witnesses were notified that they would be summoned to testify in forthcoming proceedings regarding this case. The court records are incomplete, but we can be confident that no one was subsequently convicted of the murder of Peter Kessler, Sheriff George W. Law, and W.W. Dundon. The Callaway County history published in 1884 devotes the better part of nine pages to this case. It names no members of the mob, and it is silent about any subsequent court proceedings. As with other lynchings, despite the murder of the two men, one an elected and highly respected sheriff who was guarding a prisoner, no one appears to have been convicted for his part in any aspect of the events surrounding the Fulton lynching of Peter Kessler in broad daylight by men not wearing masks. It is difficult to grasp that his underlying offense was the theft of two mules, not two horses, just two mules.

The third case of the 1870s had detailed coverage in the county history. It began on August 3, 1877, six miles north of Luray, Clark County, when one or more persons murdered five members of the Spenser family, the father and his four children: Alice, aged 20 years ; Jane, 18; Willis 10; and Charles, seven. The weapons were an ax and a pitchfork, and the motive robbery. The $1,200 that the father, as township treasurer, had in his possession was missing. Willis James, brother of long dead Mrs. Spenser, found the bodies the next day, but the missing $1,200 was never recovered. Soon reward money, $100 for each of the five victims, was offered for their killers' conviction. Initially, Willis James, the man who found the bodies, was arrested and indicted. The chief evidence against him consisted of spots of blood on his clothing and a bloody handkerchief; he explained both as the result of his nose bleeding. The prosecutor's case against James fell apart when the Iowa physicians charged with examining his clothing and handkerchief notified the prosecutor early in the trial by letter from Keokuk, Iowa, dated April 17, 1878: "Dear Sir– Upon ... a critical re-examination of the specimens which we have subjected to higher powers, we do not find sufficient evidence to justify us in putting in question the life of any human being and seeing that our visit to Kahoka [county seat of Clark County] would be of no service to either side, we have concluded to remain at home." Upon receipt of this letter, the prosecutor dismissed the case. Despite the objections of an assistant prosecutor who believed the defendant guilty, the jury agreed. It issued this statement, dated April 19, 1878: "The undersigned jurors in the case of State v. Willis James, do in this cause find no evidence on which we would have based a conviction. We fully justify the conduct of the prosecuting attorney in dismissing the case. Signed T. M. Glenn, Foreman. All the other jurors concur."[33]

The county history continues its narrative of this case. In the fall of 1878, an ex-convict recently released from the Joliet, Illinois, penitentiary arrived in Clark County, changed his name from Daniel C. Slater to Frank Lane, and proposed to solve the Spenser murders and collect the reward money. Lane met a Laura Sprouse who in February 1877 became the housekeeper for William J. Young, a widower with four children. While Young went east to visit relatives in Ohio, Laura Sprouse secretly married Walter Brown, an associate of the ex-convict Frank Lane, alias Daniel Slater. In January 1879, she swore under oath that Young had murdered the five members of the Spenser family. Upon his return from Ohio, he was arrested. His trial was lengthy; the defense consisted mainly of discrediting Laura Sprouse. She claimed that she saw Young attempting to burn bloody overalls; she stated under oath that she had rescued this vital piece of evidence and insisted, repeatedly insisted, that Young had confessed the Spenser murders to her before he left for Ohio. The overalls were never produced, and the defense put on many witnesses to impeach Laura Sprouse. Finally, on October 25, 1879, the jury found Young not guilty. He immediately celebrated his acquittal by marrying Miss Spray of Ohio. While still in Kahoka, he was warned that a mob awaited him in Luray, but this place was his home. He disregarded the warnings, and he and his bride returned to Luray by train and to their home by carriage. By 11 A.M. on the last day of his life, a mob surrounded his house and demanded his surrender. Young agreed to pay court costs and leave the county, but he refused to confess that he had murdered the Spenser family. He appeared at a window and was shot, and vigilantes entered his home and found him on the floor, surrounded by his weeping wife and children. Lane, the ex-convict, whom the county history terms the "captain of the mob,"[34] managed with his helpers to place Young on a wagon, put a rope around his neck, tie the other end of it to a cross-beam, and at 4 P.M. on October 29, 1879, the wagon was removed, and Young was hanged. His new wife asked the mob to cut down his body; its members refused and rode off on their horses.

Under the headline, "The Supposed Murderer of the Spenser Family Hung by a Mob," a Howard County news story specifies that "Lane selected nine men to hang Young." It paints a far darker portrait of the 43-year-old lynching victim than the county history. The newspaper story states of him that up to age 35 he committed many petty crimes, and in 1860 he was complicit in the murder of Whitefield, a killing the county history also mentions. The newspaper account of this lynching concludes: "It is said the mob was composed of good citizens of Clark County. There were a few from Iowa. The sentiment of the people is divided. Some approve... others are not sorry ... but do not endorse this summary method of disposing of [Young], while his friends regard it as a dastardly outrage."[35] A St. Louis newspaper chides the law enforcement officers of Clark County because they were afraid to make any arrests in the lynching of Young. It writes, "Frank Lane, the amateur detective who has made his home in Luray since being released from the Illinois Penitentiary, and who served as the captain of the lynchers seems to have a greater power than all the sheriff's posse. It is time for Gov. Phelps to interfere."[36] Presumably, whatever Governor Phelps might or might not have done about the murder of Young in Clark County would not have yielded any better results than Governor Woodson's strenuous efforts to bring the lynchers of Peter Kessler to justice in Callaway County a few years earlier.

The sheriff's timidity in arresting Frank Lane did not end the matter. The county history describes subsequent events. At the April 1880 term of the Clark County Circuit Court, Judge Anderson charged the grand jury to bring the guilty to justice in the lynching death of William J. Young. Despite the well-known fact that an ex-convict, eager to collect the reward money for solving the Spenser murders and disappointed that he had not, was the leader of the mob that murdered Young, the grand jury of Clark County did not indict Lane, alias Slater, or anyone else. However, by 1879, the Missouri legislature had changed the law. Almost certainly, the General Assembly enacted the new law in order to facilitate the prosecution of lynchers. It allowed the grand jury of an adjacent county to find an indictment in a felony, when, as the law states, "The judge of such circuit is satisfied that an impartial grand jury cannot be had in the county where the offense was committed."[37] Thanks to the new law, Judge Anderson, whose circuit also included Scotland County, transferred Lane's case there, and a month later, the grand jury of Scotland County indicted Lane and one other mob member, a Mr. Smith. The county history says that Lane escaped to Dakota Territory, but he was arrested in Yankton, and law enforcement officers returned him to the Scotland County jail in Memphis. Because this facility was inadequate, he was transferred to a sturdier jail in Mexico, seat of Audrain, a county with no known lynchings in its history. He remained a prisoner in Audrain County, under indictment in Scotland County, for a murder committed in Clark County. Lane was no saphead; he managed to hire an attorney who filed a habeas corpus petition with the Missouri Supreme Court. It heard his case and set him free. Writing for a unanimous court, Judge Norton stated the law: under the Missouri Constitution of 1875, "No grand jury can indict any offense whatsoever which doth not arise within the limits of the precincts for which they are returned.... All crimes are local ... the prosecution for them can be carried on only in the county of their commission."[38] Once the jail door was unlocked for Lane, alias Slater, he disappeared, and there ended all efforts to punish any of the murderers of Young.

The Missouri Supreme Court judge, Elijah Norton, whose decision set Lane free, made no mention of any of the particulars of the murder Lane was indicted for committing; one would never know reading this appellate decision that it had any connection to a mob murder. As discussed in Chapter 1, as a young circuit court judge in Platte County, Norton prevented the lynching of the abolitionists John Doy and his son, Charles, in Platte City in 1859. He told the mob that it could only reach these men over his dead body. Norton precisely followed the law in 1859 when he prevented the lynching of two men, and again in 1880 he once more precisely followed the law when ordering the release of "the captain of the lynch mob," as the Clark County history refers to Lane.

The three cases described in this chapter splendidly illustrate the inability of county, state, and federal authorities to secure meaningful convictions of any member of a mob who lynched a man in the 1870s in Missouri. James Botsford, the U.S. Attorney for the Western District of Missouri, was the only successful prosecutor, and his victory consisted of two $100 fines. This is a very small price to pay for committing three murders. The killing of Sheriff Law and W.W. Dundon in the process of capturing a mule thief in order to hang him remained unpunished. Last, it was not possible to do more to Frank Lane, captain of the lynch mob who murdered Bill Young, than get the ex-convict out of town. Through fear, or approval, or a combination of these sentiments, the communities did not convict lynchers, no matter how egregious the circumstances of their killings.

The next two chapters describe Missouri's lynchings of the 1880s, subsequently remembered as the decade of the greatest number of such events.

CHAPTER 6

"The brute seized her": Black Victims, 1880–1889

The matter has been referred to earlier, but it is important to emphasize that in 1881, the *Chicago Tribune* begins its annual compilations of, among other American catastrophes, such as notable shipwrecks, suicides, fires, and bankruptcies, the executed. In 1882, it adds the lynched. These separate lists of the legally and illegally executed (at times headlined respectively "The Work of Jack Ketch" and "Judge Lynch") continue for the next 38 years, or through 1918. Both begin with the newspaper's nationwide summary of the numbers by region, then state or territory, next race (or in a few instances by ethnicity), with the legally executed in one column and the lynched in another. In both groupings the entries appear chronologically; each includes the month, day, name of the deceased, race, offense, locale (either at or near a town or city) and the state and/or territory. To be sure, there are many accuracies in these giant listings, but there are also errors of every description. Virtually all compilations of American lynchings from the 1880s through 1918, including the NAACP's *Thirty Years of Lynching in the United States, 1889–1918* (April 1919), owe a huge and often unacknowledged debt to the *Chicago Tribune's* pioneering publishing of the specifics of when, who, why, and where mobs put persons to death throughout the United States. This chapter and all subsequent use the Chicago newspaper's lists as starters for research; every lynching I place in Missouri has been verified in an in-state source. After all, a daily newspaper must be put together every day, and mistakes are very easy to make under these circumstances. Likewise, the NAACP is an advocacy group for the social and political equality of persons of color, and one should not expect the dispassionate accuracy of a scholarly work in its assemblage of the lynched nationwide between 1889 and 1918.

With all this information at hand, one would anticipate that the numbers of those murdered by mobs in the 1880s would show an increase over previous time periods. This is not the case in Missouri. Despite the great likelihood that I did not discover some lynchings prior to this decade either because I missed them or the issues of newspapers which carried their stories no longer exist, the fact remains that there are fewer known mob murders of both blacks and whites here in the 1880s than in the 1870s.

Whereas between 1870 and 1879, mobs murdered at least 16 African Americans, between 1880 and 1889, they killed at least 13. This decline is largely explained by population figures. The percentage of Negroes in Missouri's population was at its highest in 1820, 18.3 percent, and in all federal censuses between 1820 and 1910, the percentage of Missourians who were black grew smaller and smaller. The decrease was from 6.7 percent in 1880 to 5.6 percent in 1890.[1] In actual numbers, there were 2,022,826 whites and 145,300 blacks counted in the 1880 federal census, and in that of 1890, there were 2,528,458 whites and 150,184 blacks.[2] This represents an increase of over 500 blacks, but the white population here increased between 1880 and 1890 by more than 500,000 persons. As emphasized earlier, African Americans in Missouri lived primarily in St. Louis, and, as Kansas City grew, there. The city of St. Louis was never the scene of a post–Civil War lynching, and Kansas City had only one known mob murder.

Unlike the 1870s, with at least one known lynching of an African American in southwestern Missouri, there are no known mob murders of blacks in any southwestern counties. Likewise, there are no known legal executions of blacks in this area of the state during the 1880s. One must conclude that African Americans were an especially small percentage of the total population in these 27 counties, and the few who lived there were both extremely law-abiding and respectful of whites. It is fact that both the known lynching and legal execution slates for African Americans are blank in 1880s southwest Missouri.

When we proceed to the northwest area, made up of 28 counties, there is one known legal execution of a black, in Lafayette County, and three known lynchings of African Americans in the 1880s. Each mob murder of a black took place in a different county. In chronological order, the first occurred in Clinton County on September 25, 1880. The documentation for it is especially solid, including as it does an account in the county history, a lengthy recounting in a Platte County newspaper, and front page coverage in two Kansas City newspapers. The crime was a sexual offense, and the victim was, expectedly, white. Though the county history does not name her, the newspapers do. The *Kansas City Times* describes her as "Mrs. Benjamin Winn, a most excellent lady and wife of one of our best citizens."

The most complete and almost certainly the most accurate account of the attack itself is the Platte City news story. According to it, on September 24, 1880, a Friday, the victim was returning home on horseback, after attending to errands a few miles distant in the town of Grayson. When she dismounted to open a gate near her home, she was "struck by a handful of mud, which was thrown in her eyes, and was so blinded she could see nothing." After her assailant temporarily deprived her of her vision, he struck her a violent blow, pulled her riding habit up over her head, raped her, and fled the scene. The Platte City paper omits any mention of how large numbers of men learned of the crime. The *Kansas City Journal* relates that after the attack on her, "Mrs. Winn mounted her horse, rode to town [Grayson] and made the fact of the outrage known." Such a spirited and purposeful journey immediately after the attack is surely omitted in the Platte City coverage because of its total inconsistency with this paper's concluding comment, "Mrs. Winn is now at her home, in a very critical condition, and ... it is doubtful if she will recover." This is a typical description of the white victim of a sex crime in a small town Missouri newspaper in the nineteenth century, when the perpetrator or alleged perpetrator, almost invariably a black male, was lynched.

The Platte City paper writes only that after the assault, "She with true courage gave the alarm ... and the whole community was aroused, nearly two hundred men being armed and in the saddle within a few hours." This paper explains that among those who joined the mob was the Winn family's hired hand, the Negro, Henry Bird. He too was in pursuit of the "awful man who would hurt his missus." By the next day, September 25, one member of this self-appointed posse noticed a "mud spot" on the back of Bird's neck, and another found a sock near the crime scene. The paper quotes Bird as asserting that the mate of the sock would locate the culprit. In due course, the leaders of the mob forced him to remove his clothing, telling him if he did not, his penalty would be death. When he stripped, as the Platte City paper describes the matter, "Large patches of mud were discovered between his shoulders and along his spine.... His boots were pulled from his feet, and one foot had no sock, while the other was covered with the mate to the one which had been found where the outrage was committed."

Initially Bird denied his guilt, but he finally admitted that he had planned his crime in advance, because of his passion for the victim. The Platte City newspaper places the number of men at 40 who tied up Bird, put him on a horse with a rope around his neck, tied the other end of it to an elm tree, drove the horse out from under him, and thereby left him to strangle to death. The county history estimates the number of hunters for the rapist at 500, with no numbers mentioned in the actual lynching. The *Kansas City Journal* lists 70 in the pursuing party, and the *Kansas City Times* includes no numbers involved in Bird's murder. We can be certain that all these sources wished to protect all participants, whatever their actual numbers may have been; none are named in any account of the lynching of Henry Bird.

All located stories about this case approve its conclusion. The *Kansas City Journal*'s story apparently went to press before the end was known. It writes, "If the perpetrator should be captured, he will summarily [be] dealt with without any process of law."[3] The *Kansas City Times* closes its account, "The community was greatly shocked over the outrage perpetrated on the lady and approve of the action of the men who so summarily dealt with the scoundrel."[4] The county history's story ends with mention that at the inquest concerning Henry Bird's death, the coroner's jury "returned a verdict of death by strangulation at the hands of parties unknown. The verdict ought to have been by an outraged and terribly enraged community."[5] The Platte City paper's lengthy coverage concludes of Bird's lynching, "He was launched into that eternity where he should meet any other demon who may in future perpetrate the same kind of crime."[6] Racism permeates every aspect of the reporting of the killing of Henry Bird. The county history's account begins, "One of the most devilish and blackest of crimes was committed by a mulatto negro man on a handsome and very accomplished young married woman of wealth and high social." There is of course no need to mention that the victim was Caucasian; no reader would have thought otherwise. The *Kansas City Times* describes the assailant as "the black fiend," and the Platte City paper terms the perpetrator, "the brutal negro demon."

The second lynching of a black in northwest Missouri in the 1880s took place in Platte County, near Weston. W.M. Paxton dates the incident as June 14, 1881. He writes that a mob hanged Charles Reese, "a mulatto boy, for the attempted rape of Miss Stillwell."[7] A Kansas City newspaper dates the rape and subsequent lynching as June 12, 1881, after 16-year-old Nancy Stillwell was attacked near her father's residence by a 21-year-old negro, Charles Diddell. The news story relates that after he "accomplished his hellish design, ... the brute seized her and with a pocket knife cut her throat, severing the wind pipe." Almost certainly Miss Stillwell's windpipe was never severed; doing so would have risked cutting either or both of her carotid arteries and almost inevitably caused her death. As a result, Paxton, whose book was initially published in 1897, or more than 15 years after the incident, would identify her as both a rape and murder victim.

As the news story continues, several ladies walking through a pasture raised the alarm, and "Miss Stillwell was taken to her home and medical aid summoned. Her injuries will certainly prove fatal." Diddell was located at a farmhouse two and a half miles distant and taken to the city jail in Weston. By 8 P.M. that same date, a mob overpowered the jail guard, tied its prisoner's hands, herded him to a railroad bridge, placed a rope around his neck, and he "was shoved from the bridge into eternity by the brother of the lady he had so foully injured." The story again mentions that "at this writing Miss Stillwell is still alive, but there is little hope of her recovery." It concludes, "While our community does not endorse mob law, it deems this action fit punishment for the crime committed."[8] I adopt the newspaper date, June 12, a Sunday, not Paxton's two-line account of June 14, a Tuesday, as the more likely to be accurate. The detailed newspaper account reflects immense community approval of the outcome; it identifies the victim's brother as a killer. Clearly, there was no thought that any one who helped to murder Charles Reese and/or Charles Diddell would be prosecuted.

The third and final lynching of an African American in the northwest section took place in Kansas City on April 3, 1882, and it remains the only known successful lynching in the second largest city in the state. It was the second and last known in Jackson County; the first took place in a rural area in 1870, and the lynched man was a white suspected horse thief. The date of April 3, 1882, was a memorable one in the history of this state and probably the nation. That morning, for a reward of $10,000, Robert Ford shot and killed America's most famous outlaw, Jesse James, as his victim dusted a picture in his parlor in St. Joseph, 54 miles north of Kansas City. The next day, one Kansas City newspaper writes that "since the assassination of President Garfield there has never been any one thing which created such a tumult of excitement as the killing of ... Jesse James. All yesterday afternoon the streets [of Kansas City] were lined with groups of men discussing ... the outlaw's death."[9] Even the Supreme Court of Missouri mentions, in a decision written one and one-half years later about a police officer killed in Kansas City on April 3, 1882, that the "deceased [Officer Patrick Jones] stood on the sidewalk" with a citizen, and "they there engaged in conversation for a few moments about the killing of Jesse James, which had occurred that day."[10]

The evening of April 3, 1882, Officer Jones attempted to arrest a man, whom one newspaper describes as a "well known colored desperado," George Grant, an ex-convict with a lengthy criminal record; he had previously been arrested at least 12 times. In 1915, or more than 30 years later, a newspaper states without any qualification that on April 3, 1882, as Officer Jones attempted to arrest George Grant, Grant "shot and killed the policeman. After the shooting the negro ran and was closely pursued by a crowd. He ran into a restaurant the back way and out the front. The mob followed at his heels. The negro porter in the restaurant got scared and ran also — ahead of the mob." The news story goes on to relate that "the negro porter was caught and without inquiry lynched.... The murderer escaped for the time."[11]

Given the all-day lathering up caused by the murder of Jesse James that morning and the police officer, only the second in Kansas City's history to die in the line of duty, that evening, the mob was especially muddle-headed. Newspaper coverage contemporary with the event describes Officer Jones as being "shot and instantly killed by an unknown colored man, whom he was pursuing." A Negro, Levi Harrington, was arrested, as this paper goes on to relate, "on suspicion of being the man who did the shooting.... A howling mob" overpowered the police, and "the prisoner was first shot and then taken to the Bluff Street Bridge, where a rope was procured, and he was hung." No evidence identified him as a cop killer, but as the newspaper writes, "He was a colored man, and that was enough for the maddened crowd, thirsting for blood."[12]

Obviously, doubt existed from the start that Levi Harrington was in any way involved in the murder of Officer Jones. John Harrington proclaimed his brother's innocence, and within a few days of this mob murder, the mayor and various other city officials investigated the conduct of the law enforcement officers guarding the murdered African American. They took testimony from a number of police officers. One testified that "there were 15 or 20 colored men in front of the mob. I thought at first they were trying to rescue Harrington, but found they were as hard after him as any of them." The investigators concluded that "the officers would have been killed had they resisted any harder" and "none of the mob were recognized by the officers."[13]

Later, George Grant was arrested on a charge of complicity with Harrington. In due course, he was tried at least three times for the first-degree murder of Officer Jones on April 3, 1882. The prosecutor's theory of the case was that Grant had stolen two pails of butter from a business and he shot the policeman in order to avoid arrest for stealing. The Missouri Supreme Court issued two decisions. Both reversed Grant's conviction. At another of his trials, the jury could not agree that he was guilty. The main difficulty was the prosecutor's inability to prove that the defendant knew the victim was a police officer *and* acting within the scope his duty.[14] The second appellate decision states that Grant's case would be retried. If so, the prosecutor was attempting for the fourth time to secure and retain a conviction for first-degree murder. This much we know. The state of Missouri never hanged George Grant, nor did any governor commute his death sentence to life imprisonment. Not until 1907 could a jury find the defendant guilty of first-degree murder and decide on a life imprisonment sentence. From 1835 until 1907, there was only one punishment for a conviction of first-degree murder in Missouri—death. We can be certain that a mob put to death an innocent man, Levi Harrington, in Kansas City's only known lynching. All other attempts to lynch anyone within the city limits of Kansas City failed.

One additional happening in the 1880s from northwest Missouri merits mention. Approximately a week prior to July 30, 1880, Thomas Word, a white man, twice shot George Quisenberry, a black man, on Main Street, in Richmond, Ray County, in broad daylight. After clinging to life a week in great pain, Quisenberry died. The provocation for this killing was Quisenberry's attempt, as the newspaper phrases it, "to raise a row with Charlie, a son of Mr. Word." According to Charlie, "the negro had been dogging his footsteps, threatening him, and on several nights had rocked him [thrown rocks at him] on his way home. Repeated warnings had no effect at all." Word's killing Quisenberry does not qualify as a lynching because the event was a one-on-one encounter. However, the community approval of a white man shooting a black is suggestive of the spirit of lynching. The news story ends, "Public spirit vindicates Mr. Word of crime, and [it] seems to consider his act justifiable, as the negro bore a bad reputation hereabouts as a bully, braggadocio of the worst type. Our city will not don the sable hue of mourning at his untimely demise."[15] Change Work, the perpetrator, to a black man and Quisenberry, the victim, to a white, and the story would have a very different ending. No circumstances would ever justify a black man shooting and killing a white in Missouri, a former slave state, in broad daylight. For example, in Chariton County, two counties east of Ray, on December 25, 1879, Noah Forest, a young white man, and other whites terrorized a former slave, John Cropp, as the black man bought Christmas gifts for his family. Later that same day, with a double-barreled shotgun, Cropp killed Forest. To no avail, the black pled self-defense to the killing. He was tried, found guilty without appeal, and he was hanged on June 11, 1880, in the county seat of Chariton County, Keytesville.[16] This was approximately 50 miles east of Richmond, the place where Word, a white man, shot and killed Quisenberry, a black, with impunity shortly after the execution of Cropp.

In the 1880s, northeast Missouri, made up of 25 counties, saw the largest number of lynched blacks, eight, and four legal executions of African Americans, including Cropp's in Chariton County. These mob murders of blacks took place in six counties: Boone, Callaway, Howard, Macon, Pike, and Randolph. Excluding Macon and Randolph, all these areas bordered one of the state's two great rivers, either the Missouri or the Mississippi. These waterways provided an easy and early way of transporting, among other personal property of this state's early settlers, their slaves. Descendants of many of these bondpersons remained in this section of Missouri.

Three black victims of mob murders, including the first two of the decade, represent unusual circumstances, those rarely mentioned in any histories. The membership of the mob was overwhelmingly African American, or so the county history states. In Randolph County, in late March 1880, two young black men, 17-year-old Henry Mitchell and 20-year-old Dick Yancy, also known as Abe Lincoln, went to the home of George Mathews, an older black man. Mathews was married to Mitchell's mother. The newspaper account suggests that Mathews beat his wife. To avenge his treatment of her, Mitchell induced a friend, Dick Yancy, to help him kill his stepfather. The young men went to Mathews's home, and both shot and beat the older man to death. Afterwards, they disposed of his body by dumping it in a nearby creek. Eventually Mathews was missed; a neighbor summoned the authorities, and they found his badly beaten body with a bullet hole in it. Shortly afterward, Mitchell, Yancy, and several others, including Alfred Cason, were arrested and lodged in the city jail in Moberly. According to two Kansas City newspapers, Mitchell and Yancy confessed to the murder of Mathews. The evening of April 21/22, 1880, a party of between 40 and 50 unmasked men rode their horses into Moberly, demanded and received the jail keys, and took Mitchell, Yancy, and Cason out of town. The mob dangled Cason from a rope, but it eventually cut him down and took him back to jail. From a railway bridge, the mob hanged Mitchell and Yancy. Afterwards, Cason swore at the inquest that he recognized none of the many unmasked men who jerked him about on a rope. The coroner's jury concluded that Mitchell and Yancy came to their deaths at the hands of unknown parties.

Though the newspapers examined (two from Kansas City and one from New York

City) do not mention the race of the mob members, it does not seem credible, given the immense racism of the time and place, that white men would be sufficiently aroused by the murder of a black to form a mob and lynch the alleged perpetrators. It makes more sense, not less, to credit the accuracy of the county history. Its story about this lynching is taken from a now non-extant issue of a newspaper, the *Moberly Headlight*. This local paper wrote that "speedy justice [was] meted out to the bloody perpetrators by an infuriated mob, composed almost wholly, if not entirely, of colored men."[17]

The third black lynched by other African Americans here during the 1880s was Harrison Mickey, a resident of Moberly (Randolph County), who attended a picnic approximately three miles east of Glasgow (Howard County) on August 2, 1884. According to the newspaper account, "Two or three thousand negroes were present, including visitors from other places." About 2 P.M., two men from Moberly began quarreling; when several others acting as police officers attempted to end the dispute, the arguing men drew weapons. One accidentally shot the acting officer, Tom Sophey, in the abdomen, and he died within 20 minutes. The newspaper describes the deceased as "immensely popular among his color, and the whites all liked him for his quiet manners, and his character as an industrious laboring man was second to none." Soon a mob formed around the shooter, Harrison Mickey, but the law abiding picnic attendees managed to convey him to the city jail in Glasgow. About 3 A.M. on August 3, 75 to 100 black men surrounded the jail. When the mob, armed with muskets and shotguns, demanded the keys from the officer of the jail, he said there was only a key to the outer door. At that point the mob began using a heavy piece of oak as a battering ram. Soon the lynchers had Harrison Mickey in their custody. They took him to a pasture south of town, conveyed him to a tree, and using a rope which they had obtained in advance, they hanged him from the tree by the neck until he was dead. The news account concludes, "The body hung until morning when it was taken down and placed in the hands of an undertaker. The inquest will be held tomorrow."[18] Presumably the coroner's jury found that Mickey came to his death at the hands of unknown men.

The remainder of the blacks lynched in northeast Missouri in the 1880s died at the hands of white mobs. One of these is reminiscent of the death of Port Cason in Howard County in 1879. He had frightened a Mrs. Capito, and a mob shot him to death when he resisted its members whipping him. On April 15, 1884, a white mob near Hatton, Callaway County, tied Julius Patterson, an African American, to a tree and whipped him, as a Callaway County newspaper reports, because he was "charged with using scandalous and slanderous language about the wives and daughters of the citizens of Liberty Township." The Linn County newspaper explains that Julius Patterson's "tormentors were arrested but acquitted." On May 3, a Saturday, about 9 P.M., a mob went in search of Julius, presumably intending to kill him because he had caused their arrest for whipping him. Its members searched the house of their intended victim's father, and when they could not find Julius, they dragged his brother or half-brother, 19-year-old Ham Patterson, out of his bed in the Patterson home, took him 15 or 20 yards from the residence, and shot him. He died several hours later. According to the Callaway County newspaper, the mob that killed Ham Patterson contained approximately 25 members. When the coroner's jury, all named in the local paper, met on Sunday, May 4, it determined, as this paper records, "that [the] deceased came to his death from gunshot wounds in the hands of parties unknown to the jury."[19] The Callaway County newspaper does not name the men arrested for whipping Julius Patterson; the Linn County paper does. It explains that the six men charged "with binding and whipping Julius Patterson" and found not guilty, only struck him "twelve or fifteen times."[20] This same paper terms the shooting death of Ham Patterson, a brother or a half-brother of Julius, "an ugly murder."[21]

Callaway County has an infamous history. It executed a 19-year-old slave who killed her owner to prevent his continuing to rape her; it sentenced a 10- to 12-year-old slave boy to death for murder; he later escaped. It was the scene of the lynching of a slave woman discussed in Chapter 2, and when, as discussed in chapter 4, members of a mob eager to lynch a mule thief accidentally killed the sheriff and at least one other person, no one was successfully prosecuted. In most Missouri counties, the perceived bad behavior that resulted in a lynching was far more serious than frightening a white woman or speaking disrespectful and slanderous words about white wives and daughters. This county's lynchings of blacks continued throughout the nineteenth century, including one in 1894 and another in 1895.

All other African Americans either lynched or reported as lynched in the northeast section of the state in the 1880s allegedly committed sex crimes against girls and women. They are discussed in chronological order. The first took place in Pike County on July 1, 1883. The lynched man was William McDowell, a 24-year-old black ex-convict. On June 25, 1883, he allegedly raped Katie McGuire, the 20-year-old adopted daughter of Mrs. Charles Murray, near Louisiana, Missouri, as she drove a cow to pasture. Initially, the wrong black man, Joe Brown, was jailed and nearly lynched. However, that same day, a Monday, McDowell was arrested and lodged in the county jail in Bowling Green. In addition to the victim identifying him, scratches found on his hand collaborated her statement that she scratched his hand. Moreover, his clothing matched her description of that worn by her assailant. About 1:30 A.M. Sunday morning, July 1, a mob of between 75 and 100 men marched to the jail. The six who demanded the keys were masked. Seeing that resistance was useless, the marshal gave the disguised men the jail keys. Once McDowell was in their custody, the mob abandoned the first plan — to hang him from a locust tree in the northwest corner of the square. Instead, he was taken to the crime scene in a wagon, and with his feet and hands pinioned and one end of a rope around his neck and the other tied to a walnut tree, the wagon was driven out from under him. That same day hundreds visited the scene of McDowell's lynching, a mile northeast of Bowling Green, on the road to Louisiana. The coroner cut his body down and held an inquest. The six jurors he assembled, all of whom the Bowling Green newspaper names, found that "Wm. McDowell, colored, came to his death by being hung to a tree with a rope until strangled by a person or persons unknown to this jury."[22]

By July 12, the *Bowling Green Times* adds, "Several of our exchanges think that hanging was too good for the negro Bill McDowell: think he should have been burned alive."[23] An out-of-state eastern newspaper reports with a St. Louis date of July 2 that McDowell's body "was put in a plain box and taken to Louisiana [MO], where it was again strung up to a tree and a photograph of the corpse taken. The head was then cut off, and the body mutilated. The head and other portions of the body are now in possession of a physician in Louisiana."[24] Whatever photograph was taken is not known to be extant. As for severing the head, the physician who obtained it presumably did so in order to further his study of the pseudoscience of phrenology, a popular belief in the nineteenth century that character, including criminality, could be understood by studying the shape of the skull, its bumps and grooves. In St. Louis, when four free blacks were executed in 1841, their severed heads were displayed in a city drugstore, and its proprietor made plaster casts of their skulls for their phrenological study.[25] Whatever disposition might have been made of the remains of McDowell is unknown.

The next mention of a black lynched for a sex crime in northeast Missouri appears in a Kansas City newspaper. It documents the shooting death of an unknown African American who happened to be working in a cornfield near Guthrie, Callaway County, on October 13, 1884. One of the black workers in the field raped a 10-year-old white child, surnamed Bennett, as she passed by the cornfield with her younger sister. The unharmed, younger child carried the news of her sister's assault home; a posse of citizens quickly organized, and it placed the three black cornfield hands under guard in a house in Guthrie. The next morning, October 14, a mob rode by this house, fired through its windows, and shot and killed one of the Negroes who ran into the street. The alleged rapist was also shot, but he feigned death and survived. The news story ends, "The party then rode off.... The survivors were taken to jail today, but are expected to be lynched tonight."[26] Presumably, law enforcement officers in Fulton, seat of Callaway County, managed to protect these men, and Fulton was not the scene of additional lynchings at this time.

Other mob murders of black males for alleged sexual assaults on white females took place in northeast Missouri. One occurred in Macon County on August 3, 1889, when Ben Smith, a 22-year-old, raped 24-year-old Mrs. William Mathews by going by her home, a residence near the Santa Fe Railroad in Richland Township, and dragging her out of her home into a patch of weeds. Afterwards, she went to the road; there she met several white men and explained her violation to them. Smith was soon captured and taken before his alleged victim for identification. One Macon newspaper quotes her as remarking, "This is the brute, burn him." According to this news story, the captured black man was turned over to a constable and two of his deputies, near La Plata about 8 P.M. that same day. They intended to catch the midnight train with Ben Smith in tow to Macon, the county seat. About two miles west of La Plata, before anyone could board a train, 50 masked men overtook the law enforcement officers and their prisoner. The mob conducted Smith to a wagon bridge, threw a rope around his neck, and hanged him from a joist of the bridge. The next morning the coroner cut the body down, and his jury came to the usual conclusion in such cases, "death by hanging at the hands of parties unknown to the jury."[27]

The other 1889 lynching of a black for a sexual crime in northeast Missouri was, by chance, for the rape of a child rumored to have a black father. Her mother was white, and she was probably biracial. The attack took place on September 5 in Columbia, Boone County. On that date 17- or 18-year-old George Bush allegedly raped the 5- or 6-year-old daughter of Lizzie Jones, a servant who, when her daughter complained of Bush's treatment of her, informed the family for whom she worked. The family in turn notified the authorities. Three physicians were summoned, and they examined the child and confirmed that she had been sexually assaulted. On the afternoon of the attack, Bush was arrested and placed in the county jail in Columbia. Very early Saturday morning, September 7, about 1 A.M., a party of 20 or so masked men appeared at the jail, demanded and obtained the keys from the sheriff. Soon they had possession of Bush. Although someone removed the wadding after his death, the lynchers placed a gag in their prisoner's mouth. Instead of taking him to a convenient tree near the scene of his alleged crime, this mob marched its victim to the nearby Boone County Courthouse, and hanged him there, leaving his body dangling from the south window of this structure. There it swung just below the inscription carved in marble over the courthouse door, "Oh justice, when expelled from other habitations, make this thy dwelling place." The mob attached a two-foot-square sign to George Bush's body: "Don't Cut Down Till Seven A.M. This is what we intend to do with all who commit this Crime [.] White Caps." Presumably the White Caps were a vigilante organization, or the mob made up a name it liked for its dirty work. When the coroner held his inquest, his jury returned its customary verdict in such cases, death at the hands of parties unknown to the jury.[28]

Southeast Missouri, made up of 34 counties and the city of St. Louis, was the scene of nine known legal executions of African Americans, mainly in St. Louis City, and one known lynching. It took place in Iron County on July 29, 1882, when 30 to 40 masked men took Henry Caldwell from the jail in Ironton, the county seat, and both hanged him from a railroad bridge and fired at least 30 shots into him. His feet had touched the ground, and the mob, fearing its strangling of him might not end his life, also shot him. On July 27, about 9:30 A.M., neighbors heard the screams of Mrs. Peck, a white woman aged more than 60 years, who struggled to free herself from Caldwell as he raped her. He was soon captured and placed in jail, but his stay was brief. The mob got him early the next morning, and soon ended his life. After the coroner summoned a jury, he cut the body down, procured a coffin, and in it conveyed Caldwell's corpse to the sheriff's room. There it lay until 10 A.M., presumably on view for all early morning spectators. From the law enforcement officer's room, the remains of the lynched man were taken to the potter's field and buried.[29]

Two foiled lynchings took place in northeast Missouri in the 1880s. The *Chicago Tribune* carries the earlier one as a completed mob murder for 1885. It lists "October 3, Si King, colored, rape, New London, Mo."[30] A newspaper from a Missouri county immediately north of Ralls, whose seat is New London, relates a different story. Si King, a black man, was believed to be guilty of the rape of a Mrs. Harris on September 29, 1885, in an open pasture in Ralls County. Pursuers had been hunting him for close to a week when several boys gathering walnuts found his body approximately three-quarters of a mile from where he allegedly attacked Mrs. Harris. Si King was not lynched; he committed suicide, perhaps as early as the evening of his crime. His body, much decayed and swollen, was found hanging from a black oak tree; his coat was hanging on the limb of a tree, and he had removed his boots and placed his socks in them. Perhaps he knew the fate that awaited him if his hunters got their hands on him, and he preferred to take his own life rather than have it taken from him by a howling mob. When his body was found on October 3, 1885, the coroner ordered it buried. As the newspaper relates, "It was exhumed last night by unknown parties, thrown upon a log-heap and brought in [to New London] some of the bones, which are now in exhibitions."[31] There is little doubt that had the mob found Si King before he hanged himself, he would have died at the hands of parties unknown to the coroner's jury.

The second failed lynching of a black male for a sexual attack on a white female took place in Columbia in 1889. On August 19, Squire Divers allegedly attempted to rape the 16-year-old daughter of Amos Henshaw of Cedar Township. The next day, a constable and a volunteer brought Divers to Columbia and turned him over to the sheriff of Boone County for safekeeping. Divers was removed from the jail in Ashland none too soon; a mob of 40 to 50 gathered the night of August 20 with the intent to lynch Divers. The mob intended to snatch him during his preliminary hearing in Ashland, but because of the danger to his life, he was moved. On August 22, the mob reassembled with one purpose in mind, but the sheriff continued to protect his prisoner. When he learned that there would be yet another attempt on Divers's life made on August 26, he secretly removed him from the jail. The mob, now swollen to 100 men, rode into Columbia at 1 A.M.; some of its members searched the jail for Divers, but he was nowhere to be found. Both the county treasurer and the former sheriff made brief speeches to the assembled on the necessity of allowing the law to take its course. The mob dispersed. Because the sheriff protected Divers, he was not lynched.[32] As related earlier in this chapter, George Bush was put to death a few weeks after Divers escaped the mob's wrath. That mob's manner of ending Bush's life, hanging him from a window in the courthouse, may have been the crowd thumbing its nose at the law because of its earlier disappointment with Divers.

Perhaps another investigator will discover additional lynchings of blacks in 1880s Missouri. One must always allow for that possibility, but as the record presently stands, the number of African Americans whom mobs put to death in this state in the 1880s, 13, decreased from the number lynched in the 1870s here, 16. This decline seems to be a function of several factors. First, law enforcement officers managed to protect their prisoners more effectively in the 1880s than the 1870s. Between 1870 and 1879, five known blacks were legally executed in this state, and between 1880 and 1889, 14 African Americans were hanged pursuant to court order. Another important factor in the decrease in blacks lynched was the decline in the percentage of Missouri's population that was African American. Coupled with the smaller percentage of the Negro population was the residence of most blacks in the state's largest metropolitan areas, St. Louis and Kansas City. These big towns had very sturdy jails; mobs could not breach them and remove their prisoners. The eastern city was never the scene of a post–Civil War lynching, and the western had only one, on April 3, 1882, the day Jesse James was shot 54 miles to the north of Kansas City in St. Joseph.

The influence of slavery surely lingered in the northeast section of the state, where two-thirds of the 1880s lynchings of blacks and two near misses took place. It is obvious that sufficient numbers of former slaves and their descendants remained in this area of Missouri to make it the scene of eight of the state's 13 known lynchings of blacks in the 1880s. In most rural areas of Missouri, there would have been insufficient numbers of African Americans to form the black mobs who put to death two young black men in Randolph County in 1880 and another black man in Howard in 1884. During this time period, only the northeast was the scene of black-on-black mob murders and two known near-lynchings of blacks; it also had as many blacks murdered by white mobs as the other three sections of Missouri combined.

The next chapter discuses the larger number of white males whom mobs put to death in 1880s Missouri.

CHAPTER 7

Railroads End Lynchings of Horse Thieves: White Victims Decrease, 1880–1889

Missouri mobs put fewer white persons to death in the 1880s than in the 1870s. There are 35 known lynchings of whites in the 1870s and 21 in the 1880s. I believe the decline is attributable to three factors. First, the rage of the Civil War gradually abated as the late 1860s became the 1870s and eventually the 1880s. To be sure, the anger aroused by the conflict was probably still on the minds of the participants, but not center stage as it had been in the first ten years after the Surrender. By the 1880s, for the most part, newspaper accounts omit the Civil War record of anyone connected to a lynching: either of the strung up perpetrator, his alleged victim(s), or the mob members. Whatever ordinary persons did or did not do during the War Between the States seems to have mattered less and less as time passed. Another factor in the decrease in the number of lynchings here in the 1880s over the 1870s was the increased effectiveness of civil govenment. All the courts were open; law enforcement officers usually placed their prisoners in jails, not in poorly guarded private residences, and sheriffs and their deputies learned from their own mistakes and those of their predecessors how *not* to lose their arrestees to mobs. To be certain there were successful attempts to lynch people charged with or suspected of serious criminal behavior, but the authorities often managed to keep them safe in secure jails, where the law, not the lawless mob, eventually took its course.

Whereas in 1870–79 the state of Missouri is known to have executed 30 persons, in the next decade, 1880–1889, the legal machinery of death here hanged 48 persons, a 63 percent increase over the numbers of the 1870s. It was not that the General Assembly added new death penalty crimes; all the legal hangings were for one offense, first-degree murder. Not surprisingly the southeast section of the state was the scene of the greatest numbers of state-conducted executions. This part of Missouri contained the city of St. Louis, and this metropolis was not only the largest in the state with its population of 350,518 in 1880 and 451,770 in 1890, it was also rank-ordered fifth in population nationwide in 1880 and fourth in 1890.[1] Hence, it is not surprising that 13 of the legal hangings of the 1880s took place in the St. Louis city jail. As emphasized earlier, this facility lost its last ever prisoner to a mob in 1836. Considering counties with legal executions, the northwest part of the state, with 12, exceeds the southwest and southeast with nine counties each. The northeast had four. Again excluding the city of St. Louis with its large number of legal hangings mainly explained by its enormous population, no other city in the state took a significant lead in the sheriff putting the condemned to death. During the 1880s the rule of law throughout the state reduced the number of lynchings from the 1870s.

A third and perhaps less obvious cause helps to explain this decrease over the previous decade in mob murders here. During the 1880s, the last known lynchings for horse stealing in Missouri took place on July 3, 1881, in Dade County, a rural area in the southwest section of the state. On that date, according to the only source I located of this event, the county history, a band of disguised individuals went to the jail in "Greenfield, and took William Underwood, James Butler, Jr., and Frank Craft, who were confined there in on a charge of horse stealing, hanged them until they were dead, and left their bodies suspended from the limbs of trees on the west side of the courthouse." The county history goes on to relate that the next morning citizens found the remains, and it concludes, "These unfortunate men were supposed to belong to a regularly organized gang of horse thieves. Though this was an unlawful and summary way of inflicting punishment, it is said that it had the effect of breaking up the horse stealing business in Dade County."[2]

When we compare this single instance of the lynching of three men in Dade County on accusations of horse stealing, an event which took place early in the 1880s, with the plethora of mob murders for the theft of horses and mules here that took place earlier, the decrease is startling. Missouri mobs put to death at least 24 boys and men between 1867 and 1874 for the theft of equines, and after July 3, 1881, there are no known instances of a mob ending anyone's life for this offense anywhere in this state.

The *Chicago Tribune* lists no fewer than 58 instances of mobs lynching, primarily, suspected horse thieves and, occasionally, cattle rustlers between 1883 and 1889. At times the numbers a single mob put to death for livestock stealing in other places exceed any known similar figures in Missouri. For example, on December 13, 1883, near Yankton, Dakota Territory, five cattle rustlers were reported as strung up; on July 30, 1884, in Cottonwood, Montana Territory, seven horse thieves were lynched; and on October 30, 1884, 17 cattle thieves met their ends near Georgetown, Colorado.[3] At the time of these mass lynchings for the alleged theft of farm and ranch animals, only the last named area had a sufficient population to have achieved statehood. The Chicago newspaper lists a few instances of lynchings south of Missouri for the theft of livestock: one for horse stealing in Mississippi in 1884, another in Arkansas in 1885, and one for cattle stealing in Florida in 1887. However the overwhelming majority of the lynchings of suspected horse thieves took place in sparsely populated areas of the West. Colorado, Dakota Territory, Kansas, Montana Territory, Nebraska, Oregon, Texas, Utah Territory, and Washington Territory were all scenes of one or more incidents of a mob murdering persons for the theft of farm and ranch animals, mostly horses. The busiest area for stringing up livestock thieves seems to have been Montana Territory. During the 1880s, the Chicago paper lists approximately 50 victims in at least 12 separate lynchings for horse stealing in this especially remote area of the United States.

U.S. census figures do not exist for Montana earlier than 1870. There is no mention of this place furnishing any troops for either the Union or the Confederate side during the Civil War. The first federal enumeration of Montana Territory's population took place in 1870: 20,595 persons lived there. In 1880, the number was 39,159 and it was 142,924 in 1890. In stark contrast, the state of Missouri's population was 1,721,295 in 1870, 2,168,380 in 1880, and 2,679,185 in 1890.[4] What the enormous numbers of Missourians as opposed to the tiny number of Montanans meant as early as the 1870s for the burgeoning railroad industry was large construction in the populated place and small in the remote mountain area of Montana Territory. By 1880, the railroads of Missouri included 3,965 miles of track, and by 1890, it was 6,142 miles. So complete was railroad building in Missouri by the end of the nineteenth century that only six of this state's 114 counties were without train service. Excluding Maries County in southeastern Missouri, the remaining five counties — Dallas, Douglas, Ozark, Stone, and Taney — which lacked locomotive transportation within their own boundaries,[5] were all in the hilly and sparsely populated southwestern section of the state. In 1880s Montana, the dominant mode of travel was not the railroad; it remained the horse. The 1900 federal census gives no figures for the number of miles of railroads in operation in Montana in either 1860 or 1870 and shows a paltry 106 miles of track for 1880 and 2,195 for 1890. This last figure was approximately the same level of railroad service Missouri had achieved by 1870 with 2,000 miles of track.[6] At this time the lynchings of horse thieves in the Show Me State were in their glory days.

It was not that the horse was forgotten once train service dominated an area. This wonderful creature was of immense importance in the past. In Shakespeare's *Richard III*, when knocked off his mount, the evil king cries out, "A horse, a horse, my kingdom for a horse." As time passed and newfangled means of transportation were devised, the memory of this animal's earlier significance survived. The railroad locomotive was initially called an *iron horse*; the automobile a *horseless carriage*, and at present the main force of our motor vehicles is spoken of in terms of *horse power.* Any political contest, if at all close, is referred to as a *horserace*; the candidates run *neck and neck.* In 2007 in additional to the human luminaries who died, Art Buchwald, Liz Claiborne, Thomas Eagleton, Lady Bird Johnson, and Luciano Pavarotti — to name but a few — both print and television necrologies also included Barbaro, winner of the 2006 Kentucky Derby and afterwards the hearts of the nation. Obviously, we continue to remember and to love the horse, but in almost all long distance travel and a great many shorter trips, journeys by train of both freight and persons replaced those by horse and mule in 1880s Missouri. As a result, horse stealing no longer presented the clear and present danger to the life and livelihood of Missouri's citizens in this decade that these forms of grand larceny had earlier. Accordingly, residents allowed sheriffs to arrest such thieves, prosecutors in courtrooms to convict them, judges to sentence them to a term of years in the state's correctional facility, and the penitentiary to punish them with confinement. In contrast, in sparsely settled Montana, where the railroad was not an easy hop, skip, and jump to board, lynchings for the theft of horses, the principal means of transporting persons and goods, continued unabated.

The last known lynchings of horse thieves in Missouri took place in a southwestern county, Dade. In the 1880s, this section of the state was the scene of more mob murders, all of white males, than any other. Not only were there more vigilante killings there, three of them had more than one victim. Indeed, except for one dual lynching of African Americans by other African Americans in northeast Missouri, all dual and triple mob murders during this decade took place in these southwestern counties. Its citizens seemed to have little confidence that the constituted legal authorities would protect the innocent and punish the guilty.

The first lynchings of the 1880s in this area occurred in Osceola, seat of St. Clair County, on May 13, 1880, at about 12:30 A.M., when a crowd of 100 men rode into town and proceeded to the county jail. One of them called for the jailer, and after he refused to turn over the keys, the mob easily smashed its way in. The mob focused on two jail cells. Each held two men; all four occupants were awaiting trial. One unit contained John Parks and Chesley Pierce; Parks was charged with the murder of William Bohon on January 20, 1880, and Pierce was charged as an accessory to Bohon's murder. The other held William R. Smith and a man surnamed Gilbert. Smith was under indictment for murdering David Triplett near Johnson City on April 10, 1880, and Gilbert was charged with horse stealing. Somehow the alleged thief managed to escape from the mob, found another horse, rode it to safe haven, and turned it loose, and its owner recovered his property that same day.

The mob intended to string up all four men in one vigilante action, and succeeded in killing three. When Smith broke away from his captors, he ran for it, and twice disobeyed the command to halt. The leader gave orders to shoot. Smith fell, riddled with approximately 100 bullets. The lynchers dragged his body with them as they proceeded to the outskirts of town, left the highway, and in a group of locust trees, hanged to death Pierce and Parks and tied about two-thirds of Smith's remains to another tree, leaving about one-third of him on the ground. At least two, perhaps three, letters were found at the scene of these three hanging bodies. The local newspaper printed two of them. The first, signed St. Clair Co. Vigilants, explains that the mob took the action it did because "justice in St. Clair County has been blindfolded by affidavits. She has been choked by legal tecknicalities [*sic*], has been thwarted by corrupt judges and attornies [*sic*]." The second contains more errors in spelling and capitalization than the first. It asserts that "Murder and Horse Stealing shall be stoped [*sic*] in this county.... Let no gilty [*sic*] man escape Justice. We are tiared [*sic*] of the Tactics in Law.... We are tiared [*sic*] of the expenses." It is signed, "Eplurubus Unum."[7]

Governor John Smith Phelps (1877–1881) had the same interest in using the legal process to punish the St. Clair County lynchers as did Governor Silas Woodson in pursuing the Callaway County mob murderers of the mule thief and the sheriff approximately seven years earlier. Despite their best efforts, neither governor succeeded. Woodson sent Attorney General Ewing to Fulton to investigate the Callaway County lynchings in 1873, and Governor Phelps dispatched Adjutant-General Mitchell to Osceola to look into the St. Clair County mob murders in 1880. In both cases, the circuit court judges of these counties were also actively involved in attempts to bring the guilty to justice.[8] Just as there was an arrest made in the Callaway County lynchings, so too in St. Clair, on June 10, 1880, less than a month after its May 13 night of terror, three men, Decatur Grimes, Hiram Curry, and Jack Barker, were taken into custody. The evidence that they were active participants in the murder of Parks, Pierce, and Smith consisted mainly of persons under oath testifying before the St. Clair County grand jury that they believed they had seen one or more of these men in incriminating activities, such as battering open the jail door. Although all three were soon released on bail, their cases were moved to adjacent Henry County.

The circuit court judge's removal action was based on the 1879 change in the law. However as discussed in Chapter 5, in October 1880, the Missouri Supreme Court held this law violated the Missouri Constitution, and it ordered the release of Daniel C. Slater, alias Frank Lane, then being held in Audrain County, under indictment in Scotland County, for a murder committed in Clark County. The grand jury of Henry County convened on August 15, 1880, at least six weeks before the Missouri Supreme Court ruled that the law allowing the judge's removal of a case to an adjacent county was unconstitutional. If Grimes, Curry, or Barker were ever indicted in Henry County for the triple lynching on May 13 in St. Clair County, the October 1880 decision of the Missouri Supreme Court nullified any legal action against them in Henry County. The court wrote, "All crimes are local.... The prosecution for them can be carried out only in the county of their commission."[9] This decision ended all attempts in Missouri to prosecute any member of a lynch mob in an adjacent county.

The St. Clair county history published in 1883 mentions the deaths of Parks, Pierce, and Smith in two places. On one page, it quotes and perhaps improves the spelling and composition of yet another letter from the mob. In this one the evildoers call themselves "The Moderators," as they justify their mob work by reiterating their grievances about the malfunctioning of the county's criminal justice system.[10] On other pages, this history concludes of the May 13, 1880, hanging of three men, "A coroner's jury decided that Judge Lynch had ordered the execution of the criminals, but could not lay their hands on this important personage, and this ended the horror."[11] Nowhere does this history name names or mention any legal action in this case in Henry County.

In February 1885, Mark Twain's *The Adventures of Huckleberry Finn* was published. The novel takes place in an indefinite antebellum time, in, among other places, Missouri. As Huck and Jim raft past St. Louis, Huck finally believes "there was twenty or thirty thousand people in St. Louis" because he saw "that wonderful spread of lights at two o'clock that still night." Based on this population figure, Twain's novel is set in the 1840s. However, the townspeople's reaction to Colonel Sherburn's shooting and killing the harmless drunk Boggs has a more modern ring to it. Twain places the failed lynching of Sherburn in Arkansas, and through this character, he denounces a common enough activity in 1880s Missouri: "A *man* goes in the night with a hundred masked cowards at his back, and lynches the rascal.... The pitifulest thing out is a mob.... But a mob without any man at the head of it is beneath pitifulness."[12] Not until 1901 did Twain take sufficient cognizance of contemporary events in Missouri to write about an actual lynching in his native state; moreover, his essay on lynchings was not published until 1923. There had been plenty of successful lynching bees to condemn here far earlier.

The same year Mark Twain's most famous novel was published, 1885, was an especially active time for mob murders in southwestern Missouri; there were five. Perhaps the most audacious lynching took place in Taney County. On April 10 in Eglinton, the Taylor brothers, Frank and Tubal, feloniously assaulted a storekeeper and his wife, Mr. and Mrs. John T. Dickenson. Both survived, badly wounded. A hunt was on for their assailants, and a reward was offered for their capture. Given Taney County's inability to secure a single conviction in even one of the 30 to 40 murders committed within its boundaries between 1865 and 1884, the Taylors assumed that courtroom history in Forsyth, the county seat, would repeat itself. As a result, on April 14 they surrendered to friends who, as planned in advance, turned them over to law enforcement officers. Their scheme was to split the reward money with their cronies, once they were, as they certainly expected to be, acquitted in Taney County Circuit Court.

A much larger group was equally aware of Taney County's failure to convict its major lawbreakers. On April 5, 1885, it held a mass recruitment on a bald knob, and its members became known as Bald Knobbers. On April 15, 100 of them on horseback rode into Forsyth, broke into the jail, took Frank and Tubal Taylor from it, and hanged them from the limbs of a tree approximately two miles from town. On Frank's dangling corpse one or more of the lynchers pinned this note: "These are the first Victims to [*sic*] the Wrath of Outraged Citizens — More will follow, the Bald Knobbers." Expectedly, the coroner's jury determined that the lynched men came to their deaths at the hands of approximately 100 unknown men.

The mob that put to death the Taylor brothers became sufficiently important for a book to be written about them.[13] According to it, at the height of the group's power its membership was 1,000 men. Those who allegedly participated in the Taylor lynching included at least seven members of the clergy: three Methodist, two Disciples of Christ, and two Baptist ministers, and a future member of the legislature. Alonzo S. Prather, the man credited with supplying the rope used to hang the Taylors,[14] represented Taney County in the General Assembly in 1888, 1896, 1902, and 1908.[15]

Heady with the success of lynching the Taylor brothers in Taney, Bald Knobbers spread into other southwestern Missouri counties. On October 1, 1886, a federal judge, Arnold Krekel, ordered an investigation into their attempts in Douglas County to deprive citizens of their homesteads. An out-of-state paper carried a story in December 1886 about the arrest of five Bald Knobbers, and noted outstanding warrants for several others by U.S. Commissioner McLain, who acted under instructions from the U.S. Attorney. The five arrested men were lodged in the jail in Springfield.[16]

These arrests by federal authorities were made possible by the U.S. Congress enacting several laws. In 1862, the 37th Congress passing the Homestead Law, and President Lincoln signed it into law that same year. This act made it possible for citizens aged at least 21 years to settle on "unappropriated public lands" for a maximum of $1.25 an acre, not to exceed 160 acres.[17] In 1870, the 40th Congress added federal protection to homesteaders when it passed and President Grant signed a Civil Rights law. One of the new law's sections prohibited two or more persons from conspiring to injure, oppress, threaten, or intimidate any citizen in the free exercise or enjoyment of any right or privilege secured to him by the Constitution or Laws of the United States. Congress allowed a fine of $5,000 and imprisonment for not more than ten years.[18]

From March 1885 until July 1889, including the time during which Judge Krekel ordered an investigation into Bald Knobber activity, the U.S. Attorney for the Western District of Missouri was Maecenas Eason Benton (1848–1924), a former Confederate soldier, an appointee of President Grover Cleveland, a future member of the U.S. Congress, and the future father of the artist Thomas Hart Benton.[19] The surviving records are incomplete, but we know that M.E. Benton prosecuted Bald Knobbers for intimidating homesteaders in two court locations: the Southern Division of the Western District of Missouri Federal Court in Springfield and its Eastern Division in Jefferson City. Federal Commissioner McLain Jones presided in Springfield and Judge Arnold Krekel presided in Jefferson City. As in the Cass County federal case of retarding the mails, many more men were hauled in these courtrooms than were convicted. In a jury trial in Jefferson City, six men were found guilty of conspiracy to intimidate citizens in the exercise of their rights.[20] Although the 1870 law allowed imprisonment for up to 10 years, in 1885, the 48th Congress made intimidation of homesteaders a misdemeanor. The fine could not exceed $1,000 and the imprisonment a year.[21] We can know the maximum punishment each might have received by examining the penalties the guilty persons in Springfield received. At least six men were sentenced to time in the Newton County, Missouri, jail in Neosho for two to six months, and one was sentenced to one year in the Missouri State Penitentiary.[22] Presumably, Judge Krekel handed down similar sentences in Jefferson City. Not until 1895 did Congress make the military prison at Fort Leavenworth, Kansas, the United States Penitentiary and transfer its administration from the Department of War to the Department of Justice.[23] Prior to this, federal offenders served their time in county and state facilities, and the federal government sometimes reimbursed the county and sometimes the state for their separate detentions of federal prisoners.

The most severe legal blow of the 1880s to this influential vigilante group took place in yet another southwestern Missouri county, Christian. On May 10, 1889, its sheriff hanged three Bald Knobber members—William Walker; his father, David Walker; and John Matthews—for the March 11, 1887, murder of two young men who were shot to death because they made disparaging remarks about Bald Knobbers.[24] Despite the federal conviction of some of its members for violation of the homestead laws in Douglas County and the legal execution of three on state charges of first-degree murder in Christian County, this powerful organization conducted at least one more Taney County lynching in the 1890s, a case discussed in Chapter 9.

The next 1885 southwestern Missouri mob murder took place in Joplin, Jasper County, on July 19, at 2 A.M., when a group of vigilantes smashed open the iron door of the jail and removed one of its inmates, Joe Thorton. In his book about Joplin, Dolph Shaner describes the lynched man as one "who ran a tough resort on the state line ... Half of his 'joint' was in Kansas and half in Missouri. Thorton kept a bad gang around him and ... declared no officer could arrest him."[25] The mob marched this man, whom the local newspaper describes as a "demon," a "desperado," and a person "of reckless habits," with a rope thrown over his head to a property in the town with several maple trees on it, and strung him up on one of them. On July 18, Thorton shot 56-year-old Daniel Sheehan, a member of the Joplin Police Department, a husband and a father of six, to avoid being arrested for selling liquor without a license. The police officer died approximately 10 hours after his assailant was lynched. The coroner's jury met shortly after daylight and determined that the hanged man had died at the hands of parties unknown to it. After the inquest was concluded, Thorton's mistress, May Ulery, claimed her lover's body, dressed it in a new suit of clothes, and hired a hearse, which took it to Galena, Kansas. In this town, the brother of the outlaw was a prominent businessman, and he, his family, and a few others followed the lynched man's remains to his burial in the city cemetery.[26]

Less than a month after the Jasper County hanging of Joe Thorton, on August 6, 1885, at 1 A.M., a McDonald County mob of between 100 and 150 men stormed the Newton County jail in Neosho. The lynchers removed Garland A. Mann from this facility, and unknown persons shot him to death. Physicians later found six bullet wounds in his remains, any one of which might have killed him. Nearly two years earlier, on September 12, 1883, Mann, a saloon keeper, allegedly murdered Dr. A.W. Chenowith in McDonald County. The victim was an enthusiastic advocate of temperance, much opposed to the sale and consumption of alcoholic beverages, and it was his opposition to saloons that was believed to have motivated a keeper of one to kill him.[27] Mann was charged with homicide, but prosecutors in Pineville were unable to convict him consistent with due process. He was initially tried and sentenced to death in Newton County on a change of venue from McDonald, but the Supreme Court of Missouri reversed and granted him a new trial.[28] According to the county history, subsequent juries hearing Mann's case could not agree, and by the time his fourth trial was beginning in Neosho, on August 3, 1885, the taxpayers of McDonald County, the locale of Dr. Chenowith's homicide, had already spent approximately $11,000 in unsuccessful attempts to convict Mann of first-degree murder.[29] The early morning work of the McDonald County citizens' committee ended any additional expenses. Its lynching of Mann is an excellent example of finances motivating a mob. Richard Maxwell Brown writes persuasively that "ordinary men formed the rank and file of the vigilante organization, but usually its direction was firmly in the hands of the local elite. The local vigilante leaders often paid the highest taxes. They had the customary desire to whittle down the tax rate and keep local expenses in check."[30] One best explains Mann's murder as the cheapest way to keep the inordinate expenses of trying him in a courtroom from reaching even more deeply into the pockets of McDonald County's wealthiest citizens.

A mob murder in McDonald County, Irwin Grubb's, followed closely on the heels of Mann's in Newton. The men who killed Grubb in November 1885 were most likely motivated by a desire to spare the county the expense of trying him. At the time of his death, he had been an inmate in the McDonald County jail in Pineville, awaiting trial for the June 1885 murder of Dorson B. Anderson. Unknown men took him from the jail, and near the scene where Mann allegedly killed Dr. Chenoweth on September 12, 1883, they lynched Grubb by hanging him to death.[31] Once more, the motive seems to have been a clear cut case of thrift.

The last confirmed southwest Missouri lynching of the 1880s took place in Springfield, seat of Greene County, on April 27, 1886, when a mob of 75 to 100 masked men on horseback rode into town, managed to secure the keys to the jail, and took George E. Graham from it to a tree, and upon it, at 2 A.M., hanged him. A note was found pinned to the corpse: "Don't Tell if Anyone Recognized." The sheriff testified before the coroner's jury that he recognized no member of the masked mob, and the coroner's jury predictably found that the deceased came to his death at the hands of unknown men. Once these six jurors had finished their work, the coroner, a longtime undertaker, took Graham's remains to his funeral parlor business and arranged his corpse for viewing. Approximately 5,000 men, women, and children filed past it prior to his 5 P.M. burial in Hazelwood cemetery, three miles southeast of Springfield, on the same day as the lynching. These numbers are higher than any of the estimates of those who gazed upon the laid-out remains of the legally executed in this state.

The intense community interest in Graham was rooted in his religious, sexual, and marital life; the hanged man was involved in immensely complicated relationships. Besides being an ex-convict, he was an associate of Mrs. Emma Molloy, a noted evangelist. He was believed to have lived in northern Kansas with his wife/ex-wife, Sarah Graham, as well as Mrs. Molloy and her foster daughter, Cora Lee. In a Kansas locale, he was apparently active in sexual relations with all three women. Graham was an adulterer if one believes that he remarried his first wife, Sarah, who divorced him during his first term as an inmate in the Indiana State Penitentiary. If he did remarry her in 1878, as her relatives certainly believe he had, he committed the crime of bigamy, when on July 18, 1885, he married Cora Lee in Springfield. Sometime after September 30 of that same year, Sarah Graham was last seen there. Four months later, after Graham was arrested for bigamy, Sarah's body was found in an old well on a farm in Greene County, acreage which Emma Molloy owned and lived on with her foster daughter and son-in-law. The three of them, George and his bride, Cora Lee, and her foster mother, Emma Molloy, had daily passed the well that held the body of Sarah Graham as they pursued their religious activities, goings-on that brought about the conversion of hundreds of the repentant. Initially, Emma Molloy and Cora Lee were held as accessories to Sarah's murder, the foster daughter as accessory before the fact and the foster mother as accessory after it. Graham confessed to the murder of Sarah and appears to have done so in an attempt to protect his wife and his mother-in-law. Nonetheless, it was while Cora Lee was an inmate in the Polk County jail in Bolivar, awaiting her trial as an accessory to the murder of Sarah Graham, that she received the news of her beloved husband's lynching. I do not know what legal action, if any, was finally taken against her. What is known is that Emma Molloy continued her religious work in Washington Territory; she conducted revival meetings and also spoke in favor of temperance and giving women the right to vote. Presumably, among the 5,000 persons who viewed her son-in-law's remains in Springfield, Missouri, on April 27, 1886, were members of the mob who strung up George E. Graham, as well as many who had been converted by Emma Molloy or the lynched man. Whatever else the townspeople of Springfield, Missouri, may have thought of him, they certainly agreed, as the local paper noted in its lengthy coverage of his death, "Graham has taken a change of venue to a higher court, and the taxpayers will be saved an enormous expense."[32]

In northwest Missouri, the sheriff put to death 11 persons between 1880 and 1889; all were white. Presumably the well-built jails of Kansas City and St. Joseph discouraged vigilante efforts to breach their doors. Mobs are known to have succeeded in murdering only three white men in this area between 1880 and 1889. This section's first lynching of the 1880s took place in Atchison County. In May 1881, the former hired hand of Alfred Angel, Thomas Reinhammer, returned for additional employment and assaulted his employer, who managed to survive his injuries despite being shot in the back four times. The assailant robbed Angel of $250 and took one of his horses. At Burlington Junction, he abandoned his mount and caught a train for Iowa. Thanks to the sheriff of Atchison County casting an interstate net of telegrams about Reinhammer, a return message from Clarinda, Iowa, approximately 11 miles north of Missouri, allowed him to apprehend and confine the hired hand in the county jail in Rock Port. At 1 A.M. June 11, a masked mob of 25 men seized his prisoner from the jail, and hanged him to death from a tree.[33]

The next lynching in northwest Missouri, that of Charlie "Omaha" Stevens on December 9, 1884, in Maryville, Nodaway County, is chiefly of interest because of the unfavorable publicity his death gave Governor Thomas Crittenden (1881–1885). This chief executive of the state was already on record as granting the most infamous pardons in Missouri's history. They went to Robert and Charley Ford, killers of Jesse James on April 17, 1882, two hours and 15 minutes after these men pled guilty to the first-degree murder of James and were sentenced to death in Buchanan County Circuit Court.[34] On January 2, 1884, Governor Crittenden's pardon released Charlie "Omaha" Stevens from the Missouri State Penitentiary. Stevens had been convicted of the March 1, 1879, second-degree murder of John Mahan during the June 1879 term of Nodaway County Circuit Court and sentenced to 12 years in prison. During his incarceration, Stevens, a handy woodworker and charming fellow when sober, had endeared himself to Caroline Crittenden, the governor's young daughter. One may ask what were the governor and Mrs. Crittenden thinking when they allowed their eight-year-old daughter to visit the penitentiary with some regularity; most parents would never have permitted their young child to leave the governor's mansion and roam the corridors of the penitentiary, where she could make friends with the likes of Charlie "Omaha" Stevens, a convicted murderer. Caroline had found a wonderful friend, and when this eight-year-old child lay dying during her last illness, she extracted a promise from her chuckle-headed father to pardon Stevens. Forthwith, after four years and six months and thanks to the wishes of his dying child, on January 2, 1884, the governor's pardon released a man from prison who was an extremely dangerous drunk.

Once free from confinement, 40-year-old Stevens returned to Maryville and resumed his old habits, including drinking to excess. At approximately 4 P.M. on December 3, 1884, he shot and seriously wounded 27-year-old Hubert Kremer in Hilgert's saloon in Maryville. Stevens was soon arrested and confined in the Nodaway County jail there. The shooter's provocation seems to have been his victim's objection to Stevens throwing wine on Kremer's clothes and in his face. Kremer appears to have survived the shooting, or if he did not, he was still alive after the man who shot him was lynched. Stevens was taken from the jail on December 9, 1884, at 2 A.M. by 60 masked men. He was marched by them from the Nodaway County jail to a railroad bridge on East Fourth Street in Maryville, and with a rope around his neck, hanged from it at least six times to insure that he was dead. The six-member coroner's jury who investigated Stevens's death concluded that the deceased "came to his death by hanging, at the hands of diverse parties unknown to the jury."[35]

The third and final lynching of a white man in 1880s northwest Missouri took place five miles from Marion in Cole County on January 18, 1889. Henry Thomas, a farmer, was a strict parent with his four daughters, Hattie, Margaret, Nancy, and Jane, aged 16, 18, 20, and 22, respectively. He often bragged that he would not have lazy sons-in-law. As a result, Samuel and Charles Hasburn, brothers, used a ladder to help 18-year-old Margaret and 20-year-old Jane out of a second story window in order to elope with and marry these young Thomas women. The girls' father spied them making their get-away, and on his best horse and armed with a shotgun, he pursued them approximately 12 miles. When he came upon his daughters and their beaus, he opened fire, killing the young men and seriously wounding Margaret. After nearly reaching home with Jane and the dying Margaret, he learned that Hattie and Nancy had also eloped with Ned Greason and Thomas Allison. He is supposed to have left Jane and Margaret with neighbors and pursued and captured 16-year-old Hattie and 20-year-old Nancy. As he was returning home with them, a mob seized him and hanged him from a tree until he was dead. All news accounts relate, "Public feeling is strongly in favor of the lynching." Shortly after her father's death, 18-year-old Margaret died. Three lives were ended and others irreparably changed because Henry Thomas was never able to remember that as the parent of four daughters, he was likely raising the wives of four husbands. The sheer horror of the matter caused its story to be carried in both in- and out-of-state newspapers. Those out-of-state mistakenly place this ghastly incident in Mercer County, an area adjacent to the Iowa border.[36] It took place in the county which is home to the state capitol, governor's mansion, prison, and other important structures, and it was Cole County's only known lynching.

Northeast Missouri in the 1880s yields only one lynching of a white man, and his death at the hands of a mob is one of the few mob murders of a *white* rapist in this state. Although the General Assembly allowed a death sentence for rape as early as 1879, no black was legally executed for this crime until 1891 and no white until 1933. Almost certainly, lynchers anticipated that the accused would not receive the death sentence they believed that he richly deserved at the hands of the law, and they made up for that perceived deficiency.

In March 1880, C.W. Corlew, an ex-convict who had served time for a sex crime, raped Mrs. Crump, who lived near Centralia, Boone County, while she was waiting for a train with her two children in Moberly, Randolph County. He used the pretext of securing her lodgings in a hotel run by his mother. She accepted his offer and accompanied him to a house across the street from train station. He waited until her children were asleep, returned, placed a pistol to her head, and worked his will upon her. Mrs. Crump survived, and let be known her violation. Her assailant was soon captured, and for safekeeping, he was held in the jail in Kansas City. Sometime thereafter he was returned to the Randolph County jail in Huntsville, and his trial was scheduled to begin at 8:30 A.M. July 29, 1880, in the Moberly court of common pleas. As the sheriff and his deputies alighted with their handcuffed prisoner at the steps leading to the courthouse, suddenly Mr. Crump, the outraged husband, pistol in hand, was on the scene. According to one newspaper, he shouted, "I've got you now, G-d d--n you, and I'm going to kill you like a dog."[37] With indignant fury, Crump pursued the cuffed man through a dry good business, a grocery store, a shoe repair shop, and into a saloon in Moberly. He felled him with at least four bullets, two to his head and two to his torso. Crump came to town with a mob of 100 men, and once he was satisfied that Corlew was dead, he and his many friends mounted their horses and rode off. No attempt was made to arrest Mr. Crump or to bring any charges against him. At the coroner's inquest, the jury concluded, "We the jury having viewed the body of Corlew, deceased, find that he came to his death by gun or pistol shots fired by unknown hands."[38] In legal executions for rape in this state, the husband of the victim always had a front row seat reserved for him, and most appeared to have filled it. In Corlew's case, the husband sought his own revenge, and as one newspaper concluded of his murder of his wife's rapist, "The sympathies of the people are in a great measure with the lynchers."[39]

In the 1880s, southeast Missouri accounts for 19 known legal executions of white persons and five lynchings of whites. In each, the victim of the mob was accused of murder. They are discussed in chronological order. The first was Mack Marsden, on April 7,

1883, near DeSoto, Jefferson County. Five men concealed in the woods surrounded him on horseback and commanded him to throw up his hands. Soon, a rider got off his horse and put a noose around Marsden's neck and led him to a tree, and the suspected robber and murderer was hanged by the neck until he was dead. Among the crimes the lynched man was believed to have committed were the March 29, 1882, arson of Joseph Yerger's house and his murder by gunshot. Yerger was postmaster and storekeeper at Antonia, Jefferson County. In addition, two years earlier in this same county, an elderly and solitary man surnamed Vall was found dead in the burned remains of his cabin, about a mile from Sandy Creek. Marsden admitted being in the vicinity of Vall's cabin just before it caught fire. Community belief was strong that after Marsden robbed and murdered Vall, he set fire to his victim's cabin to destroy the evidence. As the news account of this killing states, when the mob members were certain Marsden was dead, "They rode away in the direction of Sandy Creek."[40]

Less than two months after the disposal of Marsden in Jefferson County, shortly before midnight, a mob of 125–200 men broke into the jail at Hermann, seat of Gasconade County. They took keys from a blindfolded deputy and led J.W. Fisher, alias Whitney, from his cell through the town to a small bridge over the Iron Road. The men leading their prisoner were met by others, and in the early morning hours of June 5, 1883, Fisher/Whitney was hanged from a tree until he was dead. The lynched man was charged with the May 19, 1883, murder in the course of a robbery of William Borchard, son of the proprietor of a store in Bem. Fisher and his partner, surnamed Collier, intended to rob this small business. Collier was killed at the crime scene in Bem. After Fisher's body was cut down, the coroner placed it in the courthouse hall. There his six jurors and many citizens viewed it. The coroner's jurors concluded, "We the jury find the deceased, J.W. Whitney [alias Fisher], whose body we have viewed, came to his death on the 5th of June, at the hands of men who hung him to a tree. The names of such men are to this jury unknown."[41]

Within a few days, Governor Crittenden wrote both the judge of the judicial district which included Gasconade County and the prosecuting attorney of the county, suggesting that steps be taken to punish the lynchers.[42] The writers of the county history, first published in 1888, sneeringly comment of the governor's request for "prompt measures" to punish the mob, "It was thought by many that the anxiety of Gov. Crittenden to have these violators of the law brought to deserved punishment would have merited and received more respect and consideration if his own course in connection with the James boys had evinced the same anxiety."[43] Needless to say, nothing came of the governor's request for punishment of the mob members who lynched Fisher, alias Whitney.

In September 1886, in Malden, Dunklin County, Bowman Paxton, a prominent druggist and businessman, quarreled with, shot, and killed J. McGuillery, a blacksmith and neighbor. In order to avoid his lynching, the perpetrator was immediately taken to the county jail in Kennett. On a Sunday night, September 19, the sheriff and a posse left Kennett with Paxton en route to Malden, where his trial was set to take place. About five miles from Kennett, over 100 masked men demanded the prisoner, obtained him, and hanged him from a tree limb. Two hours later, perhaps by this time, September 20, his remains were cut down and buried in Malden. The news story concludes, "Paxton was a man of considerable wealth.... He had employed the best lawyers.... His wealth and social standing, the array of legal talent ... induced the belief that he would defeat the aims of the law and escape, and this caused the unwarrantable deed. The parties who participated in the affair are unknown."[44]

The last two southeastern lynchings of the 1880s took place in the same county, Crawford. The earlier occurred on October 4, 1886, when 100 masked men took R. Pat Wallace, a neighbor of the Logans, then in jail awaiting his trial in Steelville for the September 21 murder of six members of the Logan family, the parents and four children. He was arrested in St. Louis, after a resident of Crawford County pointed him out to a St. Louis police officer. He was returned under heavy guard, threatened by a mob in Cuba, Missouri, and almost lynched on a Thursday, September 28. Shortly after midnight five days later he was taken to the Meramec Bridge, two miles north of Crawford's county seat, and hanged beneath its trestle. After his father refused to bury his remains, the authorities interred the lynched man on a hill north of Steeleville, near the area where the youngest known person legally executed in Missouri's history was buried.[45] One newspaper account ends its coverage of Wallace's lynching, "There is no clue as to the leaders or participants in the lynching."[46]

The event which precipitated the last 1880s lynching in southeast Missouri was a January 2, 1888, crime against David Miller. He was robbed and shot in the head en route to pay his taxes. His body was found a week later with his pockets rifled. As one in-state newspaper account states of the matter, "The bullet found in [Miller's] brain fitted the pistol found on Davis ... and other circumstances pointed to Davis's guilt." On this evidence and perhaps other, Lewis Davis was arrested for the first-degree murder of Miller. He spent the next six months in the secure jail in the city of St. Louis. As his trial date neared, he was returned to Steelville; his jury had already been selected, and proceedings were set to begin on Monday, September 24, 1888. Between 2 A.M. and 3 A.M. on September 23, a mob of 40 masked men snatched Davis from the Crawford County jail and put a rope around his neck, and as the in-state newspaper continues, "hung him to the limb of a post oak tree, immediately over the grave of Pat Wallace who was hung by a mob October 4, 1886, for the murder of the Logan family." According to the Steelville paper, the mob who lynched Lewis Davis "was enraged by the acquittal of Elbert Clonts who was tried ... last week under an indictment for the murder of his father." An Atchison, Kansas newspaper writes of the lynched man, "Lewis Davis is from a family of high standing in Crawford County. His brother has been elected twice to the officer of assessor."[47]

The social status of the lynched man's family surely explains C.C. Bland, circuit court judge of Crawford County, ordering an investigation of this murder. As the in-state paper quotes him, the judge used considerable hyperbole when he exclaimed of the lynching of Lewis Wallace, "Every piece of real estate in the county is depreciated in value at least 25 percent by this act of inexcusable lawlessness." In addition, the leading citizens assembled at the courthouse to express their indignation. Those in attendance included Nathaniel G. Clark, a former state senator; F.M. Jamison, the prosecuting attorney; and a number of other notables.[48] Since the lynching of Davis occurred in the early morning hours of September 23 and the meeting did not get underway until 11 A.M. on September 24, 1888, the time lapse of 32 hours allowed any or all of the 40 masked men who strung up Davis to attend the disapproval get-together. Needless to say, I came across no evidence to suggest that anyone incurred any legal liability in this last known lynching in the 1880s in southeast Missouri.[49]

This chapter concludes with events that cannot be documented as lynchings in Missouri. As with the mob murders that we are certain occurred, those placed in Appendix 2 are discussed by the section of the state in which they occurred. In the southwest, one event happened in Rockville, Bates County, on May 24, 1887. The newspaper states that "a heavy-set white man called at the kitchen door and asked [16-year-old Jennie Anderson] for a glass of water." When the teenager returned with the water, "the brute grabbed her around the shoulders with one hand and with the other covered her mouth with a handkerchief saturated with chloroform. In a few minutes his victim was completely in his power, and his purpose was accomplished." Two days later, she screamed and fainted as she identified her attacker. The newspaper gives his name as John Vanderbaugh and his age about 30 years. The paper's headline for the story begins, "Good Subject for a Mob" and continues, "He is Extremely Liable to Lose his Life at the Hands of Judge Lynch."[50] The alleged rapist died in a Bates County courtroom after his preliminary hearing when two of the victim's brothers gunned him down. The local newspaper concludes its coverage: "There seems to be positive proof that the Anderson brothers did the shooting, and public indignation against Vanderbaugh will go a great way to help them out of the trouble."[51] Because I limit a lynching to three or more perpetrators, it cannot be said that a mob put him to death, but the community approval is very much in keeping with a lynching. Vanderbaugh's name is in Appendix 2.

One southwestern case is uncertain. Was John Davis, the man who allegedly shot and killed Mrs. Andy Savage on September 11, 1889, at Strafford, Greene County, put to death by a mob? He was arrested at the locale of the murder, but we do not know if law enforcement officers managed to protect his life. The newspaper's headline reads, "John Davis Missing and Thought to have been Lynched." The story relates that "at midnight the prisoner and guards had not arrived [in Springfield, the county seat], and as nothing has been heard of them, it is believed that they were intercepted in the woods by a mob and the prisoner lynched."[52] The fate of John Davis is not known. As with Vanderbaugh, John Davis's name is listed in Appendix 2.

From northwest Missouri, four white males, three Corber brothers, on May 7, 1889, and Alfred Grizzard, on June 21, 1889, belong in Appendix 2. The original error was made by the compilers of the *Chicago Tribune's* annual list of the lynched for 1889. They placed Tiptonville, a Tennessee town across the Mississippi River from this state, in Missouri. Most likely an in-state newspaper from southeastern Missouri, no longer extant, carried news stories about these four Tennessee lynchings, and events that did not take place here were in turn mistakenly assigned to Missouri by the NAACP when it compiled its 1919 list. Dominic J. Capeci Jr., following the lead of the NAACP, places all four in Moniteau County, probably because the town of Tipton is located there. There are no known lynchings in the history of Moniteau County.[53]

There are no uncertain cases of white lynchings from northeast Missouri to add to Appendix 2 in the 1880s. From the southwest, there is a totally convincing story about the lynching of a white man in Ironton, seat of Iron County, in a paper published hundreds of miles from the scene. However, there is an extant newspaper in the town in which this mob murder allegedly took place, and no mention is made of the lynching. It is not credible that the event took place where and when the New York City newspaper said it did. Lynchings were always good copy; they invariably sold newspapers. This is what *The New York Times* reported about John Wagoner. He was one of the men charged with the late November 1881 murder of Dr. Biggs, treasurer of the Alice Furnace Company. Wagoner's lynching took place in Ironton, seat of Iron County, when between midnight and 1 A.M. January 20, 1882, 40 to 60 masked men took Bill Zeek, the other accused murderer of Biggs, to the courthouse yard and strung him up. When Zeek implicated others, the mob allowed him to live. Next it took Wagoner to the same spot and hanged Wagoner by the neck until dead. The newspaper account concludes, "There is not the slightest clue to the perpetrators, and the public seems to approve of the lynching."[54] It is beyond the scope of this book to ascertain the town and state or territory of the mob murder of John Wagoner. Suffice it to say, no evidence suggests that it took place in Ironton, seat of Iron County in 1882.

Finally, the lynchings of two additional white men in the southeastern section did not result in death. The *Chicago Tribune* lists Joseph Gebhard [sic] as lynched on November 17, 1889, for safe breaking, in Kennett, Missouri.[55] The local paper tells a slightly different story. On November 15, masked men forced the county jailer to deliver Joe Gibheart to them for some very strenuous questioning. He and his brother, Lawrence, were charged with the October 26, 1889, burglary of a safe at Caruth. The safe and its contents, approximately one thousand dollars, were the property of the Farmer's Store. Lawrence made bond, and Joe went to jail. The mob roughed up both Joe and Lawrence in a vain attempt to learn, if these men had taken the money, where they hid it. However, both lived through the ordeal of being hanged by the neck several times. The local paper observes that Joe Gibheart's "having served a time in the penitentiary for stealing a horse is no evidence that he is guilty of robbing a safe."[56] Because the Gibhearts, Joe and Lawrence, survived their ordeal with a crowd of masked men, they too are listed in Appendix 2.

As newspapers with national coverage publicized lynchings, there were even more stories about them that were inaccurate, and more of them, discussed in later chapters, must be placed in Appendix 2. The 1880s was the last decade in this state in which suspected horse thieves were lynched. It is also the last 10-year period in which there were more white victims of mobs than black. As the next chapter shows, white men met even fewer deaths at the hands of vigilantes in the 1890s than in any nineteenth century time period after the Civil War.

CHAPTER 8

Arranged Media Coverage and Other Obscenities: Black Victims, 1890–1899

The 1890s remains the most active period for legal executions under state law in Missouri's history. Only the Union Army, guided by martial law, put to death more men and boys here in an even shorter time span, 89 between 1862 and 1865. During the last decade of the nineteenth century, Missouri sheriffs are known to have legally hanged 59 men and boys, 36 white and 23 black. Among other crimes, wife murder was vigorously prosecuted as a capital offense in the last decade of the nineteenth century; it is not today. Thus far, only two men who committed this crime have been put to death in this state by lethal injection, one in 1999 and the other in 2005. In contrast, during the 1890s, at least 11 men were legally hanged because they murdered their wives. The 1890s here also was the only time span in which a millionaire, worth approximately $25 million today, was legally executed. His crime was wife and child murder. Only in the 1890s was a former member of the Missouri legislature hanged pursuant to court order. Likewise, the sheriff of Saline County hanged the first convicted rapist in Missouri's history in 1891. Indeed, between 1890 and 1899, Judge Ketch, to use a phrase of the *Chicago Tribune,* was so busy with his legal executions that it diminished the work of Judge Lynch. In all, 31 lynchings can be confirmed as occurring in Missouri during the 1890s. This is a reduction from the years 1866–1869 with 35; 1870–1879 with 52; and 1880–1889 with 33. Of equal interest, for the first time in Missouri since the 1850s, mobs murdered more blacks, 17, than whites, 14, in the last decade of the nineteenth century.

This fact takes on additional significance when we look at census figures. The percentage of Missouri's population that was African American continued to decline. It was 5.6 percent of the population in 1890 and 5.2 percent in 1900.[1] In 1880, there were 7,185 blacks for every 100,000 whites; in 1890, 5,940; and in 1900, 5,475.[2] By 1900, the white population of Missouri was 2,944,843 and the African-American was 161,234.[3] Without specifying which cities, Missouri scholars state that "by 1890, 47 percent of the state's black population lived in cities; the figure jumped to 55 percent by 1900."[4] As repeatedly emphasized throughout this book, lynchings did not take place in the state's two largest towns, Kansas City and St. Louis; their jails were too well built for such nefarious activities. The largest percentage of African Americans lived in these metropolitan areas by

105

1890. Charles Coulter lists the black population of Kansas City as increasing from 10.3 percent (13,700) of the total in 1890 to 10.7 percent (17,567) in 1900.[5] By 1900, St. Louis ranked second only to Baltimore among American cities for the percentage of its population that was black; more than 35,000 Negroes lived in this eastern Missouri metropolis at the beginning of the twentieth century.[6] With the percentage of African Americans in Missouri's countryside continuing to decline, what best explains the increased numbers of lynched blacks during the 1890s here?

One contributing factor must have been the sprouting seeds of belief that a white man was more deserving of the legal process than a black; after all, he was white. Although the matter would become more terrible here in the twentieth century, it is worth noticing that the size of Missouri mobs lynching blacks during the 1890s also increased over previous decades. The number of lynched blacks who had committed crimes against other blacks only slightly elevated the total number; typically, this demographic mix did not arouse sufficient indignation in white men to turn them into a functioning lynch mob. Likewise depressing the numbers of both black and white mob victims was the continuing improvement of law enforcement officers in protecting prisoners.

Train service certainly aided the authorities in preventing mob murders. Once the railway car was available and frequently used to transport prisoners, fewer arrested persons were victims of vigilantes. It is true that mobs occasionally managed to remove someone from a train. However, it was far more difficult to get a man off a train than to grab him from a deputy attempting to bring his arrestee to a jail. As the guard sat astride one mount while the prisoner was on another, it was child's play to seize the suspect. As a result of several factors during the 1890s here, 59 condemned persons, all male, were kept alive, not lynched, and sheriffs hanged them pursuant to court orders. These numbers would be smaller without the combined beliefs that white guys should be tried but black men who committed crimes against other blacks need not worry about white mobs (the usual race of lynchers). The rest of the decrease was due to law enforcement officers' improved abilities to prevent lynchings by transporting prisoners by train, not by horse, statewide.

Beginning, as in earlier chapters, with southwest Missouri, an area with a small black population, the region saw six legal executions during the 1890s, and all but one were of white males. The exception was the legal hanging in 1895 in Vernon County of the African American William Wright, a former mental patient in Alabama. He axed his wife Betty to death because he believed that she had deliberately burned his dinner. Otherwise, the sheriffs in the southwestern counties in the 1890s led no black prisoners to the scaffold.

There were two known lynchings of black men in southwest Missouri in the 1890s. The first took place in Rich Hill, Bates County. Will Jackson was a resident of Kansas City, and he happened to go to Rich Hill because he found work in the mines near this town. On September 15, 1893, he allegedly attempted to rape a white child, 11-year-old Lizzie Davis, the daughter of John Davis, a farmer who lived two miles from town. Jackson was soon captured and placed in the jail in Rich Hill. A mob estimated at 300 enraged members dragged him from his cell the afternoon of September 16, 1893, and while he tearfully confessed to his crime, a rope was thrown about his neck and the other end of it over the limb of a young cottonwood tree. The limb broke, and what was probably Jackson's lifeless body fell to the ground. The mob again strung him up until there was no doubt that his life was extinct.[7]

The second southwest Missouri lynching of a black took place in Monett, Barry County, on June 28, 1894. Earlier that same month and year, Hewett Hayden and another Negro, Marshall Young, got into a fight with a white railroad brakeman, Robert Greenwood. In the course of the argument, Greenwood was shot to death, and the Negroes escaped. Hayden was captured in Neosho, Newton County, on June 27, and returned to Monett the next day. Marshall Young, perhaps the actual firer of the shot that killed Greenwood, evaded capture. The authorities attempted to convey Hayden from Monett to Cassville, the seat of Barry County, by train. A mob estimated at 300 stopped the train just outside Monett; 60 or 70 men boarded it, seized Hayden, and strung him on a telegraph pole, where shots were fired into his lifeless body. The coroner's inquest was no surprise. As the Cassville paper states, "The deceased came to his death at the hands of unknown persons." This newspaper also makes clear that the homicide of Robert Greenwood was not the killing of poor white trash. It notes that the victim was "a grandson of the late Judge Greenwood, formerly of this place and a cousin of Mrs. T.D. Steele and Mrs. Helen C. Hobbs."[8] In the southwest section of the state, these two are the only known lynchings of blacks during the 1890s.

When we turn to the northwest, a sizeable number of blacks were legally executed; out of 27 males whom county sheriffs hanged in this section during the 1890s, 13 were black. Most either murdered other blacks and/or their crimes and punishments took place in counties with secure jails, such as in St. Joseph and Kansas City. One important exception to this general rule was the legal hanging in Saline County of 23-year-old William Price, a black male, on May 8, 1891, for the November 18, 1890, rape of 19-year-old Alice Ninas, a white female. That Price lived to be tried in a court of law was thanks to law enforcement officers in Marshall, seat of Saline County, secretly removing him from the jail, concealing him in a hotel in Marshall and quietly bringing him by train from Marshall to Kansas City, where he was lodged in the jail.[9] Another factor in keeping Price alive may have been the wishes of Saline County's leading citizens to avoid yet another mob murder of a black. There had been many in the past, most sensationally the four within 24 hours in July 1859. In a Pettis County case, one in which a black committed a capital crime against a white and lived to be legally executed, the strenuous efforts of law enforcement officers prevented a mob murder. The sheriff of this county, alarmed by the threat of mob violence took his African-American prisoner by midnight train to California, the seat of Moniteau,[10] a county with no known lynchings in its history. In late 1896 or early 1897, William Joel Stone, governor of Missouri, personally went to the Cole County jail and prevailed on an integrated mob of white and black men intent on stringing up a black prisoner to disperse. The accused, Toby Lanahan, was charged with the rape and murder of a 12-year-old black girl. The governor told the assembled, "The capital city of the state must not be disgraced with a lynching."[11] As far as we know it was not; the only lynching that can be documented in Cole County took place in 1889. During the 1890s, there were three legal hangings in Jefferson City, the state capital and the seat of Cole County; all were black males, and two committed a capital crime against a white person. The authorities simply insured that no lynching took place within this county, the seat of state government. As in the southwest section of the state, so too in the northwest portion of 1890s Missouri, there were only two known lynchings of black men in the 1890s. Kansas City's well-built jail, a capable police force, and dependable railroad service surely helped to depress the numbers of the lynched in this section.

The first northwest event of the 1890s took place on August 29, 1890, near Mayview, Lafayette County, when 18-year-old Will Waters was accused of and confessed to the murder of a white storeowner in Mayview, J.W. Parker, on that same date. Waters's motive was probably robbery; the cash drawer of the business and the victim's pockets were rifled. He was arrested by a constable, and a mob took him from the law enforcement officer and hanged him to death from a tree limb.[12]

The second occurred in Kingston, Caldwell County, and it appears to have been a black-on-black affair. On February 7, 1895, George Tracy murdered his 25-year-old wife, Mary, leaving their three offspring, aged one, three, and six years, motherless children. Their father was considered a bad man. He had earlier been shot in the eye, lost both legs when he was knocked off a train, and served a long jail sentence for shooting and killing another Negro male. When he was arrested for the murder of his wife, he was held in the Caldwell County jail in Kingston. Between 1 A.M. and 3 A.M. on February 17, a mob of between 40 and 50 men obtained the jail keys, entered the facility, and, when unable to secure the key to Tracy's cell, pumped at least 17 shots into Tracy as he cowered in his compartment. The coroner's inquest produced no culprits. The local paper quotes the sheriff, who was tied up while the mob did its work and afterwards untied: "'All the men whose faces I saw were colored men; a few of the men had handkerchiefs over their faces.' These he could not tell whether they were white or colored but thinks they were also colored."[13]

In the northeast section in the 1890s, all three known legal executions were of white men. Eight blacks were lynched in four northeastern counties, or nearly as many as the three other parts of the state combined. The northeast was known as "Little Dixie." As noted earlier, much of it bordered the Missouri River. As a result, during the antebellum period, bondpersons reached the area by this waterway, and it became an especially slave-rich portion of the state. More than 25 years after slavery perished, some blacks remained. During the 1890s, Howard County was in the lead when it came to lynching them, with one in 1891 and two unrelated happenings in 1899. All of Howard County's known executions of white persons took place before the Civil War. Its most recent execution of an African American took place in 1873 when its sheriff hanged a black man, Robert Champion, convicted of the murder of his black wife. During the last decade of the nineteenth century, Howard County dispatched any blacks perceived as major wrongdoers by lynching them. No other Missouri county achieved these numbers during this decade. Another black was lynched in Fayette in 1914.

The first lynching of the 1890s was of Allie Thixton, on January 20, 1891. The local newspaper describes him as "a young yellow boy, 18 or 19 years of age" who, 18 months earlier, was suspected of the rape of "Miss Haston, a highly respected young lady residing near Glasgow." Two African-American males were involved in this attack. One was captured, convicted, and sent to the penitentiary; Thixton escaped punishment. Probably in January 1891, he allegedly held up a Miss Crews, who, with a Negro child, was driving home from Glasgow. He took the white lady's pocketbook and attempted to drag her from her buggy. Her resistance and the child's screams drove the assailant away. When Thixton was arrested, Miss Crews could not recognize him because of his disguise, but the young girl was certain of his identity. On this basis and other evidence, unspecified in the local news account, Thixton was arrested and confined in the county jail in Fayette. By Monday, January 19, rumors were reported to at least one sheriff's deputy and other law enforcement officers that a mob was organizing to remove him from the jail and hang him. The *Howard County Advertiser* relates of these warnings: "No attention was give them, either because no reliance was placed in the reports or because no one cared."

At approximately 1:30 A.M., Tuesday, January 20, 30 masked men rode into town. Most went directly to the jail, but six or so went to the room of Sheriff Crigler at the Butler Hotel and obtained the jail keys from him. The mob easily unlocked the jail door, took out its intended prisoner, and mounted him on a horse. One-half mile from the public square, the mob hanged him from an old elm tree. Once he was dead, the mob members rode off. They did so just as V.J. Hughes, the sheriff's deputy following the crowd, arrived on the scene and cut the corpse down. This news account suggests that this particular sheriff's deputy was the liaison between the vigilantes and law enforcement officers; other lynchings point to collusive activity between law enforcement officers and mob murderers. The local news story of Thixton's murder concludes that his corpse was taken to the courthouse; there, the coroner held his inquest; his jury returned its expected verdict, "Death by hanging at the hands of unknown parties," and friends of the deceased took his body to Glasgow for burial.[14] Another in-state newspaper briefly reports of Thixton's lynching, "He was a tough character and had on several other occasions attempted to assault young women."[15] A highly unreliable book on events nationwide, *100 Years of Lynchings*, garbles the name as Ollie Truxton.[16]

The second Howard County lynching of a black man, Frank Embree, during the 1890s is one of the best known in the whole awful history of such events in Missouri. It is the first in which photographs of a still-alive but soon-to-die person survive. Someone donated them to the Missouri State Historical Society in Columbia. All we know of their provenance is the anonymity of the picture-taker, original curator, and donor to a society which the Missouri Press Association organized in 1898, the year before Embree was lynched. In addition, two pictures of a living person (front and back) and one of a hanged Embree are a part of the Allen/Littlefield Collection, Special Collections Department, Robert W. Woodruff Library, Emory University, Atlanta, Georgia. They are the only positively identified photographs from Missouri in *Without Sanctuary*, a twenty-first century publication of ghastly snapshots of lynched persons in the United States.[17] When this book was published, Rick Montgomery, then a reporter for the *Kansas City Star*, wrote a lengthy and well-researched article about Frank Embree's mob murder.[18]

His alleged crime was raping 14-year-old Willie Dougherty, on Saturday, June 17, 1899, as she was riding a horse near Burton. He caught her mount by the bridle, pulled her from the saddle and into the brush, repeatedly assaulted her, and left her unconscious. When she came to, she got back on her horse, rode home, and related what had happened to her. Apparently, she knew Embree because the hunt for him was soon commenced; however, he had escaped to Garnett, Anderson County, Kansas, the residence of his parents. In due course, the sheriff of this Kansas county sent a message, presumably by telegram, that he had arrested Frank Embree.

Extradition to Missouri was not easy. The governor of Kansas, William Stanley, refused to sign the necessary paperwork unless the state of Missouri guaranteed that Frank Embree

Photographs of Frank Embree and his lynchers, July 22, 1899, near Burton, Howard County. Stripped naked and soon-to-die Frank Embree is first photographed from the front. This and other pictures of Embree's murder were arranged so as to be suitable for viewing by the entire community, including women and children. (Used by permission, State Historical Society of Missouri, Columbia.)

would be protected from any lynch mob and receive a fair trial. All Missouri's governor, Lon Stephens, could rely on when giving these assurances to a fellow governor was the word of local authorities. Initially, Embree was lodged in the county jail in Mexico, seat of Audrain County, a place with no known lynchings. When it came time to transport him to Howard County for his trial, he was awakening at 3 A.M. He begged to be taken to Kansas City for safekeeping. Obviously, a change of venue out of Howard County would have been appropriate, but when a black male was charged with the rape of a white female, he almost never received a change of venue. He was considered very fortunate if he stayed alive long enough to be tried.

The sheriff of Howard County appointed 36 deputies to guard Embree on his journey from Mexico to Fayette. These many law enforcement officers used the Chicago and Alton Railroad to take an indirect route to Fayette, i.e. via the village of Steinmetz. The train arrived in Steinmetz at 5:15 A.M. July 22. There the prisoner was removed from the train and placed in a carriage; as it started for Fayette, it was guarded by three deputies. Within two miles of Steinmetz, a large crowd of white men was waiting and ready to snatch Embree from the deputies. Almost certainly, one or more of the 36 deputized men were connected to the mob. How else was it possible that the lynchers knew the precise location of their prey? Rather easily, the already shackled and handcuffed prisoner was removed from the deputy-guarded carriage and placed in a spring wagon for the 12-mile trip to the scene of his alleged crime, near Burton. The assemblage so increased that by the time it reached Burton, it numbered 1,000 persons.

Its leaders had also arranged for appropriate media coverage. A reporter or an editor-publisher from at least two in-county newspapers appear to have been invited to observe and favorably report the key features of Embree's lynching from its start to its finish. Naturally, no member of the enormous unmasked mob is named in the press coverage of the county's big event. The Fayette paper stresses the physical decorum of the vigilantes: "A better organized or more orderly mob was never seen, not a shout nor any boisterous conduct whatever.... A funeral procession of some honored deceased could not have been more quiet." Although the technology to include photographs in newspapers did not yet exist, both in-county papers mention Embree's awareness that someone was taking pictures of him. They make clear that either Embree turned 180 degrees, or was turned, so that both his front and his back could be taken; otherwise the snapshots would not include the same hatted and bearded lyncher, his right hand resting comfortably on a wheel of the spring wagon containing the doomed man. The *Armstrong Herald* writes, "At the request of a snapshot photographer [Embree] got his face in all kinds of shape to be photographed." This paper reports his request of his lynchers, "Send one of my pictures you have to my mother so she can remember me. Please gentlemen do that much for me."[19] The Fayette paper also quotes him as asking "that his parents be notified and his picture be sent to them, that they had no likeness of him and might want one to remember him by."

Apparently in an effort to force a confession from him, as the Fayette newspaper reports, "He was ... stripped of his clothing, and half a dozen stalwart, well-muscled citizens of the community laid on the lash, buggy whips being used." It continues, "Each lash laid open the hide, and the blood trickled down his body. The negro never once winced. He gazed abstractly into the face of the crowd and never uttered a word." The

Fayette paper explains Embree's tolerance of the whippings he was subjected to by quoting an unnamed physician: "The negro was ... insensible to pain; ... he had ridden the 12 long miles sitting in a cramped position in the spring wagon, and his body was benumbed. No living man with his sense of feeling unimpaired could have stood the merciless punishment inflicted upon Embree and not winced or cried out with pain." After 105 lashes, as the Fayette paper continues, he "told the crowd that if they would not torture him any more, would not burn him, but would either shoot or hang him, he would

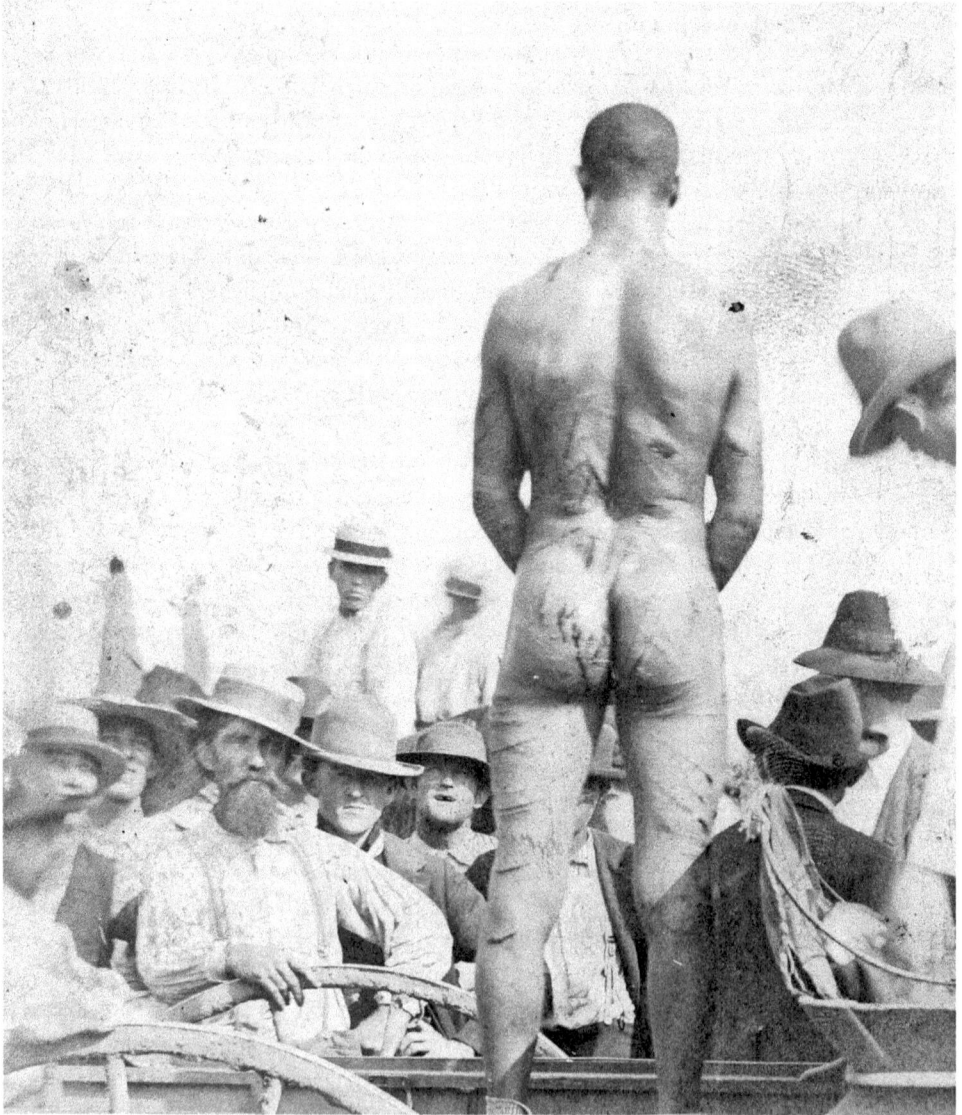

Either Embree turned 180 degrees or was turned in order to be photographed in the wagon from the back as well as the front. The bearded and hatted lyncher, with his right hand resting comfortably on the wagon wheel, and others appear in both pictures of the whipped black man. (Used by permission State Historical Society of Missouri, Columbia.)

The murdered Frank Embree with what looks to be a blanket covering him from his waist to his feet. He died wearing only shoes. They are visible amidst the folds of the coverlet. This photograph was considered suitable viewing for women and children. (Used by permission, State Historical Society of Missouri, Columbia.)

confess all. Embree then admitted that he committed the crime; that he was drunk.... It is believed that he told the truth." The news story goes on to relate that, at the request of the victim and her father, plans to burn Embree to death were abandoned. After allowing him to pray and send his goodbyes to his parents, one end of a rope was thrown about his neck and the other over a tree limb; soon his dead body was swinging in mid-air in broad daylight on July 22, 1899. It was photographed, surrounded by his unmasked white murderers.

The Fayette paper's coverage mentions that Coroner Smith cut down Embree's body by 5 P.M. and held an inquest. From this paper we learn that Negroes buried Embree's remains at a nearby black church cemetery the next day, a Sunday. As for the coroner and his jury's verdict, its six members decided, "After having heard the evidence and upon full inquiry concerning the facts and a careful examination of said body, do find that the deceased came to his death by parties unknown to us. We the jury found the dead body hanging to a limb of a tree." Once more nothing would prevent any member of the coroner's jury, all of whom were named in the Fayette paper, from earlier being a participant in the lynching of Frank Embree.[20]

Slightly over four months later, Howard County was the scene of another lynching of a black man, Tom Hayden, for the murder of a 23-year-old white male, Andrew Woods, a crime that Tom Hayden may or may not have committed. The trouble began on a Saturday night, October 28, 1899, at a craps game held in a deserted cabin four miles south of Glasgow. Both black and white young men were playing and drinking

A very large mob mills about at the scene of Frank Embree's murder. The coroner and his six-member jury could surely have recognized a number of the participants in this event, but the jury's verdict was that "the deceased came to his death by parties unknown to us." (Used by permission, State Historical Society of Missouri, Columbia.)

whiskey. Andrew Woods and Ben Hayden, Tom's half brother, were engaged in good humored bantering when Andy took off his hat and slapped Ben in the face with it. Testimony differed as to what happened next. According to Ben Hayden, after hitting him with his hat, Woods said to Ben what the local paper reported as, "You g-d-b-s-b." Some witnesses testified before the coroner's jury that Ben Hayden fired the shot that hit Andy Woods in the head, killing him instantly; others that Tom Hayden was the culprit.

The next evening at dark, Constable James B. Lewis and Deputy Joe Sartain captured Tom Hayden in Chariton Township. They put him on one horse while each of them rode other mounts as they began their journey to Fayette. Within a short time, 50 men surrounded them and easily took their prisoner from them. When the mob reached a suitable tree near the road, it stopped, threw a rope around Tom Hayden's neck and hanged him to death. The coroner and his jury soon arrived, and their findings were wholly predictable. After hearing six witnesses, the jury first found that Andrew Woods "came to his death by a gun shot in the hands of Tom Hayden, colored." After hearing a few more witnesses, including Deputy Joe Sartain, who recognized no member of the mob who took his prisoner from him, the jury found that Tom Hayden "came to his death by being hung to a tree, done by parties unknown to us."[21]

Two lynchings of black males during the 1890s took place in another northeastern county, Callaway. The first was of James Johnson, near Guthrie, on July 1, 1894, when a mob of approximately 120 men took him from Constable J.R. Reynolds, who was on one horse, while his prisoner was on another. The mob hanged Johnson from a tree at about midnight. His initial arrest was not made in Callaway County; it took place in the city of St. Louis, a locale that Johnson was known to live in. There was nothing unusual about the charge; it was the rape of a white female. However, the alleged date of the crime was anything but the usual. The allegation was that James Johnson had raped Mrs. Stella King in August 1892, *almost two years earlier.*

What the Fulton newspaper makes no mention of, but a Jefferson City paper reports, is that James Johnson was a hired hand on the farm of Mr. William King, and his wife, Mrs. Stella King, gave birth to a mulatto child the summer of 1893. Her husband eventually noticed that the baby did not look like him, and he sent his wife home to her family. It was at this point that Mrs. Stella King finally remembered that James Johnson had raped her nearly 24 months earlier. The Jefferson City news story about the matter begins, "A lynching occurred in Callaway County, near Guthrie, early Sunday morning, that would do credit to the worst and roughest locality in the state of Mississippi." It continues, "A woman who could remain silent two years after an assault, such as she charges, must have had some strong motive for trying to escape from the disgrace that had overtaken her."[22]Two other in-state newspapers differ in their coverage. One, far removed from the scene, published in Barry County, a locale in the southwestern section of Missouri bordering Arkansas, reports of the July 1894 lynching of Johnson, "The rape was said to have been committed in August 1892."[23] Much closer to the scene of the lynching, a newspaper, from Johnson County, Missouri, reports of James Johnson's mob murder, "Johnson was accused of criminally assaulting Mrs. William King two years ago, but had succeeded in avoiding arrest."[24] In July 1894, James Johnson was murdered on the false allegation of a woman who had consensual sex with him two years earlier.

At approximately this same time, Ida B. Wells (1862–1932), a courageous African-

American civil rights leader, women's suffrage advocate, and newspaper reporter, was touring England and lecturing on the lynching of black men in the South. According to a Portland, Oregon, newspaper, she "draws large audiences and the indignant expressions of the English press." The story continues, "Governor Stone of Missouri has addressed a letter to the *London Daily News* in which he asserts that in Missouri the colored people enjoy the same rights as the whites, and then adds the broad assertion that the same is true of all the Southern states and that Miss Wells has exaggerated."[25] Contrary to his assertion, she had not.

Governor Joel Stone was a good booster for his state and other former slave states. However, he was not blind to the very real danger a black man confronted when he was charged with a potentially capital offense against a white person. After Emmett Divers, a black male, was charged with the July 23, 1895, rape and murder of a 17-year-old white female, Mrs. John Cain, in Callaway County, on August 2, Governor Stone wrote the judge of this county's circuit court, John A. Hockaday: "I am led to believe there is danger of mob violence when the negro Emmett Divers is returned to Fulton.... [There is] a great deal of talk about the negro being taken from officers and burned." Governor Stone continued, "The people of the State have their eyes on Callaway County. It will be a great triumph for the law, and will add much to the already high character of your people, if they shall, in spite of provocation or persuasion, refuse to lend themselves to the cause of lawlessness."[26]

Once he was in their custody, the initial response of law enforcement officers in Callaway County was to make every effort to protect Divers from a mob. They moved him first to the Audrain County jail in Mexico; then he was placed in the Pike County jail in Bowling Green. Next, he was taken to a jail in Hannibal, and from this Marion County town, he was transferred to the Ralls County jail in New London.[27] Finally, he was moved to the city of St. Louis jail. Had he been able to secure a change of venue out of Callaway County, the odds are he would have lived to be legally executed. No change of venue took place.

When the time came to move Divers out of the St. Louis jail for his return trip to Callaway County, its citizens did not heed Governor Stone's admonitions. Divers's train ride on the Wabash Railroad to New Florence was expectedly uneventful. However, at this town, on August 15, 1895, he was removed from the train and placed in a surrey with a driver for the 35 mile journey to Fulton. Since members of a 1,000-person mob were guarding every possible road into the county seat, Fulton, any attempt to bring this man into a courtroom for any legal proceeding was doomed. The portion of the crowd who easily wrestled him from the four-wheeled pleasure carriage and hanged him from a bridge beam was a small part of the enormous group that wished to participate in the lynching of Divers. Once the far larger number of mob members learned, as the local newspaper notes, "that only a very few men had composed the lynching party, they became infuriated and their curses of rage and disappointment were heard on every hand." Once the coroner arrived and his jury brought in its usual verdict in such cases, death by parties unknown, Divers's body was loaded on a farm wagon, covered with straw, and approximately 300 men on horseback led a procession with the corpse into Fulton. The already dead black man was rehanged at the old fairgrounds. Next, the corpse was, as the local paper continues, "brought to town and hung to a telephone post on the north side of the courthouse, where thousands of people viewed the horrible, ghastly body, with black, disfigured face, with tongue protruding, and stiffened limbs. A more terrible sight was never witnessed in this community."[28] One local newspaper ran a story headlined, "A Strange Coincidence." In it the paper notes that 22 years before to the exact date of Divers's lynching on August 15, 1895, a Fulton mob lynched Peter Kessler, mortally wounding the sheriff and another man.[29]

The evidence against Emmett Divers for the rape and murder of the 17-year-old bride of two months was solid. When Divers was found shortly after the crime was discovered on July 23, he was covered with blood. The victim tore a buckle from his suspender, and a portion of his shirt was missing. These items were not a part of Divers's clothing when he was arrested; rather, they were found near the murdered woman. His shoes matched the bloody tracks leading from the crime scene. On the basis of the physical evidence, the sheriff moved him from one jail to another to prevent his being lynched shortly after the crime was discovered. Once he was finally safe inside the St. Louis city jail, Divers confessed to law enforcement officers that he had killed Mrs. Cain. His confession included this Q. & A.: "Q. Did you do it?" A. "Yes I did it." Q. "Why did you kill her?" A. "Because I did not want her to have the ring I had taken from her.... The door was open and I walked in. The woman was sitting by the bed cutting out quilt pieces.... She kept trying to fight me and I cut her throat." [30] Given the overwhelming evidence of Divers's guilt, securing a first-degree murder conviction against him in Callaway County Circuit Court would have been easy as pie. Nonetheless, the mob prevailed.

Pike was another northeastern Missouri County where black males were lynched during the last decade of the nineteenth century. The triggering event took place on June 5, 1898, when the city marshal of Clarksville boarded the tied-up excursion boat, *Ottumwa Belle*, in order to quell a disturbance that had erupted among some of its 250 African-American passengers. They had earlier boarded this boat in Quincy, Illinois, and Hannibal, Missouri. The ruckus was caused by Curtis Young, a passenger, getting into a fight with Lena Bryant. When she came ashore, he followed her, hit her, dragged her back onto the boat, and continued to beat her. The manager of the excursion came ashore and asked for help and the arrest of Curtis Young. S. Walter McLoan, city marshal of Clarksville, boarded the boat and arrested Curtis Young, and as the officer was about to depart with his prisoner, someone shouted that Young need not leave unless he wanted to. Almost immediately the prisoner pinioned his guard, and either Sam Young, brother of Curtis, or Robert Taylor, both black men, shot and killed McLoan.

Immediately after the shooting and the chaotic scattering of most passengers, a black barber on board pointed a pistol at Curtis Young's head and marched his prisoner ashore. He held him at gunpoint until the key to the city jail was fished out of McLoan's pocket and Curtis Young was confined in this facility. Soon, at least 50 white citizens had learned of the shooting and were on the scene. In addition to the arrest of Curtis Young, three other black males were arrested, Sam Young, Robert Taylor, and Charles Bohon. During the afternoon of June 5, all four were removed from the Clarksville jail, put on another river boat, taken up the Mississippi River a mile or so, landed, and interrogated concerning the shooting death of the city marshal.

None offered a satisfactory explanation of this incident, and the four men were returned to the Clarksville jail. At this point, the city of Clarksville relinquished custody of its *Ottumwa Belle* prisoners to the sheriff of Pike County. He procured six guards and the city furnished another six. In order to pacify the enraged citizens, the mayor of Clarksville explained to the townspeople that these men would receive a preliminary hearing the next morning. Nonetheless, at midnight, a mob of approximately 200 men surrounded the jail, demanded its keys from the sheriff, and unlocked its door. The mob took the Young brothers from the jail, marched them to a gravel road about one mile north of town, and hanged them to death from two walnut trees. At 7:30 A.M. the coroner arrived and in the presence of the hundreds of people, both black and white, who had gathered to observe the spectacle, cut down the swinging bodies. After the coroner and his jurors viewed the bodies, they were placed in a coffin and taken into town, where an inquest was held. Its verdict was the usual: "Curtis and Sam Young came to their death by being hung by parties unknown to us." Soon thereafter, the coroner impaneled another jury, and it inquired into the cause of the city marshal's death. Expectedly, the second coroner's jury found that the recently lynched black men, Curtis Young and his brother, Sam, bore responsibility for McLoan's death. As the local newspaper reports the matter, the finding of the second jury confirmed "the belief that the right parties had paid the penalty for committing such a cowardly deed." Robert Taylor, the jury held, was an accessory to the Young brothers' crime. When the northbound Burlington train came through town at 10:30 A.M. that June 6 morning, the sheriff boarded it with Robert Taylor in order to prevent the mob from dealing with Taylor as it had the Young brothers. Charles Bohon disappears from the news story, but presumably he was safely released, and Robert Taylor was also filtered out of the criminal justice system when a grand jury met in Bowling Green on Monday, June 7, 1898.[31]

The hanging of the Young brothers on June 6, 1898 was Pike County's first known lynching. In 1841, the sheriff of Pike County hanged a wedding gift, Slave Lewis, for the murder of his new owner. In 1911, Governor Hadley commuted Mert Holman's death sentence for a rape the convicted man never committed; Governor Stark finally paroled Holman in 1939. Other lynchings in Pike County took place in the first two decades of the twentieth century.

The final mob murder of a black male in northeast Missouri during the 1890s followed shortly after the lynching of the Young brothers in Pike County. It occurred in Macon County on June 30, 1898, when a mob, estimated at between 200 and 300 members, stormed the county jail in Macon at 12:30 A.M. The mob removed Henry Williams, a black male, and hanged him from a bridge, a Wabash Railroad viaduct. Williams was in jail on a charge of beating two daughters of Mrs. Ann Browitt in May 1898 and frightening two daughters of John Keochel, a blind broom-maker, in late June of that year. As the county history tells it, "Henry Williams, a negro ... had quite a while before been arrested for annoying some white girls, but ... had been acquitted." At the Keochel home, the intruder picked up a sack of flour, one that had a small hole in it, and tiny white specks linked the Keochel pantry to the home of Henry Williams. A detective noticed the flour trail, arrested Williams, and placed him in the jail. The mob removed him from it and lynched him. When the coroner and his jurors met and conducted the inquest, the jurors concluded, as the county history notes, "Henry Williams ... came to his death at Macon, Missouri, at the hands of two or three hundred men, whose names, identity and residence are to these jurors unknown."[32]

No known legal executions or lynchings of slaves took place in Macon County. However, in 1889 and again in 1898, black men were lynched in this county. Its executions were overwhelmingly the work of the Union Army during the Civil War. Apart from the legal execution, under state authority, of a white man for his wife's murder in 1896, Macon County's record, both official and unofficial, is of a reasonably peaceful place after the Civil War.

The lynching of blacks in southeastern Missouri during the 1890s involves five events. The earliest took place in Poplar Bluff, Butler County, on September 4, 1890. Approximately 36 hours earlier, on September 2, Tom Smith, a 25-year-old black male who was recently arrived in town from Hot Springs, Arkansas, got into an argument with his white employer, Mr. Allbright of the Gifford House. Smith was a porter at this establishment, and the disagreement involved a dime. Smith believed Allbright owed him this sum. The white man ordered the black outdoors; he left and when Mr. Allbright called him back, presumably to pay him the 10 cents, Smith returned a very angry man. He hit the white man with a rock in the back of the head, knocking him to the floor. Next he hit him over the head with a chair with sufficient force to break the chair. Between the rock and the chair, Smith rendered Allbright unconscious. However, the white man survived the attack.

Expectedly, Smith was soon arrested and lodged in the Butler County jail. A great deal of the news coverage of his lynching is devoted to the sturdy quality of the jail's locks. Needless to say, a mob gained entrance to the cell containing Smith, and eight to 10 of its members led him outside. The jail breachers were careful to relock this facility; they had no wish either to liberate or to hang any of its other prisoners, including William Harben. He was a white man, convicted of an 1888 first-degree murder in 1889, whose case was reviewed by the Supreme Court of Missouri. He was granted three respites by the governor, and finally legally executed in January 1892. The local newspaper quotes Harben that "Smith cried a little and expressed fear for his personal safety." Had the mob's motive been simply to save the taxpayers money, it would have also removed Harben and spared the people the cost of his room and board and the sheriff's fee for hanging him. However, Harben was white, and it is obvious that the mob thought he was entitled an enormous amount of due process.

Smith was a different matter; he was black and had struck and injured a white man. The mob, 150 to 200 persons strong, took him down Vine Street, out on a bridge, and hanged him from it with a new noose. Uncertain about whether his fall killed him, members of the mob riddled his body with gunshots. Afterwards, the paper notes, "There was not a weapon or tool of any kind that could be found about the jail or the place of execution. Everything had been carried away and not a sign left as evidence for ferreting out the guilty parties." The newspaper concludes that the town's best citizens disapproved of the lynching, and "it is not believed that a single man who took part in the mob is counted among our permanent citizens.... [It was composed of] a floating class of people who are always ready to join such a mob, if there are two or three to lead it."[33] Outsiders were convenient persons to blame for Butler County's first and only known lynching in its history.

The second lynching of a black took place in Clarkton, Dunklin County, on April 22, 1892. On that date, three masked men presumed to be African Americans went to the home of David Sims, also black, and shot and killed him. The three did not harm their victim's wife or another black male in the house; instead, they were, as the newspaper writes, "warned not to make an alarm. The men were tracked in a northern direction, but it is supposed they were negroes who committed the cowardly and infamous deed."[34] Nothing more is known of the matter, and the incident barely qualifies as a mob murder. Were there just one fewer person, two instead of three, it would not.

The third lynching of a black in 1890s southeastern Missouri took place in Valley Park, St. Louis County, on January 17, 1894. Not since the immediate aftermath of the Civil War was this county the scene of any known mob murder. John Buchner had recently been released from the Missouri State Penitentiary after serving a three year sentence for the rape of a black school teacher. On January 16, 1894, he allegedly raped Mrs. Albert Mingo, wife of a black farmer, early in the day, and 16-year-old Alice Harrison, daughter of a white farmer, late that same day.

The young white girl went to the home of a neighbor and related her experience; presumably, she knew her attacker. Soon the sheriff of St. Louis County, accompanied by a posse, went to Buckner's home and arrested him. The sheriff managed to convey his prisoner to the jail in Manchester; a judge placed him under a $1,000 bond and ordered that Buckner be taken to the county jail in Clayton. Fearing that a mob would wrestle the accused from him if he attempted to move him, the law enforcement officer decided to leave Buckner in the jail at Manchester until morning. An integrated mob of approximately 200 men formed about midnight. It was dispersed at the urging of several prominent citizens, but within another hour a second mob, made up of both black and white men, marched to the jail, overpowered its guard, pulled Buckner from his cell, placed a rope about his neck, seated him in a wagon, and returned him to Valley Park. There, at approximately 5 A.M. on January 17, 1894, Mrs. Albert Mingo, a black woman, identified him as her attacker on the previous day. The mob then took Buckner to the Frisco Railroad Bridge and hanged him from it. One newspaper reports of the matter, "Among the mob were many colored men, and they were wildly clamoring for Buckner's life."[35] His body was left hanging until 2 P.M. When it was cut down, the coroner's jury returned its usual verdict in such cases, as another newspaper records, "death by hanging at the hands of unknown parties."[36]

The fourth southeastern Missouri lynching of a black in the 1890s took place in Jackson, seat of Cape Girardeau County, on October 11, 1895, a Thursday, about 5 P.M. This event was set in motion on October 10, when 17-year-old Will Mance, also known as Will Henderson, allegedly attempted to rape a white girl, 14-year-old Minnie Rust. The girl's screams attracted a neighbor, Frank Long, who recognized the attacker as Will Mance, stepson of Howard Henderson. The sheriff and a city marshal went to Will Mance's residence and arrested him. The next day, both the 14-year-old victim and the neighbor who prevented her rape identified him, and the prisoner was returned to confinement. That evening, with a mob growing larger and larger outside the jail, the sheriff and a deputy attempted to remove Mance to a safe place. However, the mob captured him, took him to a pasture, and hanged him to death from a tree limb near the scene of his alleged crime. The mob's size was estimated at 100 members. The next morning, the coroner held an inquest; his jurors concluded, as a local paper notes, "that the negro was hung by parties unknown. The body hung upon the tree until ten or eleven o'clock when it was taken down by some negro men and buried, we understand, at the county's expense."[37] Mance's hanging is Cape Girardeau County's only known lynching.

The fifth and final lynching of a black male in southeastern Missouri took place in Union, Franklin County, on July 10, 1897, when a mob, estimated at 40 men on horseback and three or four in a wagon, took 23-year-old Erastus Brown from the county jail and hanged him to death from a willow tree near Villa Ridge. The lynched man was in jail awaiting court proceedings for his alleged attempted rape on July 2 of Anna Fehring, a 23-year-old white female. Franklin County saw one or two early lynchings of slaves (the record may be fused), one post–Civil War mob murder in 1865–66, the lynching of a horse thief in 1873, and the death of Erastus Brown in 1897. The known lynching record of this county ends in 1897.

This chapter concludes with a discussion of five cases that have previously been classified as lynchings of blacks in Missouri during the 1890s. For one reason or another, none were, and all are listed in Appendix 2. They are discussed by the section of the state in which they allegedly took place. Only one occurred in the southwest portion of Missouri. On January 21, 1894, near Verona, in Lawrence County, a black male raped Katie Jacob, a 12-year-old white girl, on her way home from Sunday morning church services. At least two in-state newspapers relate that *two* Negroes assaulted the child.[38] Two other newspapers located close to the scene of the attack state that *one* Negro raped a white child.[39] One in-state newspaper identifies "Pearl West, the negro brute who some time since assaulted Little Katie Jacobs near Verona" as arrested in Kansas City and taken to Lawrence County for trial. Its story ends, "There [is] strong talk of lynching."[40] It is perhaps from this statement that *100 Years of Lynchings* lists an unknown Negro as strung up in Verona, Missouri, on Jan. 22, 1894.

Nothing of the sort occurred. Twice a black man was brought before the child victim for identification. The first was one H.B. Barclay, an Alabama native. The local newspaper states that when Katie Jacobs "saw him [she] declared positively that he was not the man, and he was turned free."[41] A month or so later, a second black man, Pearl West, was brought before the victim; the newspaper states, "The little girl and others declared he was not the man."[42] Much to the young girl's credit and probably her honest parents, she made no identification. No lynching took place of anyone, black or white. The attack on her remained an unsolved crime.

No case of an incorrectly reported lynching of a black male is known from northwest Missouri in the 1890s. There are two from the northeast section during this decade. The first concerns John Hughes, a black male studying for the ministry. He was jailed in Moberly, Randolph County, on February 17, 1893, for making gross and indecent remarks to a young white woman, Drucie Sparkman. The newspaper did not publish the remarks. The next day, February 18, according to three newspapers, three brothers of the insulted girl entered the area of Hughes's cell and pumped multiple bullets into him. Their story concludes, Hughes "is not dead, but will probably die."[43] The local newspaper states that two brothers, Theodore C.A. and Samuel Sparkman shot Hughes in his cell, and "none of the wounds are dangerous, but the right leg would be stiff."[44] No person who lived after an attack on him is classified as a lynched person. The *Chicago Tribune*, *100 Years of Lynchings*, and Capeci include John Hughes as the victim of a lynching; they are in error.

The second incident from the northeast that does not rise to the level of a lynching concerns John North, a black farmer who eloped with Lena Diekamp, a 15-year-old white girl, in St. Charles County in late July or early August 1893. He was arrested in the city of St. Louis and returned to the jail in St. Charles. The charges for which he was taken into custody probably involved an illegal marriage. Missouri law punished the marriage of an eighth-part black person and a white person with two years in prison, or a fine of not less than $100, or three months in the county jail, or both a fine and imprisonment.[45] Whatever the basis for locking him in the county jail, a committee of white men was soon formed to lynch North, and it sent out approximately 100 invitations to the planned event: "Consider yourself invited to a necktie party tonight at the corner of Sixth and Clay at 10:30 P.M., Place of Business Second and Madison. Bring nerve and guns loaded for coon. Committee ... 8-3-93." One invitee, uninterested in joining this party, turned his letter over to the sheriff. Soon extra deputies were sworn in; 20 were stationed inside the jail, guarding its entrance; four additional deputies armed with Winchester rifles were posted at North's cell throughout the night, and other law enforcement officers patrolled the streets near the courthouse. Despite the fact that at least 150 armed men assembled for the purpose of lynching North, as the newspaper reports, these men "were standing across the street from the jail, waiting for someone to come along and command them to move on the jail." The headline says it all, "NO LEADER. Why a Mob at St. Charles Failed to Lynch John North."[46] This is an excellent example of life imitating art, as Twain writes in chapter 22 of *Huckleberry Finn*, "The pitifulest thing is a mob.... But a mob without any *man* at the head of it is *beneath* pitifulness."[47]

One of the final incidents from the 1890s that does not qualify as a Missouri lynching is reported as taking place in New Madrid County, Missouri, in five separate compilations.[48] It is fact that a New Madrid newspaper reports that two Negroes murdered a white man, Alex Loin, on Saturday, November 26, 1898, near Madrid Bend, for the purpose of robbing him. One of the culprits was captured and shot to death that same day near the scene of his crime, and the other escaped, only to be apprehended on a Monday evening in Dyersburg, returned to Madrid Bend, and hanged to death early Tuesday morning, November 29, 1898.[49] Another newspaper writes "that J. L. Loins, a farmer living across the Mississippi River in Kentucky, was murdered for money by two negroes, Saturday night [November 26].... One of the negroes has been captured and shot to death by a mob, which is now hunting for the other murderer."[50] The New Madrid paper reports the scene of the lynching was Madrid Bend and the second Negro was captured in Dyersburg. Any local resident would know their locations; outsiders would not. I contacted the prosecuting attorney of New Madrid County, Missouri, and he confirmed that Madrid Bend is not in the state of Missouri, it is in Kentucky.[51] Moreover, Dyersburg is in Tennessee. Missouri's only connection with this dual lynching—one that took place in an area where four states converge (Illinois, Kentucky, Missouri, and Tennessee)—is that it was reported in a newspaper published in New Madrid County.

Two other events reported in a Missouri newspaper and carried as in-state lynchings by the *Chicago Tribune* took place in yet another state. They are discussed in the next chapter, which deals with white victims of mob violence during the 1890s.

CHAPTER 9

White Victims, 1891–1899

The first 18 months of the 1890s yield no lynching of a white person in Missouri. As this decade began, all victims of Judge Lynch were African American. The first mob murder of a white man took place in the northwestern section of the state on August 31, 1891.

We begin in southwestern Missouri with the January 17, 1892, murder of Mrs. Joseph Goodley and her 11-year-old son near Kenoma, in Barton County. The murderer's motive may have been a grudge or robbery of a large sum of money he believed the husband had sent Mrs. Goodley. The killer thought that he had also ended the life of the nine-year-old Goodley daughter, but she survived and identified him as Robert Hepler, their 33-year-old hired hand, who lived one mile from their residence. Mr. Joseph Goodley, a prominent livestock dealer, was at the time of the crime in Cheyenne, Wyoming, on business with a railroad car of horses. When the homicides in his home were discovered, he was notified by telegram. He returned and is named as a member of the mob. Soon after Hepler's arrest, the prisoner was taken to the jail in Lamar, seat of Barton County. Talk of a lynching compelled its sheriff to take him for safekeeping to the jail in Nevada, Missouri, seat of the county immediately north of Barton, Vernon. Once Hepler was lodged in the supposedly safe facility, he acted insane and attempted to commit suicide by hanging himself in his cell. A prisoner in an adjacent compartment notified the sheriff, and he managed to cut Hepler's hanging rope, one that he had made from a blanket.

Mention has been made earlier of the train's importance in suppressing the number of mob murders in the last years of the nineteenth century. Such was not the case in Hepler's lynching. Rather, the railroad facilitated the event. On January 21, 1892, a mob of between 100 and 200 unmasked men arrived in Nevada on the eight o'clock Missouri Pacific passenger train from Lamar. The sheriff of Vernon County was confident that no attempt would be made to remove the Barton County murderer; as a result he had not bothered to so much as post a guard at the jail. When the train transporting the sizeable Barton County mob arrived in Nevada, its members went to the jail, put Hepler in a wagon, transported him to the village of Milo, and with their prisoner in tow, caught the southbound train back to Lamar. It arrived at 12:30 A.M., and within 25 minutes the mob hanged Hepler from a tree especially trimmed for his lynching in the northeast corner of the Barton County courthouse square on January 22, 1892.

As in the Butler County lynching of Tom Smith, in which a white man already convicted of murder was also not seized by the mob, so too in the lynching of Hepler, the mob took several ballots, and the majority was against pulling young Amos Avery from his cell in the Barton County jail and stringing him up with Hepler.[1] On September 22, 1891, 19-year-old Avery murdered 21-year-old James Miles in Barton County. The victim was from Prairie County, Arkansas, and he and two others were canvassing for a family photograph album published in Chicago. Sometime after the lynching of Hepler, the Barton County sheriff and four of his deputies lodged Avery in the Second Street jail in Kansas City. It is likely that both Avery's race and age helped him win the majority vote to allow the law, including an appeal to the Supreme Court of Missouri, to take its course. The lynching of young white boys was a rarity. Finally, Avery was returned to Lamar, and the sheriff of Barton County hanged him on May 24, 1893.[2]

Soon after the Barton County courtyard lynching of Robert Hepler, a mob murder took place in Marshfield, seat of Webster County. According to its county history, the death of Richard Cullen, on February 26, 1892, was its only lynching. I never discovered another in this county. The enmity against Cullen began after the body of four-year-old Clifford Vere Shaw was discovered in a well. The child was first noticed missing from his bed the night of February 22/23. He was the adopted son of Mr. and Mrs. Hiram Shaw. She had a 23-year-old son by a previous marriage, Richard Cullen. He was charged with his young brother's murder after discovery of his shoeprints in the snow from the family home to the abandoned well, which contained the little boy's body. The motive for the crime was the adult brother's jealousy and fear that the child would inherit Cullen's hoped-for share of the estate of his mother and stepfather.

Initially, Mrs. Shaw was jailed with her son and charged as an accomplice. When the coroner held his inquest, in the eyes of his jurors, she appeared indifferent to the loss of her young child. The Webster County prosecuting attorney first set the preliminary hearing for the last week in February, but community feeling against the accused principal, Richard Cullen, ran so high that the prosecutor postponed the first court proceeding in the case. The sheriff wished to take Cullen to the Greene County jail in Springfield for safekeeping, but he never made the journey. Groups of determined men guarded the roads and made his passage out of the county with Cullen impossible. On February 26 at approximately 10 P.M., an armed and masked mob, eventually numbering 150, gathered at the jail and demanded the keys from the sheriff. Despite the lawman's anticipation of difficulty in keeping Cullen alive and his procuring three heavily armed deputies to guard the jail, these law enforcement officers were no match for the mob. Its members included men armed with sledge hammers, if need be, to get at their victim. Under these circumstances, the sheriff surrendered the keys, and the lynchers soon had custody of Cullen. They led him out of the jail with a rope around his neck and hanged him to death from a maple tree limb near the east entrance to the Webster County courthouse. When he was asked if he had any last words, he is supposed to have replied, "Pull your rope." It was pulled. The mob's leader gave orders that the body was to hang there until morning, but by 11 P.M. it was cut down and taken inside the courthouse. Expectedly, Richard Cullen's mother was unharmed. She was quoted as remarking that she felt better with the knowledge that her son Richard was dead. She, too, shared the community's certainty that the mob hanged the actual killer of four-year-old Clifford Vere Shaw, a child so young that he was still wearing dresses.[3]

The next southwestern lynching was yet another Bald Knobber operation, and it took place in Taney County on March 12, 1892. It was set in motion when mentally ill John W. Bright murdered his wife, Matilda, in a jealous rage, by shooting her on March 1, 1892. He had earlier shot at a man named Jones; Bright thought him too friendly with Mrs. Bright. Their four small children found their mother's body; the oldest daughter alerted neighbors. Soon, these neighbors and many others were on the lookout for Bright. Approximately a week and a half after he shot his wife, Bright was captured, lodged in the county jail at Forsyth, and charged with first-degree murder. His preliminary hearing was set for March 12. However, the justice of the peace, W.H. Jones, did not hear all the evidence, so he continued the hearing until the next day. The prisoner was uneventfully returned to the Taney County jail. That evening the trouble, or as one of the lynchers termed it, the "fun," began. The mob agreed that the tree from which the Bald Knobbers had hanged the Taylor brothers seven years earlier would not be an appropriate place to string up Bright. Law enforcement officers could easily disrupt the operation there. The best place for Bright to die would be a large oak tree at the cemetery. Before the planners started to the jail for their victim, they took a Bald Knobber oath that they would kill anyone who revealed the identity of any member of the pack.

As the mob neared the jail, Deputy Sheriff George Williams grabbed the hat of one member of the mob, and he said to him, "George Taylor, I have got you spotted, damn you."[4] Shortly shots rang out, and the second one felled Williams. By the time a physician reached his body and attempted to get a pulse, there was none. Once more a law enforcement officer had died in the line of duty protecting a prisoner from a mob.

The mob easily enough sledge-hammered the jail door, breaking the padlock on it. The man Williams had recognized, Taylor, located Bright, tied a rope around his neck, and mounted him on horseback behind a man named George Friend. When the mob reached its cemetery destination, Friend helped force Bright off his mount. Soon, Bright's life was extinguished; his body was suspended by a rope. Afterwards, the sheriff ordered his men to cut it down. He conveyed it to Forsyth and deposited Bright's remains on the steps to the courthouse. On March 14, the coroner held his inquest regarding Bright's death; probably the jurors reached their usual verdict: death by hanging at the hands of unknown parties. No one particularly cared who killed him, but this was not true of the murder of Deputy Sheriff George Williams. Governor David Francis offered the maximum the law permitted him to offer, $300, for the arrest and conviction of the gang members. In due course, no fewer than 20 men were arrested and charged with first-degree murder. Governor Francis sent the attorney general of Missouri, John Wood, to assist in this large prosecutorial undertaking.

Of the 20 arrested, the circuit court judge of Taney County found probable cause to bind over 12 for grand jury indictment. One was released on a $10,000 bond, but the other 11 were held in the Greene County jail in Springfield and the Christian County jail in Ozark without bond. These prisoners managed to avoid being murdered by relatives of Bright on their return to Forsyth for their trial. The sheriff and two of his deputies transporting these 11 men passed out weapons, a gun for each unshackled prisoner. By arming the men who risked being lynched, the party reached Forsyth.

The Taney County prosecutor, James L. Davis, built his case against these multiple defendants by granting George Friend immunity in return for his testimony. The arrangement must have been highly informal because once Friend had immunity, he refused to testify. The upshot of all the to-do in Taney County produced no better results than earlier efforts to prosecute lynchers elsewhere in Missouri. Even when the case was tried in the county in which the lynching took place, the collateral damage of murdering a law enforcement officer was insufficient to secure a conviction. That a sheriff's deputy died in the line of duty did not change the rule that lynchers went unpunished in the county where they strung up their victim(s). The chief justice of the Missouri Supreme Court, Thomas Sherwood, called for an amendment to the state constitution. He knew that only by allowing the state to take a change of venue was there any chance of securing a conviction against lynchers. No change in the state constitution occurred.[5] The 1875 Missouri Constitution requires that the accused be tried "by an impartial jury of the county" in which the crime takes place. This precise language — "by an impartial jury of the county" — continues in the 1945 Missouri Constitution, and it remains Missouri law in 2008.[6] Bald Knobbers and other vigilante groups would have to be combated in other ways.

In-state news coverage includes at least six articles that appeared in a Johnson County newspaper.[7] Perhaps the most outlandish story is its last; one of the men arrested on charges of participating in the Bright-Williams mob murder filed a civil suit for false imprisonment, seeking $10,000 in damages from authorities such as the governor of Missouri, the sheriffs of several counties, and a Taney County justice of the peace.[8] Presumably, his suit did not succeed; but the fact that the arrestee had the audacity to file it argues that Bald Knobberism was still a force to be reckoned with in southwest Missouri as late as October 1892.

One Chicago newspaper, the *Daily Inter Ocean*, erroneously assumes that Bright was an African American. Its article begins with a naïve question, "Now that one of the men engaged in the lynching of a negro in Taney County, Missouri, has given the grand jury the names of all engaged in that outrageous affair, is Missouri justice strong enough to bring the lynchers to punishment?"[9] Although the *Chicago Tribune* slightly misdates Bright's lynching as March 14, not March 12, 1892, it correctly states his race, his offense (wife murder), and the place of his death, Taney County, Missouri.[10] The *Rocky Mountain News* strikes an optimistic note when it writes of the legal proceedings against the nine men charged "with the murder of Deputy Sheriff George Williams and the lynching of his insane prisoner, Bright.... The trial will last two weeks and some startling developments are expected."[11] Sadly, community approval and/or fear remained sufficiently strong in the county where the lynching took place to prevent any prosecutor, no matter how capable, from securing a conviction. That a good law enforcement officer died attempting to protect his prisoner was regrettable, but his death was insufficient grounds for sending any mob member to the Missouri State Penitentiary, or even to a county jail.

The final lynching event from 1890s southwest Missouri took place near Mountain Grove, Wright County. It is the only known lynching in this county. In the early morning hours of May 18, 1897, a mob of 20 respected farmers and other grey-haired men stormed the cabin of John Mitchell and his stepbrother, Jack Kaufman. The mob riddled the bodies of these men with multiple bullets in the presence of their wives and children. Earlier, mob members severely whipped another brother, Dave Mitchell, but he escaped with his life. The men shot on May 18 did not. According to the newspaper account of this dual lynching, the victims of it had, for at least a year prior to their deaths, engaged in petty thievery against their farmer neighbors, including stealing livestock such as hogs. One news story concludes that at least 10 arrests would be made in the next 10 days.[12] Presumably if any men were taken into custody, they were soon again at liberty.

When we turn to northwestern Missouri lynchings of the 1890s, there are six known, one more than in the southwest section from this same time period. The first took place in Lafayette County. Its triggering event was the 3:20 P.M. robbery on August 31, 1891, of the American Bank in Corder. Two men entered and obtained approximately $600. As they left the bank, the alarm was given; soon a city marshal and a deputy sheriff pursued them. One bank robber was captured in a cornfield after his horse was wounded; he gave his name as Andrew Murrell. Confusion exists regarding the actual name of the lynched Corder bank robber. In addition to Andrew Murrell, he was also known as Lon McFadden and Jesse Musser.[13] As the law enforcement officers were attempting to take the man they had arrested to the county jail in Lexington, they were overpowered by a mob of approximately 20 men. Its members seized Murrell, strung him up on a thorn tree, and riddled his body with bullets. One-half of the bank's money was found on his person. The other bank robber was never captured.

A ghoulish detail is preserved in a newspaper account of what train passengers on the Chicago and Alton Railroad would be able to see the next morning. The conductors and other trainmen were notified at Corder, as the paper notes, "that if they kept their eyes open they would 'see some unusual fruit on a tree a little way out of town.'" They saw, as the story's headline clarifies, "Murrell's Body Hanging in Full Sight of Alton Passengers."[14] As of 1957, a souvenir of the robbery remained at the bank, a wide-brimmed western hat with two bullet holes in it, the one worn by the captured holdup man.[15] A telephone call to the Corder Bank confirms that the hat, though remembered by current bank employees, is no longer in their workplace. It is officially lost. As expected, no one was so much as arrested, let alone prosecuted, for the lynching of the Corder bank robber.

Two men, James Nelson and Jesse Winner, were forcibly removed from the Lafayette County jail in Lexington on December 7, 1896. A mob, composed of 150 members, came from Ray County, overpowered the jailer, battered down the door, and conveyed its intended victims to just inside the Ray County line. According to one news account, when the leader of the lynchers was asked where he intended to string up the men who were now his and his followers' prisoners, he replied, "They were going to Ray County, so that Lafayette would not have the expense of burying them."[16] As a result, search parties from Lexington found these former Lafayette County jail inmates hanging from the limb of an oak tree with their hands tied behind them, inside Ray County. The lynchers' original plan had been to hang these men almost to death and then to throw them into a fire for their final throes. However, they had insufficient time for their original plan, and they were satisfied to allow them the ease of death by hanging.

The event which set this dual lynching in motion was Jesse Winner's October 28, 1896, murder near Richmond of his wife and two young children. James Nelson, a former hired hand of the Winners, assisted him. None of the press coverage clarifies the motive for such a horrendous crime, but clearly there were great difficulties in the marriage of the Winners and/or the father and husband suffered from extensive mental illness. Sometime after the killings, the bodies were discovered and the perpetrators confined in the Ray County jail in Richmond. By mid–November, Winner and Nelson, as a newspaper reports, "came near being mobbed the other night by angry citizens."[17] To avoid a successful repeat of the near-lynching, they were moved to an adjacent county jail, Lafayette's. Had they been moved to another adjacent county's lockup, that is the Jackson County facility in Kansas City, there would never have been a lynching. By the 1890s throughout western Missouri the Kansas City jail was known as the place "where men never get lynched."[18] At the time Nelson and Winner became Lafayette County jail inmates, at least eight mob murders had taken place within this county; its jail was easily breached.

Afterwards, the Lafayette County Prosecutor was firmly resolved to pursue the lynchers of Winner and Nelson. One newspaper quotes him as pronouncing, "If this is the last act of my life, I expect to bring the perpetrators to justice. To this end I shall ask the assistance of the attorney general and invoke the power of the state to see that such conspiracies against law are punished."[19] In this case, Lafayette County had dual jurisdiction with Ray. The crime began in one county with the kidnapping of Winner and Nelson, and it ended in another with their deaths; either was free to proceed. It is no surprise that even though the prosecution was, one presumes, held in a county adjacent to the one in which all the killings took place (the Winner family and the subsequent lynchings), the results were the same. Seven months later, a newspaper reports, "George J. Spense, of Richmond, the alleged leader of the mob that hanged Winner and Nelson near Lexington last December, was cleared by a jury recently."[20] Community approval and/or fear did not stop at the county line; both emotions spread into adjacent areas, and once more the leader of the mob and all its members escaped conviction and punishment.

Three other events took place in northwest Missouri during the 1890s. In Carroll County, 22-year-old Lewis Gordon, a white male, stopped by the farm house of the John Perretons during the day on March 11, 1892. Mrs. Perreton was home alone, and her visitor, described in news accounts as a tramp, asked for food. When informed that none was prepared, he ask for and received a glass of water, drank it, and assaulted the woman of the house. When she regained consciousness, she screamed so loudly that her husband heard her and hurried to her assistance. Soon the word spread, and a lynch mob was on the lookout for Gordon. The perpetrator was arrested at Wakenda, seven railroad miles east of Carrollton, the county seat. The sheriff dispatched deputies to bring him to the jail. The sheriff, fearing that a mob would snatch his high profile prisoner from him, waited until dusk and with two of his trusted deputies, hurried Gordon out of the west kitchen door of the jail. The law enforcement officers' intention was to secure Gordon in another county's jail by catching the Wabash evening train. Initially, their plan appeared to be working, but when the deputies reached the railroad track, 500 men were ready and waiting to make Gordon their prisoner. The scene suggests collusion between one or more law enforcement officers and the mob. How else could this prisoner's precise whereabouts be known? On March 12, 1892, the expected took place; Gordon was easily transferred from deputy to mob custody. Soon he had a rope about his neck. He asked his captors to notify his mother, a resident of Independence, Missouri, of his demise. His body hung from a telegraph pole for three hours before the coroner and sheriff together cut it down. One news story concludes, as most of the time period did when a white woman was raped, "the brutality of the assault and the mental anguish entailed by Gordon's horrible crime unite to render her recovery doubtful.... Death may follow, but universal hope is expressed that her age and vital force will win the fight for her." [21]

Carroll County's known lynchings are three: Slave George for the murder of his owner in 1855; a black man, Jim Callaway, for rape in 1875; and Lewis Gordon, a white man, for rape, in 1892. With one exception in the 1890s, death sentences returned in this county were commuted by various governors.[22] That one, William Taylor's, was actually carried out in Carrollton is much to the credit of vigorous and intelligent law enforcement officers. With the aid of excellent railroad service, they repeatedly outwitted a mob intent on lynching the Taylor brothers. Since their crimes were committed in Sullivan County, a locale in northeastern Missouri and their case came to Carroll on a change of venue, it is discussed later in this chapter.

Caldwell was another northwest Missouri county in which a mob put to death a white man, Redmund Burke, aged approximately 55 years, on September 17, 1893. His offense in the eyes of his Breckinridge neighbors was wife and child abuse, coupled with withholding necessities from his family. His wife had left him, presumably with her young son, and moved to Kansas City, where she had a married daughter. Early on the morning that Burke was found dead in his bed, neighbors heard screams. The back door of the residence was broken open, and his body was found with a piece of flour sack twisted about his neck. Fastened to a window was an unusual message for a Missouri lynching. As the county seat newspaper reports the matter, it read, "Three days to leave — or worse — Klu Klux."[23] The coroner's inquest produced the expected result, as this same newspaper reports, "The deceased came to his death by strangulation, by persons unknown."[24] Caldwell County was the scene of known lynchings only in the 1890s. Both mobs murdered men, one white, and the other black, who mistreated their families. The white man's relatives survived the abuse; the black's did not.

The final lynching of a white man in northwest Missouri during the 1890s took place in Clay County. On September 10, 1898, Benjamin Jones, aged 68 years, raped 11-year-old Annie Montgomery. He took the child to the local fair, and, probably drunk, he attacked her in the buggy on the way home. Expectedly, the weeping child told her parents what had happened to her as soon as she returned home. Her father quickly relayed news of the crime to a constable; the lawman soon arrested Jones. Some enraged citizens wished to kill the old man on the spot, but the constable was permitted to lodge him in the county jail in Liberty. The next evening, after 10:30 P.M., a crowd of approximately 75 men wearing white and black masks, with the usual sledge hammers, took their victim from the jail and hanged him to death on the courthouse lawn. The sheriff and his deputy, Ed Cave, arrived 30 minutes later and saw the corpse of Benjamin Jones dangling in the air. Several months earlier, these law enforcement officers had outsmarted a mob that wished to lynch William Foley, a Clay County man. His first trial, for the murder of his mother and sister, resulted in a hung jury. When he was retried the jury brought in a death sentence, but the Supreme Court of Missouri overturned it on June 14, 1898, and awarded him a third trial. Many Clay County citizens were angry at what they perceived as a travesty of justice, and they were intent on lynching Foley. Capable lawmen managed to lodge him in the jail in Kansas City. At his third trial, on a change of venue to Platte County, Foley was acquitted in March 1899.[25] Obviously, when a mob was disappointed that its prey escaped on an earlier occasion, it was especially determined that its next intended victim not be so lucky. Benjamin Jones was not.

There is one known lynching of a white person in northeast Missouri in the 1890s. In Rhineland, Montgomery County, on September 2, 1896, a tramp, Thomas Larkin, who later gave his residence as New York, raped an 11-year-old girl, Alta Gammon. He was quickly arrested and confined in the jail at Rhineland. By the next evening, September 4, an angry mob of masked men was not deterred by the guards refusing its members admission to the jail. The lynchers broke down the jail door, grabbed Larkin, took him to a tree near the town, and hanged him to death from one of its limbs. The coroner's inquest followed,[26] and its results were surely the usual, death by hanging at the hands of parties unknown to the coroner's jurors.

Stoddard County was the only scene of southeastern Missouri lynchings in the 1890s. The first occurred on March 1, 1892, near Bloomfield. The events which led to this mob murder began on February 27, when Marshal Sprinkle of Dexter, Missouri, was placing Amos Miller under arrest. An unknown person attempted to rescue him, and two men, A.J. Cooper and Tom Toole, began assisting the officer. Suddenly, a general gun battle erupted. Cooper was killed; Toole had his finger shot off; the unidentified man who sought to rescue Miller was wounded and shot himself to prevent his arrest, and City Marshal Sprinkle, shot three times, died several days later. Miller, though wounded, escaped, only to be subsequently recaptured.

When Sprinkle died on February 28 or 29, Bloomfield citizens held a mass meeting at city hall. At it, they raised a reward of $500, and they also telegraphed Governor David Francis, requesting that he offer an additional $300 for the arrest and conviction of Amos Miller, the man whom they held responsible for the law enforcement officer's death. The attendees also requested bloodhounds to track Miller, and additional posses were soon on the lookout for him. A Dunklin County sheriff's deputy captured him near Malden. Shortly, the much-wanted Amos Miller was lodged in the Stoddard County jail at Bloomfield. The evening of March 1, four armed and disguised men knocked at the sheriff's door at the jail and demanded the keys to Miller's cell. Threatened with death if he did not relinquish these keys, the sheriff gave them to the four men; they dragged Miller from his cell with a rope around his neck to a tree just beyond the city limits. At this locale, approximately 50 men awaited him. After the mob hung Miller to death from a tree limb, the body remained suspended for the next 10 hours. The coroner's inquest determined the deceased came to his death by hanging at the hands of persons unknown to his jurors. Afterwards, Miller's body was released to his friends for burial.[27]

The final nineteenth century lynching in Missouri, also the second and last known in the history of Stoddard County, took place on November 16, 1899. Five days earlier William Huff shot and killed Andrew Melton. He was arrested and lodged in the jail in Bloomfield. That same evening the mob removed him from the jail and put him to death, probably by hanging him. As he was being led out of the jail, he called out the names of two men whom he recognized. Several weeks later, William and John Demint, the men whose names Huff spoke, were indicted for his murder. The news account states of them: "They are both reputable citizens and stand high socially in the county."[28] The odds are overwhelming that charges against both these accused lynchers were soon dropped.

One known aftermath of Huff's lynching survives. The same evening Huff was lynched, another Stoddard County murder occurred; 19-year-old Elijah Moore shot and killed his father, an abusive minister, while he slept at 3:30 A.M. The son was arrested, indicted, tried in the county of his crime, found guilty of first-degree murder, and sentenced to death. He appealed his conviction, and the Supreme Court of Missouri reversed. It ruled that the son's confession of his crime was involuntary. The sheriff used a threat, as the appellate court noted of "the Huff matter," to obtain a confession from Elijah Moore. According to this appellate decision, the sheriff told his young prisoner, "There is a mob in the streets and one in your county, and by God I can't save you unless you do what I say." The court ruled that a confession "made under threats, either expressed or implied, of mob violence in case defendant failed to confess to the crime charged ... is wholly inadmissible."[29] The next year this same court made clear that the confession of a young black man, General Armstrong, to the rape of a white female, also under threat of mob violence, was admissible. At this time Missouri's highest court allowed such a threat to extract an admission if the accused was a Negro. Thirty years later, when the threat of a lynch mob contaminated the case, it reversed the death sentence of a black man.

The discussion of white men falsely reported as put to death by mobs begins with a sketchy account in the southwestern section, in a Henry County newspaper. The story quotes a dispatch from the *Globe-Democrat* in St. Louis to the effect that two men, on Sunday, October 27, 1894, discovered the swinging remains of a man hanging from a tree near Roscoe, St. Clair County. They reported their discovery at a nearby farmhouse, where they informed the man who answered the door of their find. Upon receipt of their news, he laughed and replied, "The people around here have organized to hang all the thieves. I suppose this is the first victim."[30] This lacks sufficient information to classify it as an actual lynching.

The only detailed account of a southwestern lynching that did not occur was set in motion by Martin Crawford, aged 39 years, when he attempted to rape 15-year-old Miss Mary Tuckley. He was a section foreman on the Missouri Pacific Railroad. On July 26, 1896, she took a train from Kansas City with the intent of departing it in Versailles, seat of Morgan County, but she got off at the wrong place. The conductor arranged for Crawford to drive the young lady, presumably in a buggy, to Versailles, and he tried to assault her en route. She reported the incident to the authorities, and he was arrested later that same day. On Monday, his preliminary hearing was held in Versailles, and he was bound over to the Morgan County Circuit Court for trial. Upon posting a bond of $5,000, he was permitted to return to his home. At noon at home in Versailles, he died of a heart attack on July 27, 1896. A local newspaper reports, "He had complained of heart disease for some time, and it is supposed that the excitement produced by the charge made against him caused his death.... There is no truth whatever in the statement that was published in a number of papers that he was lynched."[31] A Kansas City paper correctly reports that Martin Crawford "died ... while sitting in a chair at home."[32] Nonetheless, stories such as one run in a Salt Lake City, Utah, paper apparently appeared in newspapers nationwide: "The assault was attempted a few miles from Versailles. The meeting of two men [unnamed] in the roadway alone prevented Crawford from succeeding. Crawford escaped but was arrested Saturday at Tipton. Sheriff Lumpee started for Versailles with the prisoner, but was met by an unmasked mob, who took Crawford from him and hanged him to a tree."[33] On the basis of fanciful stories such as the above, the *Chicago Tribune* ran as a completed lynching, "July 27, 1896, Martin Crawford, attempted rape, near Tipton, Mo." The 1919 NAACP list includes "Crawford, M. near Tipton, Moniteau Co. ... Attempted Rape," and Capeci follows suit.[34] All three place this lynching that never occurred in the wrong county. Moniteau is adjacent to Morgan County, and a newspaper in Moniteau County accurately reported the cause of Crawford's death, a heart attack.

In the northwest section in 1892, in a Johnson County newspaper, the headline reads, "STARTLING! HORRIBLE DISCLOSURE. The town of Knob Noster on the verge of another conflagration! Theft, Arson, Murder." The story begins, "Jonathan Shockley and Henry Wills have been taken and HUNG." The account ends with the punch line: "The human fiends are dead! Dead! Dead! (?) April First."[35] None of these terrible events had taken place, but so common was this newspaper's reporting of lynching statewide and so frequent the occurrence of mob murders elsewhere in the United States that the shaggy dog story about an imaginary lynching of two white men was not inappropriate humor at that time.

From northwestern Missouri, there is one other known false report of a mob murder of a white man in the 1890s. It concerns Silas Fargo. He was the foreman at a blacksmith shop that burned on October 1, 1896, in Liberty, Clay County. Earlier, he had been fired for drunkenness and missing work. Initially, he confessed to the arson of his employer's shop, but he later repudiated his confession. He was subsequently tried, and on November 12, 1897, the jury came in with a not guilty verdict, but among many Clay County residents the belief persisted that he was guilty. Five days after his acquittal, a mob calling itself "the Clay County Benevolent Association" rode into Liberty and requested that the Liberty Electric Light Company turn its power off by 11. The lights went off as requested. Once the mob was under cover of darkness, it proceeded to Silas Fargo's home, attempted to break down its door, and shot and seriously wounded him."[36] However, it did not kill him. A Kansas City paper reports that Fargo "stated to Deputy Sheriff Ed Cave that he would be ready to leave town as soon as he was able to travel. He did not, he said, want to see any of his assailants punished."[37] The *Chicago Tribune,* the NAACP report, and Capeci list Silas Fargo as murdered by a mob on November 18, 1897.[38]

Likewise, in the northeastern section of the state, in Ralls County, Cecil Layland was charged with attempting to rape a young lady named Crome in June 1896. A warrant was sworn out for his arrest, but he could not be located. On June 29, his neighbors found his body hanging from a tree limb in the woods. According to an adjacent county newspaper, "Some of them thought a mob lynched him; others that he committed suicide."[39] Despite the uncertainty as to the cause of Cecil Layland's death, the *Chicago Tribune,* the NAACP report, and Capeci include him as a victim of lynching. All three slightly misdate his death and report it as taking place on June 30, 1896, near Hannibal [Marion County], Missouri."[40] They confused the date and place of its newspaper mention with the date and place of what might have been a suicide.

The discussion of white men reported as put to death by Missouri mobs in the 1890s ends with a lynching that did take place on February 27, 1894, but not in Missouri. Again, the *Chicago Tribune* and the NAACP report list Anderson Carter and Bud Montgomery, accused of murder, as lynched in West Plains, Howell County, Missouri.[41] An in-state newspaper relates a somewhat different story. These men were shot to death in their jail cell at Mountain Home, Arkansas. The mob came from Ozark County, Missouri, and Fulton and Baxter counties, Arkansas. Mountain Home is the seat of Baxter County. In all, three men, the two lynched and Bud Carter, son of Anderson Carter, allegedly killed Hunter Wilson in Baxter County on December 18, 1893. Their motive was robbery; $1,100 was taken from the victim's home. The man whom the mob spared confessed the criminal activity and assisted law enforcement officers in recovering most of the money. According to the in-state newspaper, the lynching took place on February 26, not February 27, 1894.[42] There is no extant newspaper from West Plains or any other town in Howell County, Missouri, that is contemporary with the lynchings in Mountain Home, Arkansas. Most likely, a West Plains newspaper covered the story of a mob murder immediately south in Arkansas.

Two other happenings in 1890s Missouri are worthy of mention. The first has been referenced earlier in this chapter's discussion of Carroll County's lynchings. On May 10, 1894, in Sullivan County in northeastern Missouri, the Taylor brothers, William and George, intended to murdered the entire Meeks family; it consisted of Gus, his pregnant wife Delora, and their three children, 18-month-old Mamie, four-year-old Hattie, and six-year-old Nellie. Their motive was to prevent the father and husband from testifying against William Taylor on charges of stealing cattle. Nellie Meeks survived and lived to tell and retell the story of how her entire family was murdered.[43] The Taylor brothers were captured in Arkansas the next month. Without train service, it is unlikely that either would have lived to be legally sentenced to death. When the train on which they were passengers arrived at Brookfield, Linn County, a mob of 1,000 men was organized and ready to lynch the sheriff's prisoners. However, lawmen got off the train with the Taylors 30 miles east of Brookfield and locked them in the Macon County jail in Macon City. Two hundred determined mob members mounted horses in Brookfield and started for Macon City, and 50 others caught a train to this town. Meanwhile, the sheriff, informed of the mob's intended arrival time in Macon City, boarded a southbound train with his prisoners; on the sheriff's signal to the engineer, the train with the Taylors as passengers pulled away from the depot just as the train with 50 lynchers reached the depot. The sheriff's train went south to Moberly, Randolph County, and then west to St. Joseph, a town with a sturdy jail, in a county, Buchanan, whose only known mob murders took place in 1850 and 1933. The Taylors had several trials, including one on a change of venue to Carroll County. In Carrollton, they were found guilty of four counts of first-degree murder and sentenced to death. The Supreme Court of Missouri affirmed the verdict; two weeks before their scheduled hanging, they escaped. George was never found, but William was recaptured and hanged on April 30, 1896.[44] It seems unimaginable that the sheriff of Sullivan County could have protected the Taylors from one mob of 1,000 members and others of 200 and 50 without the aid of multiple trains. Had he attempted to lodge his prisoner in a horse-drawn carriage, one of the mobs after these men would have gotten them and made short work of the Taylor brothers.

This chapter concludes with a mention of one Missouri legislator's bill to reduce lynchings in his state. Joab Nicholas was elected in 1898 to represented Nodaway County in the Missouri General Assembly; he served one term.[45] His home county was the scene of lynchings in 1874, 1884, and 1931. Clearly, he disapproved of such lawlessness. In late winter 1899, he introduced a startling bill; it allowed sheriffs or jailers to arm prisoners in danger of being lynched. Representative Nicholas explained the purpose of his bill: "I would give the accused man at least a chance to defend his life, and if he must die at the hands of a lawless mob, I would let him have the satisfaction of taking a few of them with him into the next world." The sheriff or jailer who refused to give a threatened prisoner a 40 caliber revolver and 49 cartridges would be liable to a fine of $500 to $1,000 and dismissal from office.[46] Perhaps the idea of arming threatened prisoners came to Representative Nicholas when he learned that the sheriff of Taney County had protected his prisoners from relatives and friends of John Bright, lynched in 1892, by giving them guns as the sheriff conveyed them in a wagon to Forsyth for their trial in 1893. It will come as no surprise that Representative Nicholas's bill to curb lynchings never became Missouri law. What is startling is a major eastern newspaper's editorial approval of it.[47]

As the next chapter demonstrates, lynchings in Missouri, already on the decline, continued to be fewer and fewer throughout the successive decades of the twentieth century, but the percentage of African Americans murdered by mobs here continued to increase.

CHAPTER **10**

Racism as Scholarship to Justify Violence: 1900–1909

Lynchings in Missouri declined between the last decade of the nineteenth century and the first decade of the twentieth: 31 lynchings between 1890 and 1899 decreased to 19 between 1900 and 1909. However, what is more startling than the decrease in numbers is the new century's increase in the percentage of blacks murdered by mobs. Between 1866 and 1889, significantly more whites (89) than blacks (30) were lynched in Missouri; between 1890 and 1899, three more blacks (17) than whites (14) were victims of mobs. Then suddenly it was a new century. During the first decade of the 1900s, there were 16 known mob murders of blacks and only three of whites. This is the smallest number of whites lynched here since the 1840s, a time from which extant records are not plentiful. By the 1900s, there is a far greater likelihood that a newspaper from these years, preserved on microfilm, would carry a lynching than one that managed to survive from two decades before the Civil War. It seems obvious that the numbers of known lynchings in the 1900s more closely match the actual numbers than in the 1840s, when only two records of white persons being murdered by a mob have survived. It is fact that between 1900 and 1909 the percentage of lynched blacks increased so dramatically that they represented 84 percent of the total. Equally important, of the 45 persons legally executed here between 1900 and 1909, 19, including four executed for rape, were black (42 percent) and 26 were white (58 percent). The mindset of this decade clearly indicates that white persons were believed to be more deserving of due process than blacks.

One factor that was not a cause of animosity toward blacks in this state was their numbers. The percentage of Missouri's population that was African American continued to decline: 5.19 percent in 1900 became 4.78 percent in 1910.[1] Moreover, black residents of this state were not equally spread among its 114 counties. As Greene, Kremer, and Holland note, "By 1910 nearly 67 percent of Missouri's blacks lived in cities, almost three times the national average."[2] As repeatedly emphasized, there were no lynchings in the city of St. Louis after its solitary event in 1836, and none in Kansas City after its only one in 1882, the same day Jesse James was murdered. In 1901, one of the most horrific, involving three almost certainly innocent men, took place in Lawrence County, an area with an African-American population of .3 percent In contrast, Thompson lists 11 black victims of lynching between 1900 and 1909 in Tunica County, Mississippi; the percentage of its population that was Negro in 1910 was 90.7 percent.[3] The fear of sheer numbers helps to explain Mississippi's lynchings of blacks, but black population density will not account for the mob murder of African Americans here in the early years of the twentieth century.

By the 1900s, respectable opinion toward blacks had become poisonous. Most likely a misapplication of the writings of Charles Darwin explains this matter. Some surviving group or race had to be more fit than another, or so it was believed at the time. It is fact that white university professors, medical doctors, economists, and other sages spewed forth hateful comments about African Americans. In 1902, the American Economic Association published a study which blamed the Negro's African heritage — not slavery — for what it called his dominant traits: "indolence, carelessness, brutality, deception, and passion."[4] Authorities on the Negro stressed his "sexual fury." One estimated, as Newby notes, "that more than 98 percent of all Negro men were 'socially impure' and that at least 95 percent had gonorrhea."[5] Newby makes clear that the "achievement of scientific racism was to strengthen this popular prejudice by clothing it in a mantle of academic and scholarly authority."[6] In 1903, an editorial appeared in a medical journal, "Genital Peculiarities of the Negro." Its author asserted that "among negroes the virile organ ... often reach[es] massive proportions.... The genital characteristics coupled with utter contempt and cynical disbelief in the existence of chastity, together with his stallion-like passion and entire willingness to run any risk ... renders the negro the menace of the rural South."[7] That same year the author of another medical journal article, Dr. William Lee Howard, proclaimed of the African American, "Freedom from control of a superior race, thirty years of attempted education, has resulted in the increase of sexual crimes and a decided revision to savage lust."[8] Robert Bennett Bean, a physician, anthropologist, and professor of anatomy at the University of Virginia, concluded in articles published in 1906 that the peculiar development of the Negro's brain caused "sexual excitement, anger, or vexation."[9] Historians, such as Columbia University's William Archibald Dunning in an article published in 1907, determined that the emancipation of slaves dramatically increased "the hideous crime against white womanhood."[10] The retired U.S. Army physician, R.W. Shufeldt, in his aptly entitled 1907 book, *The Negro: A Menace to American Civilization,* described the African American in these terms: "Everything about him, mentally, morally, and physically, is undesirable in the highest degree."[11] The Missourian Charles Carroll, author of *The Negro a Beast* (1900) *and The Tempter of Eve* (1902), argued, among much else, that the natural stupidity of the Negro can be demonstrated by weighing his brain. In Carroll's chart, entitled "State of Hybridization," pure whites, on average, have brains that weigh 1,424 grams; the brains of those three parts white weigh 1,390, and so on until those that are pure Negroes, on average, have brain weights of 1,331.[12] Most of this author's rambling text does not concern cranial matters; rather, it deals with Biblical affairs. He states, "The Bible is simply a history of the long conflict which has raged between God and man, as the result of man's criminal relations with the negro."[13] In Carroll's view, Eve's tempter was not a serpent, it was a Negro-ape. David M. Friedman summarizes Carroll's novel interpretation of how Adam and Eve came to depart paradise: his "scenario transformed the presumably red apple of Scripture into a large black penis and redefined the cause of man's fall from grace as sex with an animal."[14]

What of the clergy's views on lynching? Throughout the antebellum period, rural Missouri preachers justified slavery as "ordained of God."[15] They assured their slave-owning parishioners: "God has, nowhere in his revelation to man, mentioned slaveholding as an evil.... Legitimate human authority has sanctioned slavery."[16] Years after the "peculiar institution" had ended, the silence of the Southern Protestant churches, especially the Baptists, on mob murders of blacks led a 1920s commentator, Jerome Dowd, himself a Southerner, to conclude, "One would suppose that they did not regard lynching as comparable to the sin of dancing, playing cards, or going to a theater."[17] Obviously, the condemnation of the mob murders of blacks from white pulpits in former slave jurisdictions was at best anemic in the early years of the twentieth century.

A single event took place on October 16, 1901, which nicely illustrates the average white person's opinion of African Americans. Today, with a U.S. president who is an African American, this get-together would scarcely be newsworthy. At the time, it shattered precedent. A Memphis newspaper termed it, "The most damnable outrage which has ever been perpetrated by any citizen of the United States."[18] On this date, Theodore Roosevelt, our 26th president, invited Booker T. Washington to dinner. He was the first president in American history to entertain an African American. Lincoln had several White House meetings with Frederick Douglass in 1863 and 1864, but the interchanges between them were confined to the president's office.[19] TR's invitation was social, and no one had to guess who had come to dinner. The newspapers shouted this black/white encounter from the rooftops. In South Carolina, U.S. Senator Tillman reacted to the news in this fashion: "The action of President Roosevelt in entertaining that nigger will necessitate our killing a thousand niggers in the South before they will learn their place."[20] If scientists, economists, historians, medical doctors, and U.S. senators considered African-Americans objects of utter contempt as the twentieth century commenced, it is no wonder that the percentage of mob victims who were black in Missouri dramatically increased. Given all their historical baggage, including being the alleged cause of mankind's expulsion from the Garden of Eden, lynching blacks made sense to whites.

We begin, as earlier, in the southwestern section of the state. In the nineteenth century, this area of Missouri was the scene of either few or no lynchings of African Americans from the late 1860s through the end of the nineteenth century. Between 1901 and 1906, southwestern Missouri had seven, and all the victims were black. The earliest were the mob murders of three blacks within 24 hours in Pierce City, Lawrence County. This horror began with the discovery, on August 18, 1901, that Miss Geshel Wild, a young white woman, had been thrown off a culvert into a ditch and murdered on a Sunday as she was returning to her home from morning church services. Her body was found approximately one-half mile from the business section; her throat had been cut nearly ear to ear. According to one news story, her brother found her body near the railroad tracks. Other papers credit a farmer viewing the crime and seeing a Negro running from the scene. The assumption that only rape could explain the motive for her killing was almost instantaneous with the news of her death. When word came to the city, the tolling of the fire bell summoned an enormous crowd. As the crowd learned about Geshel Wild's death, a Will Roark stated that he had seen a black sitting on a culvert shortly before the crime was committed. The coroner held an inquest that same day, and three days later, his six jurors had not delivered a verdict regarding the perpetrator(s) of the crime. This absence of even the most rudimentary evidence regarding the young lady's killer(s) did not delay the arrest of two black men. According to the city newspaper, Will Godley, "a notorious negro," and

Eugene Barnett were arrested "on suspicion." By Monday evening, August 20, a mob estimated at 1,000 armed men went to the city jail, broke down its door, and put a rope
around Will Godley's neck. When he refused to confess that he had murdered Miss Wild,
the mob took him to the Lawrence Hotel, tied a rope to its awning, strung him up, and
fired bullets into his body/corpse. The Pierce City newspaper reported that a terrified
Barnett stated that a fellow named Flavors murdered Miss Wild.[21] The *Lawrence Chieftain* noted, "It is not claimed [Will] Godley killed the young girl, but his reputation was
of the worst." Meanwhile, according to the *Chieftain*, Barnett gave the mob a different
name; it was either Joe Lark or a man named Jim Starks, both railroad porters. Once
Barnett told this story, the authorities managed to obtain his release from the mob, and
they took him to the Lawrence County jail in Mount Vernon for safekeeping.

The inhuman fury of the crowd was not appeased by the lynching of Will Godley.
After the mob hanged and shot him, it went to the Pierce City home of Pete Hampton,
identified in the local paper as "a notorious negro criminal." Someone inside this residence may or may not have fired on the mob, but if so, no member of it was harmed.
However, this 1,000-person gathering set fire to Pete Hampton's house and burned it to
the ground. In its charred remains were found his body and that of French Godley, father
of Will Godley. For good measure, the mob also burned four other residences of African
Americans. The remaining Negroes in Pierce City ran for their lives; some were unable
to pack household goods. By Thursday, August 22, the Pierce City paper sums up the
events: "It is reported that there is not now a colored person left in Pierce City."

As for the men whom Gene Barnett confessed were Miss Wild's killers, one, Joe Stark,
was arrested and taken to the Greene County jail in Springfield. He was believed, as the
local paper reports, "to be entirely innocent." When Stark was tried for Geshel Wild's
murder in Lawrence County Circuit Court, he was acquitted.[22] The other, Joe Lark, was
arrested and held in Tulsa, Indian Territory. Meanwhile the citizens of Pierce City offered
a $1,000 reward for, as the local paper states it, "the capture of the real murderer." The
purse was anticipated to reach as high as $2,000.[23] By the end of August, Governor
Alexander Dockery had offered an additional $300 for the arrest of the murderer of Miss
Geschel Wild of Pierce City.[24] In September 1901, another local paper pronounced of the
riotous and indiscriminate behavior of the white mob against the town's black citizens,
"There is no city in the great state of Missouri that has treated its negro population with
higher considerations than Pierce City."[25] This hyperbolic statement is cast into consid-
erable doubt by population figures. By 1910, the percentage of the population in Lawrence
County that was black was .3 percent; 99.7 percent of it was white.[26]

A pogrom of this magnitude against the African-American community in Pierce
City, Missouri, did not escape the attention of out-of-state newspapers. Both the *New
York Times* and the *Hartford Courant* in Connecticut gave it front page coverage.[27] Among
many others who learned about these awful events was a famous Missouri native, Mark
Twain. He wrote a scorching essay about these Pierce City happenings entitled, "The
United States of Lyncherdom." It begins, "And so Missouri has fallen, that great state.
Certain of her children have joined the lynchers, and the smirch is upon the rest of us....
The tragedy occurred near Pierce City.... Lynching has reached Colorado; it has reached
California; it has reached Indiana — and now Missouri."[28]

It is nothing if not amazing that Twain somehow managed to avoid learning that the lynching deaths of three Negroes in Pierce City, on August 19, 1901, were not the first in the state of his birth and childhood. They numbered at least in the 190s of known lynchings in Missouri. The fact is that this wonderful writer, the "Lincoln of our literature," as his recent biographer, Fred Kaplan, describes him, left Missouri as a young man. In his home county of Marion, or so a newspaper reports, a mob lynched a man for stealing a horse in October 1859. By this early date, the Clemens family no longer resided in Hannibal. Twain's father, John Clemens, died in 1847; his sister, Pamela Clemens, was married in September 1851, and she and her husband opened a grocery business in St. Louis. Soon his mother and brother, Henry, arrived in this same city. By late 1854, another brother, Orion, had married and moved to his wife's hometown of Keokuk, Iowa. As for Twain himself, his lifelong wanderlust began early. As Kaplan writes, "In 1853 at seventeen years of age, he was restlessly ready and eager to leave Missouri."[29] He carried with him wonderful memories of his childhood in Hannibal. As noted in Chapter 7, in *Huckleberry Finn*, published in February 1885, he sets the lynching bee that failed in Arkansas. Somehow, Twain managed until the Pierce City lynchings in 1901 to remain unaware of the sizeable number of mob murders that had taken place in his native state. According to his biographer, Twain's original intention in 1901 was to write a book to be entitled *History of Lynching in America*, or in the alternative, *Rise and Progress of Lynching*. He planned to hire researchers nationwide to locate newspaper accounts of these events. Then he changed his mind; he realized that his Southern readers, who were overwhelmingly white, would likely be offended by the hateful truth of the matter and their dislike would have an adverse effect on his book sales. He wrote his publisher, "Upon reflection, it won't do for me to write that book."[30] As for his essay, "The United States of Lyncherdom," it was never published during Twain's lifetime. Written in 1901, the essay awaited the attention of Twain's early biographer, Albert Bigelow Paine, who saw to its publication in 1923, 13 years after Twain's death.

Whether or not Twain wrote a book about lynchings did not curb their continuance. The next southwestern Missouri incident took place in Jasper County; it involved 20-year-old Thomas Gilyard. On April 14, 1903, he shot and killed a Joplin police officer, Theodore Leslie. The officer was gunned down in the Kansas City Southern Railroad yards as he attempted to arrest three black men, whom he suspected of stealing. He had ordered several who had gone into a freight car to surrender, and when they did not, he fired at the car. Apparently, in so doing, Leslie shot Gilyard in the leg, and the wounded man came out of the car, shot the officer in the head, and fled the scene.[31] The black man was captured the next afternoon and confined in the jail in Joplin. A newspaper reported that the bullet in his leg corresponded to the missing bullet from the slain police officer's revolver.[32]

Word soon spread of the arrest of the cop killer. In broad daylight, several thousand assembled, broke open the jail, dragged the crippled Gilyard two blocks to the intersection of Second and Wall streets, and hanged him from a telegraph pole. The drawing that appeared in the next morning's *Joplin Daily Globe* with its headline "MURDERER OF LESLIE LYNCHED BY ANGRY MOB" illustrates the scene. The violence did not end with the death of Gilyard. The mob proceeded to the black section of town, burned homes, and drove frightened Negro residents to neighboring cities. At least 50 police officers from other Missouri and Kansas municipalities were in Joplin to attend Officer Leslie's funeral. At the request of Joplin city officials, they remained and were sworn in as deputy marshals in order to prevent even greater destruction of black-occupied and/or owned real estate. According to a Kansas City paper, a report was being circulated "that several hundred 'Negro Chasers' from Pierce City are coming this evening to assist in the extermination of the negro population."[33] No such extermination took place, but by 1910, only 1.9 percent of Jasper County, Missouri, was African American. It had become 98.1 percent white.[34]

To the credit of city and county officials, vigorous efforts were made to prevent both Gilyard's lynching and the subsequent destruction of black homes. A city attorney, P.H. Decker, made a strong plea at the jail for the mob to cease and let the law take its course. Afterwards, the coroner's jury did not come in with its usual verdict. Instead, it found

AT THE SCENE OF THE LYNCHING.
(Sketched From the East Side of Wall Street Looking to the Northwest.)

Above and opposite: This cartoon appeared in the April 16, 1903, *Joplin Daily Globe* after the April 15 lynching in Joplin, Jasper County, of the African American, 20-year-old Thomas Gilyard, charged with the April 14, 1903, shooting and killing of a Joplin police officer, Theodore Leslie. (Used by permission, State Historical Society of Missouri, Columbia.)

that the deceased "came to his death from hanging by the neck and that said hanging was done by Sam Mitchell, Ed Fields, alias' Hickory Bill,' and a man named Barnes."[35] According to James E. Cutler, "on June 4, 1903, Samuel Mitchell, white, who led the mob that lynched Thomas Gilyard, a negro, at Joplin Missouri, on April 15, preceding, was sentenced to ten years imprisonment in the penitentiary."[36] However, a check of the Register of Inmates, Missouri State Penitentiary, shows no inmate named Sam or Samuel Mitchell in the early 1900s. Likewise a check of Missouri appellate case law reveals no Sam or Samuel Mitchell as a defendant in a criminal case during this same time period. Either Cutler was mistaken, or if not, someone intervened and Mitchell's 10-year prison sentence was cancelled.

The final lynching of African Americans in southwest Missouri took place in Springfield, seat of Greene County. It was set in motion by the Good Friday, April 13, 1906, alleged rape of Mable Edwards, a 21-year-old white female. She had come to Springfield from Bolivar, Polk County; she left her husband there and was seeking employment as a maid. She later reconciled with him and returned to her life in Bolivar. On the evening of April 13, she was riding in a buggy with a young man, Charles Cooper. One or more black males attacked, robbed, and, she claimed, raped her. Despite the fact that their employers provided alibis stating that these men were elsewhere at the time of the supposed attack, Fred Coker and Horace Duncan were arrested. When they were brought before Mable Edwards, she was not able to identify them; it was only after a mob had

AT THE SCENE OF THE LYNCHING.

hanged and burned their remains that Mrs. Edwards was certain that they were the men who assaulted her.

Following Mrs. Edwards's accusation, Coker and Horace were confined in the Greene County jail, presumably during the day on Saturday, April 14. That night a mob, together with cheering spectators estimated in all at 3,000 persons, stormed the jail, placed ropes about the necks of Coker and Duncan, dragged them to the public square, and hanged them to death from the statue of the Goddess of Liberty, or almost to death. Next, the mob built a fire under their bodies and began shooting bullets into their remains. The local newspaper reports after their deaths: "It is positively stated that the two negroes burned in the public square are not the two that assaulted and ravished Mrs. Edwards on Friday night."[37]

Not content with the gruesome lynching of two almost certainly innocent men, cries arose from the enormous crowd, as the local paper reports, "Kill all the niggers. Get some more of 'em. Run 'em all out of town. We don't want any more of our men killed by the blacks, and we don't want any more of our women ravished by 'em. Burn 'em all."[38] As a result, the mob returned to the county jail with the intent of killing all of its African-American inmates. Many escaped in the confusion of the second raid on this facility, but the crowd got its hands on another African American, William Allen, charged with the murder of a white man, O.M. Rouark. By 2 A.M. Sunday morning, on Easter, the mob lynched Allen. Newspaper coverage of his death includes: "The rope was ... tied around his neck. When told to jump from the tower, he jumped without a word. The rope broke and the negro fell into the cremated remains of his former companions. He was again taken to the tower and this time let down, shot, and burned."[39] Most probably, Allen was not guilty of the murder of Rouark. According to an out-of town newspaper, Allen's last words were, "Bud Kane killed Mr. Rouark."[40] Among the many prisoners who escaped from the jail when the mob seized its third victim, Allen, was Bud Kane. One week after the lynching of Allen, the authorities were still searching for Kane.[41]

After the mob dispatched its third victim, it continued to vent its fury. The crowd went through the black neighborhoods of Springfield, as an earlier mob had in Pierce City and Joplin, destroying whatever of value it saw in its path. Many Negroes, perhaps hundreds, were forced to leave their businesses, homes, and personal property, including livestock.[42] City, county, and state authorities moved quickly to restore order in this city in turmoil. Governor Joseph Folk sent in three companies of state militia; three additional companies were expected, and 250 deputy sheriffs were sworn in to patrol the streets. The governor offered a reward of $300 for information that would bring the lynchers to justice.[43] The local paper announced that the Greene County circuit court judge berated the mob and ordered a special grand jury to investigate the events of Easter weekend. Of equal importance, the authorities declared their intention to arrest about 25 mob leaders.[44] Approximately four months later, one man was under indictment for perjury and two others were charged with first-degree murder. Only these three of the 23 men indicted in connection with the triple Easter lynching had even been arrested.[45] By August 1907, 16 months after these ghastly crimes, the prosecuting attorney of Greene County dismissed all charges in the April 1906 lynching spree. He explained, as the newspaper reports, "It was impossible to secure witnesses."[46]

Among other out-of-state newspapers, the *New York Times*, the *Washington Post*, the

Hartford Courant, and the *Chicago Tribune* ran stories on what happened in Springfield over Easter weekend in 1906. Immediately after these terrible events, the Springfield newspaper reported that the black clergy in Chicago were appealing directly to President Theodore Roosevelt for an official investigation into these Missouri lynchings and prosecution of the mob's leaders.[47] The president had no legal authority to take any action; nor did he. Like Mark Twain, who did not wish to alienate his white Southern readers and hence did not write a book about lynchings, Teddy Roosevelt, as his biographer reports, "did not want to jeopardize his new popularity in the South," and rather than using his moral authority to condemn specific lynchings, he made only a general condemnation of them in his sixth annual message to the U.S. Congress, delivered on December 4, 1906: "The spirit of lynching inevitably throws into prominence in the community all the foul and evil creatures who dwell therein."[48]

The Springfield newspaper also reported shortly after the city's triple lynching the remarks of the U.S. Senator from South Carolina, "Pitchfork" Tillman. This man advocated from the floor of the U.S. Senate, "When any negro ravages a white woman, I believe in visiting justice on the brute in the shortest possible order — aye — I would burn him."[49] By this late date, no American state, federal, or military sentencing authority allowed burning to death as a punishment. In an 1890 decision which upholds the use of the electric chair as a means of execution, the U.S. Supreme Court specifically disallows burning at the stake as a means of capital punishment.[50] Setting persons on fire was the mob's way of killing, not the law's.

Greene County had been the scene of at least eight lynchings prior to the April 1906 events, beginning with Slave Martin's in 1859. However, most of its earlier mob murders were of white men, and when blacks were lynched, the fury of the mob had not spilled over into the destruction of black neighborhoods. A Maryville newspaper ran an editorial from the *St. Joseph New-Press* condemning "the Springfield Horror." It lay part of the blame for the murder of three black men on the then-recent performance, in Springfield, of *The Clansman*, a play "calculated to inflame prejudice against the negro, and which was severely criticized in these columns when it was presented in St. Joseph this season."[51] In the five columns of its front page which the Springfield paper devotes to its headlined story, "Three Negroes Hanged and Corpses Burned," it mentions that "the production of Thomas Dixon's play, *The Clansman* ... was here only recently."[52] This fictional work, published as a book and produced as a play the same year, 1905, was authored by Thomas Dixon, Jr., a Baptist minister, North Carolina legislator, and lawyer.[53] It is the basis for D.W. Griffith's silent film, *The Birth of a Nation* (1915).[54]

According to Dixon's biographer, Anthony Slide, "*The Clansman*, opened in Norfolk, Virginia, on Friday, September 22, 1905, complete with white actors in black face playing the Negro roles and live horses in full Klan regalia, galloping across the stage, carrying the hooded Klansmen."[55] This must have been a wonderful spectacle for the entertainment-starved audiences in towns such as Springfield, Missouri. More to the point which provoked the St. Joseph newspaper's condemnation, the play contains an off-stage lynching of a black man, Gus. Under hypnosis he reveals how he has approached a 13-year-old white girl, Flora, not intending to harm her. However, she so fears him that she throw herself off a cliff to her death. What happens next, as a direct result of the child's ghastly demise, is that Gus is to die, as Slide describes the plan, "with his body hanging from the courthouse balcony until he is dead." A noble white character is given these lines: "Cut down the body — drag it at a horse's heels ... and then boldly fling him on the door step of the negro Lieutenant Governor of South Carolina."[56]

The Clansman bears some eerie similarities to the mob murders of the African Americans over Easter weekend 1906. The hanging and dragging of the bodies suggest that life was imitating kitsch art in the murders of Coker, Horace, and Allen, shortly after this horrid play was presented in Springfield. Whatever the causes of this madness, with this triple lynching, Greene County, Missouri, saw its last mob murders.

Although the black percentage of the population in each of Missouri's 114 counties in 1900 is not available, it is for 1910. The 27 counties making up the southwest section of the state on average in 1910 were less than three-fourths of one percent African American.[57] On average, they were more than 99 percent white. Six of the 27 counties had black populations of less than one tenth of one percent: Barry, Dallas, Douglas, McDonald, Stone, and Taney. The other 21 ranged from a low of .01 percent to a high of 4.1 percent in Greene County, whose seat was Springfield. In a recent book about racism in America, the author quotes an elderly Negro woman who now lives in central Missouri and avoids the southwestern section of the state. She remembers that after the Easter weekend events in Springfield in 1906 that "all blacks left out of the area." She adds that even at the present day those are "not places where I would feel comfortable going."[58]

When we turn to the northwest section of the state, between 1900 and 1909, it was the scene of one less mob murder than the southwestern section. Six occurred, five of them of blacks, and all took place in counties that had earlier been the scenes of lynchings. They are discussed in order of their occurrence. The first was in Marshall, seat of Saline County, on April 28, 1900. It was set in motion by the April 26 jailbreak of the victim. He was a 23-year-old black male named Mindo Cohnagwe, incarcerated for burglary. He was charged with smashing the windows of a shoe and jewelry store, and stolen jewelry was found on him when he was arrested. He claimed to be a Hindu of considerable education. A second Negro, John S. Smith, also made his escape, but he was not recaptured.

In the process of breaking out of jail, these men overpowered the sheriff, seized his revolver, and with it shot the sheriff's wife in the arm. Her wounds required the amputation of her limb. The Marshall newspaper quotes her opinion of the mob murder of her assailant: "It is too bad that a human being should lose his life simply because I have lost my arm. If he had killed me, it would be different. But I have only lost an arm, and he must lose his life." Cohnagwe was at liberty 24 hours or less. Hunger drove him to a farmhouse, and its occupants recognized him as a wanted man. The father-farmer and his two sons, armed with shotguns and a revolver, took him into custody, disarmed him, secured him with a rope, and returned with him to Marshall. Initially he was confined in the city jail; Saturday morning he was moved to the county jail. That same night a crowd estimated at 1,000 members stormed the jail and brought him out a manacled and helpless person. The Marshall paper describes, without naming any names, the assembled: "There was no pretense of disguise. The white glare of the electrical light revealed every face and figure in the crowd."

The mob led its prisoner to the courthouse square, specifically to a tree near the southeast corner of the courtyard. Its members had to pause long enough for a store to be opened so that a rope could be procured. Before they hanged him they allowed him to pray, and the Marshall paper quotes his words: "Merciful Heavenly Father, forgive the wrongs I have committed against others. Forgive my many sins and forgive them." These words weakened the resolve of at least one mob member, but not others. The prisoner asked for a drink of water, and an obliging young man ran to the nearby hotel and obtained a glass of water. Despite the attempts of some nastier fellows to spill it, the mob's leaders allowed him to quench his thirst before they hanged him by the neck until he was dead. His lynching took place at about 10 P.M., April 28, 1900. His body remained suspended for approximately one-half hour. The Marshall paper concludes its coverage: The usual morbid scenes [followed], the lowering of the lifeless body to photograph the distorted face by flashlight, and the scramble for bits of the rope as gruesome keepsakes. Later ... the coroner took charge of the body, and it was buried in the potter's field at the county farm."[59] The Marshall newspaper's extensive coverage was published in an extra edition. It includes the entire front page of six columns, and as with Frank Embree's lynching in Howard County the previous year, it seems clear that the newspaper reporter(s) knew in advance precisely what was going to take place well before it happened, Likewise apparent was that law enforcement officers either could not or would not prevent this lynching.

At the time, Missouri law was silent regarding the treatment of the dead body of a legally hanged man. Multiple souvenirs, such as a finger of the deceased or pieces of the rope used to end his life, were obtained by onlookers when the sheriff presided. Hence, it is not surprising that photographs of the lynched man (none of which are known to have survived) and pieces of rope were snatched as treasured mementos of what was probably the most exciting event in the lives of many of the participants.

The second lynching in northwest Missouri in the 1900s took place in Liberty, seat of Clay County, the week after the Saline County lynching of Mindo Cohnagwe. It was set in motion by Henry Darley's early afternoon, May 1, 1900, attempted rape in Excelsior Springs of a young white woman, Miss Vera Armstrong, aged, in newspaper coverage, between 18 and 22 years. She was employed as a dining room girl at Snapp's Tavern. Henry Darley, alias Henry Alecks, was a black male, aged mid–20s to 30 years, according to various news accounts; all newspaper accounts agree that he had earlier served time at the Missouri State Penitentiary for the rape of a young African-American girl. He was soon captured and brought to the county jail in Liberty. The next evening Darley was seized at this facility, and had the mob's primary intention been to reduce government money spent on criminals, it would also have snuffed out the lives of the men confined in the eastern portion of the jail: Francis Wade, killer of a man named Schammel, and his cellmate, Ernest Clevenger, convicted murderer of his cousin, Della Clevenger, and a rival, George Allen. Clevenger was legally hanged slightly more than six weeks later, on June 15, 1900. One newspaper mentions that "there was a sentiment in favor of taking them out, but the vigilantes seem to be satisfied with their work and did not molest them."[60] Not surprisingly, the undisturbed prisoners were both white men.

The night of May 2, a mob composed of men from Excelsior Springs and Liberty rode into town sometime just after 11 P.M. Two of its 60 to 75 members went to the "power house," as it was termed, and ordered the engineer to turn off the town's electric lights. He quickly did as he was told, and Liberty was dark by 11:20 P.M. The sheriff and a deputy named Ed Cave, probably a liaison between law enforcement officers and the lynchers,[61] attempted to reason with the mob, but to no avail. With the help of sledge hammers and chisels, the crowd opened the jail door within 10 minutes and plucked Darley from his cell in the northwest wing of the courthouse. His killers marched him from the north to the south side of the courthouse, and they paused at the top of the steps leading into the courtroom. As in Marshall, the newspaper reports that the black man about to be lynched was allowed to kneel and pray, and it prints what he said: "O Heavenly Father, forgive me of my sins and save my soul." The rope was run over the railing of the stairs, and the leader, unnamed in the newspapers, gave the command, "Pull the rope." Once the many rope pullers were certain Darley's life was extinguished, they dispersed. However, they left various placards on their victim. On one of his arms were the words "A Hint," and on other body parts, signs read, "All rapists look alike"; "We Treat Them All Alike"; and "We Protect our Homes." The coroner held an inquest, and his jurors concluded that Henry Darley came to his death at the hands of unknown parties.[62]

The third northwestern Missouri lynching of the 1900s took place on March 2, 1901, in Camden, Ray County. It happened in the early morning hours when a mob of 500 persons overpowered the sheriff and his deputies and took their prisoner from them. He was a Negro coal miner with several names, among them Arthur McNeal, Dewey Smith, and Bob McBrien. He was charged with the March 1 shooting and killing of a 26-year-old white coal miner named Chester Stanley. Stanley and McNeal argued over whether or not the white man had accused the black of wrecking coal in McNeal's room and doing so deliberately. Stanley called McNeal a liar; almost immediately, McNeal shot Stanley and fled the scene, Mine No. 4, just south of Richmond. McNeal was captured in Camden, still dressed in his pit clothes; his captors put him in the Burnett Hotel and telephoned the sheriff in Richmond to tell him of the prisoner's whereabouts.

Despite the protestations of the sheriff and his deputies after they arrived, they were unable to return to Richmond with McNeal and place him in the county jail. The assembled persons seized the black man at the hotel in Camden, returned him to the scene of his crime, and hanged him from a tree near Mine No. 4. According to one newspaper account, the mob insisted that McNeal admit the killing of Stanley was unprovoked. He refused, saying it was in self-defense. He asked that his body be sent to his mother at 2624 Woodland, Kansas City, Missouri, and his prayer, quoted in the newspaper, consisted of: "O God, have mercy on the soul of this poor doomed man and have pity on the soul of the murdered man gone before."[63] Soon after its utterance, Arthur McNeal, alias Dewey Smith, alias Bob McBrien was hanged by the neck until dead. His body was taken to Richmond, prepared for burial at the courthouse in the circuit courtroom on Saturday afternoon March 2, and buried at the county poor farm. The coroner's jurors held two inquests. At their first they found that Chester Stanley came to his death by a pistol shot fired from the hands of Arthur McNeal. At its second, the six jurors found that "Arthur McNeal came to his death at the hands of parties unknown to the jury, from hanging by the neck." [64]

An article appeared in an unlikely place for an event of this sort, a Missouri genealogical publication. It carried a two and one-half page article, mostly taken from the Richmond paper's contemporary coverage. The article was researched by a niece of the deceased white coal miner, Chester Stanley, Zelma Stanley Conner. It concludes, "While I was growing up, my father had talked of a Negro killing a brother of his at a coal mine and was very prejudiced toward that race."[65] Though two slaves were legally put to death in Ray County in 1837 and the lynching of McNeal was its fourth known lynching, the three earlier mob murders in this county, one in 1853 and a dual event in 1868, were of white men. McNeal's was this county's first and only known lynching of an African American.

The next lynching in northwest Missouri during the 1900s took place in Lexington, seat of Lafayette County, on August 12, 1902. A lynching in this county was a common enough event, but the stringing up of a white man, Charles Salyers, with a black, Harry Gates, was a rarity in this state's mob murders. The only other known Missouri lynching of a white and black together took place in Clay County on May 9, 1850, when a mob hanged Slave Annice and McClintock, a white abolitionist. The *Washington Post's* story of Salyers's and Gates's murder begins, "Mixed Lynching in Missouri/ White and Black Hanged Side by Side by a Masked Mob."[66] Judging from this headline, nationwide the mob murder of a white and black together was an anomaly.

The night of August 4, Salyers and Gates were gambling and losing. After one lent the other 75 cents, Gates decided to recover the money he lost by stealing chickens from George W. Johnson, a wealthy farmer. In the process of Johnson's attempting to protect his property, shots were exchanged; the farmer's wounds proved fatal, and Gates was shot in the hip. The gambling and chicken-stealing pair was soon arrested and lodged in the county jail in Lexington. Slightly over a week later, the expected mob arrived; 150 men masked men battered down the jail door and grabbed both Salyers and Gates. They took both a short distance from town, and they first hanged the white man, Salyers, and next the black, Gates, from a tree. Sometime afterwards, Governor Alexander Dockery issued a statement disapproving of the lynchings and generally condemning mob law.[67] The day after the lynchings, the *Kansas City Star* severely criticized the poor performance of Lafayette County's law enforcement officers in their sworn duty to protect their prisoners. Its headline about this dual lynching includes: "GUARDS WERE NOT ARMED / Only the Sheriff Had a Revolver at Lexington, Mo./ Five Officers in the Jail Awaited for a Week the Coming of a Mob to Lynch Two Prisoners — There Without Weapons After Midnight." In its story the paper states:

> The whole town of Lexington had known for a week that the lynching was to take place. When the mob came at 2 o'clock Tuesday morning, the sheriff, Oscar Thomas, the prosecuting attorney, Horace Blackwell, a deputy sheriff, Albert James; a deputy sheriff, Charles Kinkead, and a constable, W. Scott Thomas were in the jail. A weak protest in words was about all the protection offered the prisoners.[68]

These Lafayette County law enforcement officers appeared to have remembered that they had fees or salaries to collect, but they forgot they also had duties to perform in protecting *all* their prisoners, including Salyers and Gates. In marked contrast, when the sheriff of Clinton County learned on July 12, 1902, that an angry mob was coming for his 16-year-old black prisoner, General Armstrong, charged with the rape of a 16-year-old white girl, Ivy Turley, he took evasive action. Aware of the extreme danger to his prisoner, Sheriff John Wiser secretly removed Armstrong from the Clinton County jail in Plattsburgh and hid both himself and his young prisoner in a field of tall corn. Both the boy and his keeper were without water for 24 hours and without food or sleep for 48 hours. Finally, at Mecca, Clinton County, Wiser and Armstrong caught a train for Kansas

City, where the sheriff put his prisoner in the jail at 219 E. Missouri Avenue. Obviously, lynchings could be and were prevented. Regrettably, after a change of venue to Platte County, its sheriff, Joseph Elgin, subsequently hanged 18-year-old Armstrong pursuant to court order on April 25, 1902, for a crime, rape, that he never committed.[69] Plattsburgh, seat of Clinton County, was twice the distance from Kansas City that Lexington, seat of Lafayette was, but the Clinton County sheriff managed to get his prisoner to safety. In contrast to Lafayette County, Clinton had only one known lynching, and it took place in 1880.

The final mob murder of northwest Missouri in the 1900s occurred in Platte County, on August 2, 1909. The lynched man, George Johnson, was white, one of three Caucasian men statewide between 1900 and 1909 whom mobs murdered. On June 20, 1909, Johnson lay in ambush and shot and killed John W. Moore, a wealthy Platte County farmer. Johnson, a carpenter, had worked for Moore, and one version of the killing attributes it to a disagreement between them regarding the agreed-to pay. Another explanation was that Moore had called Johnson a horse thief. A third account, one supplied by a letter dated July 27, 1909, which Moore's sister wrote the judge from Perry Landing, Texas, was that her brother was insane and his insanity had been caused by a severe case of measles and a high fever.

Once Moore, probably a mentally unstable man, was returned to the Platte County jail, a mob consisting of masked men counted at between 60 and 300 members stormed this facility, and when the sheriff's wife, who had the keys, refused to relinquish them, the usual sledge hammers were used to bash in the jail door. At 2 A.M., August 2, the lynchers had their man, and they hanged him from a tree in front of the Wells Bank, one block from the jail. The body was not cut down until 6:30 A.M., and the coroner held his inquest soon thereafter. His jurors reached the usual conclusion: Johnson came to his death by hanging from a tree by unknown parties.[70] Soon thereafter, an assistant attorney general announced an investigation,[71] but almost certainly nothing came of his looking into this August 2, 1909, lynching in Platte City. Johnson's murder was Platte County's third known and last lynching. Of the earlier two, one took place in 1876, a black man charged with rape, and the other in 1881, a black man charged with attempted rape. There are no known mob murders of slaves in Platte County, and only one legal execution, that of Slave Abe in 1853. With only three known lynchings in its history, Platte County falls well outside the top counties for mob murders in Missouri.

In all, six men, four black and two white, were murdered by mobs in northwest Missouri between 1900 and 1909. According to the 1910 U.S. Census listing of racial percentages by county, the 28 counties making up the northwest section of this state contained an average black population of 4 percent. That is 40 times the average black percentage of the population in southwestern Missouri in 1910, which had less than one-tenth of one percent. It seems clear that sheer numbers did not necessarily motivate lynch mobs.

When we turn to the northeast section of the state between 1900 and 1909, there are only two lynchings, and they took place within several months of each other in 1902. The first occurred near Higbee, Randolph County, on Saturday, March 22, 1902, when seven or eight men, a very small mob by 1900s standards, seized a 35-year-old black male, Oliver Wright, and whipped him to death. The rumor had reached his assailants that the previous night Wright had almost killed a white man, unnamed in the local news account of this lynching. His body was brought to Higbee, and in the absence of the coroner, a justice of the peace held an inquest. The six jurors arrived at their usual verdict, death at the hands of parties unknown to the jury.[72]

Two months after the lynching of Oliver Wright in Randolph County, Abe Witherup, the black murderer of William Grow, a white man, in April 1902, was taken from the Monroe County jail in Paris by a 100-member mob in the early morning hours of May 25, 1902, and hanged from a bridge. Newspaper coverage notes that both the father and brother of William Grow were mob members. The brother tied Witherup's feet, and the father adjusted the rope. A state representative, James H. Whitecotton, made a fruitless appeal to the mob to cease and desist. [73] His doing so did not damage his service as a member of the Missouri legislature; he was initially elected to a two-year term in 1896, and he served continuously until 1906.[74] Later, county officials stated the usual about prosecuting the lynchers.[75] Presumably, if charges were actually filed, they were eventually dropped. Witherup's lynching in 1902 is the only known mob murder in the history of the county. Of interest in the 1910 census, northeast Missouri's 25 counties contained a larger percentage of blacks, 7.5 percent, than the other three sections of the state, yet had fewer lynchings between 1900 and 1901 than elsewhere in Missouri.

In the southeast Missouri, there were four known lynchings during this time period, with one white victim and three black. The mob murder of the white Rev. W.J. Malone took place near Wardell, Pemiscot County. He was about 50 years old, had previously been a Methodist minister, and then he became "sanctified." Sometime after his sanctification, he became enamored of Mrs. Mary Frield. He converted her to his religion, and the pair preached and traveled together, much to the displeasure of the minister's wife, Mrs. Malone. He installed Mary as his housekeeper, and she and Malone, as the local paper reports, went "so far as to bind Mrs. Malone hand and foot to her bed with leather thongs." Neighbors became alarmed, and eventually a warrant was sworn out against the reverend for wife abandonment, but the constable was afraid to serve it. Next, a second warrant was issued for Reverend Malone and his companion Mrs. Frield. Constable W.J. Mooneyhan went to arrest the pair on Saturday evening, May 2, 1903, on charges of adultery. An armed and disguised mob killed both Malone and the constable who tried to protect him.[76] This is the first known of Pemiscot County's three lynchings. The other two took place in later decades; they are discussed in the next chapter.

The first mob murder discussed in this book, an Indian lynched by other Indians, took place in 1803, in what was then known as New Madrid District, an area so vast that it included most of the present state of Arkansas. Nearly 100 years later, the second New Madrid County event that can be documented took place on February 16, 1902. The third and last known lynching in this county is discussed in the next chapter. The victim of New Madrid County's second lynching was 22-year-old Louis F. Wright, a member of the Richards and Pringle Georgia Minstrels, on tour in New Madrid. The trouble began innocently enough. Several of the out-of-town blacks were sightseeing near the courthouse on a Saturday, February 15, at the same time as some white boys were throwing snowballs. One, Tom Waters, threw one at the blacks, nearly hitting one, and according to the local paper, he called Tom, "You dirty s — of a b — —." To avenge, as the paper phrases it, "his vile insult," the white boys caught the insulting black after the Saturday evening performance. They were about to beat him to show him his place, when a second Negro, another member of the minstrel show, opened fire on the white boys with a pistol. His bullets grazed various clothing of the whites, including a collar, an overcoat, and a hat. One shot hit the shoulder of a white boy, and another bullet appeared to have hit the knee of one of the minstrel Negroes.

In the melee that followed, the minstrel show audience fled the Opera House in what the paper describes as a "stampede." No one was injured. Nonetheless, the hunt was on for the shooter. In the process, all 24 members of the touring group were arrested and placed in the county jail in New Madrid. After law enforcement officers interrogated the entire cast, Louis F. Wright was identified by one or more of his terrified companions as "the bad nigger with a pistol." Sunday night, a masked mob took him from the jail and 300 yards from it hanged him from a tree. His body was cut down Monday morning. That afternoon the 23 members of the tour, their manager and his assistant, were charged with aiding and abetting a riot and found not guilty. The entire black party left town on the 4:10 P.M. train. Shortly, the acting coroner held an inquest, and the six jurors determined that Louis F. Wright came to his death by hanging by parties unknown.[77] Several months later, the *Kansas City Star* carried a story with a Chicago dateline about a meeting to protest the lynching of Wright. One speaker, an assistant Illinois state's attorney, stated of the large number of lynchings in the South, "The Negro has ... come to know that the law affords him no protection." The meeting ended with the collection of funds to prosecute the lynchers.[78]

The second known lynching of a black in 1900s southeast Missouri took place on January 21, 1903, near Leeper, Wayne County. Seventy men battered down the door of the village jail, seized Andy Clark, and hanged him to death from a tree. Two days earlier, Clark ended a running dispute about land with a 60-year-old white farmer, James Herman, by going to his home with a shotgun, calling Herman to the door, and shooting his head off. Eventually, Clark was captured, jailed, and lynched.[79] Clark's mob murder is Wayne County's only known lynching.

The final mob murder in southeast Missouri of the 1900s took place on May 12, 1905, in Belmont, Mississippi County, when a 200- to 300-member mob wrestled Tom Witherspoon from town marshal Bob Zimmerman of Columbus, Kentucky, and, between 6 and 7 P.M., hanged him on the public square in Belmont. Witherspoon had recently been released from the Missouri State Penitentiary in Jefferson City after serving a five-year sentence for attempting to murder his wife. According to the county seat paper, while he was an inmate he assaulted a guard and was placed in solitary confinement. He blamed his conviction and prison sentence on Fred J. Hess, a former state legislator who represented Mississippi County in the Missouri General Assembly for three terms, 1890 and 1896–1900.[80] The morning of May 12, 1905, a heavily armed Witherspoon went to the Hess residence, found his man at his barn, and demanded $600 from him on these grounds: "You were a witness against me and helped send me to the penitentiary and you owe me $600 for it, and I want it right now." Hess realized the danger and told him that he did not have that much money, but he would get it. As surety, Witherspoon took Hess's wife and three-year-old child and held them in a deserted cabin. Hess went to Belmont, then crossed the Mississippi River to Columbus, Kentucky, where he secured the $600, paid it over to Witherspoon, and left with his wife and child. Once Witherspoon's hostages were safe, a deputy sheriff and a dozen members of his posse from Charleston, seat of Mississippi County, moved in on Witherspoon, but he escaped. With the aid of bloodhounds, they located him in a cabin and captured him, and the sheriff managed to removed his prisoner to Belmont. There a mob of 200 to 300 persons wrestled Witherspoon from law enforcement officers and hanged him to death. According to the local paper, the St. Louis newspaper coverage of the lynching was inaccurate. This large city's newspapers blamed Mississippi County residents, and the mob came from Kentucky. The deputy sheriff recognized none of the lynchers. The prosecuting attorney stated, "There were few, if any, Missourians in the mob." The local news story concludes, "After the negro had been lynched, the mob returned to Kentucky."[81] It is highly unlikely that all persons involved in the lynching of Witherspoon were residents of Kentucky. Unlike the local newspaper, the *St. Louis Post-Dispatch*, in both an editorial and a front-page story, discusses the governor of Missouri's great opportunity to see that all the laws are obeyed, not just "the enforcement of a hundred laws regulating the conduct of people on Sundays and holidays."[82] Governor Folk ordered his attorney general, as the *Post-Dispatch's* front page story notes, "to institute immediately an investigation of the lynching of ... Tom Witherspoon. The governor proposes to prosecute vigorously all those responsible for the negro's death."[83] Nothing came of the governor's efforts, but he tried harder than did any local authorities to bring the chief members of the mob to justice.

Witherspoon's lynching was the first of four known in Mississippi County; the remaining three are discussed in the next chapter. In the 1910 census, the 34 counties in the southeast section of Missouri had, on average, a black population that was 2.98 percent of the total. Two of the counties where lynchings of African Americans took place, New Madrid (10.8 percent) and Mississippi (13.8 percent), had far larger black populations than the average. On the other hand, Wayne County's black population was miniscule, .2 percent of the total; 99.8 percent of this county was white.

This account of the lynchings in Missouri that took place between 1900 and 1909 would not be complete without an account of those erroneously reported to have occurred here during this time period. None are known from southwestern Missouri. There are four in the northwest section. The first concerns a reported event on March 26, 1900, in Bellair, Cooper County. A Connecticut newspaper ran a story headlined "Lynching in Missouri/ Sheriff Fired upon the Mob and Wounded Two." Its story relates that "Lewis Harris, colored, arrested last night for a felonious assault on Miss Anne McIlvaine, a recluse, was lynched tonight. Sheriff Kinart and his deputy fought to protect the prisoner and fired into the mob, wounded two of them. The officers were overpowered."[84] Mob murders were *always* newsworthy events, especially in the county in which they took place. There was a weekly newspaper published in Boonville, seat of Cooper County, at the time this alleged lynching occurred. The local newspaper carries no mention of this mob murder. Further, the *Official Manual, State of Missouri* for the year of this event, 1900, lists no sheriff in any Missouri county named Kinart. There is one and only one reasonable conclusion: no lynching took place on or near this date in this state. If a mob put to death a Lewis Harris any place in the United States, it is beyond the scope of this book to ascertain where this event took place. It did not happen in Missouri.[85]

The other northwestern non-events of the 1900s are not invented out of whole cloth. The first began on a Wednesday night, July 10, 1901, when an 18-year-old white girl, Miss Grace Davis, claimed that she was raped and her white male companion, 20-year-old Vernon Newton, assaulted. The crime scene appears to have at times been 19th and Woodland streets, and at others 20th and Michigan streets. The named streets are adjacent, and the numbered sequential. As a result, the activities complained of took place within a four block area, and all possible locations of alleged evildoing were well within the city limits of Kansas City, Missouri. The police interrogated three black males and arrested two. One was Joseph Robertson, described as "young" in newspaper coverage, and the other was 17-year-old Frank Holland. By the evening of July 12, with the temperature at least 100 degrees and the city under a boil order for its water,[86] a crowd of 300 men and boys surrounded the county jail at 219 E. Missouri Avenue, where the two suspects were incarcerated. With a police force of 251 members, it was possible to police the city and simultaneously post 50 police officers at the jail. At 11 P.M. on Friday, July 12, the tricky part took place. In an arrangement quietly worked out between the fire and police departments, the police smuggled their endangered prisoners through an underground passageway from the jail to the county courthouse a few blocks distant at 5th and Locust streets, placed them in a carriage, and drove off with them. They were clandestinely taken to one of the city's 19 fire stations, No. 18, at 26th and Prospect streets. At the time, this station was as far to the east from the jail as one could go and still be within the city limits; the countryside was nearby. Outside this fire station, the party waited for two hours. Finally, and on orders from higher-ups, the prisoners and their guard or guards took at least one hour to return to the jail on Missouri Avenue. They arrived at approximately 3 A.M. July 13, long after the mob previously assembleld there had dispersed.

By 1901, Kansas City was a sizeable place; its population, according to the 1900 federal census, was 163,752. Leaders such as Chief of Police John Hayes and Fire Chief Edward Trickett vehemently opposed any lynchings and were determined to prevent them by protecting *all* prisoners. To that end, the underground passageway between the jail and the courthouse must have been secretly built, and its existence remained generally unknown. Otherwise sufficient members of the mob would have been stationed at the courthouse in order to gain possession of Robertson and Holland, whichever way anyone attempted to remove them. Only in a city was this precise deception of the mob possible.

Once the two young black men were returned from No. 18 fire station to the Jackson County jail, they were secretly removed to Harrisonville, and there lodged in the Cass County jail. The following Thursday, July 18, a deputy marshal returned them to Kansas City for their preliminary hearing. At it, the state and the defense were both represented by capable counsel. The defendants put on a number of witnesses to show that Holland and Robinson were elsewhere when the crimes were committed, namely that they were at the Robinson residence and had gone to bed early because they planned to go fishing the next day. The defense also put on a Kansas City, Missouri, police officer, Detective Halderman, who had examined the young men separately after their arrest. He stated, "Their statements tallied pretty well."[87] Another earlier news story states, "The authorities are in doubt as to the two negroes who escaped being mobbed Friday night being the men guilty of assaulting Miss Davis."[88] Further doubt is cast on their guilt by the published statement of a resident of 19th and Woodland who wrote, "I did not know that an outrage ... had been committed within a stone's throw of my residence until I read an account of it in the papers the following evening. Nor can I find one of my neighbors who did — not even the policeman on the beat."[89] Finally an out-of-state paper ran a story headlined "Would-Be-Lynchers Mistaken/ Negroes Who are Held in Kansas City Said to be Innocent."[90] The combination of a 251 member police force, a fire department with 19 stations, capable and careful investigation of reported crimes and pseudo-crimes, a sturdy jail with an underground passage to the courthouse, and cooperation between officials of different Missouri counties, all came together to avert a lynching in Kansas City on July 12/13, 1901.[91]

The third would-be northwestern Missouri lynching of two men was prevented on March 29, 1909, in Daviess County. On this date, Earl and Ray Chism, along with a third brother, Harvey, attempted to blow up the safe at the Spickard Bank in Spickardville, Grundy County. As they made their getaway on a freight train, George Caraway, the city marshal of Jamesport, Daviess County, was in their way, and one of the robbers and the marshal apparently exchanged shots at approximately 11:30 A.M. Initially it was believed that the law enforcement officer's wounds were mortal. The first Chillicothe newspaper's headline states, "City Marshal at Jamesport Shot Down by Robbers."[92] The *New York Times* account credits the pleas of Mrs. Wood, wife of a farmer, to let the law take its course as preventing a posse of farmers who had captured the two wounded men from lynching them in the yard of the Wood home. This story states that these men were "accused of shooting and mortally wounding Marshall Caraway of Jamesport."[93] The captured Chism brothers were secured in the Daviess County jail at Gallatin, and the sheriff saw to it that this facility was adequately guarded. Soon the third Chism brother, Harvey, was arrested in Bloomington, Illinois, and the Daviess County sheriff planned to go there to get his prisoner. As it turned out, the bullet wounds that Earl Chism sustained proved mortal. As this would-be bank robber was dying, he confessed to the shooting of George Caraway, Jamesport's city marshal. Meanwhile, the city marshal was sufficiently out of danger to give a local reporter a detailed statement regarding the gun battle in which he was wounded. The bullets that struck him hit no vital organ. This story is headlined "Caraway will Recover."[94]

No false accounts of lynching are known from the northeast section of the state, and from southeast Missouri, only one. The *Chicago Tribune* lists Nelson Simpson as lynched on January 3, 1901, because of "race prejudice, by White Caps, Neelyville, [Butler County] Mo." The NAACP list precisely follows the Chicago paper, and both *100 Years of Lynchings* and Capeci repeat the NAACP error.[95] The newspaper of Butler County's seat, Poplar Bluff, ran this headline: "White Caps/ Terrorizing Negroes in Vicinity of Neelyville/ Ordered to Leave/ Notice Posted on Residence of Nelson Simpson and Others Threatening Them with Violence if They Disobey." The story concludes, "There is not the least suspicion as to who comprises the Whitecaps, but the gang is supposed to be composed of men who are jealous of the negroes and are determined to drive them out of the country."[96] Simpson was surely terrified, but he lived through his December 31, 1900, ordeal. Once more the date of the local newspaper coverage, January 3, 1901, was mistaken for the date of the event. Since there was no fatality, it cannot be classified as a lynching.

The next two chapters resemble my first two because they cover a far longer time period than a single decade. The records from the antebellum period are surely inadequate and hence the paucity of confirmed lynchings. In contrast to the pre–Civil War period, mob murders in Missouri from the second through the fourth decades of the twentieth century are well documented. During these years, 1910 to 1942, lynchings were on the decline throughout the United States, including the state of Missouri.

CHAPTER 11

Black and White Victims, 1910–1919

This chapter and the next are echoes of Chapter 3, wherein two blacks could be confirmed as lynched between 1866 and 1869 and all 33 others were white. The extralegal deaths of 35 persons took place in Missouri within a four-year period immediately following the Civil War. In this same state, between 1910 and 1919 only two whites can be confirmed as murdered by mobs and all eight others were black. This is a paltry total of 10. Further, if error exists in these numbers, the likelihood is great that the undercount is a feature of the late 1860s. Often in the Civil War's sputtering conclusion, newspapers that contained stories of other lynchings had either been destroyed by the Union Army or vanished long before they could be microfilmed. In contrast, by 1910, any lynching within this state's borders and many outside them were carried in the presently extant newspapers of Missouri's two largest cities, St. Louis and Kansas City, both without a mob murder in 74 and 28 years, respectively. In these metropolises, the newspapers not only reported all in-state lynchings, they also totally condemned them. If their censure did not suppress these awful events, they did not encourage them. The count of 10 lynchings in Missouri between 1910 and 1919 and six between 1920 and 1942 are probably more accurate numbers than during any earlier time periods.

Missouri's only lynchings of white persons during this decade took place in 1915 and 1919, and both occurred in western counties, those which bordered Kansas. Because there are only two, the usual start of my coverage with the southwestern section is dispensed with, and the two mob murders of whites are discussed in chronological order.

The first took place in Pleasant Hill, Cass County, a locale in the northwest section of the state, during early Sunday morning hours, 3:30 A.M. to 5 A.M., February 21, 1915, when a mob of approximately 100 persons stormed the city jail, retrieved W.F. Williams from it, and hanged him from a bell tower above city hall. Early churchgoers were the first to notice his dangling body. Williams was already wounded by gunfire in his head and shoulder, when put in the facility from which his lynchers removed him. He may have been nearly finished off in the jail before his bullet-riddled and dying body was strung up in plain view. The previous day, Williams, who gave his residence as Hot Springs, Arkansas, had come by train to Pleasant Hill. He and a companion were suspected in the robbery of the crew of a Kansas City Southern freight train in Richards,

Vernon County, Missouri. A city marshal, J.E. Evans, and a police officer, Clarence Poindexter, had been alerted by persons in Richards to be on the look out for the bandits. Soon after the train carrying the suspected robbers pulled into the Pleasant Hill depot, bullets began flying. In the shootout with two law enforcement officers, one of the robbery suspects and one of the officers were shot and killed. The slain officer, Clarence Poindexter, was the son of a wealthy, retired Cass County farmer and recently married. Judging from the separate pictures of Mr. and Mrs. Poindexter, Clarence, the husband, looks to have been in his early twenties, and Lois, his wife, still a teenager. The newspaper with photographs of them refers to her as "the girl-widow." Its story includes this headline, "Mrs. Lois Poindexter Only Person in Pleasant Hill who Expresses Regret at Lynching."[1] Not surprisingly, when the coroner held his inquest, his jurors concluded, "that Williams came to his death at the hands of parties unknown."[2] By 1915, the nation-wide increasing rarity of mob murders of white persons is illustrated by a New York City newspaper's headline: "Lynched by Missouri Mob/ White Man Taken from Jail and Hanged Over City Hall."[3] Mrs. Lois Poindexter, wife of the murdered policeman, expressed unusual sentiments about the death of her husband. Not only did she disapprove of lynching, she stated, "Capital punishment is a terrible crime.... Let him [Williams] go to the penitentiary ... that is where he belongs.... But don't kill him."[4] Obviously, the demise of Missouri's death penalty was in the air; otherwise this young widow would never have voiced these sentiments. On April 13, 1917, the week after the U.S. entered World War I, the Missouri legislature abolished the death penalty, and it reinstated it on July 8, 1919.

The reinstatement was intimately connected to the lynching of the other white man murdered by a mob in this state in the second decade of the twentieth century. This event took place in Lamar, Barton County, a locale in the southwestern section of the state. It was set in motion on March 3, 1919. On that date, Jay Lynch killed the sheriff of Barton County, John Harlow, and his son, Walter Harlow. He was arrested in Colorado and kept in the Bates County jail in Butler. On May 28, 1919, Lynch pled guilty to these killings without an attorney at a hearing in the circuit court of Barton County. The judge accepted the plea and sentenced him to life imprisonment, the only penalty then available for first-degree murder. Immediately thereafter, a mob entered the courtroom, took the defendant to the courtyard, and in the presence of 500 to 1,000 spectators, including cheering women and children, lynched Jay Lynch by hanging him from an elm tree in the Barton County courtyard. No one was able to identify any of the men who strung up the prisoner. An elderly viewer of this enterprise gave as his opinion that five or six of the legislators who voted to abolish capital punishment should meet the same fate.[5] The headline of the *New York Times* connects this lynching to Missouri's abolition of legal hangings: "Mob Enters Court and Hangs a Life Convict/ Sentenced under Law Banning Death Penalty."[6] The Missouri General Assembly appears to have gotten the message. With all deliberate speed it called an extra session, and the legislature reinstated the death penalty less than two months after the death of Jay Lynch. Among its motives was punishing capitally the murderers of law enforcement officers, the precise crime that the two white men murdered by mobs between 1910 and 1919 committed here.

After Lynch, there were no additional mob murders of white persons in this state until 1981. Of equal interest, only two white persons were legally executed in this state between 1910 and 1919. To find as few or fewer of the dominant race legally hanged here in any earlier decade, one must go to Missouri's territorial period. Likewise diminished were the number of African Americans whom this state's sheriffs hanged pursuant to court order between 1910 and 1919; there were seven. There were eight blacks lynched in this state during the second decade of the twentieth century, or one more than those legally put to death. This figure of eight is also a decline from earlier periods. The percentage of Missouri's population that was African American rose from 4.78 in 1910 to 5.23 in 1920[7]; the increase was so slight as to not be a factor.

There are no known lynchings of blacks in any of the 50 counties of western Missouri, either in the southwest or the northwest between 1910 and 1919. These sections of the state saw, from the 1870s through the 1910s, the great majority of this state's mob murders. This is a puzzling development, and other than noting the probable absence of blacks from small towns and rural areas of western Missouri, the lynch-proof quality of the jail in Kansas City, and law enforcement officers' increased skills in protecting the prisoners in the western half of the state, I have no ready explanation for the absence of lynched blacks in both the southwestern and northwestern sections of the state during the second decade of the twentieth century.

There were no mob murders of blacks in northeast Missouri between 1910 and early 1914. There were four in this section between March 17, 1914, and November 16, 1919; all took place in counties that had earlier been the scenes of lynchings. They are discussed in chronological order.

The first was Dallas Shields, in Fayette, seat of Howard County. On March 17, 1914, he was reported as being drunk, carrying a revolver, and involved in a spat with another black man with whom he had been quarreling for several months. Constable John W. Gaines responded to the disturbance, and in the process of the law enforcement officer attempting to arrest him, Shields shot and killed Gaines. Within two hours of the shooting, the perpetrator was an inmate in the county jail. That same evening, 150 men subdued the sheriff and his deputy, obtained the keys to the facility, removed Shields, and at approximately 8 P.M. hanged him from a locust tree in the north end of the courthouse square. After dangling from a rope for several hours, Shields's body was cut down and taken to the home of his parents. The local newspaper devotes considerable space in its coverage of this mob murder to the slain constable, John W. Gaines, a married father of four and deacon in the Christian Church.[8] It should be noted that both white men lynched during the 1910 to 1919 time period were guilty of this same offense, the killing of a law enforcement officer.

The next northeast Missouri mob murder of a black took place near Louisiana, Pike County, on September 8, 1915, when 40 masked men took Love Rudd from an automobile driven by a constable from Louisiana. Four days later, September 12, two fishermen saw the body of a Negro in the Mississippi River. When it was recovered it was assumed to be the body of Love Rudd, but two of his brothers failed to identify the body as Love Rudd's. Rudd had been charged with the September 5, 1915, burglary of the Randolph Bankhead residence in Clarksville. He was arrested in Louisiana on a complaint from Clarksville.[9]

Rudd's or another African American's Pike County lynching was followed by the April 5, 1916, mob murder of Lafayette Channel, in or near St. Charles, St. Charles

County. The local paper describes him as "a no-account nigger," and its story about him involves yet another gun battle. This exchange of bullets took the life of John H. Dierker, the sheriff of St. Charles County, and it also seriously wounded one of his deputies, Joe Ollendorf, as these law enforcement officers attempted to extract Channel from his hiding place and arrest him. The black man had earlier attempted to shoot Ernest Placke-meier, a white farmer, and sought refuge in the barn of another white farmer, Ed Bosehert. A number of neighbors gathered, and Channel died in a hail of gunfire.[10] The coroner's jury came in with the cause of Channel's death as suicide. The local paper registers its surprise at the verdict since "hundreds of weapons were raining bullets down on him," but it applauds the verdict, pronouncing it "one of great merit, as it protects all citizens who took part against any technical charge of murder in the case."[11]

The fourth and final lynching of a black in northeast Missouri in the second decade of the twentieth century took place in Randolph County, when a masked mob of 100 to 200 persons in 12 different automobiles took James Anderson, of Chicago, Illinois, from the sheriff. The incident which set this mob murder in action was the assault and robbery just east of Moberly of a Randolph County farmer, Ed Thompson, on a Thursday evening, November 13, 1919. By the next day, four African-American males were arrested for these crimes and held in the county jail at Huntsville. One of the four was James Anderson, whose home address was 3122 Federal Street, Chicago, Illinois. The other three were Richardson Hailey and George Adams, both of Chicago, and Sanford Taylor of East St. Louis, Illinois. The four waived their preliminary hearing, and they were returned to the jail in Huntsville to await their next court appearance.

The sheriff of Randolph County moved them to the Macon County jail in Macon City on Saturday, November 15, in order to avoid the mob murder of all four. When the sheriff of Macon County received a 3 A.M. phone call asking him if he had the four prisoners, he believed that it came from another law enforcement officer, and he answered in the affirmative. Shortly, 12 automobiles of masked men arrived at the Macon County jail and demanded the four African-American inmates.

The Macon County sheriff attempted to persuade the mob, estimated at between 100 and 200 members, to disperse. Its leaders informed him that if they were not given the jail keys, they would blast their way into his facility with the dynamite they had brought with them. The sheriff then directed his deputy to turn the four blacks over to the masked men. Soon, the lynch mob placed the four Negroes in one of the cars, and all 12 vehicles departed south for Moberly. When the mob reached Randolph County, it lined up its four prisoners with their hands tied behind their backs. At approximately 5 A.M. Sunday, November 16, 1919, mob members placed a rope around James Anderson's neck; suddenly he tried to escape. He was shot four times in the head and killed instantly. The other three intended victims escaped; they were later recaptured, but all were kept safe from the mob.

The positive identity of James Anderson was ascertained by the Moberly chief of police who sent this telegram: "Chief of Police, Moberly, MO. Wire me collect, particulars of James Anderson. His father, James Anderson, 3122 Federal, Chicago." The father, James Anderson responded that he had a son with his name. Shortly, the father received another telegram, presumably from a Moberly funeral home. It read, "Your telegram to chief of police handed us. James Anderson was taken from jail by a mob, shot and killed.

The body is in our possession. Martin & Mahan." Meanwhile, the coroner's jury met and determined that James Anderson "came to his death from pistol shot wounds at the hands of persons unknown."[12]

When we turn to southeast Missouri between 1910 and 1919, there are four completed lynchings, all of African-American males. They took place in the bootheel counties of New Madrid, Mississippi, and Pemiscot between May 29, 1910, and October 11, 1911. The first occurred in the town of New Madrid, and the victim of this mob murder was and remains unknown. On May 28, 1910, the city marshal arrested a man whom the newspaper describes as a "refractory negro." When the African American was asked to "move on" after standing in front of Sheehy's saloon, he attempted to draw a knife and offered to fight the law enforcement officer. The black was subdued and placed in the city jail. The next day, Sunday, May 29, 1910, the police judge was notified that the body of a Negro was hanging from a tree limb in the western part of town. The newspaper is silent about any of the particulars of how the incarcerated man came to the tree from which his body was found hanging. It mentions that the coroner's jury held an inquest on Monday, May 30, 1910, and it surmises that "the negro came to his death by hanging at the hands of parties unknown." The story concludes that the acting coroner buried the body of the unknown black man in the East Side Cemetery."[13]

The next southeastern incident was a dual lynching. It was set in motion by the Saturday, July 2, 1910, robbery and murder of William Fox, a prominent and wealthy farmer in Mississippi County. Robert Coleman, from Memphis, Tennessee, and Sam Fields, from Hopkinsville, Kentucky, were working during harvest time as field hands in the area. They asked Mr. Fox for a ride in his wagon as he was returning to his home from Charleston, the county seat. They told him that they were employees of Ben Anderson, another farmer, and Fox gave them a ride. Soon, one grabbed him, and the other shot and mortally wounded him. Their robbery of Fox gave these men $2. The wounded man pointed his team in the direction of home, and he called for help at the first farmhouse. Soon law enforcement officers were summoned, and with the aid of bloodhounds, the sheriff tracked the culprits to the barn of Ben Anderson. Fox, though weakened from his injuries said, "Hold them." Two other Negroes went to the jail the next day, and they identified Coleman and Fields as the men who had stopped them immediately before Fox was shot. According to a constable, shoeprints near the wagon crime scene matched the prisoners' footwear.

On Sunday afternoon, July 3, 1910, a mob of 1,000 stormed the jail in Charleston, battered its doors down with a board, and obtained Coleman and Fields. Each, about to be hanged by the neck until dead, said that his companion had done the shooting. Coleman was strung up on a shade tree at the southwest corner of the courthouse, and Fields was hanged from a railroad crossing sign in the Bad Land suburbs. Not surprisingly, no member of the mob could be identified. The local newspaper phrases the matter quite deftly: "It is very doubtful if any member of the mob could be identified, as there was such a mix-up in trying to defend the prisoners that it would be almost impossible to distinguish those defending the prisoners from those who were members of the mob." The coroner's jury returned the expected verdict, "death was caused by hanging by unknown persons." The *Charleston Weekly Enterprise*'s lengthy story states, "The punishment given the negroes by the mob Sunday seems to meet with the approval of many of our good citizens." It also mentions that soon after this dual mob murder, approximately 100 Negroes left their harvesting jobs in Mississippi County.[14] Sheer terror must have caused their departure.

The third incident was reported as a dual lynching, but it was not. It took place in or near Carthursville, Pemiscot County, during the early morning hours on October 11, 1911, when a mob of 75 members took two black males, A.B. Rich and "High Pockets" or "Ben" from the county jail. The *St. Louis Post-Dispatch*, an evening paper, ran this headline that same day: "Mob storms Jail, Lynches 2 Negroes in Missouri Town." In smaller print the story continues, "Body of One found in River ... Second Body Missing."[15] Presumably from this first account in the *Post-Dispatch*, both an in-state paper, the *Knob Noster Gem* and an out-of-state paper, the *New York Times*, reported two victims of this lynching. The *Gem* gave their names as A.B. Rich and Hiram Pickets, and it reported that after they were shot by a mob, their bodies were pitched in the Mississippi River. The *Times* identified them as A.B. Richardson and Ben Woods. It stated that Richardson's body was found in the Mississippi River, and "that Woods met a like fate is the accepted belief."[16] Both newspapers were partially in error. The local paper identifies the man whose body was found as A.B. Rich. He was jailed on charges of stealing, and he had frequently been locked up on a variety of minor charges. The other has no surname, only "High Pockets" or "Ben." He was arrested and incarcerated because he had annoyed Misses Josie Faulk and Bessie Gee, two young white clerks employed at the Supply Store as they walked home from work on Tuesday, October 10. All we know is what the local headline proclaims, the Negro "had insulted young ladies." In the body of the story, he followed the young women, and "they became very much frightened at the peculiar actions of the negro."[17]

A subsequent *Post-Dispatch* story headlined, "Caruthersville Lynchers Safe From Prosecution," reports that the "Mayor, Sheriff, and Prosecuting Attorney Refuse to Act Against Mob that Stormed the Jail, Killed One Negro, Lashed Another, and Burned a House." Buried in the St. Louis newspaper's account is mention that "High Pockets" or "Ben" "was released by the mob after being whipped and has fled to Tennessee."[18] The local paper identifies the burned structure as a "Negro Hotel," but it avoids the use of the word *lynched.* Instead its story is headlined: "Mob Whips Bad Negroes.... One Negro Found Dead in Mississippi River." It explains that the coroner's jury could not agree on the cause of the death of A.B. Rich. Doing so protected any member of the mob from a charge of murder. It seems reasonable to classify Rich's demise as a lynching. After all he was removed from the jail and whipped near the Mississippi River. If by chance, Rich accidentally fell in the river, the mob's action made that possible. Equally likely is that the members of the mob tossed A.B. Rich's already dead body in the Mississippi River. Not so with "High Pockets." In approximately the middle of the Caruthersville newspaper's account we read that he "showed up for work at Gid Kinnon's on Wednesday morning, Oct. 12." It goes on to relate that he "took his belongings and disappeared. It is believed that he will manage to avoid Caruthersville in the future."[19] The proximity of Caruthersville to the state immediately east of Missouri makes credible that the man who survived the mob's whipping crossed the Mississippi River into Tennessee. We have no definitive knowledge about where he went; all we know for certain is that he survived the whipping.

The *Chicago Tribune*, the NAACP list, and *100 Years of Lynchings* carry Ben Woods as the victim of a lynching, and Capeci repeats the error.[20] "High Pockets" or "Ben" belongs in Appendix 2, not Appendix 1. A.B. Rich's lynching and "High Pockets" survival ends Missouri's known lynchings between 1910 and 1919, two whites and eight blacks, or 60 percent black. One must revisit the 1840s to find so few mob murders in this state.

Six falsely reported and/or foiled mob murders between 1910 and 1919 are known. In the southwest there are two, Paralee and Isaac Collins, both white. The NAACP list of 1919 includes them as being murdered by a mob. On June 10, 1914, a band of masked men knocked at the door of the Collins cabin. They managed to live through the attack, but Isaac was shot in the head and lost a part of his right ear and Paralee was shot in the leg. Further, their cabin was burned; all this took place in Douglas County, on Noblett Creek. The *Howell County Gazette*, published in a county adjacent to Douglas County, where Paralee and Isaac Collins were victims of assault, arson, and other evil doing, carried a story about the incident; hence the placement of these happenings as completed lynchings in Howell County. The newspaper reported that unknown persons had committed these deeds, and done so "as a warning that such undesirable citizens are not wanted in the community."[21]

In northeast Missouri between 1900 and 1919, there were two foiled lynchings. The first occurred on April 20, 1915, in Louisiana, when a 150-member mob stormed the jail in an attempt to lynch John Eaton, an African American charged with the April 10 stabbing of William Prettyman, a white employee in a shoe factory. The would-be lynchers managed to splinter the jail door with their axes, but law enforcement officers dispersed the crowd, and the county sheriff brought Eaton and two other black prisoners from Louisiana to the jail in Bowling Green, seat of Pike County.[22]

The second prevented mob murder also took place in Pike County. Harrison Rose, a black man, was charged with the August 31, 1915, murder of Dudley Davidson, a white farmer, near Clarksville. While Rose was at work on Davidson's farm, the owner criticized Rose's threshing machine skills, and the black hit the white in the head with a club, fracturing his skull. Rose escaped, and Davidson died that same evening. Soon, the hunt was on for Rose. Both the Pike County sheriff and prosecuting attorney were among the 500 men and boys searching for him. On Wednesday, September 1, he was captured, placed in a car, and brought to the county jail in Bowling Green. Instead of taking a direct route to the county seat, the authorities took evasive action by traveling south to Cyrene, before head northwest to Bowling Green. Nonetheless as the local paper reports, the car carrying the prisoner "was followed closely by several others filled with would-be lynchers."[23]

Harrison Rose's residence in the Pike County jail appears to have been brief. Authorities secretly removed him to New London and placed him in the Ralls County jail. Ralls is north of and adjacent to Pike County, and there are no known lynchings in Ralls County's history. Once the time came for court proceedings against Rose, a deputy sheriff brought him from New London to Bowling Green on the 6:45 A.M. Short Line train, probably on Monday, October 4. At approximately 1:10 A.M., on October 5, 1915, a small mob began forming outside the jail. Both Sheriff and Mrs. Hawkins helped prevent a lynching. She was the first to hear the unwelcome sounds of a man moving about in the yard near the jail. She awakened and alerted her husband. While the sheriff slipped out and went to the Cottage Hotel in order to telephone prominent persons who were opposed to vigilante action, his wife, in possession of the jail keys, refused to surrender them. Among the many citizens who came to the sheriff's aid at this early morning hour were the circuit court judge, Champ Clark and his son, and other notables, whom the local paper names. At this time Champ Clark, a skilled orator, was Speaker of the U.S. House of Representatives and had earlier been Woodrow Wilson's chief rival for the Democratic nomination for president in 1912. According to the *New York Times*, Clark's eloquent pleas on both the occasion of Rose's initial jailing in early September and the mob action against him in early October helped disperse the men intent on lynching this black prisoner. The newspaper's September story is headlined, "Clark Prevents Lynching/ Speaker Saves Negro by Eloquent Plea to Missouri Mob," and its October account, "Clark Prevents Lynching/ Speaker and Son in Posse which Disperses Mob in Front of Jail." These stories praise a high federal official for doing the right thing among his constituents.[24]

The local news stories mention that the presence of 40 to 50 eminent citizens at the jail, including Champ Clark and his son, caused the five- to six-member mob to cease its jail demolition work and flee the scene in an automobile. The lynchers manqué had handkerchiefs over their faces and could not be recognized, but most likely they were neighbors of Dudley Davidson, the white man whom Rose clubbed to death a month earlier. Both Bowling Green newspapers praise the avoidance of a mob murder. One concludes its story, "Let Rose have a fair trial. The law will certainly be strong enough to punish him as he deserves. That is the feeling of the people, outside of a few immediate neighbors of the dead man."[25] The other local paper's story, headlined, "Too Much Mob/ A Disgrace to the County./ Time/ to Stop It," concludes, "The people guilty of these attacks are doing the county much harm.... All good citizens should back [Sheriff Hawkins]." On the same front page as the above is another story headlined "Circuit Court," and it states that the judge appointed two lawyers to represent the accused in a forthcoming trial, *State* v. *Harrison Rose*.[26]

In southeast Missouri there were two instances in which a mob murder did not take place. One concerns "High Pockets;" it has been discussed earlier. The other averted lynching took place in Mississippi County, when, in the early morning hours, Lee Gardner, a black male, allegedly attempted to rape Geneva, a 12-year-old white girl, the daughter of Mr. and Mrs. Drinkwater, on July 5, 1910, approximately 10 miles northeast of Charleston. The father heard the screams of his children and found the culprit in his home. The father telephoned the authorities at 3:30 A.M., reached a deputy sheriff, and by the time law enforcement officers arrived at the Drinkwater residence, Lee Gardner had been captured and a large crowd of farmers had also arrived. They were ready to lynch him, but "cooler heads," as the local paper reports, pleaded with the crowd and "the negro's life [was] not taken." The news story's headline about the matter states: "Attempted Assault/ Lee Gardner, a Negro, Came Near Being Lynched by Angry Mob."[27]

Increasing numbers of failed lynchings may have been a Missouri phenomenon, but declining numbers of lynchings were nationwide. Any figures are suspect, but their dwindling is not. A black Kansas City newspaper contains a chart of essentially decreasing numbers from 1893, with 200 lynchings nationwide to 45 from 1903 to mid–1905.[28] A black Chicago newspaper relates that 61 persons were lynched in 1920, and that is 22 less than in 1919. These numbers may have been picked out of a hat, but the figures tell the same stories. Fewer and fewer persons were murdered by mobs as the 1910s became the 1920s, the 1930s, and the early 1940s. No decade in Missouri earlier than 1910–1919 had six foiled and/or falsely reported mob murders and only 10 actual events.

The nation, including Missouri, appears to have been losing its appetite for necktie and other lethal parties. The next chapter explores some of the reasons that enthusiasm for mob murders was waning in this state and throughout the United States.

CHAPTER 12

Declining Numbers and Black Victims Only, 1920–1942

The numbers of lynchings in Missouri and nationwide decreased in the 1920s, 1930s, and 1940s from one decade to the next. In this state, only African Americans were lynched: six in the 1920s, two in the 1930s, and the last in 1942. What caused this reduction in numbers? Two authors of an interesting book state their belief that KKK membership and hence lynchings declined because Klan members became embarrassed by the parody of their activities in a children's radio program, which aired after World War II. They quote a KKK member who saw children playing their games, youngsters with inside information about the Ku Klux Klan: "When I asked them what they were doing, they said they were playing a new kind of cops and robbers called Superman against the Klan. Gangbusting, they called it. Knew all our secret passwords and everything. I never felt so ridiculous in my life. Suppose my own kid finds my Klan robe someday."[1] I find all of this interesting, but being made to feel ridiculous seems an insufficient explanation of a complicated matter. Persons filled with sufficient hateful energy to form themselves into mobs and kill their fellow humans were not the sort to be embarrassed; quite the contrary, they saw themselves as fighting to protect white rights, including the rights of white women to be safe from black rapists. These groups were very far removed from being embarrassed.[2] The explanation for these smaller numbers of lynchings is a more complex matter than that the lynchers were ridiculed out of existence.

Every post–Civil War Missouri governor in whose administration a lynching occurred condemned it, and there is nothing to suggest that antebellum governors of this state applauded mob murders. All U.S. presidents from Theodore Roosevelt (already discussed) through FDR denounced lynchings. President William Howard Taft stated on one occasion that "if one man could commit a lynching there would be fewer of them; but 300 or 400 men banded together seem to lose their conscience." On another he said, "I cannot speak too strongly of my utter detestation of the crime of lynching."[3] During World War I, President Woodrow Wilson declared that lynchings furnished Germans with propaganda. He stated, "No man who loves America, ... who is truly loyal to her institutions, can justify mob action while the courts of justice are open and the government of the States and the Nation are ready and able to do their duty."[4] President Warren Harding favored a law to make lynching a federal crime,[5] as did President Calvin Coolidge, who said, "The Congress ought to exercise all its power of prevention and punishment against the hideous crime of lynching, of which the Negroes are by no means the sole sufferers, but for which they furnish a majority of the victims."[6] President Herbert Hoover agreed with his predecessors when he commented, "Every decent citizen must condemn the lynching evil as an undermining of the very essence of both justice and democracy."[7] Unlike Presidents Harding and Coolidge, Hoover was against a federal anti-lynching law.[8] While Eleanor Roosevelt favored this law on grounds that "it puts us as a whole, against something we should all be against,"[9] her husband, while abhorring mob rule, did not actively support any federal lynching legislation. In a word, all American presidents between the years covered in this chapter, 1920 through 1942, vigorously spoke out against mob murders.

These words from multiple bully pulpits no doubt helped to diminish the numbers of the lynched during these six administrations, but it seems likely that there were other factors at work. The explosive technological growth, new forms of communication and improved transportation dispelled the explosive force of boredom in rural places and small towns, areas that saw the great majority of earlier lynchings. Movies were one new gathering spot, less volatile because groups were no longer left to their own devices, and for the most part, they were a harmless and wonderful pastime. Actors such as Tom Mix in his cowboy flicks, Charlie Chaplin as the little tramp, and Rudolph Valentino as the great lover thrilled audiences. However, one silent film played a more sinister role, D.W. Griffith's *The Birth of a Nation* (1915).

As mentioned in Chapter 10, this movie was based on Thomas Dixon's book and play, *The Clansman* (1905). Dixon wrote the script and gave the title to this infamous motion picture. Both Griffith and Dixon were Southerners; each had a father who fought in the Civil War on the Confederate side, and more than 40 years after Lee's surrender to Grant at Appomattox Courthouse, they felt that Harriet Beecher Stowe's *Uncle Tom's Cabin* (1852) was a malicious slander of their beloved homeland. Between them they set out to tell the "true story" of the Civil War and Reconstruction.[10]

From its first showing, Griffith's movie produced a storm of controversy. Among other newspapers that excoriated its racist message was the *Kansas City Times*. After praising the "wonderful spectacle" of the film, then showing in Kansas City, the paper asks, "What is to be thought of an author who would deliberately bring all the resources of his art to bear on a spectacle founded on race hatred? Who would seek popularity by inflaming the worst passions of the human heart.... The whole tendency of ... the [movie] is to arouse loathing and contempt of whites against blacks." The editorial continues, "Mr. Dixon has ... invented ... some revolting episodes and made them typical. In so doing this he has succeeded in picturing the negro as wholly degraded and bestial, with unlimited possibilities of evil."[11] The *Chicago Tribune's* headline tells a similar story, "Clansman Film Objected to as Peril to Negro."[12] Jane Addams, the famous Chicago social worker and founder of Hull House, denounced the movie as exciting racial prejudice. She stated, "The producer ... gather[ed] the most vicious and grotesque individuals he could find among colored people and showed them as representative of the truth about the entire race.... This film appeals to race prejudice."[13]

I first saw *The Birth of a Nation* in the early 1960s at Henry Ford's Greenfield Village, just outside Detroit, in Dearborn, Michigan. I remember that a piano player produced all the sound which accompanied this silent film. My dominant memory is of clansmen riding horses, and in 2008, seeing this movie again, those wonderful horses, all decked out in their clan regalia galloping across the screen with hooded and robed clan riders on them, remain the best part of this ridiculous movie.

Early in this silent film, much of it set in South Carolina, the screen message tells the viewer that this movie will "take the liberty to show the dark side of the wrong." Significant chunks of American history, such as Lincoln signing the Emancipation Proclamation, Lee's surrender to a cigar-smoking Grant, and Lincoln's assassination at Ford's Theater, are interspersed with many a scene of white Southerners and their good, docile slaves and former slaves living in wonderful harmony, mostly before and during, but a bit after the Civil War. Many white persons play African-American roles in black face. Then the War Between the States ends, and harmony is no more. Carpetbaggers and uppity blacks cause all the trouble. When a black legislature passes a law which provides for the intermarriage of white and black, we can be sure that an assault of a young white female will soon be suggested on the screen. Gus, lynched off-stage in *The Clansman* (1905), is now an officer in the Union Army and wearing his uniform he tells the white ingénue Elsie, "I'm a captain now. I want to marry you." She fights him off, runs, and jumps off a cliff to her death.

The KKK appears to end the life of Gus off-stage. Another sinister character, named Silas Lynch, a mulatto, announces to Flora, another white young beauty, "I want to marry a white woman." Again the KKK on its horses outfitted in KKK garb, comes to the rescue. Those horses, wonderful horses, the theft of which led to so many lynchings in Missouri from the late 1860s through the early 1880s, repeatedly fill Griffith's screen. The piano player hammers out songs such as "The Star-Spangled Banner." There is no doubt that young white women are victims and lustful black males are aflame with sexual desire for them. As far as I could make out, there is no black male who actually rapes a white girl or woman in this movie, but as Charlene Regester notes, "*The Birth of a Nation* constructed the white female as victim, positioned the black male as monster, created and whipped up the white males' hysterical zest for violent physical attacks against the 'Monster,' and justified the white man's lawlessness and vicious behavior."[14]

The same year this silly movie was all the rage or the outrage, R.W. Shufeldt, retired U.S. Army medical doctor, published yet another of his hateful books: *America's Greatest Problem, The Negro* (1915). In it, he confidently informs his reader, "As a rule, the youth of the negro people are liars by nature; they are nearly all predisposed to gambling, and the majority of them will steal."[15] More to the point of the special nature of their depravity, as this learned M.D. explains, "In the negro, all passions, emotions, and ambitions are almost wholly subservient to the sexual instinct."[16] Shufeldt does not endorse lynching as a remedy to curb Negro rapists of white girls and women; lynching was never an activity which learned persons such as Dr. Shufeldt praised in print. Instead, he recommends that the black male who rapes the white female be tried in a court of law and put to death within a few hours of the jury reaching its verdict.[17] To be sure, a rush to judgment characterized the trials and punishments of black boys and men charged with the rape of white girls and women. The first legal execution in Missouri after the legislature restored capital punishment was the March 26, 1920, hanging of Adam Jackson in Butler County for the February 9, 1920, rape of Mrs. Emma Mann.[18] This interval of six weeks would surely have been too slow to satisfy Dr. Shufeldt and his admirers. Further, the time lapse in this state between the crime of the black raping the white and his legal punishment of death typically took far longer than six weeks. It would seem that Shufeldt recommended the punishment for rape be considerably speeded up, and there was just one way to do that.

Did the movie *The Birth of a Nation* (1915) and the book *America's Greatest Problem: The Negro* (1915) encourage lynch mobs? To argue that there is a direct link between viewing this enormously popular and silly movie and/or reading this horrible book and participating in the lynching of a black male is a considerable stretch. Too many lynchings took place earlier than the appearance of this movie, this book, and other anti-black propagandistic works to establish any direct link between them. What can be shown, however, in Missouri, is that from 1920 until 1942, *all* victims of lynchings were black males and *all* were alleged to have committed a crime against a white girl or woman. That crime was either attempted rape, rape, murder, or both rape and murder. There is no doubt that lynching was growing less frequent in both Missouri and nationwide, but where it took place in this state, the lynching always avenged the crime hinted at in *The Birth of a Nation* (1915), which *American's Greatest Problem the Negro* (1915) urged as properly legally punished within a few hours of the jury reaching its guilty verdict.

In April 1919, the NAACP published its hurriedly assembled book *Thirty Years of Lynching in the United States, 1889–1918.* Probably because many 1890s mob victims were white, the compilers of this publication omitted the race of the lynched. They almost certainly did so in order to call attention to the plight of the African American at the hands of a white mob. The timing of the NAACP publication was surely in anticipation of the introduction in 1920 of an anti-lynching bill in the U.S. House of Representatives. Though there had been furtive attempts earlier, the 1920 bill was the first widely publicized effort to make lynching a federal crime. It was introduced by Leonidas Carstarphen Dyer (1871–1957), better known as L.C., a Republican member of the House from Missouri. Dyer attended Missouri's common schools, Central Wesleyan College, Warrenton, and Washington University, St. Louis. He studied law and was admitted to the bar in 1893. He was first elected to the House in 1911 and again in 1915, and he served in the next eight succeeding Congresses (March 4, 1915–March 3, 1933).[19] He represented a heavily black constituency in St. Louis City. Of equal importance, he was born and raised in Warren County, Missouri, a locale that had no known lynching in its history and a rarity in its use of the death penalty. Eight days after Dyer celebrated his fifth birthday, William Foster, a white man, after two jury trials and an appeal to the Supreme Court of Missouri, was hanged by the sheriff of Warren County on June 19, 1876, for the murder of an unknown black man. Among the headlines in the St. Louis newspapers' extensive coverage was "First Execution of a White for the Slaughter of a Black."[20] Surely, Dyer heard this execution discussed as he grew up; he came from a Missouri county where the equal protection of the law meant something real to its residents.

Under the legislation which Dyer proposed, any persons charged with a crime would be able to appeal to federal courts for protection if they had a reasonable belief that they would be denied the equal protection of the law, a right guaranteed against the states in the 14th Amendment to the U.S. Constitution. Further, participants in mobs (defined as three or more persons) would be subject to fines of not more than $10,000 and imprisonment for not more than 10 years. Counties in which lynchings took place would be subject to a forfeiture of $10,000, and the federal government would compensate the surviving family members of the lynched person.[21] Those who actually caused the death would be tried for murder. In the event that the prisoner was taken from one county and lynched in another — and there are several instances of this taking place in Missouri — both counties would be held responsible.[22]

The bill was favorably reported out of the House Judiciary Committee in November 1921. In 1922, it was passed by the House and was declared constitutional by Harry Daughtery, President Harding's attorney general. It hit a snag in the U.S. Senate. Among those who voted against it was James A. Reed of Missouri, a member of the Senate Judiciary Committee. Senator Reed stated, "No man is any more opposed to lynching than I am," but said he could not and would not vote in favor of a bill that he considered unconstitutional. Reed insisted that the matter should be left to the states; he added that he would be in favor of a state bill.[23] Other members of congress were more direct in their opposition to the Dyer Anti-Lynching Bill. Congressman John Rankin of Mississippi believed the bill should have a new name, "a bill to encourage rape."[24] This bill and others that followed it were repeatedly filibustered in the Senate,[25] principally by Southern members. Numerous attempts to pass any federal anti-lynching legislation were defeated.[26]

Finally, on June 13, 2005, 80 members of the U.S. Senate officially apologized for this body's failure to enact any anti-lynching laws of the many that were introduced over the past 105 years. This time period includes one proposed in January 1900 by Representative George H. White of North Carolina, an African-American member of the U.S. House of Representatives. His bill would have made participants in mobs that murdered persons guilty of treason and subject to prosecution in federal courts.[27] White's bill failed to become law; likewise, every other bill introduced in the U.S. Congress to make lynching a federal crime failed, and these failures extended over a period of 40 or more years.

Meanwhile, at the same time the Dyer Act was being introduced and reintroduced throughout the 1920s, lynchings continued to decline nationwide and in Missouri. Five of the six in Missouri between 1920 and 1929 took place in counties with earlier mob murders of blacks. There are none known from the southwestern section of the state and only one from northwestern Missouri. It took place just outside the city limits of Excelsior Springs, Clay County, on August 7, 1925.

The triggering incident was the alleged 1:30 A.M. attempted rape of 18-year-old Blanche Holt, a white girl, on August 7, 1925. She was the daughter of a farmer living near Lawson. Miss Holt and her white male companion, 20-year-old Leonard Utt, claimed the identification of Walter Mitchell was easy because the black man had worked in their environs for several weeks prior to his attempted rape of her. Both said that they recognized him immediately when they saw him at the Excelsior Springs jail. Mitchell arrived at this facility at an early hour; he had been arrested as early as 5 A.M., the same morning as the alleged attack. Soon after he was placed in the city jail, a crowd began to collect. Miss Holt and her companion arrived shortly after noon, and they identified Mitchell as her attacker. By then, the jail crowd had already reached 300 persons, and it continued to grow. Had the local authorities anticipated a lynching, they would have taken Mitchell to Liberty, the county seat. His crime, if a crime did take place, had occurred

POST SPEEDED TO EXCELSIOR SPRINGS

Coverage of mob murders always boosted newspaper sales in the vicinity of the event. The text under this photograph explains that "Within an hour after Walter Mitchell, Negro, had been hanged in Excelsior Springs yesterday, copies of the *Post* containing a complete account of the tragedy were being distributed on the streets of that town. This photograph shows a group of Excelsior Springs residents reading the *Post*. The papers were loaded in the back of a high powered touring car as they came from the press." From the *Kansas City Post*, August 8, 1925. (Used by permission, State Historical Society of Missouri, Columbia.)

outside the Excelsior Springs city limits, out in the country near Larson. Belatedly, those in charge realized the seriousness of the lynching threat. A false fire alarm was turned in to distract the crowd, but since the jail and the fire station occupied the same building, the removal of the fire truck, pretending to respond to a blaze somewhere, created space for the mob to move in. In addition to the false fire alarm, the Clay County prosecutor, Ray Cummins, made a telephone call to the Kansas City, Missouri, chief of police and requested police assistance in controlling the crowd.

Estimates vary as to how many minutes — five, eight, and 20 — after the strangulation death of Mitchell did 50-plus Kansas City police officers arrive on the scene. Well before the big city cops got there, the mob and spectators numbered 1,000 members. A sizeable number of them stormed the city jail, and in all five attacks were necessary before the mob gained entrance and grabbed Mitchell. It rushed him handcuffed to its designated hanging tree. There, in addition to the 1,000 men, women, and children on the ground, a Wabash passenger train of two cars arrived just before Mitchell was hanged. The locomotive stopped, enabling both its passengers and crew to view the spectacle. The photograph of the mob immediately before the noose was tightened about the prisoner's neck was made by a newspaper photographer concealed in the train. Three other photographers attempting to take snapshots of the lynching were attacked by the mob, and one camera was destroyed. Later, the *Kansas City Post* rushed newspapers, as it stated, "in the back of a high powered touring car as they came from the press," and it photographed eager residents of Excelsior Springs reading about the big event.[28]

The Kansas City police officers cut down Mitchell's body, and the undertaker who laid out the lynched man's remains for viewing kept the doors of his business open until midnight in order to accommodate the crowds of men, women, and children who waited their turn to see the dead man. Afterwards, residents of Excelsior Springs blamed outsiders for Mitchell's death, but the sentiment about this town was that the black man got what he deserved. The county prosecutor stated of the matter, "We feel that justice has been done.... Of course the method was crude. I would have preferred that the negro could have been hanged legally, and I am convinced that it would have been done." The prosecutor had no knowledge of the individual members of the mob. He said, "I don't know who they are, and I am unable to find out." This news story concludes with a statement from the county coroner as he signed Mitchell's death certification, "This is Clay County, not Jackson. There will be no inquest."[29]

The first incident from 1920s northeast Missouri was set in motion by 19-year-old Roy Hammonds's attempting to rape an unnamed 14-year-old white girl on April 27, 1921, in or near Booth, Pike County. His attack on the child was interrupted by the victim's father and brother. Two days later, Hammonds pled guilty to this offense before a circuit court judge, and he was sentenced to ten years in the Missouri State Penitentiary. The sheriff, Charles P. Moore, and six deputies took the young black man to the train depot. The locomotive was due at 7:45 P.M., but by 7:25 P.M. or so, a mob of 200 unmasked boys and men broke into the railroad station, seized the prisoner, put him in one of a number of waiting automobiles, and drove off with him. The mob hanged him from a tree near the Bowling Green Road at approximately 8 P.M. on April 29, 1921. Shortly afterward the authorities were notified of the location of Hammonds's body. The coroner took charge of the remains, and the usual assurances of an investigation into the lynching were given. The sheriff communicated the event to Governor Arthur Hyde, and he in turn ordered the state's attorney general to conduct an investigation. Hammonds's was Pike County's last mob murder.[30]

The other 1920s lynching in northeast Missouri took place in Columbia, Boone County, and it was this county's third and last. All of its mob murder victims, Slave Hiram in 1853, George Bush in 1889, and James T. Scott in 1923, were African American and charged with a sexual offense. In Hiram's case it was the attempted rape of a 15-

year-old white female; in Bush's the rape of a five- or six-year-old biracial child, and in Scott's, the attempted rape of a 14- or 15-year-old white girl.

The crime took place on April 20, 1923, when a black male attempted to rape a young girl as she was returning home from school. She was Regina Almstedt, the daughter of Hermann B. Almstedt, professor of German literature and chairman of the German Department at the University of Missouri. Her would-be assailant lured her toward the railroad tracks below the Stewart Bridge, but he was frightened by persons passing by, and no rape took place. According to a Kansas City newspaper, in the week following this incident, Regina Almstedt made three positive identifications of James T. Scott as her assailant. Among the clues which led to her pointing him out was the odor of formaldehyde, which she claimed she smelled on his clothing both at the time he attacked her and when the police brought him before her. Scott was employed as a janitor at the University of Missouri's medical building,[31] and in this capacity he would have been surrounded by many chemicals in the medical school's laboratories, including the pungent disinfectant and preservative formaldehyde. In a well-written and thoroughly researched article about this lynching, Patrick J. Huber concludes that Scott "appears to have been innocent." However, Huber notes that between 3 and 5 P.M. on the day of the attack, as Miss Almstedt was homeward bound from school, Scott's whereabouts could not be ascertained; "no one had seen [Scott] in the intervening two hours."[32]

Apart from the guilt or innocence of the perpetrator, if one changes the demographics in the case and makes Scott white and his victim African American, the threat of a lynching is as remote as that of the sky falling in. When the mob came for him on Sunday, April 29, at an early morning hour, he had been an inmate of the Boone County jail since at least Saturday, April 28. On this date, a circuit court judge ordered him held without bond and set his trial for May 21. The mob gained access to the jail by using an acetylene torch and cold chisels, those used to cut through stone. According to a Kansas City paper, when the mob grabbed Scott, he was "in a cell with two other negroes charged with similar crimes against negro girls. These negroes were not harmed."[33]

The mob began gathering about the jail at approximately 9 P.M., and by 11 P.M. a committee of approximately 100 persons called on the sheriff, Fred Brown, to surrender Scott. He refused. By 12:30 A.M. the mob had its man, and it marched him to the Stewart Bridge, the place where he allegedly attempted to rape Regina Almstedt. The authorities notified her father, Professor Almstedt, and he tried his best to persuade the assembled that they should not lynch Scott; rather they should allow the law to take its course. He had no success. By approximately 1:40 A.M. April 29, 1923, Scott's lifeless body dangled from a rope attached to the Stewart Bridge. The coroner cut it down that same morning. Who were the members of the mob that lynched James Scott? According to a Kansas City newspaper, the crowd was estimated at 1,500, but separating those who were active participants from those who were spectators was difficult. It notes that the witnesses included "some women and girls and many university students."[34] The acting university president, Isidor Loeb, insisted that no student had been a participant in this execrable event. The *New York Times* story about it is headlined, "Missouri Students See Negro Lynched/ Co-eds Join Crowd Which Cheers the Storming of the Columbia jail."[35]

The same day as the lynching the coroner's jury came in with its customary verdict, "death at the hands of a man or men unknown to this jury."[36] In early May, there were a series of indictments. A Kansas City newspaper's headline proclaimed, "Five Indicted in Lynching; Arrests Due/ Names Suppressed While Probe Is Extended." The story itself clarifies that "George Bankwell [was] arrested yesterday on a charge of carrying cold chisels and a hammer into the jail ... for the purpose of releasing Scott." The account concludes that Bankwell is "at liberty on bail."[37] This same newspaper's next day story about this matter states that a farmer, Hamp Rowland, had been charged with "obstruct[ing] an officer of the law in the performance of his duty." It concludes that "numerous farmers came to Columbia and offered to go on Rowland's bond, which was quickly arranged."[38] In May, the Boone County prosecutor announced he would seek a first-degree murder indictment from the special grand jury that he had called into session to investigate Scott's lynching.[39]

In July 1923, George Bankwell was acquitted on the murder charge. This came as no surprise to Congressman L.C. Dyer, author of the anti-lynching bill then stalled in the U.S. Congress. Dyer stated, "The verdict furnishes more evidence of the failure to punish mob violence, especially in cases of negro lynchings. It is a failure to give the equal protection guaranteed by the Fourteenth Amendment of the United States Constitution."[40] Dyer believed that a federal court would be far more likely to secure a conviction than a state court. Perhaps he was right. Kansas City's black newspaper *The Call* got to the heart of the matter shortly after Scott's mob murder. Its editorial is headlined "Lynching is the Flower of which Hate is the Seed." In this piece the newspaper states the truth of mob murders in 1920s Missouri, "Lynching is the logical working out of race prejudice. This nation teaches its babies, its youths, its men, that there is no good in Negroes. It suppresses their contribution to a common civilization and magnifies their weaknesses."[41] In hindsight, a change of heart was called for, and whether a state or a federal court was given jurisdiction to try the lynchers seems less important than that succeeding generations unlearn the prejudices of their forbears.

In southeastern 1920s Missouri there were three mob murders. The earliest occurred at Centerville, Reynolds County, on July 7, 1920, when an armed posse of citizens from Centerville and Ellington shot and killed Fred Canafex. He was a convict from the Missouri State Penitentiary in Jefferson City and a member of prison road camp No. 5, working on the state highway out of Ellington. The previous day, July 6, he was alleged to have "attacked" a young white girl, Miss Verla Simmons, daughter of Frank Simmons, a prominent farmer, as she was homeward bound after carrying the mail on a rural route. Armed with a knife, he took hold of her team, forced her into the woods, and there "assaulted" her; presumably, he raped her. Local coverage of this lynching includes: "We have never had any negro residents in this county, and the people here have as much use for a colored man as they have for rattlesnakes and copperheads." The news story concludes, "Our people are law abiding citizens. If the negro had been captured by the sheriff, we doubt if any attempt would have been made to take the case out of the hands of the law. But ... when [Canafex] tried to escape, they had one sure method of stopping him, and they were forced to resort thereto."[42] The *New York Times* coverage of this lynching mentions that Fred Canafex was sentenced to prison for 20 years on a charge of first-degree robbery in 1914.[43]

The next southeastern lynching of the 1920s was set in motion by the December 18, 1924, attempted rape of a 15-year-old white girl, daughter of a onetime candidate for the state legislature from Mississippi County. As she was returning home at approximately 6 P.M., a Negro appeared and grabbed her, but he soon disappeared, frightened from the scene by passing automobile traffic. The young victim was able to describe her attacker in minute detail, and Roosevelt Grigsby, a 20-year-old African American, was soon under arrest. He was taken first to the sheriff's office in Charleston, where the sherriff and his deputies later asserted that their prisoner confessed his crime to them. Next he was taken to the young girl's home, and she positively identified him. He was then returned to the sheriff's office, and in what could only have been collusion between lawmen and a mob, someone in the sheriff's office dropped a copy of Grigsby's alleged confession from an upstairs window of the courthouse to one of the mob leaders on the street. He read it aloud to the assembled, and the 200-member crowd soon stormed the courthouse. The mob tied up and later untied the sheriff and his deputies, seized Roosevelt Grisby, dragged him out of the courthouse to a tree 50 feet from the sheriff's office, and hanged him from it. Next, after a bullet was fired through his remains, his body was cut down, tied to an automobile, dragged through the streets of Charleston's Negro section, and later hanged from a post in front of a grocery store. Afterward, the body was cut down, thrown into a bonfire, and consumed by its flames. By 10 P.M. that same night, December 18, 1924, the city of Charleston, seat of Mississippi County, was quiet.[44]

The Kansas City branch of the NAACP sent a telegram to Governor Arthur Hyde; it urged him to do all in his power to punish Grigsby's lynchers.[45] The governor offered the usual $300 reward for the apprehension and conviction of each person guilty of this crime.[46] There ended the matter of the last of Mississippi County's four known mob murders, all of black males, between 1905 and 1924: Witherspoon in 1905, Coleman and Fields in 1910, and Grigsby in 1924.

The next and last lynching of a black male in southeastern Missouri in the 1920s took place in Braggadocio, Pemiscot County, on May 22, 1927. Will Sherod, a 30-year-old African American, was suspected of the rape of a 31-year-old white widow with two children, Mrs. Ella Henderson. The alleged attack took place some time after midnight, and Sherod was apprehended early that same morning, brought down by bullets fired by a local constable. He was taken to the county jail in Caruthersville, and that same evening, a mob of 100 members removed him from this facility, took him to Braggadocio, hanged him from a tree, and riddled his body with bullets. The coroner's inquest found that Sherod came to his death at the hands of unknown persons.[47] This was the last of Pemiscot County's known lynchings. They were all twentieth century events: Reverend Malone, a white male adulterer and wife abuser, in 1903; A.B. Rich, a black robbery suspect in 1911; and Sherod in 1927. It was also Missouri's last lynching of the 1920s.

The only falsely reported event of this decade concerns a Saline County matter. According to a May 31, 1928, *New York Times* story headlined "Negroes Lynch Negro," 12 African-American men took another black man, Ocie Wilson, from lawmen as they were en route with him in a motor car from south of Slater to Marshall. Wilson allegedly had killed Romeo Logan, a Negro railroad shop worker, in a gambling game. The story about Wilson concludes, "His body was found hanging from a tree near the highway."[48] This item must be placed in Appendix 2 for three reasons. First, there is no coverage about it in any Saline County newspaper. Further, it is unmentioned in a roll call of Missouri lynchings that appeared in an in-state newspaper two and one-half years later. The story lists the mob murder of Hammonds (1921), Scott (1923), Grigsby (1924), Mitchell (1925), Sherod (1927), and Gunn (1931) as those that occurred here in the past 10 years.[49] Beginning in the 1920s, newspapers statewide kept box scores of the lynched, and every time a new name was added, the entire list of the 1920s was repeated with the date, name, race, place, and alleged crime. Finally, no other researcher has discovered any previously unknown mob murders in Missouri that took place here after 1920.

In 1930s Missouri only two mob murders occurred; both took place in the northwestern section, and they remain notoriously well-known nearly eight decades later. The first happened in Nodaway Count, just outside Maryville, on January 12, 1931, at 10:30 A.M. Its trigger was the December 16, 1930, rape and murder of a 20-year-old white female, a school teacher, Miss Velma Coulter. Her body was found mutilated, beaten and slashed in her place of employment, the one-room Garrett School, after her pupils had left for the day, on a Tuesday. The locale of her murder was three miles southwest of Maryville. She was then living with Mr. and Mrs. T.H. Thompson, and when she did not arrive at their home as expected by supper, Mr. Thompson went to the Garrett School and found the young woman's body in a pool of blood. He quickly informed others of his hideous discovery, and by 7 P.M., Sheriff Harve England, the coroner, and others, including bloodhounds from Savannah, in Andrew County, had arrived. In addition, National Guard members volunteered their assistance, and the St. Joseph police detective unit was also involved in the search for the rapist-killer of Velma Coulter.

Lawmen were interested in a 27-year-old black male, Raymond Gunn. Earlier he had been convicted and served time in the Missouri State Penitentiary for a 1925 attempted rape of a white college girl from Mound City, Holt County, when she was a student at Northwest Missouri State Teachers College in Maryville. He was released January 28, 1928, married a Negro woman, and they moved to Omaha, where she died. He returned to Maryville and was afterwards arrested and convicted of carrying a concealed weapon. Gunn had not been seen on December 17, a Wednesday, the day after the murder. On December 18, Velma Coulter was buried, after an enormous crowd attended her funeral. That same day, a Thursday, Gunn was picked up in a cornfield by a law enforcement officer, interrogated for the entire afternoon, and at 6 P.M. he confessed and signed a written statement that he had killed Velma Coulter. In addition to his confession, a heel print found near the scene matched Gunn's shoe. The coroner's jury concluded on December 18 that Raymond Gunn killed Velma Coulter on December 16, 1930.

The confessed murderer was immediately and hurriedly taken to the St. Joseph city jail, and he was soon transferred to the Buchanan County jail, also in St. Joseph. The next day, when a 150-member mob attempted to seize him from the Buchanan County jail, he was moved to the Jackson County jail at 219 E. Missouri Ave., Kansas City. This was Gunn's second confinement in St. Joseph. When he was arrested in October 1925 for the attempted rape of a college student in Maryville, he was removed and taken to St. Joseph in order to avoid mob violence.

Gunn remained in the Jackson County jail in Kansas City on a charge of the first-degree murder of Velma Coulter until the early morning of December 26, 1930, when he was returned to Maryville, appeared before a justice of the peace, and waived his preliminary hearing. His case was set for trial on the second Monday in January, the 12th. Afterwards he was quickly returned to the security of the Jackson County jail in Kansas City.

On Saturday, January 10, at 8:30 P.M., lawmen returned him to Maryville. Rumor had it that he was kept at the Farmers Trust Company, but deputies stated that this high-profile prisoner was confined in the Nodaway County jail in Maryville. By Sunday, January 11, the streets and restaurants of Maryville, Nodaway County's seat, were thronged. It was the largest Sunday crowd in the history of the town. Even more persons arrived in Maryville as early as 4 A.M. Monday, January 12. Some official, unnamed in the Maryville newspaper coverage, had announced that Gunn would be brought from the jail to the courthouse at 9 A.M. As early as 7 A.M., the courthouse crowd was immense: corridors, stairs, and the courtroom itself were packed. As per the earlier announcement, Sheriff England was bringing Gunn from the jail to the courthouse when a mob of 500 grabbed him at 9:30 A.M. No law enforcement officer fired so much as a single shot. Next, the mob walked Gunn the three miles southwest of Maryville to the Garrett School; he was led by a chain attached to a handcuff.

Well before the mob had Gunn in its custody, it had made extensive preparations for his death. Some persons had removed all the Garrett School's equipment; even the slates on its wall were gone. Someone had brought or built a ladder to the roof in order to get Gunn on top of it. Once he was hoisted up, led there by the chain, he was secured on the school's roof by other chains. In order to insure proper ventilation, holes had been cut in the school roof. Shingles were torn off it in order to chain him to the rafters. Once all was ready, the mob poured gasoline on the school floor, on the roof, and on Gunn's body. There at 10:30 A.M. January 12, 1931, in the presence of nearly 3,000 witnesses, Raymond Gunn was burned to death.

Photographs of this horror, a repetition of the burning to death of Francis McIntosh in St. Louis nearly a century earlier, survive. They did not appear in the Maryville newspaper of January 12, 1931. Rather, the *St. Joseph News-Press* ran an above-the-fold six column photograph on its front page below its enormous headline: "NEGRO GUNN BURNED TO DEATH BY MOB ON ROOF OF VICTIM'S SCHOOL." Among other front page stories in the St. Joseph newspaper is one headlined, "Mob Precautions against Taking Any Photographs;" presumably the *Maryville Daily Forum* compiled with the mob's request and ran none, at least not on the day the mob burned Gunn to death. On the other hand, the *St. Joseph News-Press* ran a number of photographs of this ghastly event.

In Gunn's death, his lynchers exhausted every refinement of cruelty. They also did a great deal of advance planning. Five hundred persons seized him from the sheriff, and he died in the presence of 3,000 witnesses. These viewers were not casual sightseers in the vicinity by chance. Rather, large numbers knew of the plan long before it took place. Among others concerned that Gunn would meet foul play at the hands of a mob was Henry Caulfield, governor of Missouri. He had sent Adjutant General A.V. Adams, commander of the Missouri National Guard, to Maryville to protect this reviled prisoner from the well-publicized threat of violence. At the very moment that Sheriff England's arrestee was snatched from him on the threshold of the courthouse, 60 armed and uniformed guardsmen were marching about as they drilled nearby. Under Missouri law at that time, National Guardsmen were powerless to undertake any action unless county officials requested their assistance.[50] That there was an urgent need for massive assistance to protect Gunn had to be obvious to any officials charged with this responsibility. The Maryville newspaper quotes Sheriff England as saying that he was unaware that there was

The caption under this front page photograph states: "The *News-Press*, sensing the spirit of the populace in Nodaway County, sent its staff photographer to Maryville [43 miles north of St. Joseph] this morning. The above picture shows the mob getting ready to burn Raymond Gunn, Negro slayer of Velma Coulter, on the roof of Garrett school house, where the teacher was murdered Dec. 16. The picture shows the school and the mob just before the Negro was taken to the roof, where he was chained and the building set on fire. Insert: Raymond Gunn, Negro victim of mob." (Reprinted by permission of the *St. Joseph News-Press*. Used by permission, State Historical Society of Missouri, Columbia.)

a mobilized unit of the National Guard in Maryville at the time he lost his prisoner to the mob, a unit one block distant from where the mob seized Gunn.[51]

The reaction to this horror was one of outrage. The *St. Louis Argus*, a black newspaper, ran this headline: "Missouri Mob Lynches Negro with State Militia But Block Away." Its lead story's headline read, "Sheriff Says He Failed to Act for Fear Someone Would be Killed." This paper also ran a large, above-the-fold photograph entitled, "Funeral Pyre of Raymond Gunn Who Died at Hands of Maryville Mob." This paper's story excoriates the 63-year-old sheriff's pathetic performance in protecting Gunn. It quotes the lawman, at home in bed suffering from a sprained back and arm, as the result of his tussle with the mob: "It is too bad it happened, but there were just too many of them for us."[52] The out-of-state press ran very large headlines about the unspeakable event in Nodaway County, Missouri. "Mob Burns Killer of School Teacher" proclaimed the *Washington Post*[53]; "Missouri Mob Cremates Man," stated the *Chicago Defender*'s headline, and its lead story's headline read, "Troops Drill Blocks Away as Cannibals Disgrace State." This story mentions that a resolution in the state legislature concerning this awful event had been tabled. It was introduced by a Kansas City Democrat, Gil. P. Bourk, and it called on the governor and attorney general to conduct an investigation to determine the cause of the flagrant breakdown in law enforcement.[54] Likewise, the Missouri House refused to pass a resolution condemning the lynching and the Nodaway County officials for their failure to resist the mob more effectively. The *Chicago Tribune* states that Representative William Job of Nodaway County "was loudly applauded when he spoke against the resolution."[55]

Something needed to be done to prevent another disgrace in this state. In early February 1931, two anti-lynching bills were introduced in the Missouri legislature. One was HB 207, sponsored by two state representatives from Kansas City. It empowered the governor to remove from office any sheriff, deputy sheriff, or jailer who permitted a prisoner to be taken and lynched. Senator Kinney, who represented a heavily black senatorial district in the city of St. Louis, introduced SB 259. On February 25, 1931, hearings were held on both bills. They lasted from 4 P.M. until 10 P.M., and they were attended by a number of black citizens from St. Louis and Kansas City.[56]

The Missouri General Assembly passed SB 259. It received its first reading on February 16, its second on February 18, and it was reported out of the Committee on Criminal Jurisprudence with the recommendation that the bill be passed on condition that its sections 4, 5, and 6 be stricken. Section 4 required that the county in which the lynching occurred forfeit $10,000, recoverable in a lawsuit in the name of the state against the county, for the benefit of the lynched person's survivors; otherwise for the use of the state. Section 5 held that if a person was seized in one county and transported to another, where he was put to death, both counties were jointly and severally liable to pay the forfeiture. Section 6 required that if one or more sections of this law were held invalid by a court, the entire act should not be held invalid.

The portion of the law which the legislature passed, one to "assure to persons the equal protection of the laws, and to punish the crime of lynching," began by defining a "mob or riotous assemblage" as composed of three or more persons acting in concert "without authority of law, for the purpose of depriving any person of his life, or doing him physical injury." The main thrust of this bill, one clearly motivated by the sheriff of Nodaway County's failure to protect Raymond Gunn, required that "any state or municipal officer" charged to protect a prisoner who "fails, neglects, or refuses to make appropriate efforts to prevent such person from being injured or put to death shall be guilty of a felony, upon conviction, imprisoned for five years or fined up to $5,000 or both such imprisonment and fine." With sections 4, 5, and 6 removed, SB 259 was ordered engrossed (that is a final and fair copy made of it) and printed on April 6, 1931.[57] Momentarily, it appeared as if Missouri would finally have a law on the books to punish officials who failed to prevent lynchings. At least as early as 1879, legislative efforts to curb mob murders were begun here by allowing the state to take a change of venue when prosecuting the lynchers. The Missouri Supreme Court struck down this legislation in 1880. Again in 1899, a state representative from Nodaway County introduced a bill to permit sheriffs or jailers to give prisoners in danger of being lynched guns to protect themselves. This legislation never became law.

Nor did Senate Bill No. 259. Governor Henry Caulfield vetoed it on May 12, 1931. In his message, the governor explained his veto as necessary because the state cannot take a change of venue, and in the county where the lynching took place, "the state of the public mind is not favorable to conviction." Likewise important, wrote the governor, is that in the opinion of the Missouri Supreme Court and the attorney general, the sheriff is not "a state or municipal officer; he is a county officer." Hence, "the very officer charged with protecting the prisoner from mob violence could not be prosecuted." The governor closed by suggesting that the legislature enact a law that would provide a tribunal, outside any county, to remove "derelict officers."[58]

The state of Missouri never established a tribunal to remove negligent lawmen from office, including those who failed to prevent the lynching of their prisoners. However, already in the legislative hopper and signed into law by Governor Caulfield on April 24, 1931, approximately three weeks before he vetoed Senate Bill 259, was a new 20-section law; it created the Missouri State Highway Patrol. Its first part explains that this new agency's "powers and duties ... shall be supplementary to and no way a limitation on the powers and duties of sheriffs, police officers, and other peace officers of this state." As is well known, the highway patrol's primary responsibility is the state's highways. However, the law's original 13th section declares that "members of the patrol are ... officers of the state [and they] shall have authority to arrest ... any person detected by [them] in the act of violating any law of the state." Further, they are "authorized to continue in pursuit of such violator or suspected violator into whatever part of this state may be reasonably necessary to ... arrest such violator or suspected violator."[59] This legislation was passed and signed into law slightly less than four months after the Maryville event that took the life of Raymond Gunn. The governor and the General Assembly surely reasoned that a law enforcement agency with statewide policing powers, one not dependent on the request of local law enforcement to act, could much more effectively suppress a lynching than the county authorities. However, with an initial highway patrol work force limited by law to one superintendent, 10 captains, and 115 patrolmen (or 126 officers), and the actual initial appointment of 55 officers and a few civilians,[60] the newly formed state police was not able to overpower any sizeable mob. Just how ineffective it was at preventing a lynching can be shown by the next horrendous happening here.

It took place in St. Joseph, Buchanan County, on November 28, 1933. The victim was a 19-year-old black male, Lloyd Warner, charged with the Sunday, November 26, rape of a 21-year-old white female, the daughter of a tailor and a member of a prominent Jewish family. She is the only Jew in Missouri history whose assailant was known to be subsequently murdered by a mob. She is never named in the voluminous newspaper coverage of this matter. She identified Warner as the man who approached her with a knife as she got off a bus; later she hoped that her identification had been correct. After her assailant's mob murder, she regretted his death and wished that the law had been allowed to take its course. The young woman had been dragged into an alley between Jule and Francis streets, just west of 22nd Street, at knife point, beaten, tied with her own stockings, and raped. In his haste to make his getaway, Warner dropped his bloody knife in an alley. The police recovered the weapon, and they traced its ownership to another African American. He in turn told them that he had lent it to Warner. The police stated that this key piece of physical evidence led to the perpetrator's arrest.

Warner had a prior arrest for the rape of the daughter of a black minister. Because the father of his victim did not want his daughter involved in court proceedings, Warner was never prosecuted for this crime. He was arrested the morning of November 28, a

Tuesday, and he confessed to both the police and members of the prosecutor's staff. When brought before a JP, he once more confessed. When the justice of the peace certified Warner's case to circuit court, he yet again confessed that he had attacked the young woman. The judge refused to accept his guilty plea without a defense attorney representing him; his crime was potentially capital. The judge appointed an attorney for Warner, and the prisoner was taken to the county jail.

By 7 P.M. that same evening, a crowd of at least 100 persons had gathered at this facility. Earlier, despised prisoners housed in the Buchanan County jail had not been captured by any mob. The Taylor brothers, killers of the Meeks family in Sullivan County, were briefly inmates in this facility in 1894 and kept alive; a black prisoner, Joseph Burries, also in 1894, charged with the rape of a child, was not surrendered to the mob; and Raymond Gunn, both in 1925 and in December 1930, lived through his residence at the Buchanan County jail. Given this background, the sheriff surely assumed that the structure was sufficiently sturdy to protect Warner in 1933. After all, there had been no successful lynching in either the city of St. Joseph or Buchanan County within anyone's memory. The only known event was the stringing up of two horse thieves in St. Joseph in September 1850, more than 83 years earlier. The sheriff could only have assumed that what had not been would not be. He was mistaken.

The crowd around the jail grew larger and larger, and the situation more dire. Newspaper estimates of the mob's numbers range from 5,000 to 8,000 to 10,000. At the sheriff's request the reporter for the *St. Joseph News-Press* phoned Governor Guy P. Park, and he sent a tank company of two vehicles staffed by National Guard members; they were under orders not to fire. As it turned out, the lynchers easily captured these guardsmen and held them prisoner. At a minimum, the crowd now numbered at least 5,000 persons. At 11:32 the sheriff finally turned Warner over to the lynchers. He did so in order to protect other black prisoners and spare the county the expense of even more property damage to the structure of the jail, its fixtures, furniture, and equipment.

The mob marched its prisoner to the approximate location of his attack on the young woman. He was hanged from a tree at Fifth and Jule streets at 11:38 P.M., just six minutes after his tormentors gained custody of him. His killers had no fear of being identified; they allowed a photographer from the Kansas City newspaper, the *Journal-Post*, to snap a number of shots of many unmasked men. This newspaper stated, "Members of the throng at the lynching made a passage way for camera men, so they reach vantage points to take pictures of the scene of horror."[61] In addition to gouging out Warner's eyes, the mob also procured seven gallons of gasoline from a filling station across the street and poured the fuel over his body before igniting him. Next, small branches from a tree were added to the fire in order to increase its fury. Shortly, someone cut the rope by which Warner's charred body was hanging, and his remains fell into the bonfire. There it stayed in full view for nearly two hours. The mob would not allow a white undertaker to retrieve it. Finally the proprietor of a black funeral home arrived, collected what was left of Warner, placed it in a basket, and drove off. An original copy I own of the *St. Joseph Gazette* states the matter in an eight-column, above-the-fold headline: "MOB HANGS NEGRO ATTACKER AT FIFTH & JULE; BODY SATURATED WITH GASOLINE AND BURNED."[62] Likewise, the *Kansas City Journal* had a similarly immense headline: "MISSOURI MOB BURNS NEGRO ALIVE."[63]

What were members of the new statewide policing agency doing during the entire evening of lawlessness in St. Joseph? According to the *Call*, a black Kansas City newspaper, "State highway police augmented by some of Kansas City's traffic officers directed traffic after the mob murder of [Warner]."[64] Governor Park quickly appointed the chief of the State Highway Patrol, Colonel Marvin Casteel, to investigate. Casteel arrived at 4 A.M. on November 29. He stated that in all, and in response to a radio order, 18 members of the highway patrol came to St. Joseph. The first to arrive came from Kansas City. He managed to get there at the same time the mob was lynching Warner. There were never enough highway patrolmen, city police, sheriff's deputies, or other law enforcement officers on the scene to intimidate a 5,000- to 10,000-member mob. Casteel almost immediately stated, as did the St. Joseph chief of police, that the sheriff of Buchanan County was guilty of no wrongdoing in releasing Warner to the mob. As expected, Governor Park declared his opposition to the lynchers and ordered an investigation, and the attorney general pledged to aid the prosecution of the responsible parties in the murder of Lloyd Warner.[65]

On January 18, 1934, a Buchanan County grand jury was called, and it indicted eight men for the first-degree murder of Lloyd Warner. One of the eight was tried. His name was Walter Garton, aged 43 years, a World War I veteran, white, and illiterate. Newspaper coverage at times lists his occupation as cook and at others as dishwasher. Garton was charged with chaining the jail door to a truck during the murder of Warner. When the state announced that four other men, all facing murder charges in connection with the lynching, would turn state's evidence and testify for the state, it looked as if the case against Garton was a solid one. His trial began in Buchanan County Circuit Court on February 1, 1934. The first evidence the prosecutor introduced against him was eight photographs of the awful scene taken by a cameraman for the *St. Joseph News-Press*. Presumably, Garton was one of many unmasked men captured on film that night who would be readily recognized by anyone looking at him in the courtroom and looking at some, if not all, of the eight snapshots of the lynching. A St. Joseph police officer testified for the state that Garton had boasted of his role in the death of Warner. A courthouse reporter for the *News-Press* who was present in the jail during the hours immediately before and after the removal of Warner also testified for the prosecution. The judge gave the jury instructions on verdicts of murder in the first degree, murder in the second degree, manslaughter, and not guilty. Well before the jury began its deliberations, a photograph of the 12 male members of the jury — all identified by name, all white, all married, and all wearing suits and ties — appeared in the local newspaper. On Saturday, February 3, it came in with its not guilty verdict in *State* v. *Walter Garton*. On Monday, February 5, 1934, the other lynching cases were dismissed. However, Walter Garton was not a free man. He had earlier been sentenced in an Iowa court to five years in prison for breaking into a car; he was paroled, and following his acquittal in St. Joseph, he was returned to the State Penitentiary at Anamosa, Iowa, as a parole violator. With Garton returned to Iowa, the official inquiry into the lynching of Lloyd Warner concluded. Once more the mob, not the law, prevailed.[66]

The only happening placed in Appendix 2 from the 1930s took place in Ste. Genevieve County early in the decade. On October 12, 1930, two white men, Harry Panchot and Paul Ritter, were victims of robbery and murder two miles north of the town of Ste.

Genevieve. Panchot's body was thrown in the Mississippi River, and Ritter died in a St. Louis hospital a few days later. Shortly after this crime was discovered, Lonnie Taylor (known also as Lee Guy), Columbus Jennings (known also as J.C.), and Vera Rogers were arrested. Jennings and Rogers confessed to being present during the shooting, but both fingered Taylor as the actual killer. When Taylor was confronted with the statements of his accomplices, he too confessed. Once their confessions were obtained, local authorities spirited them out of Ste. Genevieve County, taking them first to the Jefferson County jail in Hillsboro and later to the St. Louis City jail. The first removal of them came on fear of their being taken from the Ste. Genevieve jail and lynched; their removal from Hillsboro to St. Louis came on a rumor that the Jefferson County jail would be attacked. In addition to moving his prisoners to several different jails and doing so because of threats of a triple lynching, the sheriff contacted Governor Caulfield and asked for assistance. The governor sent National Guard troops. Some came from Festus; others from DeSoto and Cape Girardeau, and no lynching occurred.[67]

On a change of venue to St. Francois County, the state tried Lonnie Taylor for the first-degree murder of Paul Ritter. The jury found him guilty and set his punishment at death. On appeal, the Supreme Court of Missouri reversed; it granted Taylor a new trial. It reasoned:

> In the present case reference was made in the testimony that a mob had formed in Ste. Genevieve County, shortly after the alleged crime was committed for the purpose of lynching the defendant. This evidence was introduced to show that the defendant made incriminating statements in fear of the mob. Under these circumstances the argument under discussion tended to improperly influence the jury and persuade them to return a verdict of guilty and assess the death penalty to satisfy the wishes of the mob. Such argument is highly improper.... The trial court should have declared a new trial on account of the argument.[68]

In St. Francois County, on December 5, 1932, Lonnie Taylor pled guilty to two counts of murder in the first degree. He was sentenced to the Missouri State Penitentiary for life. He was received at the prison on December 28, 1932, aged 34 years. He was released on parole on July 23, 1946, to the Illinois authorities, and for all but one of the next nine and one-half years, he was a steady employee of the Schulze Baking Company in Chicago. His work consisted of maintenance duties between 5 A.M. and 1 P.M. He lived with his sister and mother, and he avoided any arrests or other difficulties with the law. On January 5, 1956, Governor Phil Donnelly commuted his sentence,[69] and presumably Lonnie Taylor continued his bakery employment. He was one lucky fellow to stay alive long enough to be tried. Earlier, his story most likely would not have had such a happy ending. However, from the infrequency of falsely reported, doubtful, and foiled lynchings in the 1930s here, it is clear that mob murders in Missouri were falling into greater and greater disfavor.

The final lynching of a black man in Missouri took place in Sikeston, Scott County, in the southeastern section of the state. The surprise is the precise locale. The Sunday, January 25, 1942, mob murder of Cleo Wright, a 30-year-old, is the only known untoward happening of this kind in the county's history. Scott County's use of the death penalty is equally meager: a white man, Harris Travis, was executed in 1875 for the murder of his father-in-law; and a black man, Will Burns, was executed in 1899 for the murder of his wife. One expects at least one prior event to have taken place in this vicinity;

in all other twentieth century lynchings in this state, the county of the mob murder had been the scene of earlier lynchings. This was not true in Scott County.

The incident that preceded Cleo Wright's death was the 1:30 A.M. January 25, 1942, attempted rape of a 29-year-old white female, Mrs. Dillard Sturgeon, the wife of a sergeant in the U.S. Army then stationed in California. This crime took place less than two months after the Japanese bombed Pearl Harbor and America entered World War II. Wright, a cotton mill worker and an ex-convict, was captured soon after he attacked his victim. In the process of being taken into custody, he stabbed a Sikeston police officer, Jess Perrigan, and the patrolman in turn shot Wright three times. The local paper reported that a physician stated that Perrigan's injuries were less serious than Wright's. The doctor who treated the black man's wounds at 5 A.M. said his condition "was critical, and he had only an outside chance of recovery."

By daybreak, men were gathering outside the city hall, a structure with two entrances built in 1901. Given the absence of any lynchings in the county's history, its architects never foresaw the need to erect a lynch-proof structure. Wright had been lodged in a detention room in this facility; presumably, law enforcement officers intended to transfer him to the Scott County jail in Benton, but they never had an opportunity to convey their prisoner to a more secure facility. By Sunday morning at 11:30 A.M., as the local paper describes the scene, "Ignoring pleas that they refrain from bloodshed, the men, some roughly dressed and others in their Sabbath-best shoved into two entrances of [city hall] and emerged with Cleo Wright, the Negro himself thrice-wounded by pistol fire and reported by an officer to have admitted the ... knifing [of Perrigan]."

Despite the efforts of the state highway patrol to repel the crowds, the mob, 500 members strong, smashed through both the front entrance and a side door of city hall, easily grabbed the wounded Wright from the detention room, and as the local paper reports, "dragged and bounced his body through the front doors, down the steps and off the curb." Next the mob threw him into the trunk of a car. The vehicle was driven to Sunset Addition, a black section of town. There, one of Wright's ankles was attached to the car's rear bumper, and his body dragged through the streets. Again the local paper reports, Wright's "apparently lifeless ... form was doused by gasoline, and a match flipped unto the body. It was several minutes before the flames subsided and for several hours the charred body lay in plain view of hundreds of the curious who drove by." This story also adds that finally his body was retrieved by a city truck, "returned to the City Hall, awaiting the arrival of [the coroner], who held a formal inquest to be unnecessary."[70]

Press coverage was extensive. In addition to its story about this awful occurrence, the *New York Times* concludes its editorial, "Sikeston Disgraces Itself," with these timely words, "How sadly do such events tarnish the cause of democracy at war. There are few happenings in the United States that afford more comfort to the Nazis than evidence of lawlessness. Lynchings are their prize exhibit in proof of the alleged hypocrisy of the free societies."[71] We know from newspaper sources that the inevitable investigation of Wright's lynching occupied city, county, state, and even federal authorities. In March 1942, this headline stated the expected, "Scott County Grand Jury Fails to Find Sufficient Evidence to Cite Anyone in Sikeston Lynching."[72] By May, a federal grand jury investigation was underway in U.S. District Court for the Eastern District of Missouri in St. Louis, but no indictment came out of the federal investigation.

Dominic J. Capeci, Jr., is unquestionably *the* authority on Missouri's last mob murder of a black man. His first publication on this case was in 1992.[73] In his 1998 book, *The Lynching of Cleo Wright*, he discusses the founding of Sikeston, the importance of blacks in the cotton fields in the area, the role of local authorities, Governor Forest Donnell's concern, the efforts of Troop E of the highway patrol headquartered at Poplar Bluff to prevent the lynching, the NAACP's protests after the event, and the operative federal statutes that might have been used had it been certain that Wright was still alive when the mob violence against him commenced. No one can murder a dead body. It is a well-written, wonderfully documented, exhaustive analysis. It includes a number of interesting photographs of the entire case, including several Missouri State Penitentiary mug shots of Cleo Wright in 1940. As noted in earlier chapters, my disapproval of this author's work in no way concerns the main subject matter of his book, *The Lynching of Cleo Wright*. Rather, my objections are entirely with its map of Missouri lynchings and its Appendix, Table 1: "Lynching Victims in Missouri, 1889–1942."[74]

Had any experts on Missouri's dark side — historians, true crime story writers, sheriffs, police chiefs, governors, members of the legislature, judges, or most anyone else — been asked if there would be additional lynchings in this state after Scott County's last hurrah, the answer would have been in the negative. As time passed and World War II, the Korean War, and the Vietnam conflict ended, the idea of yet another mob murder in this state seemed more and more remote. However, as my conclusion explains, there was another big event here 39 years after the mob murder of Cleo Wright.

Missouri's Last Lynching, 1981

The last lynching in Missouri seems anachronistic. It might have taken place 100 years earlier, and at that time, it would have been characteristic of its period. For example, when a mob strung up two white men, Frank Taylor and his brother Tubal in Taney County, southwest Missouri, on April 15, 1885, the vigilantes feared that the court system would not punish these troublemakers. Five days earlier, the Taylors had shot a white storekeeper and his wife, Mr. and Mrs. John Dickenson. The husband lost four teeth as one bullet passed out of his neck, and he sustained a shoulder injury with another. His wife lost a finger in the shooting, and a random shot grazed her neck. The couple was alive, but they were badly wounded. The Taylors had been major hellcats for a long time before the Bald Knobbers hanged them. These brothers were suspected of, among many criminal acts, chopping the tongues out of prized cattle, who died of starvation because they could not eat. The cattle's owner, a rancher and a miller, had earlier argued with one of the Taylors.[1] Or take the case of John Mitchell and his stepbrother, Jack Kaufman, other white men. A group of angry farmers shot them to death on May 18, 1897, in Wright County, in southwestern Missouri. Both were suspected of repetitive stealing of hogs, among other larcenous crimes.

Nearly a century, later, in northwest Missouri, history repeated itself. Kenneth R. McElroy, a white man, first met the Kansas City attorney, Richard McFadin, who represented him in his many scrapes with the law, in a St. Joseph courtroom in the 1960s. This lawyer was then defending a man on cattle-rustling charges. McElroy asked McFadin's fee to represent him on three counts of hog-theft. In response, he said $5,000 per charge, and his new client paid him $15,000 in cash. Thus began a lengthy attorney-client relationship between McFadin and McElroy.[2]

On July 8, 1980, McElroy continued his lawbreaking ways when, in Skidmore, Nodaway County, he shot a 70-year-old grocer in the neck and shoulder. His victim was Ernest Bowenkamp, and the badly injured man claimed that he had done nothing to provoke the assault. According to a former Andrew County prosecutor, "McElroy was a vicious criminal.... [He] openly supported himself by stealing livestock and farm equipment from his neighbors. In 1971, I had him arrested eight separate times for felony theft, but I had to drop the case when my witnesses decided not to testify against him." Alden Lance, the former prosecutor continued: "Look at his record: dozens of arrests for everything from arson, theft, and rape, to assault with intent to kill. And not a single conviction. The man never spent a night in prison in his life."[3]

Following the wounding of Bowenkamp, the Nodaway County prosecutor filed felony charges against McElroy. The defendant requested and received a change of venue to Harrison County; its seat, Bethany, is 60 miles northeast of Skidmore. At his trial there on June 26, 1981, he admitted that he shot the elderly grocer, but he claimed that he did so in self-defense because his victim had attempted to attack him with a knife. The jury came in with a mild verdict; it found him guilty of second-degree assault and recommended that he serve a two-year prison term. The jury that returned with this lenient sentence had not heard any evidence regarding McElroy's prior record. If it had, its recommendation would have been in favor of a far lengthier sentence.

Since this was not a capital case, under Missouri law, the defendant could post bond.[4] He was allowed 25 days in which to file a motion for a new trial, and during this interval, he remained a free man. McElroy posted the $40,000 bond, and once more he was at liberty. Harry MacLean, author of a book about this case, quotes a man who had a conversation with McElroy after his trial. "The jury convicted me, and they gave me two years. But I'll tell you what. I'll never go to jail. I'll appeal and get off.... I been fighting prosecutors since I was 13 years old, and I'm almost 50. I've been arrested for over 53 felonies, and this is the first one I ever lost." McElroy continued, "My f...... lawyer better get me off. I've already paid him $30,000, and he wants another $20,000 for an appeal."[5] McElroy was referring to Richard McFadin, the Kansas City lawyer who had served his client with warm zeal in his many involvements with the legal system.

Photograph of the grave marker of Kenneth McElroy, the last person lynched in Missouri, on July 10, 1981, in Skidmore, Nodaway County. The marker states, "Beloved Ken/ Ken Rex McElroy/ Brave, Fearless and Compassionate/ 1934–1981." McElroy avoided a conviction for at least his first 53 felony arrests. His first felony conviction, for second-degree assault, came on a change of venue. He was convicted by a Harrison County jury, but after posting bond, he was once more a free man. McElroy is buried in the Last Supper section, Memorial Park Cemetery, 4950 Frederick Ave., St. Joseph, Missouri (photograph by the author).

Meanwhile, back in Skidmore, following McElroy's posting of his bond, the towns-people became alarmed that once more the court system had failed them. This serial trou-blemaker was again free to torment them. The handful of witnesses who had testified against him in the Bowenkamp shooting—the one that led to his first conviction ever—were especially concerned. On a Friday morning, July 10, 1981, a number of local men held a meeting at the American Legion hall in Skidmore. They invited the sheriff of Nod-away County, and he assured these concerned citizens that he and his deputies would be on the alert for any trouble that McElroy might cause. At 10 A.M., the meeting, a sort of neighborhood watch group, ended.[6] Less than two hours later, McElroy and his wife, Trena, left the D&G Tavern in Skidmore, got into their Chevy Silverado parked nearby, and Ken, in the driver's seat, stuck a Camel cigarette in his mouth, and started his vehi-cle. A crowd estimated at approximately 60 persons surrounded them, and one or more persons opened fire. The gunman or gunmen lynched Kenneth R. McElroy very near the scene where approximately a year earlier the victim shot the grocer. In taking action, these vigilantes chose to end McElroy's life in the same easy manner as many white men in Missouri's past had died at the hands of a mob. They shot him to death. Two bullets hit his neck and back, and when the ambulance came to retrieve him, his body was placed in it with the sheet pulled up over his head. McElroy, aged 47 years, was no longer a tor-ment to anyone. Unlike most victims of mob murders, we know where this man is buried. He has a marked grave in the Last Supper section at Memorial Park Cemetery, 4950 Fred-erick Avenue, St. Joseph, Missouri.

According to MacLean, within one hour of the fatal shooting of this detested bully,

> three or four men gathered at a farm west of town, ... took the murder weapons out back to the barn, smashed the stocks off with a sledge-hammer, and threw them into a stove. One of the men then fired up a blow torch and cut each barrel into 15 or 20 pieces. The men divided up the pieces and threw half of them in wells 70 or 80 feet deep on farms west of town, and the other half in equally deep wells on farms south of town.[7]

Despite hundreds of man-hours of investigation by county, state, and federal agen-cies, during which they tracked down many leads, every aspect of the inquiry into the murder of Kenneth R. McElroy led to a dead end. No witnesses were talking then; nor have any talked since. On September 25, 1981, the grand jury of Nodaway County met, and it returned no indictments in the case.[8]

That did not settle the matter. Represented by Richard McFadin, Trena McElroy, Kenneth's widow, filed a wrongful death action in her husband's murder in Nodaway County Circuit Court; in it she sought $6 million in damages. In July 1984, she filed a second lawsuit in U.S. District Court for the Western District of Missouri. In the fed-eral case, she sought $5 million for deprivation of Kenneth McElroy's civil rights through his death. In the federal suit, she named the mayor of Skidmore, the sheriff of Nodaway County, and the former owner of the D&G Tavern, a man she claimed was her husband's shooter. In September 1985, the defendants jointly settled the federal suit for $17,500. The amount each paid was kept secret, but since the settlement required the approval of the Nodaway County probate judge, it was filed as a public record. Under its terms Mrs. McElroy, now remarried and living elsewhere, dismissed the wrongful death action she had filed in Nodaway County Circuit Court and released all the defendants in the fed-eral suit from any additional civil legal action.[9]

It is probably no more than wildly coincidental that the only certain punishments I discovered in the course of a long investigation into lynchings in Missouri came out of the same court: U.S. District Court for the Western District of Missouri. In 1874, a jury in this court in a criminal case found two men guilty of retarding the mails in Cass County in 1872, at the same time three men were shot to death, when a train on which they were passengers was stopped. Judge Arnold Kregel, an appointee to the federal bench of President Lincoln, fined each man $100 plus court costs. In 1985, the parties in a civil suit filed in this same court agreed to the dismissal of the case when they reached a settlement of $17,500, in the death of the last person lynched in Missouri in 1981 in Nodaway County.

With McElroy's death, this county's total mob murders number only four: Tansey in 1872, Stevens in 1884, Gunn in 1931, and McElroy in 1981. As such Nodaway falls well below those counties with the highest number of lynchings in this state. Two top counties ceased to be places of mob murders in the mid–1870s: Johnson (11 of its 12 victims of lynching were white) and Vernon (all of its seven lynched persons were white). The remaining nine with the largest number of mob murders — Callaway, Clay, Franklin, Greene, Howard, Jasper, Lafayette, Randolph, and Saline — all were scenes during the antebellum period of one of these three: the legal execution of one or more bondpersons, or the extra legal deaths at the hands of mobs of one or more slaves, or both the legal and the illegal executions of slaves.

In Callaway County, Slaves Jakes and Conway were executed in 1836, and Slave Celia in 1855. Slave Teney was lynched in this county in 1860. In 1895, Emmett Divers, a black male, was the victim of an enormous mob; 1,000 men marched into Fulton with his already dead body. Clay County executed Slave Annice in 1828, and in its county seat, Liberty, her daughter Slave Annice (1850) and Slave Peter (1855) were lynched. Its last mob murder was of a black man, Walter Mitchell, in Excelsior Springs in 1925. In Franklin County, Slave Frank was sentenced to death for the murder of his master in 1819 but he escaped, and there is no record of his recapture. In 1818, Slave Leonard was lynched in this county, and the 1847 mob murder of Slave Eli, in Franklin County, may be fused with Leonard's death almost 30 years earlier. In 1897, Erastus Brown, a black male, was lynched in Franklin County. In Greene County, Slave Martin or Mart was murdered by a mob in 1859 in Springfield, the county seat. In 1906 a 3,000 member mob in Springfield murdered two or three almost certainly innocent black males, Fred Coker, Horace Duncan, and William Allen. In Howard County, the sheriff hanged Slave Hampton in 1832 and Slaves Washington Hill and David Gates, probably in 1837. In 1899, Frank Embree died a vividly photographed death at the hands of unmasked men. In 1914, Dallas Shields, a black man, was lynched in Fayette, Howard County's seat, by hanging him from a tree in the courthouse square. In 1853 in Jasper County, a mob put Slaves Sam and Colley to death by burning them at the stake in Carthage, the county seat. In 1903, a mob of several thousand lynched Thomas Gilyard, a black man, in this same county, by taking him from the jail in Joplin and hanging him from a telegraph pole. In Lexington, seat of Lafayette County, the sheriff hanged Slave Henry in 1856 and Slaves Larrell and John in 1858. In 1905 a mob ended the life of Henry Gates, a black man, and Charles Salyers, a white, a short distance from Lexington. In Randolph County, the sheriff hanged Slave George in 1859, and a mob lynched James Anderson, a black man, in this county in 1919.

Finally, in Saline County four slaves were lynched within 24 hours in 1859. A mob murdered an unnamed slave in Arrow Rock, and Slaves John, Holman, and James in Marshall, the county seat. In 1900, Mindo Conagwe, a black man, was lynched by a 1,000-member mob by hanging him from a tree in Marshall, near the southwest corner of the courtyard.

All nine of these preeminent counties account, at a minimum, for at least six lynchings, and most were the scenes of seven or more mob murders. Six of the nine border the Missouri River, an easy conduit for transporting slaves in the antebellum period. In all of them, their extralegal killings took place both before the Civil War and either late in the nineteenth century or in the twentieth century. Within these nine counties, 79 lynchings, or slightly more than one-third of this state's 229 known mob murders, can be documented, and of these 43, or 54 percent, were of African-Americans, including the only women, both slaves, ever known to have been murdered by mobs in the history of Missouri. Vigilantism obtained an early grip in these places, and its hold was tenacious.

Four counties, Randolph (1880), Howard (1884), Dunklin (1892), and Caldwell (1895) were the scenes of black-on-black lynchings. In all African-American mobs murdered five black males in these locales between 1880 and 1895. Likewise, in Johnson (1874) and St. Louis County (1894) a mob composed of both white and black lynchers put to death a black male. No instance of a wholly black or partially black mob killing an African-American is known in Missouri earlier than 1874, and none later than 1895. The phenomenon is best explained as the minority imitating the majority. The fact is that only 3 percent of this state's mob murders were carried out by black and/or integrated lynching parties. Moreover, excluding the only known Native American on Native American incident in 1803, all other known Missouri lynch mobs (97 percent) were white.

Some counties were free of vigilantes. In all, 41 of Missouri's 114 counties saw a reported lynching. Likewise, the state's two major cities, St. Louis and Kansas City, had a significant scarcity of these atrocities. These large population centers were each disgraced only once with mob murders, both of black men, in 1882 in Kansas City and in 1836 in St. Louis. In these metropolises on November 4, 2008, an African-American received an overwhelming majority of the ballots cast for the highest office in the land. President Barack Obama received 119,609 (78.4 percent) of the votes in Kansas City and 132,260 (83.7 percent) in St. Louis. His rival, John McCain, carried the state of Missouri by less than one percentage point.[10] These numbers and percentages are a remarkable achievement for a former slave state and for our country.

When we examine the 50 entries in Appendix 2, 12 of them should be filtered out; we known in nine of them that a lynching took place in a state that bordered Missouri: Arkansas, Kentucky, and Tennessee. In three others, one in Iron County in 1882, another in Cooper in 1900, and a third in Saline in 1928, no in-state source mentions the occurrence of a mob murder, and nothing is classified as a lynching in Missouri without at least one in-state source. These 12 account for slightly more than 25 percent of the names in Appendix 2.

Of the remaining 38, one has too few numbers for a lynching; in another the deceased died of a heart attack at home sitting in a chair; four were certain or possible suicides, and two were spared in Lawrence County in 1894 because a 12-year-old girl refused to identify either of the black males paraded before her as the person who raped her, Finally, in seven incidents, we have insufficient information to classify the death as a lynching. Of the 26 remaining entries in Appendix 2, no lynching took place. Frequently a sheriff, once a judge, once the Speaker of the U.S. House of Representatives, and/or a combination of officials and upright citizens protected the intended victim of a mob. At least 14 persons were not lynched because one or more officials, usually sheriffs and their deputies, kept persons in their custody out of the clutches of vigilante men. Several law enforcement officers, most sensationally the sheriff of Callaway County in 1873, lost their lives attempting to protect their prisoners. The remainder of victims of mobs in Appendix 2 lived because they survived their injuries. Surviving a mob happened in the late nineteenth and early twentieth centuries, or at least the sources that document such survivals derive from these time periods. All in all, the 50 entries in Appendix 2 and the 229 in Appendix 1 total 279 persons, with Appendix 2 representing 21 percent. It is still 21 percent if we assume that twice lynchings in the antebellum period are fused, that there was one, not two, in both Franklin and Jefferson counties. Hence the total should be 227. The fact remains that 21 percent of that total (277, 278, or 279) cannot be classified, for a wide variety of reasons, as lynchings in Missouri. It is important to describe the circumstances that prevent any alleged lynching in Missouri from being the real thing. It is also important to describe the many untoward events in Missouri's history that were mob murders. Both are very much a part of the total picture.

In conclusion are there more undiscovered mob murders in this state's past? Most likely. Will there ever be another lynching here? Who knows? However, if one does take place within Missouri's borders, the odds are that it will occur within a county that was earlier the scene of fatal vigilante action and the place of it on more than one occasion.

Appendix 1: Lynchings in Missouri, 1803–1981

Abbreviations

I	Indian	F	Female	LE	Law Enforcement Officer
W	White	A	Adult	Att.	attempted
B	Black	C	Child	U	Unknown
M	Male	HS	Horse Stealing	"	Same Lynching as Above

Name, race, sex, and age on date of alleged crime or unacceptable activity	Date, if known; crime; sex and age of victim(s)	County	Method	Relationship, if any, between victim and perpetrator of crime(s) or unacceptable activity	Number of mob members and spectators	Date of lynching
1. U IMA	Theft of rifle	New Madrid	Beaten with clubs	U	U	Nov. 1803
?2. Slave Leonard, BMA	Rape and murder of WFA	Franklin	Hanged	U	U	1818
3. McIntosh, Francis L., BMA	April 28, 1836, manslaughter and assault, 2 WMA (LE)	St. Louis	Burned	LE and prisoner	2,000	April 28, 1836
4. U Slave	March 1840 rape of WFA and April 12, 1840, att. rape or rape, WFA	Washington	Hanged	Owner and slave; U	300–400	April 15, 1840
?5. U Negro	1842 murder of WMA	Jefferson	Hanged	Victim and robber	U	1842
6. Layton, James, WMA	Jan. 1841 murder of WFA	St. Francois	Hanged	Wife and husband	3,000	June 17, 1843
?7. U Slave, BMA	March 3, 1844, murder of WMA and WFA	Jefferson	Hanged	Victims and robber	300	March 5, 1844
8. Smith, Abraham, WMA	Late 1843 murder of WMA	Madison	Hanged	Neighbors	U	Aug. 6, 1844

Name, race, sex, and age on date of alleged crime or unacceptable activity	Date, if known; crime; sex and age of victim(s)	County	Method	Relationship, if any, between victim and perpetrator of crime(s) or unacceptable activity	Number of mob members and spectators	Date of lynching
?9. Slave Eli, BMA	Feb. or March 1847 att. rape and murder of WFA and att. murder of WMC	Franklin	Hanged	U	U	April 1847
10. Slave Annice II, BF38	April 1, 1850, att. murder	Clay	Hanged	Owner and slave	U	May 9, 1850
11. McClintock,___, WMA	"	"	"	U	"	"
12. U WMA	Late summer 1850 HS	Buchanan	Hanged	Victim and thief	"	Late summer 1850
13. U WMA	"	"	"	"	"	"
14. Slave Sam, BM19/20	July 3, 1853, murder and att. rape of WFA	Pettis	Burned	U	100	July 6, 1853
15. Slave Colley, BM19	July 16, 1853 murder and rape, WMA, WFA and WC	Jasper	Burned	Co-defendant of scolded slave	U	July 30, 1853
16. Slave Bart, BMA	"	"	"	Scolder and slave	"	"
17. Slave Hiram, BM	Aug. 12, 1853, att. rape of WF15	Boone	Hanged	U	1,000	Aug. 22, 1853
18. Wingo, Obediah, WMA	Oct. 10, 1853, murder of WMA	Ray	Hanged	Acquaintances	250	Oct. 14, 1853
19. Shackelford, William, WMA	Earlier HS and Aug. 7, 1854, murder of 2 WMA	Clay	Hanged	U	200–300	Aug. 7, 1854
20. Callaway, John, WMA	"	"	"	"	"	"
21. Shackelford, Samuel, WMA	"	"	"	"	"	"
22. Slave Peter, BMA	Feb. 12, 1855, murder of WMA	Clay	Hanged	Victim owned and severely beat Peter's wife	U	March 5, 1855
23. Slave George, BMA	Oct. 10, 1855, murder of WMA	Carroll	Hanged	Owner and slave	U	Oct. 11, 1855
24. Ray, James, WMA	Summer 1856 suspected of poisoning spring water; 20 children and teacher who drank it got ill	Morgan	Hanged	Children of witnesses against him in civil suit	100	July 8, 1856
25. Kessler, Jeff, WMA	Mid-June, 1858 murder of WMA (LE)	Gentry	Hanged	Old grudge against LE	"A great crowd"	June 25, 1858

Name, race, sex, and age on date of alleged crime or unacceptable activity	Date, if known; crime; sex and age of victim(s)	County	Method	Relationship, if any, between victim and perpetrator of crime(s) or unacceptable activity	Number of mob members and spectators	Date of lynching
26. Milligan, James, WMA	"	"	"	Co-defendant of Kessler	300	July 5, 1858
27. Slave Giles, BMA	Dec. 24, 1858, murder, WMA	Lincoln	Burned	Owner and slave	U	Jan. 1, 1859
28. U Slave, BMA	July 18, 1859, att. rape of WF14	Saline	Hanged	U	4–5; large concourse of people	July 18, 1859
29. Slave John, BM23	May 13, 1859, murder of WMA	Saline	Burned	U	U	July 19, 1859
30. Slave Holman, BM30	June 21, 1859, assault, WMA	"	Hanged	"	"	"
31. Slave James, BM32–35	July 12, 1859, att. rape of WFA	"	"	"	"	"
32. Slave Martin, BMA	Aug. 13, 1859, rape of WFA	Greene	Hanged	U	300–400	Aug. 17, 1859
33. U WMA	Oct. 1859 HS	Marion	Hanged	U	U	Oct. 1859
34. Sexton, Sim, WM35/40	HS, robbery and assault, WMA	Randolph	Hanged	U	300–400	Oct. 22, 1859
35. Slave Teney, BFA	Oct. 27, 1860, murder of WFA	Callaway	Hanged	Lessor and slave	40–50	Oct. 28, 1860
36. Stewart, Judson, WMA	Murder, WMA	Johnson	Hanged	U	U	Early 1861
37. Husher, Samuel, WMA	Aug. 31, 1861, murder of WMA	Livingston	Hanged	Neighbors	100s	Sept. 4, 1861
38. Hall, William, WMA	1858 murder of WMA and July 1862 murder of WFA	Franklin	Hanged	1st unknown; 2nd sister	50	July 18, 1862
39. U Slave, BMA	Nov. 1862 rape and murder, WFC and att. murder, WMC	Andrew	Hanged	U	U	Nov. 1862
40. U BMA	WFA rape	Franklin	Hanged	U	U	1865–1866
41. Robertson, William WMA	March 22, 1866, murder, WMA	Atchison	Hanged	Buyer and seller of wood	Band of armed men	April 4, 1866
42. Phillips, Green, WMA	Accomplice of wrongdoers	Greene	Shot	U	3 shot him; 280 in group organizing killing	May 23, 1866
43. Rush, John, WMA	Stealing and robbery suspect	Greene	Hanged	U	280 in group organizing killing	May 26, 1866
44. Gorsuch, Charlie, WMA	"	"	"	"	"	"

Name, race, sex, and age on date of alleged crime or unacceptable activity	Date, if known; crime; sex and age of victim(s)	County	Method	Relationship, if any, between victim and perpetrator of crime(s) or unacceptable activity	Number of mob members and spectators	Date of lynching
45. Ewing, Tucker, WMA	Aug. 29, 1866, murder, WMA	Morgan	Shot	Love triangle	15–20 masked men	Aug. 30, 1866
46. Sanders, Dick, WMA	Feb. 25, 1867, robbery and murder, WMA	Johnson	Hanged	U	100 citizens	March 1, 1867
47. Stevens, Bill, WMA	Desperate character	Johnson	Shot	U	20 men	March 4, 1867
48. Collins, Jeff, WMA	HS and murder	Johnson	Hanged	U	20 citizens	March 4, 1867
49. Stevens, Tom, WM18/19	Accomplice, Feb. 25, 1867, murder of WMA	Johnson	Hanged	U	Party of 400	Late March, 1867
50. Andrews, Morg, WM18/19	"	"	"	"	"	"
51. Wood, Joe, WMA	Murder, WMA	Pettis	Beat, dragged, hanged, and shot	Saloon patron and proprietor	A number of citizens	March 23, 1867
52. Hall,___, WMA	Murder, several WMA	Johnson	Hanged	U	U	Late March, 1867
53. Ingram, Tom, WMA	March 26, 1867, murder, WMA (LE), accessory after the fact	Vernon	Hanged	U	U	March 29, 1867
54. U WMA	HS	Vernon	Hanged	U	U	Spring 1867
55. Scott, Bill, WMA	HS	Johnson	Hanged	U	U	May 12, 1867
56. Conner, Allen, WM	HS	Camden	Hanged	Mob came from Moniteau Co., where theft occurred	31–37	June 23, 1867
57. Jones, Daniel, WM	"	"	"	"	"	"
58. Little, Thomas, WMA	Assault and robbery	Johnson	Hanged	U	15 to 20	Aug. 1867
59. Sims, James, WMA	HS	Johnson	Hanged	U	50	Sept. 1867
60. Devers, James, WMA	Aiding in bank robbery	Ray	Hanged	U	15	March 18, 1868
61. McGuire, Andrew, WMA	"	"	"	"	"	"
62. Myers, Lewis, WMA	HS	Callaway/ Montgomery Co. line	Hanged	U	U	Mid-April 1868

Name, race, sex, and age on date of alleged crime or unacceptable activity	Date, if known; crime; sex and age of victim(s)	County	Method	Relationship, if any, between victim and perpetrator of crime(s) or unacceptable activity	Number of mob members and spectators	Date of lynching
63. Quick, James, WMA	Murder, WMA	Jefferson	Hanged	U	Judge Lynch and disciples	Spring 1868
64. Hutton, George, WMA	Spring 1868 murder, WFA	Jasper	Shot and hanged	Son-in-law and mother-in-law	Group of armed and disguised men	April 28, 1868
65. Budd, Bill, WMA	Robber and peace disturber	Lafayette	Shot	U	Party of armed men	July 24, 1868
66. Bickford, Charles, WMA	Murder, WMA	Jefferson	Hanged	U	Judge Lynch and disciples	Fall? 1868
67. Carlisle,___, WMA	Murder, WMA	Saline	Hanged or drowned	Drinking acquaintances	Angry citizens	Jan. 6, 1869
68. Simmons, William, WMA	Feb. 1868 HS	Bates	Hanged	U	20 to 25 disguised men	March 2, 1869
69. Simmons, David, WMA	"	"	"	"	"	"
70. Chrisman, John, WMA	Mule stealing	Vernon	Hanged	U	U	Late 1860s
71. Wilson, John, WMA	"General principles"	Vernon	Hanged	U	U	Late 1860s
72. Howard, Harry, WMA	Confidence man	Clay	Hanged, shot and drowned	U	Vigilance committee	June 15, 1869
73. Colman, Anthony, BM16/18	Sept. 11, 1869, att. rape, WFA	St. Louis	Shot	U	10–15	Sept. 12, 1869
74. Moore, George, WMA	Dec. 1869 murder, WMA and WFA	Barry	Hanged	U	U	Dec. 1869
75. Childs, Bill, WMA	Desperate outlaw	Lafayette	Hanged	U	U	Dec. 1869–Jan. 1870
76. Black, Martin, WMA	HS	Jackson	Hanged	U	6	April 14, 1870
77. Taylor, A.D., WMA	Ill treatment of family	Jasper	Hanged	Family members	U	June 1870
78. Tolliver, John, BMA	June 6, 1870, rape of WF7	Lafayette	Hanged	U	U	June 13, 1870
79. Sears, John, alias Coleman, John, BMA	July 5, 1870, rape of WF18	Henry	Hanged	U	Hundreds	July 6, 1870
80. Shadle, Henry, alias Wright, Henry, WMA	Summer 1870 HS	Laclede	Hanged	U	U	July 6, 1870
81. Dayho,___, WMA	Murder of WM2/3	Ripley	Shot	U	U	July 1870

Name, race, sex, and age on date of alleged crime or unacceptable activity	Date, if known; crime; sex and age of victim(s)	County	Method	Relationship, if any, between victim and perpetrator of crime(s) or unacceptable activity	Number of mob members and spectators	Date of lynching
82. Hawkins, West, BMA	Sept. 21, 1870, att. rape of WFA	Saline	Hanged	U	U	Oct. 20, 1870
83. Walton, Ben BMA	Feb. 1868 murder of WM40	Washington	Hanged	U	U	Nov. 1, 1870
84. U BMA	Nov. 18, 1870, att. rape, WF16	Saline	Hanged	U	U	Nov. 18, 1870
85. Isbell, Bud, BM21	June 19, 1871, rape of WFA	Greene	Hanged and shot	U	U	June 24, 1871
86. Fleming, Jacob, WMA	June 17, 1871, murder of WMA	St. Clair	Hanged	U	75 to 100	June 30, 1871
87. King, Aleck, WMA	U	Barry	Hanged	U	U	Oct. 1871
88. Swinn/Swany, Louis, WMA	Dec. 30, 1871, att. murder of WMA	Newton	Hanged	U	U	Jan. 2, 1872
89. Morris, Martin, alias Buckskin, WM22/25	"	"	"	"	"	"
90. Cline, James, WMA	Bond fraud	Cass	Shot	Brown, Robert and Beck, Giles guilty of retarding the mail, March 1874	70–80 armed and masked men and 200 spectators	April 24, 1872
91. Stephenson/ Stevenson, Jehiel, WMA	"	"	"	"	"	"
92. Detroe, Thomas, WMA	"	"	"	"	"	"
93. Sharp, James WMA	Late July 1872 murder, WMA	Johnson	Hanged	U	100	Late July, 1872
94. Tansey, Alexander, WMA	Aug. 18, 1872, murder and robbery of 2 WMA, 1 WFA and 2 WC	Nodaway	Hanged	U	300–400	Late Aug. 1872
95. Sweney, Swinny, John, BMA	Jan. 1873 arson	Saline	Hanged	U	U	Jan. 22, 1873
96. Brezan, Joe BMA	Rape of WF	Livingston	Hanged	U	U	March 26, 1873
97. Howard, Joseph C., WMA	HS	Franklin	Hanged	U	200–300	June 17, 1873
98. Fields, George, BM	June 21, 1873, rape of WF	St. Charles	Hanged	U	U	June 21, 1873
99. Buis, Greenberry, WMA	Sheep stealing and sale of meat to butchers	Greene	Hanged	U	25	Early July 1873
100. Kessler, Peter, WMA	June 19, 1873 mule stealing	Callaway	Hanged and shooting of 4 guards, 2 of whom, including sheriff, died	U	U	Aug. 15, 1873

Name, race, sex, and age on date of alleged crime or unacceptable activity	Date, if known; crime; sex and age of victim(s)	County	Method	Relationship, if any, between victim and perpetrator of crime(s) or unacceptable activity	Number of mob members and spectators	Date of lynching
101. U WMA	HS stealing	Benton	Hanged	U	U	Aug. 30, 1873
102. U WMA	"	"	"	"	"	"
103. Box, Thomas, WMA	Oct. 20, 1873, HS	Cedar	Hanged	U	U	Oct. 27, 1873
104. Steigall or one of two men at his house, WMA	HS	Cedar	Hanged	U	U	Nov. 8/9, 1873
105. Onan, Alfred, WMA	Robbery of the home, WMA	Jasper	Hanged	U	15	Nov. 13, 1873
106. Stanton, Tom, WMA	Dec. 17, 1873, robbery and murder, WMA	Saline	Hanged	U	U	Dec. 17, 1873
107. U WMA	"	"	"	"	"	"
108. U WMA	"	"	"	"	"	"
109. Cox, Joe, BMA	HS	Hickory	Hanged	U	U	Late Dec. 1873– early Jan. 1874
110. Hardy, David, WMA	June 27, 1874, murder, WMA (LE)	Bates	Hanged	Officer and arrestee	70	June 28, 1874
111. Ross, James, WM17	HS	Holt	Hanged	U	5–6	July 17, 1874
112. Frakes, Oliver, WMA	HS and robbery	Vernon	Hanged and shot	U	8	July 19, 1874
113. Divers, Monroe, BM	Rape, WF6	Johnson	Hanged	U	Integrated mob	Aug. 7, 1874
114. Hall,___, WM25	HS	Lafayette	Hanged	U	U	Aug. 16, 1874
115. Hardice/Hardin, Joe, BM	HS	Lafayette	Hanged	U	U	Aug. 17, 1874
116. Osborne, Harvey, WMA	HS	Lafayette	Hanged	U	U	Aug. 26, 1874
117. Harris, James, WMA	U	Vernon	Shot	U	U	Oct. 1874
118. Teague, James, WMA	HS	Lincoln	Shot off horse and dragged by animal	U	50 in 1st attempt and 4 in 2nd	Shot Nov. 13; died Nov. 19, 1874
119. Dr. Rush, WMA	Arson in town of Concordia and att. poisoning, WMA	Lafayette	Hanged	U	U	Dec. 3, 1874
120. Callaway, Jim, BM	April 3, 1875, rape, WF16	Carroll	Hanged	U	Large body of masked horsemen	April 4, 1875

Name, race, sex, and age on date of alleged crime or unacceptable activity	Date, if known; crime; sex and age of victim(s)	County	Method	Relationship, if any, between victim and perpetrator of crime(s) or unacceptable activity	Number of mob members and spectators	Date of lynching
121. Dudley,___, WM20	Theft in Bates County	Vernon	Shot	U	Party from Bates County	July 1875
122. Williams, Raphael or Ralph, BMA	July 27, 1876 rape, WFA	Platte	Hanged	U	120	July 31, 1876
123. Moore, Edmond, BM	Sept. 23, 1876, rape, WFA	Chariton	Hanged	U	120	Sept. 28, 1876
124. Green, John, WMA	July 6, 1877, murder, WFA	Randolph	Hanged	Husband and wife	40–75	July 9, 1877
125. Cason, Port, BM30	Late Aug. 1879, frightening WFA	Howard	Shot	U	U	Aug. 29, 1879
126. Young, William J., WMA	Acquitted on Oct. 25, 1879, of Aug. 3, 1877, murder of father and 4 children	Clark	Shot and hanged	U	Slater, alias Lane, captain of the mob	Oct. 29, 1879
127. Mitchell, Henry, BM17	Late March, 1880, murder, BMA	Randolph	Hanged	Stepson and stepfather	Party of 40–50, black mob	April 20/21, 1880
128. Yancy, Dick, alias, Lincoln, Abe, BM20	"	"	"	Friend of stepson	"	"
129. Parks, John, WMA	Jan. 20, 1880, murder, WMA	St. Clair	Hanged	U	100 masked men	May 13, 1880
130. Pierce, Chesley, WMA	Accessory to Jan. 20, 1880, murder, WMA	St. Clair	"	"	"	"
131. Smith, William, WMA	April 10, 1880, murder, WMA	St. Clair	Shot and body tied to tree near hanging of Parks and Pierce	U	100 masked men	May 13, 1880
132. Corlew, C.W., WMA	March 1880 rape, WFA	Randolph	Shot	Husband shot Corlew and rode off with many friends	100 men	July 29, 1880
133. Bird, Henry, BM	Sept. 24, 1880, rape, WFA	Clinton	Hanged	Employee/ employer	40? 70? 500?	Sept. 25, 1880
134. Reinhammer, Thomas, WMA	May 1881 assault, WMA	Atchison	Hanged	Former employee/ employer	25 masked men	June 11, 1881
135. Reese, Charles, alias Diddell, Charles, BM	June 12, 1881, att. rape, WF16	Platte	Hanged	U	Mob included victim's brother	June 12, 1881
136. Butler, James Jr., WMA, BM21	HS	Dade	Hanged	U	U	July 3, 1881

Name, race, sex, and age on date of alleged crime or unacceptable activity	Date, if known; crime; sex and age of victim(s)	County	Method	Relationship, if any, between victim and perpetrator of crime(s) or unacceptable activity	Number of mob members and spectators	Date of lynching
137. Craft, Frank, WMA	"	"	"	"	"	"
138. Underwood, William, WMA	"	"	"	"	"	"
139. Harrington, Levi, BMA	Innocent of April 3, 1882, murder, WMA (LE)	Jackson	Hanged	Policeman and arrestee; George Grant guilty, murder WMA (LE)	U	April 3, 1882
140. Caldwell, Henry, BM	July 27, 1882, rape, WF60	Iron	Hanged and shot	U	30 to 40 masked men	July 29, 1882
141. Marsden, Mack, WMA	March 29, 1882, arson of home and murder, WMA	Jefferson	Hanged	U	Five men	April 7, 1883
142. Fisher, J.W., alias Whitney, WMA	May 19, 1883, murder, WMA	Gasconade	Hanged	U	125–200	June 5, 1883
143. McDowell, William, BM24	June 25, 1883, rape, WF20	Pike	Hanged	U	75–100	July 1, 1883
144. Patterson, Ham, BM19	April 15, 1884, brother or half brother spoke disrespectfully to whites	Callaway	Hanged	U	25	May 3, 1884
145. Harrison, Mickey, BM	Aug. 2, 1884, murder, BMA (LE)	Howard	Hanged	U	75–100, black mob	Aug. 3, 1884
146. Unknown, BM	Innocent of Oct. 13, 1884, rape, WF10	Callaway	Shot	Actual rapist avoided capture	U	Oct. 14, 1884
147. Stevens, Charlie, WM40	March 1, 1879, murder, WMA and Dec. 3, 1884, assault, WM27	Nodaway	Hanged	U	60 masked men	Dec. 9, 1884
148. Taylor, Frank, WMA	April 10, 1885, assault, WMA and WFA	Taney	Hanged	U	100	April 15, 1885
149. Taylor, Tubal, WMA	"	"	"	"	"	"
150. Thorton, Joe, WMA	July 18, 1885, murder, WM56 (LE)	Jasper	Hanged	U	U	July 19, 1885
151. Mann, Garland, WMA	Sept. 12, 1883, murder, WMA	Newton	Shot	U	100–150 mob from McDonald County	Aug. 6, 1885
152. Grubb, Irwin, WMA	June 1885 murder, WMA	McDonald	Hanged	U	U	Nov. 1885
153.Graham, George WMA	Fall 1885 suspicion of murder, WFA	Greene	Hanged	U	75–100	April 27, 1886

Name, race, sex, and age on date of alleged crime or unacceptable activity	Date, if known; crime; sex and age of victim(s)	County	Method	Relationship, if any, between victim and perpetrator of crime(s) or unacceptable activity	Number of mob members and spectators	Date of lynching
154. Paxton, Bowman, WMA	Sept. 1886 murder, WMA	Dunklin	Hanged	U	100	Sept. 19/20, 1886
155. Wallace, Pat, WMA	Sept. 21, 1886, murder, 4 WC, WMA, and WFA	Crawford	Hanged	U	100	Oct. 4, 1886
156. Davis, Lewis, WMA	Jan. 2, 1888, murder, WMA	Crawford	Hanged	U	40	Sept. 23, 1888
157. Thomas, Henry, WMA	Jan. 18, 1889, murder, 2 WMA and WF18	Cole	Hanged	U	U	Jan. 18, 1889
158. Smith, Ben, BM22	Aug. 3, 1889, rape, WF24	Macon	Hanged and shot	U	50	Aug. 3, 1889
159. Bush, George, BM17/18	Sept. 5, 1889, rape, 5/6 mulatto	Boone	Hanged	U	20	Sept. 7, 1889
160. Waters, Will, BM18	Aug. 29, 1890, robbery and murder, WMA	Lafayette	U	U	U	Aug. 29, 1890
161. Smith, Tom, BM25	Sept. 2, 1890, assault, WMA	Butler	Shot and hanged	U	150–200	Sept. 4, 1890
162. Thixton, Allie, BM18/19	Jan. 1891 att. rape and robbery, WF	Howard	U	U	U	Jan. 20, 1891
163. Murrell, Andrew, McFadden, Lon and Musser, Jesse WMA	Aug, 31, 1891 bank robbery	Lafayette	Hanged and shot	U	20	Aug. 31, 1891
164. Hepler, Robert, WM33	Jan. 17, 1892, murder, WFA and WMC	Barton	Hanged	Husband of deceased in mob	100	Jan. 22, 1892
165. Cullen, Richard, WM23	Feb. 22/23, 1892, murder, WM4	Webster	Hanged	U	150	Feb. 26, 1892
166. Miller, Amos WM	Feb. 27, 1892, murder, WMA (LE)	Stoddard	Hanged	U	54	March 1, 1892
167. Bright, John WMA	March 1, 1892, murder, WFA	Taney	Hanged	Husband and wife. Mob also killed George Williams, a deputy sheriff	125 and 20 later arrested	March 12, 1892
168. Gordon, Lewis, WM22	March 11, 1892, rape, WFA	Carroll	U	U	500	March 12, 1892
169. Sims, David, BMA	U	Dunklin	Shot	U	3 blacks	April 22, 1892
170. Jackson, Will, BM	Sept. 15, 1893, att. rape, WF11	Bates	Hanged	U	300	Sept. 16, 1893
171. Burke, Redmond, WM55	Ill treatment of family	Caldwell	Strangled in bed	U	U	Sept. 17, 1893
172. Buchner, John, BMA	Jan. 16, 1894, rape, BFA and WF16	St. Louis	Hanged	U	Integrated mob of 200	Jan. 17, 1894

Name, race, sex, and age on date of alleged crime or unacceptable activity	Date, if known; crime; sex and age of victim(s)	County	Method	Relationship, if any, between victim and perpetrator of crime(s) or unacceptable activity	Number of mob members and spectators	Date of lynching
173. Hayden, Hewett, BM	June 1894 murder, WMA	Barry	Hanged	U	300	June 28, 1894
174. Johnson, James, BMA	Aug. 1892, consensual sex, WFA	Callaway	Hanged	Summer 1893, she gave birth to a mulatto baby	120	July 1, 1894
175. Tracy, George, BMA	Feb. 7, 1895, murder, BF25	Caldwell	Shot	U	40 to 50 in black mob	Feb. 17, 1895
176. Divers, Emmett, BM	July 23, 1895, rape and murder, WF17	Callaway	Hanged	U	100 in mob; 1000 marched with his body	Aug. 15, 1895
177. Mance, Will, alias Henderson, Will, BM17	Oct. 10, 1895, att. rape, WF14	Cape Girardeau	Hanged	U	100	Oct. 11, 1895
178. Larkin, Thomas, WM	Sept. 2, 1896, rape, WF11	Montgomery	Hanged	U	U	Sept. 4, 1896
179. Winner, Jesse, WMA	Oct. 28, 1896, murder, WFA and 2 WC	Lafayette/Ray county line	Hanged	Husband and wife	150	Dec. 7, 1896
180. Nelson, James, WMA	Accessory to Winner's murders	"	"	Hired hand	"	"
181. Mitchell, John, WMA	Hog and other petty stealing	Wright	Shot	U	20	May 18, 1897
182. Kaufman, Jack, WMA	"	"	"	"	"	"
183. Brown, Erastus, BM23	July 2, 1897, att. rape, WF23	Franklin	Hanged	U	40 on horseback; 3 or 4 in wagon	July 10, 1897
184. Young, Curtis, BM	June 5, 1898 murder, WMA (LE)	Pike	Hanged	U	200	June 6, 1898
185. Young, Sam, BM	"	"	"	"	"	"
186. Williams, Henry, BMA	May-June 1898 beating and frightening, 4 WFs	Macon	Hanged	U	200–300	June 30, 1898
187. Jones, Benjamin, WM68	Sept. 10, 1898, rape, WF11	Clay	Hanged	U	75	Sept. 11, 1898
188. Embree, Frank, BMA	June 17, 1899, rape, WF14	Howard	Hanged	U	1,000	July 22, 1899
189. Hayden, Tom, BM	Oct. 28, 1899, murder, WM23	Howard	Hanged	U	50	Oct. 29, 1899
190. Huff, William H., WMA	Nov. 11, 1899, murder, WMA	Stoddard	U	U	U	Nov. 16, 1899
191. Cohnagwe, Mindo, BM23	April 26, 1900, assault, WFA (wife of LE)	Saline	Hanged	U	1,000	April 28, 1900

Name, race, sex, and age on date of alleged crime or unacceptable activity	Date, if known; crime; sex and age of victim(s)	County	Method	Relationship, if any, between victim and perpetrator of crime(s) or unacceptable activity	Number of mob members and spectators	Date of lynching
192. Darley, Henry, alias Alecks, Henry BM26/30	May 1, 1900, att. rape, WF18/22	Clay	Hanged	U	60–75	May 2, 1900
193. McNeal, Arthur, alias Smith, Dewey and McBrien, Bob, BMA	March 1, 1901, murder, WM26	Ray	Hanged	U	500	March 2, 1901
194. Godley, Will, BMA	Aug. 18, 1901, murder, WF	Lawrence	Hanged and shot	U	1,000	Aug. 20, 1901
195. Godley, French, BM	"	"	Burned	"	"	"
196. Hampton, Peter, BM	"	"	"	"	"	"
197. Wright, Louis F., BM22	Feb. 15, 1902, assault, WM	New Madrid	Hanged	U	U	Feb. 16, 1902
198. Wright, Oliver, BM35	March 21, 1902, rumor of murder, WMA	Randolph	Whipped to death	U	7 or 8	March 22, 1902
199. Withrup, Abe, BMA	April 1902 murder, WM21	Monroe	Hanged	U	100	May 25, 1902
200. Salyers, Charles, WMA	Aug. 4, 1902, murder, WMA	Lafayette	Hanged	U	150	Aug. 12, 1905
201. Gates Harry, BMA	"	"	"	"	"	"
202. Clark, Andy, BMA	Jan. 19, 1903, murder WM60	Wayne	Hanged	U	70	Jan. 21, 1903
203. Gilyard, Thomas, BM20	April 14, 1903, murder, WMA (LE)	Jasper	Hanged	U	2,000	April 15, 1903
204. Malone, Rev. W.J., WMA	Wife abandonment and adultery, WFA	Pemiscot	Shot	Mob also killed W.J. Mooneyhan (LE)	U	May 2, 1903
205. Witherspoon, Tom, BMA	May 12, 1905, $600 demand on WMA and taking hostage, WFA and WC	Mississippi	Hanged	U	200–300	May 12, 1905
206. Coker, Fred, BM	April 13, 1906, rape, WF21	Greene	Hanged, burned and shot	U	3,000	April 14, 1906
207. Duncan, Horace, BM	"	"	"	"	"	"
208. Allen, William, BM	1906 murder, WM	Greene	Hanged, shot and burned	U	U	April 15, 1906
209. Johnson, George, WMA	June 20, 1909, murder, WMA	Platte	Hanged	U	60–300	Aug. 2, 1909
210. Unknown Negro	May 28, 1910, assault, WMA (LE)	New Madrid	Hanged	U	U	May 29, 1910

Name, race, sex, and age on date of alleged crime or unacceptable activity	Date, if known; crime; sex and age of victim(s)	County	Method	Relationship, if any, between victim and perpetrator of crime(s) or unacceptable activity	Number of mob members and spectators	Date of lynching
211. Coleman, Robert, BM	July 2, 1910, robbery and murder, WMA	Mississippi	Hanged	U	1,000	July 3, 1910
212. Fields, Sam, BM	"	"	"	"	"	"
213. Rich, A.B., BM	Stealing and minor charges	Pemiscot	Shot	U	75	Oct. 11, 1911
214. Shields, Dallas, BM	March 17, 1914, murder, WMA (LE)	Howard	Hanged	U	150	March 17, 1914
215. Williams, W.F., WMA	Feb. 20, 1915, murder, WMA (LE)	Cass	Hanged and shot	U	100	Feb. 21, 1915
216. Rudd, Love, BM	Sept. 5, 1915, burglary of home, WMA	Pike	Hanged	U	40	Sept. 8, 1915
217. Channel, Lafayette, BMA	April 5, 1916, murder, WMA (LE) and assault, WMA (LE)	St. Charles	Shot	U	100s	April 5, 1916
218. Lynch, Jay, WMA	March 3, 1919, murder 2 WM, 1 (LE) and son	Barton	Hanged	U	500–1,000	May 28, 1919
219. Anderson, James, BM	Nov. 13, 1919, assault and robbery, WMA	Randolph	Shot	U	100–200 in 12 cars	Nov. 16, 1919
220. Canafex, Fred, BMA	July 6, 1920, rape, WF	Reynolds	Shot	U	U	July 7, 1920
221. Hammonds, Roy, BM19	April 27, 1921, att. rape, WF14	Pike	Hanged	U	200	April 29, 1921
222. Scott, James, BM30/35	April 20, 1923, att. rape, WF14/15	Boone	Hanged	U	1,500	April 29, 1923
223. Grigsby, Roosevelt, BM20	Dec. 18, 1924, att. rape, WF15	Mississippi	Hanged, dragged, shot and burned	U	200	Dec. 18, 1924
224. Mitchell, Walter, BM30	Aug. 7, 1915, att. rape, WF19	Clay	Hanged and shot	U	1,000	Aug. 7, 1925
225. Sherod, Will, BM30	May 22, 1927, rape, WF31	Pemiscot	Hanged and shot	U	100	May 22, 1927
226. Gunn, Raymond, BM27	Dec. 16, 1930, rape and murder, WF20	Nodaway	Hanged, and burned	U	500 in mob and 3000 witnesses	Jan. 12, 1931
227. Warner, Lloyd, BM19	Nov. 26, 1933, rape of WF21	Buchanan	Removed eyes, hanged and burned	U	5,000? 8,000? 10,000?	Nov. 28, 1933

Name, race, sex, and age on date of alleged crime or unacceptable activity	Date, if known; crime; sex and age of victim(s)	County	Method	Relationship, if any, between victim and perpetrator of crime(s) or unacceptable activity	Number of mob members and spectators	Date of lynching
228. Wright, Cleo, BM30	Jan. 25, 1942, att. rape, WF29	Scott	Dragged and burned	U	500	Jan. 25, 1942
229. McElroy, Kenneth, WM27	Earlier stealing and July 8, 1980, assault, WM70	Nodaway	Shot	U	60	July 10, 1981

Appendix 2: Falsely Reported, Doubtful, and Foiled Lynchings in Missouri, 1857–1930

Abbreviations

W	White	A	Adult	U	Unknown
B	Black	HS	Horse Stealing	"	Same Incident as Above
M	Male	LE	Law Enforcement Officer		
F	Female	att.	Attempted		

Name, race, sex and age on date of alleged crime or unacceptable activity	Date, if known; crime; sex and age of victim(s)	County	Relationship, if any, between victim and perpetrator of crime(s) or unacceptable activity	No. of mob members, spectators	Reason not a Missouri lynching	Date
1. Tucker, alias Matheny, George, WMA	1857 HS	Howard	U	300–400	Suicide	Sept. 5, 1857
2. Doy, Charles, WMA	Feb. 1859 abolitionist activity	Platte	U	300	Newspaper reported intended as completed lynchings; Judge prevented them	Feb. 1859
3. Doy, John, WM25	"	"	"	"	"	"
4. Harris, Marcellus, WMA	1860 murder, WMA	St. Clair	U	U	Insufficient information	1861
5. Hired Hand, BMA	Being free	Boone	U	U	Insufficient information	Mid-Feb. 1865
6. Munkirs, Redmund B., WMA	U	Clay	U	U	Insufficient information	May 18, 1867
7. White, William, WM	U	Macon	U	U	Insufficient information	Nov. 10, 1870
8. Markham,___, WMA	U	Vernon	U	6	Insufficient information	Jan. 30, 1877
9. Robinson, WMA	U	Dunklin	U	U	Insufficient information	Feb. 1878

Name, race, sex and age on date of alleged crime or unacceptable activity	Date, if known; crime; sex and age of victim(s)	County	Relationship, if any, between victim and perpetrator of crime(s) or unacceptable activity	No. of mob members, spectators	Reason not a Missouri lynching	Date
10. Wagoner, John, WMA	Nov. 1881 murder, WMA	Iron	U	40–60	No local newspaper coverage; event did not take place in Missouri	Jan. 20, 1882
11. King, Si, BM	Sept. 29, 1885, rape, WFA	Ralls	U	U	Suicide	Sept.-Oct. 1885
12. Vanderbaugh, John, WM30	May 17, 1887, rape, WF16	Bates	U	2	Insufficient numbers for a lynching	May 24, 1887
13. Corber brother, WM	Murder		U	U	Lynching in Tennessee	May 7, 1889
14. Corber brother, WM	"		"	"	"	"
15. Corber brother, WMA	"		"	"	"	"
16. Grizzard, Alfred, WM	Gambling		U	U	Lynching in Tennessee	June 21, 1889
17. Divers, Squire, BM	Aug. 19, 1889, att., rape, WF16	Boone	U	U	LE protected prisoner	Aug. 1889
18.Davis, John, WM	Sept. 11, 1889, murder of Mrs. Andy Savage	Greene	U	U	Insufficient information	Sept. 1889
19. Gebhard/Gibheart, Lawrence, WM	Oct. 26, 1889, safe-breaking	Dunklin	U	U	Survived injuries	Nov. 15, 1889
20.Gebhard/Gibheart, Joe, WM	"	"	"	"	"	"
21. Hughes, John, BM	Feb. 17, 1893, insulting WF	Randolph	Brothers of WF	2	Survived injuries	Feb. 18, 1893
22. North, John, BMA	Late July, 1893, eloping with WF15	St. Charles	U	150	LE protected prisoner	Aug. 3, 1893
23. Montgomery, Bud, WMA	Dec. 18, 1893, murder, WMA	Fulton and Baxter counties, AR	U	U	Lynching took place in Arkansas	Feb. 26, 1894
24. Carter, Anderson, WMA	"	"	"	"	"	"
25. Barclay, H.B., BMA	Jan. 21, 1894, rape, WF12	Lawrence	U	U	Child said he was not the man who raped her.	Late Jan. 1894
26. West, Pearl, BMA	"	"	"	"	"	Feb. 1894
27. Taylor, George, WMA	May 10, 1894, murder, WMA, WFA, WF1, WF4	Sullivan	U	1,000, 200, and 50	LE protected prisoner and confined in Buchanan County jail	1894; sentenced to death but escaped

Name, race, sex and age on date of alleged crime or unacceptable activity	Date, if known; crime; sex and age of victim(s)	County	Relationship, if any, between victim and perpetrator of crime(s) or unacceptable activity	No. of mob members, spectators	Reason not a Missouri lynching	Date
28. Taylor, William, WMA	"	"	"	"	"	Executed April 30, 1896, Carroll County
29. Unknown, WMA	Thievery	St. Clair	U	U	Suicide?	Oct. 27, 1894
30. Layland, Cecil, WMA	June 1896, att. rape, WF	Ralls	U	U	Suicide?	June 29, 1896
31. Crawford, Martin, WM39	July 26, 1896, att. rape, WF15	Morgan	U	U	Fatal heart attack at home sitting in chair	July 27, 1896
32. Fargo, Silas, WMA	Oct. 1, 1896, arson, black-smith's shop; acquitted Nov. 12, 1897	Clay	U	U	Survived injuries	Nov. 17, 1897
33. Foley, William, WMA	Nov. 17, 1896, murder, WFA and WF	Clay	U	U	Prisoner confined in Jackson County jail, Kansas City	July 1898
34. Unknown Negro	Nov. 26, 1898, murder, WMA	Ballard County, Kentucky	U	U	Madrid Bend is in Kentucky, not Missouri	Nov. 26, 1898
35. Unknown Negro	"	"	"	"	"	Nov. 29, 1898
36. Harris, Lewis, BM	March 25, 1900, rape, WFA	Cooper			No local news cov-erage; event did not take place in MO	March 26, 1900
37. Nelson, Simpson, BM	Racial prejudice	Butler	U	U	Survived injuries	Dec. 31, 1900
38. Robertson, Joseph, BM	July 10, 1901, alleged rape, WM18 and assault of WM20	Jackson	U	300	Police and fire departments protected prisoners and moved them to Cass County jail	July 12/13, 1901
39. Holland, Frank, BM17	"	"	"	"	"	"
40. Anderson, Joshua, WMA	Murder, WFA				Lynching took place in Kentucky	July 17, 1902

Name, race, sex and age on date of alleged crime or unacceptable activity	Date, if known; crime; sex and age of victim(s)	County	Relationship, if any, between victim and perpetrator of crime(s) or unacceptable activity	No. of mob members, spectators	Reason not a Missouri lynching	Date
41. Chism, Earl, WM	March 29, 1909, att. murder, WMA (LE)	Daviess	U	U	Farmer's wife talked posse out of lynching and LE protected prisoner	March 30, 1909
42. Chism, Ray, WM	"	"	"	"	"	"
43. Gardner, Lee, BM	July 5, 1910, att. rape, WF12	Mississippi	U	U	Mob talked out of lynching	July 5, 1910
44. Ben, alias "High Pockets," BM	Annoying young WFs	Pemiscot	U	75	Survived injuries	Oct. 11, 1911
45. Collins, Isaac, WM	Undesirable citizen	Douglas	U	U	Survived injuries	June 18, 1914
46. Collins, Paralee, WF	"	"	"	"	"	"
47. Eaton, John, BM	April 10, 1915, assault, WM	Pike	U	150	LE prevented lynching	April 20, 1915
48. Rose, Harrison BM	Aug. 31, 1915, murder, WMA	Pike	U	U	Champ Clark, then Speaker of U.S. House dissuaded mob and LE protected prisoner	Sept. 2, 1915, and Oct. 5, 1915
49. Wilson, Ocie, BM	May 1928 murder, BM	Saline	U	12	No local news coverage; event did not take place in Missouri	May 1928
50. Taylor, Lonnie, BMA	Oct. 12, 1930, robbery and murder, 2 WMA	Ste Genevieve County	U	U	LE protected prisoner	Oct. 1930

Chapter Notes

Abbreviations

CT   *Chicago Tribune*
DAB   *Dictionary of American Biography*
DMB   *Dictionary of Missouri Biography*
DSM   Frazier, *Death Sentences in Missouri,*
        1806–2005
KCS   *Kansas City Star*
KCT   *Kansas City Times*

KNG   *Knob Noster Gem*
LT   *Liberty Tribune*
MCL   Mid-Continent Library, Web Portal
MORE   *Missouri Republican* (St. Louis)
NYT   *New York Times*
RC   *Randolph Citizen* (Huntsville)
SDD   *Sedalia Daily Democrat*

Chapter 1

1. Stoddard to Clairborne, *Glimpses of the Past*, 102–03.

2. Frances Paul Prucha, *The Great White Father*, 43.

3. By the 1920s the U.S. government had paid, as Congressman Dyer notes in his anti-lynching bill report, $792,499.39 to foreign governments for less than 100 foreign lives "to compensate the murder by lynching of their citizens by American mobs; and there are now with the Department of State unadjusted claims to a large amount for similar murders of Austrians, Greek, Japanese, and Italians." See Chapter 12, note 21.

4. William Foley, *Genesis of Missouri*, 234.

5. *Missouri Statesman* (Columbia), June 30, 1843, 2:3 and *History of Southeast Missouri*, 846.

6. Geraldine Sanders Smith, St. Louis, Mo., gave me several news stories from the *Democrat-News* (Fredericktown) concerning the lynching of the man who murdered the husband of her grandmother's sister. They date from 1900, and as such they are even more remote in time from the events they relate than the *History of Southeast Missouri*'s description of the lynching of Abraham Smith in 1888, 340–41.

7. *MORE* (St. Louis), Oct. 2, 1844. 2:2.

8. 1 Stat. 119.

9. *Laws of a Public and General Nature of the District of Louisiana, of the Territory of Louisiana, of the Territory of Missouri, and of the State of Missouri Up*

to the Year 1824, chap. 65, sec. 10 and 30, 211 and 216 (1808).

10. *Laws*, chap. 65, sec. 13–14, 18–19 (1804).

11. *Louisiana Gazette* (St. Louis) Dec. 26, 1809, 2:2

12. *Missouri Gazette* (St. Louis), June 22, 1816, 3:2.

13. See chapters 1 and 6, *Runaway and Freed Missouri Slaves and Those Who Helped Them* (2004) for accounts of William Wells Brown's and John Anderson's escape from slavery in Missouri.

14. Missouri Revised Statutes, art. 3, secs. 30–31 (1835).

15. *Missouri Intelligencer* (Columbia), Dec. 11, 1830, 3:1 and *Jefferson Republican* (Jefferson City), June 16, 1833, 2:1.

16. *Laws*, chap. 58, secs. 1–12, 195 (1817).

17. Missouri Revised Statutes, chap. 172, sec. 2 (1845) and chap. 154, sec. 2 (1855).

18. See *Missouri Gazette* (St. Louis), Sept. 28, 1816, 3:4; March 22, 1817, 1:2; and Nov. 1, 1820, 4:2.

19. *Missouri Gazette* (St. Louis), Sept. 2, 1815, 4:3.

20. *St. Louis Enquirer*, March 17, 1819, 3:3.

21. *LT*, Sept. 20, 1850, 2:1.

22. *History of Clay and Platte Counties, Missouri*, 165.

23. *LT*, Aug. 11, 1854, 2:2 and *Brunswicker* (Brunswick), Aug. 12, 1854, 2:2.

24. *LT*, Oct. 21, 1859, 2:1.

25. *RC* (Huntsville), Oct. 28, 1859, 2:1.

26. *LT*, Sept. 11, 1857, 1:2. See also *Kansas City*

Enterprise, Sept. 12, 1857, 2:4 and *RC*, Sept. 10, 1857, 1:5.

27. *LT*, Oct. 28, 1853, 1:4.

28. *Ibid.*

29. *History of Ray County, Missouri,* 481.

30. *RC*, July 24, 1856, 2:5.

31. *RC*, July 17, 2:5 and July 31, 1856, 3:2 and *LT*, July 25, 1856, 2:6.

32. *RC*, July 18, 1858, 2:5.

33. *RC*, July 12, 1858, 2:5; *Palmyra Whig*, July 15, 1858, 3:2; and *History of Gentry and Worth Counties, Missouri*, 240–42.

34. *NYT*, March 8, 1859, 2:1. Hereinafter MCL follows all stories obtained through Googling "Lynchings in Missouri" on the Mid-Continent Library's website. I found material for this book in *The New York Times* and the *Chicago Tribune* both personally and through the service.

35. Lois Stanley, George F. Wilson, and Maryhelen Wilson, *Death Records from Missouri Newspapers, January 1854-December 1860,* 64.

36. *History of Henry and St. Clair Counties, Missouri,* 937

37. *California News,* March 2, 1861, 2:1.

38. *History of Caldwell and Livingston County, Missouri*, 772.

39. *History of Franklin, Jefferson , Washington, Crawford, & Gasconade Counties,* 281.

40. *Ibid.*

41. *MORE*, July 22, 1862, 2:2.

42. *LT*, Aug. 1, 1862, 1:2.

Chapter 2

1. James Cutler, *Lynch-Law, An Investigation into the History of Lynching in the United States,* 124.

2. Lawrence M. Friedman, *Crime and Punishment in American History,* 190.

3. Michael Fellman, *Inside War,* 70.

4. Edward L. Ayers, *Vengeance & Justice: Crime and Punishment in the 19th-Century American South,* 237.

5. Peter H. Wood, *Black Majority: Negroes in Colonial South Carolina From 1670 Through the Stone Rebellion,* 135.

6. Philip Schwarz, *Twice Condemned: Slaves and the Criminal Laws of Virginia, 1705–1865,* 92.

7. William H. Perrin, ed. *History of Crawford and Clark Counties, Illinois,* 38.

8. *Missouri Gazette* (St. Louis), April 5, 1820, 1:5 and *Missouri Herald* (Jackson) April 8, 1820, 1:3.

9. *Southerner* (Tarboro, NC), Aug. 31, 1830, 1:4.

10. "Acts Relating to Slaves," No. 314, *The Statutes at Large of South Carolina,* 1840, 7:355.

11. George M. Stroud, *A Sketch of the Laws Relating to Slavery,* 78.

12. William Blackstone, *Commentaries on the Laws of England,* 4:18.

13. Leon Radzinowicz, *History of English Criminal Law and Its Administration from 1750,* 1:4.

14. Blackstone, *Commentaries,* 4:75 and 204.

15. Gen. 38:24 and Lev. 21:9.

16. Lev. 20:14.

17. Harriet Beecher Stowe, *Uncle Tom's Cabin,* 382

18. *LT*, Dec. 13, 1849, 2:5.

19. Janet S. Hermann, "The McIntosh Affair," 126. This careful and detailed discussion, 123–43, is the origin of any quoted material regarding this case not attributed to another source. See also the *Pittsburgh Gazette,* May 12, 1836, 2:1, which reprints a *MORE* story about McIntosh's lynching.

20. Cited in Hermann, 133.

21. *Liberator* (Boston), May 14, 3:5 and May 21,1836, 3:3.

22. Theodore Weld, *American Slavery as It Is,* 156–57.

23. Abraham Lincoln, "Address before the Young Men's Lyceum of Springfield Illinois," 1:148–50.

24. Harriet Martineau, *Retrospect of Western Travel,* 2:206–09.

25. Madeline House, Graham Storey, and Kathleen Tillotson, eds., *Letters of Charles Dickens,* 3:197 (emphasis in the original).

26. Reprinted in *Jefferson Republican,* May 7, 1836, 2:3.

27. William Hyde and Howard L. Conrad, *Encyclopedia of the History of St. Louis,* 4:1913.

28. Cutler, *Lynch Law,* 108–112.

29. *Jefferson Republican* (Jefferson City), Dec. 17, 1836, 3:2–6; there are no extant official state census records for Missouri until 1868; all that survive are in newspaper form.

30. *Franklin County Tribune* (Union), July 16, 1897, 1:3.

31. *History of Franklin, Jefferson, Washington, Crawford & Gasconade Counties Missouri,*283.

32. *Ibid.,* 405.

33. *Missouri Statesman* (Columbia), March 15, 1844, 2:4.

34. *MORE*, March 7, 1844, 2:2.

35. *Ibid.,* March 8, 1844, 2:1.

36. *Jefferson Republican* (Jefferson City), May 2, 1840, 1:4 and *Salt River Journal* (Bowling Green), May 2, 1840, 1:5 reprint an identical story about this case from *MORE*.

37. *MORE*, Nov. 3, 1820. 3:5 and *Missouri Intelligencer* (Fayette), Oct. 30, 2:5 and Nov. 6, 1829, 2:4.

38. *Estate of Shubael Allen,* Clay County Probate Court Records, April 1842.

39. *LT*, April 5, 1850, 2:1.

40. *Ibid.,* May 3, 1850, 2:2.

41. *Ibid.,* May 10, 1850, 2:2 and May 17, 1850, 1:5.

42. *Springfield Advertiser,* May 25, 1850, 2:6.

43. *History of Clay and Platte Counties, Missouri,* 159.

44. *Boonville Weekly Observer,* Nov. 10, 1860, 1:8.

45. *History of Callaway County,* 286–87, published in 1884, quotes a lengthy news story from the *Missouri Telegraph* (Fulton) and misdates its story about Teney's crime and punishment as Oct. 2, 1860. This date is more than three weeks before the events the story describes. Contemporary newspaper stories about it —*Louisiana Journal,* Nov. 8, 1860, 2:2; *LT*, Nov. 9, 1860, 2:5; *Boonville Weekly Observer,* Nov.

10, 1860, 1:8; and *California News,* Nov. 10, 1860, 2:2 — describe events that occurred on Oct. 27 and 28, 1860.

46. *LT,* Dec. 5, 1862, 2:3.

47. Missouri Revised Statutes, art, 2, secs. 23–28 (1835).

48. *Sentinel* (Columbia), Aug. 25, 1853, 2:1; see also *LT,* Aug. 26. 2:5, 1853 and *Jefferson Examiner,* Aug. 30, 1853, 2:4, and *History of Boone County,* 371–74.

49. *LT,* Sept. 2, 1853, 2:5, quoting a lengthy news story by the *Missouri Statesman* (Columbia).

50. *LT,* Sept. 2, 1869, 2:4.

51. *History of Greene County, Missouri,* 265–66. See also *LT,* Sept. 2, 1859, 2:4.

52. *LT,* Feb. 16, 2:2; Feb. 23, 2:2; March 9, 1855, 2:1; and *History of Clay and Platte Counties, Missouri,* 166–67.

53. Missouri Revised Statutes, "Costs," art. 2, sec. 16 (1845).

54. *Calhoun* v. *Buffington,* 25 Mo. 443 (1857).

55. Missouri Revised Statutes, "Fees," chap. 64, sec. 2 (1855).

56. *RC,* Oct. 18, 1855, 2:4. See also *Brunswicker,* Oct. 13, 1855, 2:1 and *LT.* Oct. 26, 1855, 1:4.

57. *Liberator,* Jan. 18, 1856, 12:4 and Cutler, *Lynch-Law,* 119.

58. *LT,* July 22, 1853, 1:6; *History of Pettis County, Missouri,* 931–32; and Michael J. Cassidy, *Defending a Way of Life,* 42–43.

59. *LT,* Aug. 5, 2:6 and 19, 1853, 2:6; *Sentinel,* Aug. 4, 1853, 2:1; *Jefferson Examiner,* Aug. 9, 1853, 2:5; *Joplin Globe,* Feb. 14, 1954, 7E:1; and *History of Newton, Lawrence, Barry and McDonald Counties, Missouri,* 453–54. The history misdates this event as having occurred in August 1854 when it took place in August 1853.

60. *History of Lincoln County, Missouri,* 365–67; Harrison Trexler, *Slavery in Missouri,* 72; *RC,* Jan. 7, 1859, 3:5; *California News,* Jan. 22, 1859, 4:1; *LT,* Jan. 18, 1859, 1:7.

61. *Boonville Weekly Observer,* July 23, 1859, 2:1 and *California News,* July 23, 2:2 and July 29, 1859, 1:2.

62. *History of Saline County, Missouri,* 259–65; *Missouri Statesman,* July 29, 1859, 2:4; *Boonville Weekly Observer,* May 28, 1859, 3:2; *California News,* July 30, 1859, 2:3; and *LT,* July 29, 1859, 1:2; and *Louisiana Journal,* July 28, 1859, 2:4.

63. *State* v. *John,* Saline County Circuit Court Records, May-Dec. 1859.

64. *State* v. *Holman,* Saline County Circuit Court Records, June-Nov. 1859.

65. *State* v. *James,* Saline County Circuit Court Records, July-Nov. 1859.

66. Thomas G. Dyer, "A Most Unexampled Exhibition of Madness and Brutality: Judge Lynch in Saline County, Missouri, 1859," 98, initially appeared as an article in the *Missouri Historical Review* 89 (April and July 1995), 269–89, 367–83 and later as a chapter, 81–108, in *Under Sentence of Death: Lynching in the South,* ed. W. Fitzhugh Brundage.

67. In his *Celia, A Slave,* Melton McLaurin also explains the Callaway County execution of a slave in 1855 as in part caused by the Missouri-Kansas border warfare. The causality of Celia's lynching was far more complex than any events unfolding more than 100 miles west of Fulton, Missouri.

68. *Scott (a man of color)* v. *Emerson,* 15 Mo. 576, 586–87 (1852).

69. Edmund Wilson, *Patriotic Gore: Studies in the Literature of the American Civil War,* 3.

70. *California News,* Oct. 13, 1860. 2:5.

71. *Southern Quarterly Review,* Jan. 1853, 82.

72. Wilson, *Patriotic Gore,* 4.

73. *LT,* July 22, 1853, 4:1

74. *Jefferson Examiner,* Aug. 2, 1853, 1:5.

75. Joan D. Hedrick, *Harriet Beecher Stowe, a Life,* 269.

76. *RC,* Dec. 10, 1857, 2:7.

77. *LT,* Nov. 25, 1859, 2:4.

78. Missouri Revised Statutes, chap. 50, secs., 6–13 (1855).

79. *Glasgow Times,* March 15, 1860, 2:1.

80. *Charlotte* v. *Chouteau,* 11 Mo. 193, 200–01 (1847).

Chapter 3

1. Fredrick H. Dyer, *A Compendium of the War of the Rebellion,* 11.

2. See Lois Stanley, George F. Wilson, and Maryhelen Wilson, *Death Records from Missouri Newspapers: The Civil War Years, Jan. 1861-Dec. 1865,* 193 pages. Each page contains at least 30 different entries of one or more deaths. There are probably in excess of 5,800 named dead in this single volume.

3. All census figures concerning Negroes, slave and free, up to and including the 1910 census, derive from U.S. Department of Commerce, *Negro Population, 1790–1915.*

4. Annette W. Curtis, *Jackson County, Missouri in Black and White: Census of Slaves, Their Owners and Free Colored, 1850 and 1860,* 1–5.

5. Earl J. Nelson, "Missouri Slavery, 1861–1865," 260, 268.

6. *KCS,* April 16, 2003, F 4:1.

7. *Mitchell* v. *Wells,* 37 Miss. 235, 263 (1859) and Helen Catterall, ed., *Judicial Cases Concerning Slavery and the Negro,* 3:278–80 and 360–62.

8. W.M. Paxton, *Annals of Platte County,* 337–38.

9. Report of the State Auditor of Missouri for 1865, cited in Trexler, *Slavery in Missouri,* 206.

10. 13 Stat. 11

11. 13 Stat. 200.

12. Ron Chernow, *Alexander Hamilton,* 121

13. Dyer, *A Compendium of the War of the Rebellion,* 11. See also Nelson, "Missouri Slavery, 1861–1865," 264.

14. *Ibid.,* 264. The State Historical Society of Missouri has recently acquired from the National Archives six reels of microfilm with the "Descriptive Recruitment Lists of Volunteers for the U.S. Colored Troops for the State of Missouri, 1863–65."

15. Julius E. Thompson, *Lynchings in Mississippi, A History, 1865–1965,* 6–7.

16. Greene, Kremer, and Holland write, "Jim Jackson ... led his gang into Boone County in mid–February 1865 and lynched one of Dr. John Jacobs' black hired hands. This was a warning both to freedman who sought work and whites who hired them." *Missouri's Black Heritage,* 76. Had the means existed to capture and punish Jim Jackson and his gang, their careers would have ceased immediately. The war was still being fought in February 1865, and fractured as the community was at that time, law-abiding citizens did not approve of criminals murdering an employee of a physician. For this reason, the murder of Dr. Jacobs's hired hand is listed in Appendix 2.

17. *Franklin County Tribune,* July 16, 1897, 1:3.

18. *St. Louis Times,* Sept. 14, 1869, 4:2.

19. *MORE.* Sept. 14, 1869, 3:4.

20. In using directional divisions of Missouri's many counties, I have adopted those used by Bruce Nichols, *Guerrilla Warfare in Civil War Missouri, 1862,* 2.

21. *History of Greene County,* 498–501 and Roy D. Blunt, *Historical Listing of the Missouri Legislature,* 74.

22. This account comes from the *Morgan County Banner,* Sept. 8, 1866, but no copies of that paper remain from before 1867. The *Morgan County Banner* story appeared in the *Daily Evening Bulletin* (San Francisco, Calif.), Oct. 10, 1866, 3:5 and the *Daily News Herald* (Savannah, Ga.) Sept. 24, 1866, 2:2, MCL.

23. *Missouri State Times* (Jefferson City), July 5, 1867, 2:2.

24. *Laws of a Public and General Nature of the District of Louisiana, of the Territory of Louisiana, of the Territory of Missouri, and of the State of Missouri Up to the Year 1824,* chap. 37, secs. 1–9 (1807).

25. *Warrensburg Standard,* April 12, 1867, 1:4 and 3:2. See also *History of Vernon County,* 371.

26. *History of Vernon County, Missouri,* 371–72.

27. *Missouri Weekly Patriot* (Springfield), May 7, 1868, 2:2. See also *History of Newton, Lawrence, Barry, and McDonald Counties, Missouri,* 453.

28. *History of Cass and Bates Counties, Missouri,* 1002–03.

29. *History of Newton, Lawrence, Barry and McDonald Counties, Missouri,* 629–630.

30. All quoted material concerning the lynching of Robertson is taken from the *History of Holt and Atchison Counties, Missouri,* 1018–19.

31. *Warrensburg Standard,* March 1, 1867, 3:2.

32. *Ibid.,* March 8, 1867, 3:3.

33. On pages 368–85, *History of Johnson County, Missouri* relates all but one of these lynchings, Bill Scott's. All quotations identified as coming from the county history derive from this source.

34. *KCS,* Oct. 16, 1992, F1:2.

35. *Journal of Commerce* (Kansas City), May 19, 1867, 2:2.

36. *Warrensburg Standard,* March 29, 1867, 3:3.

37. *Richmond Conservator,* March 30, 1867, 2:3.

38. *LT,* June 18, 1869, 2:3.

39. *Morning Herald* (St. Joseph), July 28, 1868, 1:6.

40. *Ibid.,* Jan. 9, 1869, 1:5.

41. *LT,* March 27, 1868, 2:5.

42. *Louisiana Journal,* May 2, 1868, 2:3.

43. *History of Franklin, Jefferson, Washington, Crawford and Gasconade Counties, Missouri,* 502.

44. *Ibid.,* 497.

45. *LT,* May 24, 1867, 2:3.

46. Alexander Hamilton, *The Federalist Papers; Alexander Hamilton, James Madison, John Jay,* 208.

Chapter 4

1. *Morning Herald* (St. Joseph), Jan. 12, 1870, 4:5.

2. Thompson, *Lynchings in Mississippi,* 11–12.

3. *Daily Bazoo* (Sedalia), July 14, 1870, 1:2; *Warrensburg Standard,* July 21, 1870. 2:5, and *History of Henry and St. Clair Counties,* 218.

4. *History of Greene County,* 536–38 and *Springfield Leader,* April 28, 1886, 1:3.

5. *Saline County Weekly Progress* (Marshall), Sept. 30, 1870, 3:2.

6. *Ibid.,* Oct. 28, 1870, 1:3. See also *History of Saline County,* 382.

7. *Ibid.,* Nov. 25, 1870, 3:2 and *History of Saline County,* 382.

8. *SDD,* Jan. 31, 1:2 and Feb. 1, 1873, 3:3.

9. *Warrensburg Standard,* June 16, 1870, 3:5.

10. *SDD,* Aug. 18, 1874, 1:6.

11. *Weekly Caucasian* (Lexington), Aug. 22, 1874, 2:1.

12. Henry C. Fike Papers, Vol. 4, 301, Collection 2215 and *KCT,* Aug. 9, 1874, 1:2.

13. *LT,* Aug. 14, 1874, 1:4.

14. *KCT,* March 29, 1873, 1:2.

15. *Evening Mail* (Kansas City), April 8, 1875, 2:1.

16. *NYT,* Aug. 1, 1876, 5:3 and Paxton, *Annals of Platte County,* 623.

17. Missouri Revised Statutes, art. 2, sec.1253 (1879); *Coker v. Georgia,* 433 U.S. 584 (1977); and *Kennedy v. Louisiana,* slip opinion, (2008).

18. *SDD,* June 23, 1873, 1:2.

19. *KCT,* Oct. 2, 1876, 2:3.

20. *Howard County Advertiser* (Fayette), Sept. 4, 1879, 3:2.

21. *Washington County Journal* (Potosi), Nov. 3, 1870. 2:4.

22. *SDD,* Jan. 6, 1874, 1:5.

23. *Ibid.,* Aug. 18, 1874, 1:6 and *Weekly Caucasian* (Lexington), Aug. 22, 1874, 2:4.

24. *NYT,* Feb. 4, 1877, 9:7.

25. *History of Newton, Lawrence, Barry and McDonald Counties,* 259. The *Savannah* (GA) *Morning News,* June 13, 1870, 4:1 mentions the lynching of A.D. Taylor in Jasper County, MO.

26. *History of Newton, Lawrence, Barry and McDonald Counties,* 630.

27. *Ibid.,* 630.

28. *Ibid.*, 260 and *KCT,* Jan. 3, 1872, 1:1.
29. *History of Vernon County,* 372.
30. *Ibid.*, 372.
31. *Osceola Herald,* July 6, 1871, 2:2.
32. *History of Jasper County,* 243–44. The *SDD,* Nov. 22, 1873, 1:4 agrees with the county history's version of events regarding Onan's lynching. The newspaper makes no mention of Quantrill.
33. *SDD,* June 29, 1:5 and June 30, 1874, 1:3.
34. *History of Greene County,* 542 and *Osceola Herald,* July 17, 1873, 3:4.
35. *Herald* (Rolla), July 14, 1870, 3:2.
36. *SDD,* Sept. 2, 1873, 1:2 and *Saline County Progress,* Sept. 17, 1:4 and March 26, 1873, 3:1, and *CT,* Sept. 2, 1873, 5, MCL.
37. *Boonville Weekly Advertiser,* Nov. 7, 1873, 1:2.
38. *SDD,* Nov. 12, 1873, 1:5.
39. *History of Vernon County,* 372.
40. *Bates County Record* (Butler), April 23, 1870, 3:2.
41. *Holt County Sentinel* (Oregon), July 24, 1874, 2:2.
42. *Ibid.*
43. *Missouri Valley Times* (Oregon), July 28, 1874, 3:4.
44. *Ibid.*
45. *SDD,* Aug. 19, 1874, 1:4.
46. *SDD,* Aug. 29, 1874, 1:5.
47. *Saline County Weekly Progress* (Marshall), Dec. 11, 1874, 2:5 and *Weekly Caucasian* (Lexington), Dec. 19, 1874, 1:4.
48. *History of Nodaway County,* 347–50. See also James J. Fisher, *KCS,* Jan. 18, 1991, E1:2
49. *LT,* Aug. 2, 1872, 1:6.
50. *SDD,* Dec. 18, 1873, 1:3 and *NYT,* Dec. 20, 1873, 1:4.
51. *History of Lincoln County,* 368–69; see also *SDD,* Nov. 15, 1:7 and Nov. 20, 1874, 1:5.
52. *History of Randolph and Macon Counties, Missouri,* 244–45.
53. *NYT,* July 12, 1877, 5:6.
54. *Messages and Proclamations of the Governors of the State of Missouri,* 4: 548–49.
55. *NYT,* March 1, 1878, 1:6.
56. *Washington County Journal* (Potosi), July 7, 1870. 2:5.
57. *Franklin County Tribune* (Union), July 16, 1897, 1:3.
58. *SDD,* June 18, 1873, 1:2.

Chapter 5

1. *KCT,* April 25, 1872, 4:2.
2. *NYT,* May 3, 1872, 4:5.
3. *History of Cass and Bates Counties,* 206.
4. Allen Glenn, *History of Cass County, Missouri,* 208.
5. I am indebted to Thomas Larson, co-author with Jeffery Lay, both assistant U.S attorneys for the Western District of Missouri, for background information on James Botsford. They are the authors of a forthcoming book on the history of the federal

court for the Western District of Missouri. Its chapter six concerns James S. Botsford.
6. 3 Stat. 653 and 11 Stat. 197.
7. *DMB,* s.v. Arnold Krekel.
8. *DAB* and *DMB,* s.v., George G. Vest.
9. U.S. Constitution, art.1, sec. 8, cl., 7.
10. 4 Stat. 109.
11. *SDD,* March 11, 1874, 4:1.
12. *U.S. v Robert Brown, Jr. et al.*, Complete Record, Vol. D; U.S. District Court for the Western District of Missouri (Jefferson City: Records of District Courts of the United States, Record Group 21; National Archives and Records Administration–Central Plains Region (Kansas City), 193. Page reference to additional quoted material follows it in the text.
13. *SDD,* March 11, 1874, 4:1.
14. Glenn, *History of Cass County, Missouri,* 208.
15. *State* v. *Peter Kessler* and *State* v. *Killing Kessler, et al.,* July–October 1873, Callaway County Circuit Court Records, July–Oct., 1873.
16. *NYT,* Aug. 19, 1873, 5, MCL.
17. *SDD,* Aug.. 16, 1873, 1:4.
18. *Osceola Herald,* Aug. 31, 1873, 2:1.
19. *SDD,* Aug. 20, 1873, 4:2.
20. *Ibid.*, Aug. 19, 1873, 4:2 prints the full text of Woodson's letters of Aug. 17, 1873, to Judge Burkhardt and Attorney General Ewing.
21. *Ibid.*, Aug. 21, 1873, 4:2.
22. *Fulton Telegraph,* Aug. 29, 1973, 2:1.
23. *Ibid.*, Sept. 10, 1873, 3:2.
24. *SDD,* Sept. 12, 1873, 2:3.
25. *Ibid.*, Oct. 24, 1873, 2:5.
26. *SDD,* Sept. 12, 1873, 2:3.
27. *Fulton Telegraph,* Sept. 19, 1873, 2:1
28. Wagner's Missouri Statutes, Chap. 111, art. 9, sec. 22 (1869).
29. *SDD,* Sept. 25, 1873, 2:1.
30. *Fulton Telegraph,* Sept. 26, 1873, 2:4.
31. *NYT,* Sept. 6, 1873, 4, MCL.
32. *Ibid.*, Dec. 19, 1873, 1:1.
33. *History of Lewis, Clark, Knox and Scotland Counties* quotes the physicians' letter and jurors' statement, 323–24.
34. *Ibid.*, 331.
35. *Howard County Advertiser,* Nov. 6, 1879, 1:5.
36. *St. Louis Globe-Democrat,* Nov. 5, 1879, 4:1.
37. Missouri Revised Statutes, art. 15, chap. 24, sec. 1804 (1879).
38. *Ex Parte Slater, alias Lane,* 72 Mo. 102, 106–07 (1880).

Chapter 6

1. U.S. Department of Commerce, *Negro Population, 1790–1915,* 51.
2. *Ibid.*, 44.
3. *Kansas City Daily Journal,* Sept. 27, 1880, 1:1.
4. *KCT,* Sept. 28, 1880, 1:3.
5. *History of Clinton County, Missouri,* 428.
6. *Landmark* (Platte City), Oct. 1, 1880, 3:3.
7. W.M. Paxton, *Annals of Platte County, Missouri,* 732.

8. *KCS*, June 13, 1881, 1:2.

9. *Kansas City Daily Journal*, April 4, 1882, 8:5.

10. *State v. Grant*, 79 Mo. 113, 115 (1883). On a 2008 calendar, which lists an important event in Missouri's history for each day of the year, printed for and distributed by individual members of the Missouri Senate, including my own, Senator Jolie L. Justus, the murder of Jesse James on April 3, 1882, remains the most important event on April 3 in more than 325 years of this state's history.

11. *Kansas City Post*, Jan. 29, 1915, 5:6.

12. *Kansas City Daily Journal*, April 4, 1882, 8:4.

13. *KCS*, April 7, 1882, 1:6.

14. *State v, Grant*, 76 Mo. 236 (1882) and 79 Mo. 113 (1883).

15. *KCT*, July 31, 1880, 1:4.

16. *History of Howard and Chariton Counties, Missouri*, 620–25.

17. *History of Randolph and Macon Counties, Missouri*, 266. See also *Kansas City Daily Journal*, April 22, 1880, 4:6; *KCT*, April 22, 1880, 1:3; and *NYT*, April 22, 1880, 8:3.

18. *Howard County Advertiser* (Fayette), Aug. 7, 1884, 3:4.

19. *Callaway Gazette* (Fulton), May 9, 1884, 3:3.

20. *Linn County News* (Linneus), May 8, 1884, 1:4.

21. *Ibid.*, May 15, 1884, 1:4.

22. *Bowling Green Times*, July 5, 1883, 2:1. See also news stories in this same paper on June 28, 3:1 and 3:5 and July 5, 1883, 2:5.

23. *Ibid.*, July 12, 1883, 1:7.

24. *Hartford* (Connecticut) *Daily Courant*, July 3, 1883, MCL.

25. See my *Slavery and Crime in Missouri, 1773–1865*, 219–21.

26. *KCS*, Oct. 14, 1884, 1:5.

27. *Macon Times*, Aug. 9, 1889, 2:3. See also *Macon Republican*, Aug. 8, 1889, 4:4 and *KCT*, Aug. 5, 1889, 1:3.

28. *Missouri Herald* (Columbia), Sept. 12, 1889, 1:1.

29. *Iron County Register* (Ironton), Aug. 3, 1882, 5:3.

30. *CT*, Jan. 1, 1886, 14:3.

31. *Marion County Herald* (Palmyra) Oct. 8, 1885, 1:2.

32. *Missouri Herald* (Columbia). Aug. 29, 1889, 3:4.

Chapter 7

1. *Historical Statistics of the United States*, 1:1–110–24.

2. *History of Hickory, Polk, Cedar, Dade and Barton Counties, Missouri*, 455–56.

3. *CT*, Dec. 30, 1883, 3:2 and Dec. 31, 1884, 1:6.

4. *Negro Population*, 840.

5. *Encyclopedia of the History of Missouri*, 5:277.

6. The 1900 U.S. Census contains these earlier numbers of railroad mileage for each state and territory by decade between 1860 and 1880 and in five shorter intervals between 1887 and 1891. See 364, 374–75, and 382 of this document.

7. *Osceola Sun*, May 13, 1880, 1:3. See also *NYT*, May 14, 1880, 5:4. The *Osage Chigger* (Lowry City), Feb. 1992, 8:1, ran a retrospective on this triple lynching, largely taken from the *Osceola Sun's* contemporary coverage.

8. *Osceola Sun*, June 17, 1880, 4:1.

9. *Ex Parte Slater, alias Lane*, 72 Mo. 102, 107 (1880).

10. *History of Henry and St. Clair Counties, Missouri*, 937–38.

11. *Ibid.*, 992.

12. Mark Twain, *The Adventures of Huckleberry Finn*, 72 and 161–62, italics in the original.

13. Mary Hartman and Elmo Igenthron, *Bald Knobbers* is a detailed study of this group. I have relied heavily on it for my discussion of this vigilante group's illegal activities.

14. *Ibid.*, 56.

15. Blunt, *Historical Listing of the Missouri Legislature*, 98. To date, no killers who committed their murder(s) in Taney County have been legally executed in the history of Missouri. Darrell Mease was convicted and sentenced to death in Greene County on a change of venue from Taney for the May 15, 1988, triple murder of his former drug partner, Lloyd Lawrence, his wife, Frankie Lawrence, and their 19-year-old paraplegic grandson, Willie. Mease had exhausted every appeal, and he was to be executed on January 27, 1991. Suddenly, he was rescheduled for lethal injection on February 10. This change in dates came about because the first visit of a pope in the history of Missouri was scheduled. John Paul II, a vigorous opponent of capital punishment, arrived in St. Louis on January 27. At his personal request, on January 28, 1999, Governor Mel Carnahan commuted Mease's death sentence to life without possibility of parole. See Michael W. Cuneo, *Almost Midnight*, a book-length study of Mease's case and *DSM*, 172–73.

16. *NYT*, Dec. 11, 1886, MCL.

17. 12 Stat. 392–93.

18. 16 Stat 141.

19. *Biographical Directory of the United States Congress, 1774–2005*, S.W. Maecenas Eason Benton.

20. *Springfield Herald*, Sept. 16, 1887, 8:1.

21. 23 Stat. 321–22.

22. Criminal Record, No 1, U.S. District Court, Western District of Missouri, South Division, Springfield, National Archives and Records Administration–Central Plains Region, 87–90. See also Hartman and Igenthron, *Bald Knobbers*, 189–94.

23. 28 Stat. 957.

24. *DSM*, 123.

25. Dolph Shaner, *The Story of Joplin*, 67.

26. *Joplin Daily Herald*, July 19, 1:1 and 4:3 and July 21, 1885, 2:2.

27. *Encyclopedia of the History of Missouri*, 1: 575.

28. *State v. Mann*, 83 Mo. 589 (1884).

29. *History of Newton, Lawrence, Barry and McDonald Counties, Missouri*, 747–48.

30. Richard Maxwell Brown, *Strain of Violence,* 117.

31. *History of Newton, Lawrence, Barry and McDonald Counties, Missouri,* 748.

32. *Springfield Leader,* April 27, 1886, 1:3. See also *NYT,* April 3, 1887, 8:1, MCL nearly a year later, in its coverage of the continuing evangelical work of Mrs. Emma Molloy in Washington Territory and her earlier alleged complicity in the murder of Sarah Graham, near Springfield, Missouri, in September 1885.

33. *Atchison County Journal* (Rock Port), June 25, 1881, 1:4.

34. *DSM,* 166–67.

35. *Nodaway Democrat* (Maryville) Dec. 11, 1884, 1: 4 See also this same paper, Dec. 18, 1884, 1:3 about Crittenden's pardon of Stevens and the *NYT,* Dec. 10, 1884, 1:2. The New York paper also discusses the governor's pardon, but it incorrectly states that Stevens shot and killed Hubert Kremer.

36. See *Kansas City Daily Journal,* Jan. 19, 1889, 1:3; *LT,* Jan 25, 1889, 1:7; *Los Angeles Times,* Jan. 21, 1889, 1: MCL; and *Milwaukee Sentinel,* Jan. 22, 1889, 3:2, MCL. In *The Lynching of Cleo Wright,* 194, Capeci confuses the date of the lynching of Henry Thomas (Jan. 18, 1899) with its out-of-state news coverage (Jan. 21, 1889), mistakenly identifies Thomas as black, and misplaces his mob murder in Mercer County.

37. *KCT,* July 30, 1880, 1:1.

38. *Moberly Headlight,* July 29, 1880, quoted in *History of Randolph and Macon Counties, Missouri,* 247. See also *NYT,* July 30, 1880, 5:6.

39. *Kansas City Daily Journal,* July 30, 1880, 1:5.

40. *NYT,* April 9, 1883, 1:5.

41. *Advertiser Courier* (Hermann), June 6, 1883, 2:1.

42. *CT,* June 9, 1883, 3:1, MCL.

43. *History of Franklin, Jefferson, Washington, Crawford and Gasconade Counties, Missouri,* 651. See also *NYT,* June 6, 1883, 2:1 and *Galveston Daily News* (Houston, Tex.), June 6, 1883, MCL.

44. *NYT,* Sept. 22, 1886, 2:3.

45. Slave Mary was either 13 or 14 years old when she drowned two-year-old Vienna Jane Brinker on May 14, 1837. The sheriff of Crawford County hanged her on August 11, 1838. See my *Slavery and Crime in Missouri,* 170–74.

46. *NYT,* Oct. 6, 1886, 5:3. I have also relied on an article, which Lorene Davis wrote and sent me a typed copy of, about Wallace's lynching. She condensed her piece from the September and October 1886 *Crawford Mirror* (Steelville), and the *Star Crawford Mirror* published it on Dec. 2, 1987.

47. *Atchison Daily Globe,* Sept. 25, 1888, 3:1, MCL.

48. *Rolla Weekly Herald,* Sept. 27, 188. 3:4.

49. See also coverage of these separate Crawford County lynchings in James Ira Breuer, *Crawford County and Cuba, Missouri:* 22–23 for Wallace and 249–55 for Lewis. *History of Franklin, Jefferson, Washington, Crawford & Gasconade Counties, Missouri* covers only Wallace's death, 565–66; it mentions Lewis Davis's crime, but this history went to press before Davis was lynched.

50. *KCS,* May 21, 1887, 1:5. See also *Weekly Times* (Butler), May 25, 1887, 5:4.

51. *Weekly Times* (Butler), June 1, 1887, 2:1.

52. *KCT,* Sept. 13, 1889, 2:4 and *Joplin Daily Standard,* Sept. 14, 1889, 2:4 ran identical stories about this incident.

53. One of Capeci's 85 entries in his table in *The Lynching of Cleo Wright,* "Lynching Victims in Missouri, 1889–1942," 194–196, is mentioned in note 36, this chapter. The great majority of his entries contain the date, race, name, county, and crime of the mob-murdered person(s). He and I agree in every particular on 15 of his entries, or 18 percent of the time. We disagree on 70 entries, or 82 percent, often on the exact date, at times on the race, the name, the county, the crime, whether the person survived and occasionally in which state the event took place — Missouri, Kentucky, or Tennessee. For example, he places the July 17, 1902, lynching of Joshua Anderson in Lafayette County, MO. It occurred on July 17, 1902, but it took place in Owensboro, KY. See *Hartford Courant,* July 18, 1902, 8:1, MCL. His book also has a map of Missouri's counties showing lynchings between 1889 and 1942, 176. He and I disagree about some aspect or another of these events in 20 of the counties.

54. *NYT,* Jan. 21, 1882, 2, MCL.

55. *CT,* Jan. 1, 1890, 14:6.

56. *Kennett Clipper,* Nov. 2, 1889, 6:2.

Chapter 8

1. *Negro Population,* 51.

2. *Ibid.,* 52.

3. *Ibid.*

4. Lorenzo J. Greene, Gary R. Kremer, Anthony F. Holland, *Missouri's Black Heritage,* 95.

5. Charles Coulter, *Take Up the Black Man's Burden,* 26.

6. John Wright, *African-Americans in Downtown St. Louis,* 39.

7. *Kingston Times,* Sept. 22, 1893, 2:2.

8. *Cassville Republican,* July 5, 1894. 3:4. See also *KCT,* June 30, 1894, 3:4.

9. *DSM,* 135–36.

10. *Ibid.,* 76.

11. *Ibid.,* 72.

12. *KNG,* Sept. 5, 1890, 7:2 and *Washington Post,* Aug. 30, 1890, MCL. The lynching of Waters on Aug. 29, 1890, in Lafayette County, is the earliest, chronologically, of nine mob murders in Missouri between 1891 and 1920 that Capeci omits from his table, "Lynching Victims in Missouri,1889–1942."

13. *Kingston Times,* Feb. 22, 1895, 1:1. See also this same newspaper Feb. 8, 1895, 1:3 and 2:3.

14. *Howard County Advertiser* (Fayette), Jan. 22, 1891, 1:1.

15. *KNG,* Jan. 30, 1891, 7:1.

16. In his *100 Years of Lynchings,* Ralph Ginzburg organizes his "State by State Partial List of 5,000 Negroes Lynched in the United States Since 1859" by imperfect alphabetical order of the last name of

the victim. His 55 Missouri entries include no lynched persons earlier than 1889. His dates are usually those of the newspaper account relating the matter, not the date of the event. At times his names are misspelled; at others, completely wrong. A number of his "lynched" persons lived through their ordeals. Some of the Missouri lynching victims alleged to be Negroes were white.

17. *Without Sanctuary: Lynching Photography in America.* Santa Fe, N.M: Twin Palms Publishers, 2000, contains almost 100 photographs and related matter of mob victims put to death nationwide between 1883 and 1960. Most are pictures of lynched black males taken during the first 20 years of the twentieth century.

18. *KCS*, Feb. 27, 2000, 1:5.

19. *Armstrong Herald*, July 27, 1899, 1:1.

20. *Democrat-Leader* (Fayette), July 27, 1899, 1:1 contains the most detailed coverage of Embree's lynching. See also *KCT*, July 23, 1899, 1:5 and *Kansas City Daily Journal*, July 23, 1899, 1:7.

21. *Democrat-Leader* (Fayette), Nov. 2, 1899, 1:1. See also *KNG*, Nov. 3, 1899, 6:3 and *LT*, Nov. 3, 1899, 2:7.

22. *State Republican* (Jefferson City), July 5, 1894. 3:4. See also *Fulton Sun*, July 2, 1894, 1:1.

23. *Republican* (Cassville), July 12, 1894, 2:6.

24. *KNG*, July 31, 1894, 2:4.

25. *Morning Oregonian* (Portland), July 17, 1894. 4:6, MCL.

26. *Gazette* (Fulton), Aug. 6, 1895, 1:3.

27. *KNG*, Aug. 2, 1895, 6:4.

28. *Ibid.*, Aug. 17, 1895, 1:2.

29. *Fulton Sun*, Aug. 20, 1895. 2:2.

30. *KCT*, Aug. 16, 1895, 1:4. See also *Gazette* (Fulton), Aug. 2, 6:4; Aug. 13, 1:5 and Aug. 15, 1:5, 1895; *Kansas City Daily Journal*, Aug. 16, 1895, 1:5; *KNG*, Aug. 9, 6:4 and Aug. 23, 1895, 2:4; and *Fulton Sun*, Aug. 20, 2:2, Aug. 23, 1:2, and Aug. 27, 1895, 1:3.

31. *Sentinel* (Clarksville), June 10, 1898, 2:2. See also *Atchison Daily Globe* (Atchison, KS), June 6, 1898, MCL.

32. *General History of Macon County, Missouri*, 217–20. See also *KNG*, July 8, 1898, 3:5.

33. *Poplar Bluff Citizen*, Sept. 4, 1890, 1:1.

34. *Kennett Clipper*, April 28, 1892. 4:2.

35. *NYT*, Jan. 18, 1894, 9:6.

36. *Appleton City Journal*, Jan. 25, 1894, 2:4. See also *KNG*, Jan. 26, 1894, 3:1. John Buckner's mob murder is the earliest chronologically of the 14 Missouri lynchings discussed by Michael J. Pfeifer's "The Ritual of Lynching: Extralegal Justice in Missouri, 1890–1942." All 14 mob murders he covers in his article took place in this state between 1890 and 1942. However, Pfeifer states that, "Between 1882 and 1968, 122 people were reported lynched in Missouri," 23. This statement has no documentation, and my numbers for these years total 93, or 29 fewer. My chief objection to his article is a map of Missouri's 114 counties. His map is entitled, "Deaths by Lynching, Missouri, 1890–1942." Pfeifer writes of it, "Eighty-two confirmed lynchings occurred in Missouri during those years," 24. I count 71, and there

is no way to ascertain if he counts all 71 that I can confirm. He and I agree that between 1890 and 1942 there were neither attempted nor completed lynchings in 68 Missouri counties. We also agree on both the race of victims and number that took place in 20 counties, but between 1890 and 1942, there are discrepancies between his research and mine in 26 counties. By way of illustration, I can document no lynchings in Howell County in its history; Pfeifer has four. Two appear to be Carter, A. and Montgomery, B. Both were lynched in Arkansas. Their case is discussed in Chapter 9. Two others appear to be Isaac and Paralee Collins. They survived their ordeal; their case is discussed in Chapter 11.

37. *Cash Book* (Jackson), Oct. 17, 1895. 3:2. See also 2:1, same paper and date; *KNG*, Oct. 18, 1895. 2:4; and *Commercial Appeal* (Memphis, Tenn.), Oct. 13, 1895, 3:4, MCL.

38. *KNG*, Feb. 2, 1894, 2:4 and *Palmyra Spectator*, Jan. 25, 1894. 2:4.

39. *Fountain and Journal* (Mt. Vernon), Jan. 25, 1894, 3:2 and *Lawrence Chieftain* (Mt.Vernon), Jan. 25, 1894, 3:3.

40. *KNG* , March 23, 1894. 7.1.

41. *Lawrence Chieftain*, Feb. 1, 1894, 3:3.

42. *Ibid.*, March 15, 1894, 3:5.

43. *KCS*, Feb. 18, 1893, 2:3; *Kansas City Daily Journal*, Feb. 19, 1893, 5:3; and *Bosworth Sentinel* (Bosworth, Carroll County, Mo.), Feb. 24, 1893, 3:3.

44. *Moberly Monitor*, Feb. 18, 1893, 2:3.

45. Missouri Revised Statutes, art. 8, chap. 24, sec. 1540 (1879).

46. *St. Louis Post-Dispatch*, Aug. 14, 1893, 1:6.

47. Twain, *Huckleberry Finn*, 161–62, italics in the original.

48 *CT*, Dec. 31, 1898, 20:2; NAACP, *Thirty Years of Lynching in the United States*, 81. Ginzburg, *100 Years of Lynching*, 266; Capeci, *The Lynching of Cleo Wright*, 195, and Michael J. Pfeifer's "Partial List of Lynchings in Missouri, 1836–1981, obtained on my computer by Googling, "Lynchings in Missouri." After the *Chicago Tribune* listed among its lynchings for 1898, "Nov. 29, Negro, near New Madrid, Mo.," each subsequent compiler appears to have followed the leader.

49. *Southeast Missourian* (New Madrid) Dec. 1, 1898, 1:1 and 6:3.

50. *Moberly Daily Monitor*, Nov. 30, 1898, 1:3.

51. Personal correspondence, H. Riley Bock, then prosecuting attorney, New Madrid Co., MO.

Chapter 9

1. *Daily Mail* (Nevada), Jan. 18, 2:8; Jan. 19, 2:6; Jan. 20, 2:7; and Jan. 21, 2:2, 1892. See also *NYT*, Jan. 24, 1892, 2, MCL.

2. *DSM*, 73.

3. Floy Watters George, *History of Webster County, Missouri, 1855 to 1955*, 38–39. *Springfield Leader*, Feb. 27, 1892, 1:3; and *KNG*, March 4, 4:4 and 7:1 and March 11, 1892, 7:1.

4. Hartman and Ingenthron, *Bald Knobbers,* 274.

5. *Ibid.,* 285. I have relied heavily on Hartman and Ingenthron, *Bald Knobbers,* 271–85, for my discussion of the shooting death of Deputy George Williams, the lynching of Bright, and the unsuccessful efforts to convict anyone of these murders. The *NYT* carries the story, but it incorrectly places the murder of Williams in the Taney County courtroom, March 15, 1892, 3:3.

6. Missouri Constitution, art. 2, sec. 22 (1875), in Francis N. Thorpe, ed., *Federal and State Constitutions,* 4: 2232, and Missouri Constitution, art. 1, sec. 18a (1945), in Missouri Revised Statutes, vol. 20, Constitution of Missouri (2000).

7. *KNG,* March 18, 4:4; April 8, 4:5; April 29, 4:4, and May 13, 1892, 7:1.

8. *Ibid.,* Oct. 7, 1892, 6:4.

9. *Daily Inter Ocean* (Chicago) March 28, 1892, 4:5, MCL.

10. *CT,* Jan. 1, 1893, 30:3.

11. *Rocky Mountain News* (Denver), June 1, 1892, 2:3, MCL.

12. *Globe-Democrat* (St. Louis), May 22, 1897, 1:6. See also this same paper, May 20, 1897, 3:3.

13. *KNG,* Sept. 1, 1891, 2:4 and July 8, 1892, 6:4.

14. *KCT,* Sept. 2, 1891, 1:6.

15. *KCS,* Aug. 25, 1957, 4D:1.

16. *Kansas City Daily Journal,* Dec. 7, 1896, 1:7. See also *Hartford Courant,* Dec. 8, 1896, 2, MCL.

17. *KNG,* Nov. 20, 1896. 3:1.

18. *KCT,* March 12, 1892, 8:3.

19. *KNG,* Dec. 18, 1896. 6:4.

20. *Franklin County Tribune* (Union), July 9, 1897, 2:4.

21. *KCT,* March 13, 1892, 1:6; see also *Los Angeles Times,* March 13, 1892, 1 MCL.

22. *DMS,* 241, n. 23 and 27 and 244, n. 60.

23. *Kingston Times,* Sept. 22, 1893, 2:2.

24. *Ibid.,* Sept. 22, 1893, 1:5.

25. *LT,* Sept. 12, 1898, 1:1; *Butte Weekly Miner* (Butte, Mont.), Sept. 15, 1898, 15, MCL; *State v. Foley,* 46 SW 733 (1898); and *LT,* Sept. 19, 1974, 1B:1.

26. *Kansas City Daily Journal,* Sept. 4, 1896, 2:3 and *St. Joseph Weekly Gazette,* Sept. 8, 1896, 3:4.

27. *KCT,* March 2, 1:5 and March 4, 1892, 2:5; *KNG,* March 22, 1892, 7:2; and Cletis R. Ellinghouse, *Old Bollinger,* 28.

28. *KNG,* Dec. 1, 6:3 and Dec. 8, 1899, 7:1.

29. *State v. Moore,* 61 SW 199, 203 and 205 (1901).

30. *Daily Democrat* (Clinton), Nov. 6, 1894, 2:4.

31. *Tipton Times,* July 30, 1896, 1:5.

32. *KCS,* July 28, 1896, 1:7.

33. *Salt Lake Semi-Weekly Tribune,* July 31, 1896, 6:3, MCL.

34. *CT,* Jan. 1, 1897, 20:6; NAACP, *Thirty Years of Lynching in the United States, 1889–1918,* 81; and Capeci, *The Lynching of Cleo Wright,* 195.

35. *KNG,* April 1, 1892, 1:1.

36. *Kansas City Daily Journal,* Nov. 19, 1897, 2:3 and *KCT,* Nov. 19, 1897, 1:7.

37. *KCT,* Nov. 20, 1897, 8:3.

38. *CT,* Jan. 1, 1898, 20:7; NAACP, 81, and Capeci, 195.

39. *Palmyra Spectator,* July 2, 1896, 1:2.

40. *CT,* Jan. 1, 1897, 20:6; NAACP, 81, and Capeci, 195.

41. *CT,* Jan. 1, 1895, 10:1 and NAACP, 80.

42. *St. Louis Post-Dispatch,* Feb. 28, 1894, 9:1.

43. Nellie Meeks married Albert Spray, a collateral ancestor of my friend Brenda Toothman. From Brenda I learned that Hattie Spray, daughter of Nellie and Albert and named for the murdered four-year-old, had a daughter who attended dancing school with the actress, singer, and dancer, Mitzi Gaynor.

44. *DMS,* 78–79.

45. Blunt, *Historical Listing of the Legislature,* 90.

46. *Washington Post,* April 16, 1899. 13:1, MCL.

47. *NYT,* March 10, 1899, 6, MCL. See also *Milwaukee Sentinel,* March 19, 1899, 5:4, MCL.

Chapter 10

1. Susan B. Carter et al., *Historical Statistics of the United States,* 1–281.

2. Lorenzo J. Greene, Gary R. Kremer, and Anthony F. Holland, *Missouri's Black Heritage,* 100.

3. Thompson, *Lynchings in Mississippi,* 49 and U.S. Department of Commerce, *Negro Population,* 817–18.

4. Cited in John S. Haller, *Outcasts from Evolution,* 203.

5. Cited in I.A. Newby, *Jim Crow's Defense,* 123.

6. *Ibid.,* 20.

7. Unsigned editorial, *Atlanta Journal-Record of Medicine,* 842–44.

8. William Lee Howard, M.D., "The Negro as a Distinct Ethnic Factor in Civilization," 424.

9. *Ibid.,* 39.

10. *Ibid.,* 67.

11. Robert W. Shufeldt, M.D., *The Negro: A Menace to American Civilization,* 91. In her *Hitler's Vienna: A Dictator's Apprenticeship,* Brigitte Hamann discusses the nutty racial theories that were current in early twentieth century Vienna, the heart of the Austro-Hungarian Empire. Among other groups, Serbs and Jews were found deficient. See especially her Chapter 7, "Theoreticians of Race and Explainers of the World." In it she writes, "Around 1900 the new race theories were ubiquitous. Writers and philosophers dealt with the subject ... and assigned to the 'white race' superiority in beauty, intelligence, and strength, proclaimed it was destined to bring order into the world," 203.

12. Charles Carroll, *The Negro a Beast.* This chart appears twice, 48 and 102.

13. *Ibid.,* 221.

14. David M. Friedman, *A Mind of Its Own,* 113.

15. *LT,* May 9, 1856, 2:1.

16. *Ibid.,* Dec. 2, 1859, 2:2.

17. Cited in Newby, *Jim Crow's Defense,* 104.

18. Cited in Edmund Morris, *Theodore Rex,* 54.

19. Doris Kearns Goodwin, *Team of Rivals,* 551–53, 649–51.

20. Cited in Morris, *Theodore Rex*, 55.

21. *Pierce City Enterprise*, Aug. 22, 1901, 3:6.

22. *Springfield Leader*, April 30, 1906, 1:7.

23. *Lawrence Chieftain* (Mt. Vernon), Aug. 22, 1901, 1:1.

24. *KNG*, Aug. 30, 1901, 6:2.

25. *Pierce City Enterprise*, Sept. 5, 1901, 3:2.

26. *Negro Population*, 818.

27. *NYT*, Aug. 21, 1901, 1:4 and *Hartford Courant*, Aug. 20, 1901, 1, MCL.

28. Mark Twain, *Complete Essays of Mark Twain*, edited by Charles Neider, 673–75.

29. Fred Kaplan, *The Singular Mark Twain*, 34.

30. *Ibid.*, 591.

31. *NYT*, April 16, 1903, 2:3.

32. *KCS*, April 16, 1903, 1:6.

33. *Ibid.*

34. *Negro Population*, 818.

35. *KNG*, April 24, 1903, 3:1.

36. Cutler, *Lynch-Law*, 255.

37. *Springfield Leader*, April 15, 1906. 1:1.

38. *Ibid.*

39. *KNG*, April 20, 1906. 6:2.

40. *NYT*, April 16, 1903, 1:3.

41. *Springfield Leader*, April 22, 1906, 1:7.

42. Clate Baker, "The Exodus from Springfield."

43. *NYT*, April 16, 1906, 1:3.

44. *Springfield Leader*, April 16, 1906, 1:1.

45. *KNG*, Aug. 10, 1906, 2:4.

46. *Ibid.*, Aug. 30, 1907, 2:3.

47. *Springfield Leader*, April 17, 1906, 1:6.

48. Morris, *Theodore Rex*, 455 and 472.

49. *Springfield Leader*, April 20, 1906, 5:3.

50. *In Re Kemmler*, 136 U.S. 436, 446 (1890).

51. *Maryville Republican*, April 19, 1906.

52. *Springfield Leader*, April 15, 1906, 1:2.

53. A news story in an out of-state-paper is headlined "Drama Inspires Negro Lynching/ Bainbridge, Ga., Mob, fired by *The Clansman*, avenges shooting of sheriff," *CT*, Oct. 30, 1905, 4, MCL.

54. Michele K. Gillespie and Randal L. Hall, eds., "Introduction," *Thomas Dixon Jr. and the Birth of Modern America*, 1.

55. Anthony Slide, *American Racist*, 59.

56. *Ibid.*, 57.

57. *Negro Population*, 817–819.

58. James Loewen, *Sundown Towns*, 344.

59. *Weekly Democrat-News* (Marshall), May 1, 1900, 1:1–6. See also *KNG*, May 4, 1900, 3:2.

60. *Kansas City Daily Journal*, May 3, 1900, 2:1.

61. Ed Cave arrived on the scene immediately after several lynchings. He was the law enforcement officer that the nearly lynched victim told he did not wish to press charges, and was also the person to whom General Armstrong allegedly confessed that he had raped Ivy Turney. The sheriff of Clinton County, who guarded Armstrong for 48 hours, never secured a confession from Armstrong. Cave was clearly cozy with the mob.

62. *KCT*, May 3, 1900, 1:5; see also *KNG*, May 11, 1900, 6:3.

63. *Democrat* (Pineville), March 8, 1901, 2:2.

64. *Richmond Conservator*, March 7, 1901, 2:1.

65. Al McKemy, "Negro Murderer Lynched," 168–170.

66. *Washington Post*, Aug. 13, 1902, 2, MCL.

67. *KNG*, Aug. 22, 1902, 7:2.

68. *KCS*, Aug. 13, 1902, 1:5. See also *Kansas City Daily Journal*, Aug. 12, 1902, 1:7.

69. *DSM*, 127–28.

70. *KCS*, Aug. 2, 1909, 1:7; *Post* (Kansas City), Aug. 2, 1909, 1:1; and *KCT*, Aug. 2, 1909, 4:2.

71. *KNG*, Aug. 20, 1909, 3:1.

72. *Higbee Weekly News*, March 28, 1902, 3:3. See also *KNG*, March 28, 1902, 6:1.

73. *NYT*, May 26, 1902, 2:4; *KNG*, May 30, 1902, 3:4; and *Los Angeles Times*, May 25, 1902, 2, MCL.

74. Blunt, *Historical Listing of the Missouri Legislature*, 129.

75. *KNG*, June 13, 1902, 2:4. and *Twice-A Week Democrat* (Caruthersville), May 5, 1903, 1:3.

76. *KNG*, May 8, 1903, 2:2 and *Twice-A-Week Democrat*, May 5, 1903, 1:3.

77. *Weekly Record* (New Madrid), Feb. 22, 1902, 4:2.

78. *KCS*, May 23, 1902, 1:6.

79. *St. Louis Globe-Democrat*, Jan. 23, 1903, 7:4.

80. Blunt, *Historical Listing of the Missouri Legislature*, 55.

81. *Charleston Courier*, May 19, 1905, 1:4.

82. *St. Louis Post-Dispatch*, May 15, 1905, 6:1.

83. *Ibid.*, May 14, 1905, 1:2. See also the *Post-Dispatch*, May 15, 1:4 and May 18, 1905, 10:4 and *St. Louis Globe-Democrat*, May 13, 1905, 1:4 and 1:6.

84. *Hartford Courant*, March 27, 1900, 1:1, MCL.

85. My thanks to Kimberly Harper, reference librarian, Missouri State Historical Society, Columbia, Mo., for checking at my request the *Missouri Democrat* (Boonville), and for her initiative in also checking the official manual for 1900 for any sheriff named Kinart in any of this state's 114 counties.

86. *KCT*, July 12, 1901, 1:1

87. *Ibid.*, July 18, 1901, 3:1.

88. *Ibid.*, July 14, 1901, 3:3.

89. *Ibid.*, July 16, 1901, 10:2.

90. *NYT*, July 19, 1901, 2:4.

91. Material which Ray Elder, historian for the Kansas City (Missouri) Fire Department, sent me and my conversation with him as well as correspondence with Kevin Boehm of the Kansas City Police Department's Chief's Office were invaluable aids in research about this foiled lynching.

92. *Chillicothe Constitution*, March 29, 1909, 1:1.

93. *NYT*, March 31, 1909, 1:5.

94. *Gallatin North Missourian*, April 9, 1909, 4:3. See also this same paper April 2, 1909, 1:1 and *Chillicothe Constitution*, March 30, 1:6 and April 2, 1909, 1:1.

95. *CT*, Jan. 1, 1902, 21:4; *NAACP*, 81; Ralph Ginzburg, *100 Years of Lynchings*, 266; and Capeci, 195.

96. *Poplar Bluff Citizen*, Jan. 3, 1901, 5:1.

Chapter 11

1. *Kansas City Post,* Feb. 23, 1915, 1:6.
2. *KCT,* Feb. 22, 1915, 1:3. See also *KCS,* Feb. 21, 1915, 1:1.
3. *NYT,* Feb. 22, 1915, 4:6.
4. *Kansas City Post,* Feb. 23, 1915, 1:6.
5. *Lamar Democrat,* June 5, 1919, 2:3. See also this issue's front page and June 5, 1919, front page.
6. *NYT,* May 29, 1919, 1:3.
7. Susan B. Carter, et al., *Historical Statistics of the United States,* 1–281.
8. *Democrat-Leader* (Fayette) March 19, 1914, 1:1.
9. *Pike County News* (Louisiana), Sept. 16, 1915, 1:1.
10. *St. Charles Banner,* April 6, 1916, 1:1.
11. *Ibid.,* April 13, 1916, 1:1.
12. *Moberly Monitor-Index,* Nov. 18, 1:6. See also this paper's coverage on Nov. 14, 1:5 and Nov. 17, 1:1 and *NYT,* Nov. 17, 1919, 3:4.
13. *Southeast Missourian* (New Madrid), June 2, 1910, 4:2.
14. *Weekly Enterprise* (Charleston), July 8, 1910, 1:1. See also *KNG,* July 8, 1910, 2:2 and *NYT,* July 4, 1910, 14:6.
15. *St. Louis Post-Dispatch,* Oct. 11, 1911, 1:6.
16. *KNG,* Oct. 20, 1911, 6:1 and *NYT,* Oct. 12, 1911, 1:3.
17. *Twice-A-Week Democrat* (Caruthersville), Oct. 13, 1911, 1:1.
18. *St. Louis Post-Dispatch,* Oct. 13, 1911, 1:1.
19. *Twice-A Week-Democrat* (Caruthersville) Oct. 13, 1911, 1:1.
20. CT, Dec. 31, 1911, sec. x, 6:2; NAACP, 82; Ralph Ginzburg, *100 Years of Lynchings,* 266, and Capeci, 196.
21. *Howell County Gazette* (West Plains), June 18, 1914, 1:1.
22. *Pike County Post* (Bowling Green), April 21, 1915, 1:4 and *NYT,* April 21, 1915, 13:6.
23. *Pike County Post* (Bowling Green), Sept. 8, 1915, 1:6.
24. *NYT,* Sept. 3, 1915, 4:7 and Oct. 6, 1915, 7:4.
25. *Bowling Green Times,* Oct. 7, 1915, 8:2.
26. *Pike County Post* (Bowling Green), Oct. 6, 1915, 1:1 and 1:5. See also this same paper, Sept. 8, 1915, 1:6 and *Bowling Green Times,* Sept. 2, 1915, 1:3.
27. *Weekly Enterprise* (Charleston), July 8, 1910, 1:4.
28. *Rising Sun* (Kansas City), July 10, 1905, 7:1.

Chapter 12

1. Steven D. Levitt and Stephen J. Dubner, *Freakonomics,* 65.
2. I attended a Ku Klux Klan meeting in Lawrenceville, Ga., in the early 1960s. The assembled told me that they were fighting for their rights just as the "niggers" were. When asked if I'd mind living next door to a nigger, I did not give the correct response. My friends and I were isolated and driven out of town by honking horns and blinking lights. It was a frightening and dangerous experience; none of the Klanspersons — men, women, and children — seemed the least embarrassed. More recently, on March 21, 1981, in Mobile, AL, a 19-year-old African American, Michael Donald, was the victim of a Klan-inspired lynching. In 1987, Morris Dees, of the Southern Poverty Law Center (SPLC) successfully sued the United Klans of America in federal court on behalf of Beulah May Donald for the wrongful death of her son. Among other stories, the *New York Times* ran the following headlines about this case: "U.S. Jurors Award $7 Million Damages in Slaying by Klan" and "Black Is Handed Deed to Offices of Klan Group/Jury Had Awarded Her Site Over Son's Death." Feb. 13, 1:6 and May 20, 1987, 18:6. A trial was set to begin on Nov. 12, 2008, in Brandenburg, KY, against the Imperial Klans of America. The SPLC is bringing it on behalf of Jordan Gruver, a teenager and U.S. citizen of Panamanian Indian descent. Gruver was savagely beaten by Klansmen who thought him an illegal Hispanic immigrant at a county fair in July 2006 (*SPLC Report,* Fall, 2008, 1:2). The Klan may be suffering financially from court decisions, but contrary to the authors of *Freakonomics,* it has not been laughed out of existence.
3. *NYT,* Dec. 4, 1911, 5 and July 27, 1912, 1, MCL.
4. *Boston Globe,* July 27, 1918, 6, MCL.
5. *NYT,* Dec. 2, 1922, 2, MCL.
6. *Chicago Defender,* Dec. 15, 1923, 11, MCL.
7. *Ibid.,* Aug. 30, 1930, 13, 1 and *Pittsburgh Courier,* Aug. 30, 1930, 3, MCL.
8. *Pittsburgh Courier,* Jan. 1, 1931, A6, MCL.
9. *Chicago Defender,* Jan. 21, 1939, 2, MCL.
10. Slide, *American Racist,* 3.
11. *KCT,* Oct. 25, 1915, 12:1.
12. *CT,* March 27, 1915, 3, MCL.
13. *Chicago Defender,* March 20, 1915, 1, MCL.
14. Charlene Regester, "The Cinematic Representation of Race in *The Birth of a Nation,*" 164–182, 180, in Gillespie and Hall, eds., *Thomas Dixon Jr. and the Birth of Modern America.*
15. R.W. Shufeldt, *America's Greatest Problem, the Negro,* 131.
16. *Ibid.,* 145.
17. *Ibid.,* 224–225.
18. *DSM,* 137.
19. *Biographical Directory of the United States Congress, 1774–Present, s.v.* Dyer, L.C.
20. *St. Louis Globe-Democrat,* June 20, 1876, 1:3.
21. 66th Congress, 2nd Session, House Report, Pts. 1 & 2, Anti-Lynching Bill, May 22, 1920. See also *Chicago Defender,* May 29, 1920, 1:1, MCL.
22. *Chicago Defender,* May 29 and June 18, 1921, 3:1, MCL.
23. *St. Louis Argus,* March 24, 1922, 1:9.
24. Congressional Record, 67th Congress, 2nd Session (Jan. 19, 1922), 1426.
25. *NYT,* June 14, 2005, A 15:1.
26. George C. Rable, "The South and the Politics of Antilynching Legislation, 1920–1940," 201–220.
27. *Montgomery Enterprise* (Montgomery, AL),

Jan. 26, 1900, 2:3. See also Congressional Record, 56th Congress, 1st Session (Jan. 20, 1900), 1017.

28. *Kansas City Post*, Aug. 8, 1935, 5:2–5.

29. *KCT*, Aug. 8, 1925, 1:7. See also *Kansas City Daily Journal*, Aug 8, 1925, 2:1–5; *KCS*, Aug. 8, 1925, 1:7; *Call* (Kansas City), Aug. 14, 1925, 1:1; *Daily Standard* (Excelsior Springs), April 4, 1991, 1:1; *NYT*, Aug. 8, 1925, 3:4; and *Los Angeles Times,* Aug. 9, 1925, MCL.

30. *KCS*, April 30, 1921, 1:1; *Kansas City Daily Journal*, April 30, 1921, 1:7, and *NYT*, April 30, 1921, 1:2.

31. *Kansas City Daily Journal*, April 30, 1923, 1:8.

32. Patrick J. Huber, "The Lynching of James T. Scott," 21 and 34.

33. *KCS*, May 2, 1923, 1:7.

34. *Ibid.*

35. *NYT*, April 30, 1923, 1, MCL.

36. Cited in Huber, "The Lynching of James T. Scott," 28.

37. *Kansas City Daily Journal*, May 4, 1923, 1:8.

38. *Ibid.*, May 5, 1923, 1:3.

39. *NYT*, May 3, 1923, 3, MCL.

40. *Ibid.*, July 14, 1923, 2:5.

41. *Call* (Kansas City), May 4, 1923, 9:1.

42. *Ellington Press* (Ellington, Reynolds County), July 15, 1920, 1:2.

43. *NYT*, July 9, 1920, 11:5.

44. *Kansas City Daily Journal*, Dec. 19, 1924, 1:4; *KCS*, Dec. 19, 1924, 1:3; *NYT*, Dec. 19, 1924, 8:1; and *Los Angles Times,* Dec. 19, 1924, 1, MCL.

45. *Call* (Kansas City), Dec. 26, 1924, 1:1.

46. *Kansas City Daily Journal*, Dec. 24, 1924, 1:3.

47. *Call* (Kansas City), May 27, 1927, 1:5 and *NYT*, May 24, 1927, 27:5.

48. *NYT*, May 31, 1928, 25:5.

49. *Maryville Daily Forum*, Jan. 12, 1931, 1:3.

50. Missouri Revised Statutes, art. 5, sec. 15039 (1929).

51. My in-state coverage of Gunn's lynching is based on the *St. Joseph News-Press*, Jan.12, 1931, front page, "50 Years Later: Memories of Gunn Burning;" *Maryville Daily Forum,* Jan. 10, 1981, 1:1, and an actual copy of the entire front page of the *Maryville Daily Forum*, Jan. 23, 1931.

52. *St. Louis Argus*, Jan. 16, 1931, 8:3.

53. *Washington Post*, Jan. 13, 1931, 1, MCL.

54. *Chicago Defender*, Jan. 17, 1931, 1, MCL.

55. *CT*, Jan. 17, 1931, 1, MCL.

56. *Pittsburgh Courier*, Feb. 17, 1931, 5, MCL and *St. Louis Argus*, Feb. 27, 1931, 1:7.

57. Senate Bill No. 159, Missouri State Archives.

58. *Messages and Proclamations of the Governors of the State of Missouri*, Vol. 13, 132–133.

59. 1931 Missouri Laws, 230–236.

60. *Official Manual, State of Missouri, 2007– 2008,* 586.

61. *Kansas City Journal-Post*, Nov. 29, 1933, 3:3.

62. *St. Joseph Gazette*, November 29, 1933, 1:1–8.

63. *Kansas City Journal-Post*, November 29, 1933, 1:1–8.

64. *Call*, Dec. 1, 1933, 1:1.

65. Out-of-state newspapers followed this story. See *Washington Post*, Nov. 30, 1933, 4, MCL and *Los Angeles Times,* Nov. 30, 1933, 1, MCL.

66. Among other sources, I benefited from a 40-page *St. Joseph News-Press* vertical file, dating from Nov. 28, 1933, through Feb. 5, 1934, obtained by my friend, the late Warren Chelline, from the St. Joseph Public Library. The late Fred Slater sent me his excellent article, "46 Years Later, St. Joseph still wants to forget the Lynching," *St. Joseph News-Press*, Dec. 2, 1979, Sec. C, 1:1. See also *NYT*, Jan. 2, 1934, 8:4.

67. *Ste. Genevieve Herald*, Oct. 18, 1930, 1:6; *Fair Play* (St. Genevieve), Oct. 18, 1:1 and 8:3, Oct. 25, 1930, 1:6; and *Chicago Defender*, Oct. 18, 1930, MCL.

68. *State* v. *Taylor*, 51 SW2d 1003, 1007 (1932).

69. Record Group 5, Series- Commutations of Sentence, Box 338, Folder 1 (January 1956), Missouri State Archives.

70. *Sikeston Standard*, Jan. 27, 1942, 1:3.

71. *NYT*, Jan. 27, 1942, 20:3. See also this paper's Jan. 26, 1942, 17:2 coverage of the lynching itself.

72. *Weekly Citizen Democrat* (Poplar Bluff), March 12, 1942, 4:7.

73. Dominic J. Capeci Jr., "The Lynching of Cleo Wright: Federal Protection of Constitution Rights during World War II," 47–73.

74. Dominic J. Capeci, Jr., *The Lynching of Cleo Wright,* 176 and 194–96.

Conclusion

1. Hartman and Ingenthron, *Bald Knobbers*, 21 and 50.

2. *KCS*, July 10, 2001, Compilation, Kenneth McElroy Murder.

3. Carl Navaree, "High Noon in Skidmore," 111.

4. Missouri Revised Statutes 547.170 (1986).

5. Harry N. MacLean, *In Broad Daylight,* 262. I have relied heavily on this book, the most lengthy of the many writings about McElroy, in describing the circumstances of the last lynching in Missouri.

6. *St. Joseph News-Press,* July 18, 1981, 1:2.

7. MacLean, *In Broad Daylight*, 304.

8. *St. Joseph News-Press,* Sept. 25, 1981, 1:2.

9. *KCS*, July 10, 1984, and Sept. 5, 1985, Compilation, Kenneth McElroy Murder.

10. Election results information obtained by Internet search on "State of Missouri, Election Night, 2008, County Reporting." See also *KCS*, Nov. 19, 2008, B1:1.

Bibliography

Books

Allen, James, et al. *Without Sanctuary: Lynching Photography in America*. Santa Fe, N.M: Twin Palms Publishers, 2000.

Ayers, Edward L. *Vengeance & Justice: Crime and Punishment in the 19th-Century American South*. New York: Oxford University Press, 1984.

Blackstone, William. *Commentaries on the Laws of England: A Facsimile of the First Edition of 1786–1769*. Vol. 4. Chicago: University of Chicago Press, 1979.

Breuer, Ira. *Crawford County and Cuba, Missouri*. Cape Girardeau: Ramfre Press, 1972.

Brown, Richard Maxwell. *Strain of Violence: Historical Studies of American Violence and Vigilantism*. New York: Oxford University Press, 1977.

Capeci, Dominic J., Jr. *The Lynching of Cleo Wright*. Lexington: University Press of Kentucky, 1998.

Carroll, Charles. *The Negro a Beast*. St. Louis: American Book and Bible House, 1900.

_____. *The Tempter of Eve or The Criminality of Man's Social, Political, and Religious Equality with the Negro, and the Amalgamation to which these Crimes Inevitably Lead*. St. Louis: Adamic Publishing Co., 1902.

Carter, Susan B., et al. *Historical Statistics of the United States: Earliest Times to the Present*. Vol. 1. New York: Cambridge University Press, 2006.

Cassidy, Michael. *Defending a Way of Life. An American Community in the Nineteenth Century*. Albany: State University of New York Press, 1989.

Catterall, Helen, ed. *Judicial Cases Concerning Slavery and the Negro*. Vol. 3. New York: Octagon Books, 1968.

Chernow, Ron. *Alexander Hamilton*. New York: Penguin Books, 2004.

Christensen, Lawrence, et al. *Dictionary of Missouri Biography*. Columbia: University of Missouri Press, 1999.

Conard, Howard L., ed. *Encyclopedia of the History of Missouri: a compendium of history and biography for ready reference*. 5 vols. St. Louis: Southern Historical Press, 1901.

Coulter, Charles. *Take Up the Black Man's Burden: Kansas City's African American Communities, 1865–1939*. Columbia: University of Missouri Press, 2006.

Cuneo, Michael. *Almost Midnight: An American Story of Murder and Redemption*. New York: Broadway Books, 2004.

Curtis, Annette W. *Jackson County, Missouri, in Black and White: Census of Slaves, Their Owners and Free Colored, 1850–1860*. Independence, Mo: Annette Curtis, 1995.

Cutler, James Elbert. *Lynch-Law: An Investigation into the History of Lynching in the United States*. 1905. Reprint. New York: Negro Universities Press, 1969.

Demuth, I. McDonald. *History of Pettis County, Missouri*. N.p., 1882.

Dictionary of American Biography. 11 vols. New York: Charles Scribner's Sons, 1964.

Dyer, Frederick H. *A Compendium of the War of the Rebellion*. Broadfoot Publishing Co., 1908. Reprint. N.p., 1994.

Ellinghouse, Cletis R. *Old Bollinger : a collection of historical articles taken from the pages of the Banner-Press, Bollinger County's weekly newspaper, and published in celebration of the bicentennial of the American Revolution*. Marble Hill, Mo.: Banner Press, 1975.

Fellman, Michael. *Inside War: The Guerrilla Conflict in Missouri during the American Civil War*. New York: Oxford University Press, 1990.

Foley, William E. *Genesis of Missouri: From Wilderness Outpost to Statehood*. Columbia: University of Missouri Press, 1989.

Frazier, Harriet C. *Death Sentences in Missouri, 1803–2005*. Jefferson, N.C.: McFarland, 2006.

_____. *Runaway and Freed Missouri Slaves and Those Who Helped Them*. Jefferson, N.C. McFarland, 2004.

_____. *Slavery and Crime in Missouri*. Jefferson, N.C: McFarland, 2001.

Friedman, David M. *A Mind of Its Own: A Cultural History of the Penis*. New York: Free Press, 2001.

Friedman, Lawrence M. *Crime and Punishment in American History*. New York: Basic Books, 1993.

General History of Macon County, Missouri. Chicago: Henry Taylor & Co., 1910.

George, Floy Watters. *History of Webster County, Missouri, 1855 to 1955*. Marshfield, Mo.: Historical Committee of the Webster County Centennial, 1955.

Gillespie, Michele, and Randal L. Hall, eds. *Thomas Dixon Jr. and the Birth of Modern America*. Baton Rouge: Louisiana State University Press, 2006.

Ginzburg, Ralph. *100 Years of Lynchings*. Baltimore: Black Classic Press, 1988.

Glenn, Allen. *History of Cass County, Missouri*. Topeka, Kan.: Historical Publishing Co., 1917.

Goodwin, Doris Kearns. *Team of Rivals: The Political Genius of Abraham Lincoln*. New York: Simon and Schuster, 2005.

Greene, Lorenzo J., Gary R. Kremer, and Anthony F. Holland. *Missouri's Black Heritage*. St. Louis: Forum Press, 1980.

Haller, John S. *Outcasts from Evolution: Scientific Attitudes of Racial Inferiority, 1859–1900*. Urbana: University of Illinois Press, 1971.

Hamann, Brigitte. *Hitler's Vienna: A Dictator's Apprenticeship*. New York: Oxford University Press, 1999.

Hamilton, Alexander, Clinton Rossiter, intro. *The Federalist Papers; Alexander Hamilton, James Madison, John Jay*. New York: New American Library, 1961.

Hartman, Mary and Elmo Ingenthron. *Bald Knobbers: Vigilantes on the Ozarks Frontier*. Gretna, La.: Pelican Publishing Co., 1988.

Hedrick, Joan D. *Harriet Beecher Stowe, a Life*. New York: Oxford University Press, 1994.

History of Boone County, Missouri. St. Louis: Western Historical Co., 1882.

History of Caldwell and Livingston Counties, Missouri. St. Louis: National Historical Society, 1886.

History of Callaway County, Missouri. St. Louis: National Historical Co., 1884.

History of Cass and Bates Counties, Missouri. St. Joseph, Mo.: National Historical Co., 1883.

History of Clay and Platte Counties, Missouri. St. Louis: National Historical Co., 1885.

History of Clinton County, Missouri. St. Joseph, Mo.: National Historical Co., 1881.

History of Franklin, Jefferson, Washington, Crawford & Gasconade Counties, Missouri. 1888. Reprint. Greenville, S.C: Southern Historical Press, 2001.

History of Gentry and Worth Counties, Missouri. St. Joseph, Mo.: National Historical Co., 1882.

History of Greene County, Missouri. St. Louis: Western Historical Co., 1883.

History of Henry and St. Clair Counties, Missouri. 1883. Reprint. Clinton, Mo.: Henry County Historical Society, 1968.

History of Hickory, Polk, Cedar, Dade and Barton Counties, Missouri. Chicago: Goodspeed, 1889.

History of Holt and Atchison Counties, Missouri. St. Joseph, Mo.: National Historical Co., 1882.

History of Howard and Chariton Counties, Missouri. St. Louis: National Historical Co., 1883.

History of Jasper County, Missouri. Des Moines, Iowa: Miller & Co., 1883.

History of Johnson County, Missouri. Kansas City: Kansas City Historical Co., 1881.

History of Lewis, Clark, Knox and Scotland Counties, Missouri. St. Louis: Goodspeed, 1887.

History of Lincoln County, Missouri. Chicago: Goodspeed, 1888.

History of Newton, Lawrence, Barry and McDonald Counties, Missouri. Chicago: Goodspeed, 1888.

History of Nodaway County, Missouri. St. Joseph, Mo.: National Historical Co., 1882.

History of Randolph and Macon Counties, Missouri. St. Louis, National Historical Co., 1884.

History of Ray County, Missouri. St. Louis: Missouri Historical Society, 1881.

History of Saline County, Missouri. St. Louis: Missouri Historical Society, 1886.

History of Southeast Missouri. Chicago: Goodspeed Publishing Co., 1888.

History of Vernon County, Missouri. Vol. 1. Chicago: C.F. Cooper & Co., 1911.

House, Madeline, Graham Storey, and Kathleen Tillotson, eds. *Letters of Charles Dickens*. Vol. 3. Oxford: Clarendon Press, 1974.

Hyde, William and Howard L. Conrad, eds. *Encyclopedia of the History of St. Louis*. Vol. 4. St. Louis: Southern History Co., 1899.

Kaplan, Fred. *The Singular Mark Twain: a Biography*. New York: Doubleday, 2003.

Levitt, Steven D. and Stephen J. Dubner, *Freakonomics*. New York: William Morrow, 2005.

Lincoln, Abraham. *The Writings of Abraham Lincoln*. Vol. 1. Edited by Arthur Brook Lapsley. New York: B.F. Collier & Son, 1905.

Loewen, James W. *Sundown Towns: A Hidden Dimension of American Racism*. New York: New Press, 2005.

MacLean, Harry N. *In Broad Daylight: A Murder in Skidmore, Missouri*. New York: Dell, 1988.

McLaurin, Melton. *Celia, a Slave*. Athens: University of Georgia Press, 1991.

Martineau, Harriet. *Retrospective of Western Travel*. Vol. 2. 1838. Reprint. New York: Greenwood Press, 1969.

Missouri Historical Society. *Glimpses of the Past*. St. Louis, Mo.: Jefferson Memorial, 1935.

Morris, Edmund. *Theodore Rex*. New York: Random House, 2001.

NAACP. *Thirty Years of Lynching in the United States, 1889–1918*. New York: NAACP, April 1919.

Newby, I.A. *Jim Crow's Defense: Anti-Negro Thought in America, 1900–1930*. Baton Rouge: Louisiana State University Press, 1967.

Nichols, Bruce, *Guerrilla Warfare in Civil War Missouri, 1862*. Jefferson, NC: McFarland, 2004.

Paxton, W.M. *Annals of Platte County, Missouri*. Kansas City: Hudson-Kimberly 1897.

Perrin, William H., ed. *History of Crawford and Clark Counties, Illinois*. Chicago: O.L. Baskin, 1883.

Prucha, Frances Paul. *The Great Father: The United States Government and the American Indians*. Lincoln: University of Nebraska Press, 1986.

Radzinwicz, Leon. *A History of English Criminal Law*

and Its Administration from 1750. Vol. 1. New York: Macmillan, 1948.

Schwarz, Philip J. *Twice Condemned: Slaves and the Criminal Laws of Virginia, 1705–1865.* Baton Rouge: Louisiana State University Press, 1988.

Shaner, Dolph. *The Story of Joplin.* New York: Stratford House, 1948.

Shufeldt, Robert W. *America's Greatest Problem: The Negro.* Philadelphia: F.A. Davis Co., 1915.

_____. *The Negro: A Menace to American Civilization.* Boston: Gorman Press, 1907.

Slide, Anthony. *American Racist: The Life and Films of Thomas Dixon.* Lexington: University Press of Kentucky, 2004.

Stanley, Lois, George F. Wilson, and Maryhelen Wilson. *Death Records from Missouri Newspapers: Jan. 1854–Dec. 1860.* Greenville, SC: Southern Historical Press, 1990.

_____. *Death Records from Missouri Newspapers: The Civil War Years, Jan. 1861–Dec. 1865.* Greenville, SC: Southern Historical Press, 1990.

Stowe, Harriet Beecher. *Uncle Tom's Cabin.* New York: Harper & Row, 1965.

Stroud, George M. *A Sketch of the Laws Relating to Slavery.* 1856. Reprint. New York: Negro Universities Press, 1968.

Thompson, Julius E. *Lynchings in Mississippi, A History, 1865–1965.* Jefferson, N.C: McFarland, 2007.

Trexler, Harrison. *Slavery in Missouri, 1804–1865.* Baltimore: Johns Hopkins Press, 1914.

Twain, Mark. *Complete Essays.* Edited by Charles Neider. Garden City, N.J: Doubleday& Co., 1963.

_____. *The Adventures of Huckleberry Finn.* New York: Penguin Books, 1985.

Weld, Theodore. *American Slavery As It Is; Testimony of a Thousand Witnesses.* 1839. Reprint. New York: Arno Press and The New York Times, 1968.

Wilson, Edmund. *Patriot Gore: Studies in the Literature of the American Civil War.* New York: Oxford University Press, 1966.

Wood, Peter. *Black Majority: Negroes in Colonial South Carolina from 1670 through the Stone Rebellion.* New York: Alfred A. Knopf, 1974.

Wright, John. *African-Americans in Downtown St. Louis.* Chicago: Arcadia Publishing Co., 2003.

Articles

Atlanta Journal-Record of Medicine 4 (1903), 842–44.

Capeci, Dominic J. Jr. "The Lynching of Cleo Wright: Federal Protection of Constitutional Rights during World War II." In *Lynching, Racial Violence, and Law,* Vol. 9, edited by Paul Finkelman, 47–75. New York: Garland Publishing Co., 1992.

Clate, Baker. "The Exodus from Springfield, Missouri." *Osage County Historical Society Newsletter* 8 (February 1993): 1.

Dyer, Thomas G. "A Most Unexampled Exhibition of Madness and Brutality: Judge Lynch in Saline County, Missouri, 1859." In *Under Sentence of Death: Lynching in the South,* edited by W.

Fitzhugh Brundage, 81–108. Chapel Hill: University of North Carolina Press, 1997.

Hermann, Janet S. "The McIntosh Affair." *Bulletin of the Missouri Historical Society* 26 (July 1970): 123–43.

Howard, William Lee. "The Negro as a Distinct Ethnic Factor in Civilization." *Medicine* 9 (1903): 423–26.

Huber, Patrick J. "The Lynching of James T. Scott: The Underside of a College Town." *Gateway Heritage* 12 (Summer 1991): 18–37.

McCord, Louisa S. Review of *Uncle Tom's Cabin,* by Harriet Beecher Stowe. *Southern Quarterly Review,* January 1853.

McKemy, Al. "Negro Murderer Lynched." *Missouri State Genealogical Association. Journal* 13, no. 3 (Summer 1993): 168–170.

Navaree, Carl. "High Noon in Skidmore." *Playboy Magazine,* July 1982.

Nelson, Earl J. "Missouri Slavery 1861–1865." *Missouri Historical Review* 28 (July 1934): 260–74.

Pfeifer, Michael J. "The Ritual of Lynching: Extralegal Justice in Missouri, 1890–1942." *Gateway Heritage* 13 (Winter 1993): 23–33.

Rable, George C. "The South and the Politics of Antilynching Legislation, 1920–1940." *Journal of Southern History* 51, no. 2 (May 1985): 201–20.

Videos

Griffith, D.W. *The Birth of a Nation.* Epoch Film Co. (1915).

Newspapers

Advertiser Courier (Hermann)
Appleton City Journal
Armstrong Herald
Atchison County Journal (Rock Port)
Bates County Record (Butler)
Boonville Weekly Advertiser
Boonville Weekly Observer
Bosworth Sentinel (Carroll County)
Bowling Green Times
Brunswicker (Brunswick)
California News
Call (Kansas City)
Callaway Weekly Gazette (Fulton)
Cash Book (Jackson)
Cassville Republican
Chicago Tribune
Charleston Courier
Chillicothe Constitution
Daily Bazoo (Sedalia)
Daily Democrat (Clinton)
Daily Mail (Nevada)
Daily Herald (St. Joseph)
Daily Herald (Savannah, Ga.)
Daily Standard (Excelsior Springs)
Democrat (Pineville)
Democrat-Leader (Fayette)

Democrat-News (Fredericktown)
Ellington Press (Reynolds County, Mo.)
Evening Mail (Kansas City)
Fair Play (Ste. Genevieve)
Fountain and Journal (Mt. Vernon)
Franklin County Tribune (Union)
Fulton Sun
Fulton Telegraph
Gallatin North Missourian
Gazette (Fulton)
Glasgow Times
Herald (Rolla)
Globe-Democrat (St. Louis)
Higbee Weekly News (Randolph County)
Howard County Advertiser (Fayette)
Holt County Sentinel (Oregon)
Howell County Gazette (West Plains)
Iron County Register (Ironton)
Jefferson Examiner (Jefferson City)
Jefferson Republican (Jefferson City)
Joplin Daily Herald
Joplin Daily Standard
Joplin Globe
Journal of Commerce (Kansas City)
Kansas City Daily Journal
Kansas City Enterprise
Kansas City Journal-Post
Kansas City Star
Kansas City Times
Kennett Clipper
Kingston Times
Knob Noster Gem
Landmark (Platte City)
Lamar Democrat
Lawrence Chieftain
Liberator (Boston)
Liberty Tribune
Linn County News (Linneus)
Louisiana Gazette (St. Louis)
Louisiana Journal
Macon Republican
Macon Times
Marion County Herald (Palmyra)
Maryville Daily Forum
Maryville Republican
Missouri Democrat (Boonville)
Missouri Gazette (St. Louis)
Missouri Herald (Columbia)
Missouri Herald (Jackson)
Missouri Intelligencer (Columbia and Fayette)
Missouri Republican (St. Louis)
Missouri Statesman (Columbia)
Missouri State Times (Jefferson City)
Missouri Telegraph (Fulton)
Missouri Valley Times (Oregon)
Missouri Weekly Patriot (Springfield)
Moberly Headlight
Moberly Monitor
Moberly Monitor-Index
Morning Herald (St. Joseph)
Montgomery Enterprise (Montgomery, Ala.)
The New York Times
Nodaway Democrat (Maryville)

North Missourian (Gallatin)
Osage Chigger (Lowry City)
Osceola Herald
Osceola Sun
Palmyra Spectator
Palmyra Whig
Pittsburgh (Pennsylvania) *Gazette*
Pierce City Enterprise
Pike County News (Louisiana)
Pike County Post (Bowling Green)
Poplar Bluff Citizen
Post (Kansas City)
Randolph Citizen (Huntsville)
Republican (Cassville)
Richmond Conservator
Rising Sun (Kansas City)
Rolla Weekly Herald
St. Charles Banner
St. Joseph News-Press
St. Joseph Weekly Gazette
St. Louis Argus
St. Louis Enquirer
St. Louis Post-Dispatch
St. Louis Times
Ste. Genevieve Herald
Saline County Weekly Progress (Marshall)
Salt River Journal (Bowling Green)
Savannah (Georgia) *Morning News*
Sedalia Daily Democrat
Sentinel (Clarksville)
Sentinel (Columbia)
Sikeston Standard
Southeast Missourian (New Madrid)
Southerner (Tarboro, N.C.)
SPLC Newsletter (Montgomery, Ala.)
Springfield Advertiser
Springfield Herald
Springfield Leader
Star Crawford Mirror (Steelville)
State Republican (Jefferson City)
Tipton Times
Twice-A-Weekly Democrat (Caruthersville)
Warrensburg Standard
Washington County Journal (Potosi)
Weekly Caucasian (Lexington)
Weekly Citizen Democrat (Poplar Bluff)
Weekly Democrat-News (Marshall)
Weekly Enterprise (Charleston)
Weekly Record (New Madrid)
Weekly Times (Butler)

Newspapers made available through the
Internet portal of the Mid-Continent
Library, Independence, Mo.

Atchison Daily Globe (Atchison, Kan.)
Boston Globe
Butte Weekly Miner (Butte, Mont.)
Chicago Defender
Chicago Tribune
Commercial Appeal (Memphis, Tenn.)
Daily Evening Bulletin (San Francisco, Calif.)
Daily Inter Ocean (Chicago)

Daily News Herald (Savannah, Ga.)
Galveston Daily News (Houston, Tex.)
Hartford (Connecticut) *Courant*
Inter Ocean (Chicago)
Los Angeles Times
Milwaukee Sentinel
Morning Oregonian (Portland, Ore.)
The New York Times
Pittsburgh Courier
Rocky Mountain News (Denver)
Salt Lake Semi-Weekly Tribune
Savannah (Georgia) *Morning News*
The Washington Post

Government Documents

Biographical Directory of the American Congress, 1774–1996. Alexandria, Va.: CQ Staff Directories, 1997.

Blunt, Roy D. *Historical Listing of the Missouri Legislature.* Jefferson City, Mo.: Missouri State Archives, 1994.

Congressional Record: Washington, D.C.: Government Printing Office, 1918 and 1922.

Official Manual, State of Missouri, 2007–2008. Jefferson City, Mo.: Secretary of State, 2008.

Penn, Dorothy and Floyd C. Shoemaker, compilers and eds. *The Messages and Proclamations of the Governors of the State of Missouri.* Vol. 13. Columbia, Mo.: State Historical Society of Missouri, 1947.

Thorpe, Francis N., ed. *Federal and State Constitutions, Colonial Charters, and Other Organic Laws of the States. Territories, and Colonies Now or Heretofore forming the United States of America.* Vol. 4. Washington, D.C.: Government Printing Office, 1909.

U.S. Congressional Serial Set, 66 Congress, 2nd Session, H. Rpt. 1027, pt. 1 & 2, Anti-lynching bill, May 22, 1920.

U.S. Department of Commerce. *Negro Population, 1790–1915.* Washington, D.C.: Government Printing Office, 1915.

Archival Material

Compilation. Kenneth McElroy Murder, Missouri Valley Room, Kansas City Public Library, Kansas City, Mo.

Compilation, Raymond Gunn Lynching, St. Joseph Public Library, St. Joseph, Mo.

Missouri State Archives: Record Group 5, Series-Commutations of Sentence, Box 338, Folder 1.

Senate Bill 259.

Western Missouri Manuscript Collection, Columbia, Mo.: Henry C. Fike Papers, Collection 2215.

Statutory Law

Laws of Missouri (1804–2008).

South Carolina, "Acts Relating to Slaves" (1840).

Statutes at Large of the United States of America, 1789–1873. 17 vols. Washington, D.C., 1850–73.

Handwritten Court Records

Federal

U.S .v. Robert Brown Jr. et al. (1873–1874), U.S. District Court, Western District of Missouri, Central Division, Jefferson City, Central Plains Regional, National Archives, Kansas City, Mo.

Criminal Record No. 1, U.S. District Court, Western District of Missouri, South Division, Springfield, Central Plains Region, National Archives, Kansas City, Mo.

State

Callaway County: *State* v. *Peter Kessler* and *State* v. *Killing Kessler et al.* (July-October, 1873).

Clay County: *In Re Estate of Shubael Allen* (1842).

Saline County: *State v. Holman* (1859); *State v. James* (1859); *State v. John* (1859).

Printed Court Records

Federal

Coker v. *Georgia*, 433 U.S. 584 (1977); *In Re, Kemmler,* 136 U.S. 436 (1890); *Kennedy* v. *Louisiana*, slip opinion (2008).

State

Mississippi: *Mitchell* v. *Wells*, 37 Miss. 235 (1859).

Missouri: *Calhoun* v. *Buffington*, 25 Mo. 443 (1857); *Charlotte* v. *Chouteau*, 11 Mo. 193 (1847); *State* v. *Foley*, 46 SW 733 (1898); *State* v. *Grant*, 76 Mo. 236 (1882) and 79 Mo. 113 (1883); *State* v. *Mann*, 83 Mo. 589 (1884); *State* v. *Moore*, 61 SW 199 (1901); *Scott (a man of color)* v. *Emerson*, 15 Mo. 576 (1952); *Slater, alias Lane, Ex Parte*, 72 Mo. 102 (1880); *State* v. *Taylor*, 51 SW2d 1003 (1932).

Index

www.ingramcontent.com/pod-product-compliance
Lightning Source LLC
Chambersburg PA
CBHW080552270326
41929CB00019B/3278